95

ℬROOKS
Sale Calendar

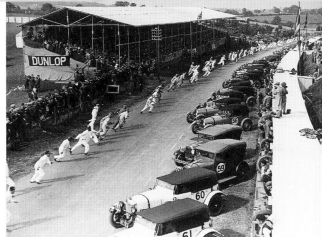

23-24 May
Collectors Motor Cars and
Automobilia, Monaco

23 June
Sports, Competition and
Collectors Motor Cars,
Goodwood Festival of Speed

28 July
Summer Vintage Collectors
Motor Cars and Automobilia

14 September
Collectors Motor Cars and
Automobilia Olympia, London

19-28 October
Collectors Motor Cars and
Automobilia, London Motor
Show, Earls Court, London

9 November
Collectors Motor Cars and
Automobilia a Rolls-Royce
and Bentley event

2 December
Pioneer, Vintage, Sports
and Classic Motorcycles
and related material, London

4 December
Important Collectors Motor
Cars and Automobilia, London

Brooks continues the year with an exciting calendar of sales for 1995. The full programme promises action throughout the year with the now traditional Goodwood Festival of Speed and the popular London Motor Show sales promising to be two highlights.
If you are interested in entering a motor car, motorcycle, automobilia or related collectable items in any of our sales, please call Malcolm Barber, Stewart Skilbeck, James Knight or Robert Brooks on 0171-228 8000 or Michael Worthington-Williams on 01559 370928.

Sale catalogues can be ordered individually in advance. Annual subscriptions are available at a special offer price of £100 (post paid UK..).

Please call 0171-228 8000 and ask for catalogue sales.

ℬROOKS
81 WESTSIDE, LONDON, SW4 9AY
TEL: 0171 228 8000. FAX: 0171 585 0830

MILLER'S
Collectors Cars
PRICE GUIDE

MILLER'S
Collectors
Cars
PRICE GUIDE

1995-96

Volume V

Consultants: Judith and Martin Miller

General Editor: Robert Murfin

Foreword by Lord Montagu of Beaulieu

MILLER'S COLLECTORS CARS PRICE GUIDE 1995–96

Created and designed by
Miller's Publications
The Cellars, High Street
Tenterden, Kent TN30 6BN
Telephone: 01580 766411

Consultants: Judith and Martin Miller

General Editor: Robert Murfin
Editorial and Production Co-ordinator: Sue Boyd
Editorial Assistants: Marion Rickman, Jo Wood, Sue Montgomery
Artwork: Jody Taylor, Kari Reeves, Matthew Leppard, Shirley Reeves
Advertising Executive: Melinda Williams
Display Advertisements: Elizabeth Smith, Joanne Daniels
Material Collators: Gillian Charles, Karen Taylor
Additional Photographers: Neill Bruce, John Colley, Paul Cross, Geoff Goddard/GP
Bob Masters, Martin McGlone, Midland Motor Museum, Robin Saker, Stanland, Julius Weitmann
Index compiled by: DD Editorial Services, Beccles

First published in 1995
by Miller's
an imprint of Reed Consumer Books Limited
Michelin House, 81 Fulham Road, London SW3 6RB
and Auckland, Melbourne, Singapore and Toronto

Bromide output by Perfect Image, Hurst Green, E. Sussex
Illustrations by G. H. Graphics, St. Leonard's-on-Sea, E. Sussex
Colour origination by Scantrans, Singapore
Printed and bound in England by William Clowes Ltd,
Beccles and London

Miller's is a trademark of
Reed International Books Limited

ACKNOWLEDGEMENTS

The publishers would like to acknowledge the great assistance given by our consultants.

Malcolm Barber	Tel: 01883 626553
Stephen Boyd	Scootacar Register, 18 Holman Close, Aylsham, Norfolk NR11 6DD
Michael Chapman	Tel: 01789 77897
Tom Falconer	Claremont Corvette, Snodland, Kent. Tel: 01634 244444
Paul Foulkes-Halbard	Foulkes-Halbard of Filching, Filching Manor, Jevington Road, Wannock, Polegate, Sussex. Tel: 01323 487838/487124
Tony Leslie	Holmesdale Sevens, Fareham, Chilsham Lane, Herstmonceux, E. Sussex. Tel: 01323 833603
Stanley Mann	Tel: 01923 852505

HOW TO USE THIS BOOK

Miller's Collectors Cars Price Guide presents an overview of the collectors cars market during the past twelve months. The cars are listed alphabetically by make and then chronologically by model within each make. In the case of manufacturers renowned for producing both sports and saloon cars, for example Bentley and MG, we have grouped the sports and saloon cars together and then listed these cars chronologically.

Each illustration is fully captioned and carries a price range which reflects the dealer/auctioneer sale price. The prefix 'Est.' indicates the estimated price for the cars which did not sell at auction. Each illustration also has an identification code which allows you to locate the source of that particular picture by using the Key to Illustrations.

In the Automobilia section, objects are grouped alphabetically by type, for example clothing, garage equipment, and so on, then chronologically within each grouping. Competition cars, commercial vehicles, military vehicles, fire engines and micro cars all follow the same format. The Automobile Art section is listed alphabetically.

Also included in *Miller's Collectors Cars Price Guide* are price boxes, compiled by our team of experts, (including Malcolm Barber, a well-known car historian), car clubs and private collectors, which give the value of a particular model, dependent on condition.
Condition 1. A vehicle in top class condition but not 'Concours d'élégance' standard, either fully restored or in very good original condition.

Condition 2. A good, clean roadworthy vehicle, both mechanically and bodily sound.
Condition 3. A runner, but in need of attention, probably to both bodywork and mechanics. Must have current MOT.
We have also included restoration projects, which cover vehicles that fail to make the condition 3 grading.

Remember, we do not illustrate every classic or collectors car ever produced. Our aim is to reflect the marketplace, so if, for example, there appears to be a large number of Lotus's and only a few Volvos, then this is an indication of the quantity, availability and, to an extent, the desirability of these cars in the marketplace over the last twelve months. If the car you are looking for is not featured under its alphabetical listing, do look in the colour sections and double-check the index. If a particular car is not featured this year, it may well have appeared in previous editions of *Miller's Collectors Cars Price Guide,* which provide a growing visual reference library.

Lastly, we are always keen to improve the content and accuracy of our books. If you feel that a particular make or model or other aspect of classic and collectable vehicles has not been covered in sufficient detail, if you disagree with our panel of experts, or have any other comments you would like to share with us about our book, please write and let us know.

We value feedback from the people who use *Miller's Collectors Cars Price Guide* to tell us how we can make it even better.

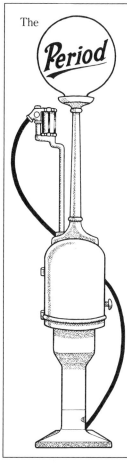

KEY TO ILLUSTRATIONS

Each illustration and descriptive caption is accompanied by a letter-code. The source of any item may be immediately determined by referring to the following list, in which Auctioneers are denoted by *, Dealers by •, Advertisers by †, and Clubs and Trusts by ‡. In no way does this constitute or imply a contract or binding offer on the part of any of our contributors to supply or sell the goods illustrated, or similar articles, at the prices stated.

If you require a valuation for an item, it is advisable to check whether the dealer or specialist will carry out this service and if there is a charge. Please mention Miller's when making an enquiry. Having found a specialist who will carry out your valuation it is best to send a photograph and description of the item to the specialist together with a stamped addressed envelope for the reply. A valuation by telephone is not possible.

Most dealers are only too happy to help you with your enquiry, however, they are very busy people and consideration of the above points would be welcomed.

AAOC ‡ Austin Atlantic Owners Club, 124 Holbrook Road, Stratford, London, E15 3DZ. Tel: 0181 534 2682

ACC • Albert's, 113 London Road, Twickenham, Middx. Tel: 0181 891 3067

ADT * † ADT Auctions Ltd., Classic & Historic Automobile Division, Blackbushe Airport, Blackwater, Camberley, Surrey. GU17 9LG. Tel: 01252 878555

AG * Anderson & Garland, Marlborough House, Marlborough Crescent, Newcastle-upon-Tyne. Tel: 0191 232 6278

ALC * Alcocks, Wyeval House, 42 Bridge Street, Hereford. HR4 9DG Tel: 01432 344322

BA • † Balmoral Automobile Co. Ltd., 260 Knights Hill, West Norwood, London, SE27. Tel: 0181-761 1155

BCA • † Beaulieu Cars Automobilia, Beaulieu, Hants. Tel: 01590 612689

Bea * Bearnes, Rainbow, Avenue Road, Torquay, Devon. Tel: 01803 296277

BKS * † Robert Brooks (Auctioneers) Ltd., 81 Westside, London SW4 9AY. Tel: 0171 228 8000

BLE • † Ivor Bleaney, PO Box 60, Salisbury, Wilts. Tel: 01794 390895

Bro • John Brown, Letchworth, Herts. Tel: 01763 852200

C * Christie, Manson & Wood, 8 King Street, St James's, London SW1Y 6QT. Tel: 0171-839 9060

C(A) * Christie's Australia Pty. Ltd., 1 Darling Street, South Yarra, Victoria 3141, Australia. Tel: (613) 820 4311

CARS • † Classic Automobilia & Regalia Specialists, 4-4a Chapel Terrace Mews, Kemp Town, Brighton, Sussex. Tel: 01273 601960

Car • † Chris Alford Racing & Sports Cars, Newland Cottage, Hassocks, West Sussex. Tel: 01273 845966

CBG • Cropredy Bridge Garage, (exclusively Jensen), Riverside Works, Cropredy, Banbury, Oxon. Tel: 01295 758444

CCK • Castle Cars (Kingswood). Tel: 01622 842577

CCTC • † Classic Car Trade Centre, 47 Ash Grove, Chelmsford, Essex. Tel: 01245 358028

CGB • Cars Gone By, Maidstone, Kent. Tel: 01622 630220

CGOC • † Capital & General Omnibus Company Ltd. Tel: 01260 223456

CLP ‡ Club Peugeot UK, Beacon View, Forster Road, Soberton Heath, Southampton. SO32 3QG. Tel: 01329 833029

CNY * Christie, Manson & Woods International Inc., 502 Park Avenue, New York, NY 10022. Tel: (212) 546 1000 (including Christie's East).

COR • † Claremont Corvette, Snodland, Kent. Tel: 01634 244444

COYS * Coys of Kensington, 2-4 Queen's Gate Mews, London SW7 5QJ. Tel: 0171 584 7444

CR • † Classic Restorations, Arch 124, Cornwall Road, Waterloo, London SE1. Tel: 0171 928 6613

CSK • Christie's South Kensington Ltd., 85 Old Brompton Road, London SW7 3LD. Tel: 0171 581 7611

CVPG ‡ Chiltern Vehicle Preservation Group, Chiltern House, Ashendon, Aylesbury, Bucks. Tel: 01296 651283

DaD * David Dockree, 224 Moss Lane, Bramhall, Stockport, Cheshire. Tel: 0161 485 1258

DJR • † DJR Services, Unit N4, Europa Trading Estate, Trader Road, Erith, Kent. Tel: 01322 442850

DKE • † D. K. Engineering, Unit D, 200 Rickmansworth Road, Watford, Herts. WD1 7JS. Tel: 01923 255246

EP * Evans & Partridge, Agriculture House, High Street, Stockbridge, Hants. SO20 6HF. Tel: 01264 810702

FHD • † F. H. Douglass, 1a South Ealing Road, Ealing, London W5. Tel: 0181 567 0570

FHF • † Foulkes-Halbard of Filching, Filching Manor, Jevington Road, Wannock, Polegate, Sussex. Tel: 01323 487838/487124

FYC ‡ † Ford Y & C Model Register, Castle Farm, Main Street, Pollington, Goole, Humberside DN14 0DJ.

GAR • † Guild of Automotive Restorers, 18-37 Woodbine Avenue, R.R. No. 1, Sharon, Ontario, LOG 1BO. Tel: (905) 895 0035

GEC ‡ Granada Enthusiasts Club, 515a Bristol Road, Bournbrook, Birmingham, B29 6AU. Tel: 0121 426 2346

GES * G. E. Sworder & Sons, 15 Northgate End, Bishop's Stortford, Herts. Tel: 01279 651388

H&H * † H & H Auctions, 385 London Road, Appleton, Nr Warrington, Cheshire. WA4 5DN. Tel: 0161 747 0561 & 01925 860471

HOLL * † Holloway's, 49 Parsons Street, Banbury, Oxon. OX16 8PF. Tel: 01295 253197

HRR	•†	Historique Race & Rally, 47 Ash Grove, Chelmsford, Essex. CM2 9JT. Tel: 01245 358028
JAR	•	Jarrotts, Hales Place, Woodchurch Road, High Halden, Kent. TN26 3JQ. Tel: 01233 850037
JNic	*	John Nicholson, 1 Crossways Court, Fernhurst, Haslemere, Surrey. Tel: 01428 653727
KSC	•†	Kent Sports Cars, High Street (A257), Littlebourne, Canterbury, Kent. Tel: 01227 832200
LF	*	Lambert & Foster, 77 Commercial Road, Paddock Wood, Kent. TN12 6DR. Tel: 01892 832325
MAN	•†	Stanley Mann. Tel: 01923 852505
MCh	•†	Michael Chapman. Tel: 01789 773897
Mot	•†	Motospot, North Kilworth, Lutterworth, Leics. Tel: 01455 552548 or 01831 120498
MSMP	•	Mike Smith's Motoring Past, Chiltern House, Ashendon, Aylesbury, Bucks. Tel: 01296 651283
N	•	Neale's, 192-194 Mansfield Road, Nottingham. Tel: 0115 962 4141
NTC	•	Northern TR Centre, Sedgefield Industrial Estate, Sedgefield, Cleveland. Tel: 01740 621447
OMH	•†	The Old Motor House, Andover Road, Whitchurch, Hants. RG28 7RL. Tel: 01256 896483/895444
ONS	*	Onslows, Metrostore, Townmead Road, London SW6. Tel: 0171-793 0240
PC		Private Collection.
PJF	•	P. J. Fischer Classic, Dyers Lane, Upper Richmond Road, Putney, London SW15. Tel: 0181 785 6633
PMB	•†	Pook's Motor Bookshop, Fowke Street, Rothley, Leics. Tel: 01533 376222
PRD	•	Prototype Research & Development, 230 Albert Lane, Box 1330, Campbellford, Ontario, Canada. KOl 1LO. Tel: (705) 653 4525
RT	•†	Richard Thorne, Classic Cars, Unit 1, Bloomfield Hatch, Mortimer, Reading, Berks. RG1 3AD. Tel: 01734 333633
S	*†	Sotheby's, 34-35 New Bond Street, London W1A 2AA. Tel: 0171 493 8080
SC	•	Sporting Classics, Phil Hacker, The Oast, Shears Farm, North Road, Goudhurst, Kent. Tel: 01580 211275
ScR	‡	Scootacar Register, 18 Holman Close, Aylham, Norwich, Norfolk. NR11 6DD. Tel: 01263 733861
SIG	•	Sigma Antiques, Water Skellgate, Ripon, Yorks. Tel: 01765 603163
SJR	•†	Simon J. Robinson (MGA) 1982 Ltd., Ketton Garage, Durham Road, Coatham Munderville, Darlington. Tel: 01325 311232
STAR	‡	Sunbeam Talbot Alpine Register, 84 High Brooms Road, Tunbridge Wells, Kent.
TAR	•	Lorraine Tarrant Antiques, 7–11 Market Place, Ringwood, Hants. Tel: 01425 461123
TVM	•	Theresa Vanneck-Murray, Vanneck House, 22 Richmond Hill, Richmond, Surrey. TW1 6QX Tel: 0181 940 2035
VIC	•†	Vicarys of Battle Ltd., 32 High Street, Battle, East Sussex. Tel: 01424 772425
WP	•	West Promotions, PO Box 257, Sutton, Surrey. Tel: 0181 641 3224

CONTENTS

FOREWORD

The car is an essential element of modern day life. Perhaps more than anything else this century, it has changed the way in which we live. A practical necessity, the car can also be an object of romance, beauty and an endless source of fascination.

At the same time as technological advances are being made to develop the vehicles of the 21st Century, so interest in automobile history continues to expand. At the National Motor Museum at Beaulieu we welcome half a million visitors every year and our special programme of events for children is introducing a new generation of young enthusiasts to the exciting story of motoring. Increasingly, visitors are coming to Beaulieu not only to admire the exhibits, but also to buy and collect for themselves. We host two major auto-jumbles – the Spring Classic in May, and the International Auto-Jumble in September, a massive event which, in the space of one hectic and fun-filled weekend, brings forty thousand enthusiasts to the museum.

As I know from both personal and professional experience collecting is a great joy, but in the same way that a driver needs a good road map, so a collector needs a reliable guide to conduct him or her safely around a varied and expanding market. *Miller's Collectors Cars Price Guide* is the only illustrated manual of its kind and an invaluable aid to both buyer and seller. It covers the breadth of vehicles available from vintage buses to bubble cars and offers an in-depth pictorial survey and price guide to the ever-growing automobilia market.

As the pictures in this book show, cars can be magnificent objects. However, nothing equals the excitement of seeing them, and I would like to take this opportunity to invite Miller's readers to come and visit both the National Motor Museum and Beaulieu's auto-jumbles. There you will be able to witness and experience the pleasures of collecting at first hand and, armed with this enjoyable and informative book, you can learn to buy as carefully as you would learn to drive.

Montagu of Beaulieu

1995

RESTORATION

Many who find vehicle restoration a rewarding and satisfying exercise are also left with an appreciating asset and a vehicle which will provide years of pleasure. On the other hand it can sometimes be a frustrating and expensive business involving more time and capital outlay than the value of the finished vehicle warrants.

The condition of the car to be restored will indicate the extent of work required and hense the expense involved. With this in mind, the cost of re-trimming a saloon or limousine is higher than that for a touring car or two seater, but the cost of restoration is generally much the same for a luxury or an economy car, if their condition is similar.

If you want to keep costs to a minimun choose a well known make or model where spares and advice are cheap and plentiful. Avoid exotic cars which may require costly specialist work as well as expensive parts. Decide at the outset what you can afford to spend and stick to it.

If you have certain restoration skills then the more jobs you can complete yourself the cheaper the restoration will be. Specialist labour charges can vary enormously from £7–30 an hour. But be warned, since the boom years of the late '80s the restoration business has acquired its own share of 'cowboy' operators.

Before you commit yourself to the services of a specialist restorer ask if they will put you in touch with previous customers. A personal recommendation from a satisfied customer is worth more than all the paid advertising in the world. But do not be put off by appearances. The best work is often done in the most primitive looking workshops as well as the brand new purpose-built factory unit.

Make sure the professional you are going to use is a specialist in the area of work you want carried out. If they are not it is extremely likely your job will be sub-contracted to someone who you have not vetted and approved.

If your interest lies in concours and shows then you will want a higher standard of restoration and finish than someone who may want a car in sufficient mechanical condition to take part in rallies or trials. Decide on what standard you require at the outset and inform your restorer accordingly.

Shop around and get several quotes. You will be surprised at the wide differences between prices and requirements. However, the cheapest is not always the best, and here personal recommendation is always useful. Remember, that your restorer cannot see the extent of some of the work required until full dismantling is complete. It is sometimes better to accept a fixed price for the cost of dismantling and then a firm estimate for the cost of work needed. This will avoid the nightmare problem of being left with a vehicle in a hundred pieces, if you then cannot agree, or cannot afford, the price of the quote.

Always obtain a firm written estimate before work commences. There are many half-completed restoration projects where owners received such a shock upon receipt of their first invoice for progress payments that they have been forced to call a halt to the restoration. Monitor the work regularly, not when it is too late to change things and do not pay for everything in advance. Progress payments ensure high standards by giving you a lever to insist on poor work being rectified.

If you are undertaking the majority of the work yourself, avoid the temptation to strip the car down completely. A dismembered motor car is a daunting prospect which has sufficiently disheartened many would-be restorers into abandoning their projects for good. Instead keep the car in 'large lumps', dismantling only those components upon which you are currently working. It is important to photograph all assemblies before you start to dismantle them. These photographs will prove invaluable when the time comes for re-assembly. It is also a useful visual record of the restoration project which you can show to prospective buyers.

The UK is probably better served with specialist or one-make clubs than any other country in the world, and it is always a good idea to join the club specialising in your vehicle before your restoration commences. Many of these clubs maintain supplies of spares, or even manufacture obsolete parts, and many of their members will have already trodden the restoration path. Their experience and advice will prove invaluable, and will inevitably help save you time and money.

STATE OF THE MARKET

Auction activity in the classic vehicle market has been at high a level recently as in the boom years of the late eighties. There are a number of reasons for this, not the least of which is the surplus of cars in the collectors' category still seeking buyers. The early 1990s saw a recession in trade following three years in which collectors' vehicles experienced an unprecedented increase in prices. It is natural therefore that many who had bought when the market was at its peak were reluctant to sell until prices improved.

For some, the decision on when to sell was taken out of their hands, as banks, finance companies and receivers repossessed vehicles and sold them for what they could fetch. For most however, it was only recently the realisation has dawned that prices from late 1987–89 were artificially high – largely manufactured by fugitives from the stock market after Black Monday 1987, and unlikely in real terms to return.

The problem of surplus collectors' vehicles in Britain is exacerbated by the fact that during the period when the dollar was weak against the pound many collectors, both dealers and private individuals alike, went car hunting in the USA and, in UK terms, bought more affordable cars. As a result hoards of left hand drive MGs, Jaguars, Austin Healeys and other British sports cars returned to the UK, and the resultant glut is still being sold. Today many dealers remain over stocked, and have been relying on the collectors' vehicle auctions as a means of improving cash flow, and this too, has increased auction activity.

Prices of lower range and mediocre condition cars have fallen, and the buying public have become a great deal more discriminating. The result of this trend may be seen in the auction results. These show immediately that good quality cars, of whatever make, will invariably make their reserve, whereas cars of indifferent quality can be bought very cheaply.

The influx of 'brass age' cars from America, where the inter-State highway system and vast distances between cities inhibit their use, have also had its effect on veteran and Edwardian vehicle prices, and with the exception of high powered multi-cylinder high quality veterans – especially those eligible for the London to Brighton Run – are generally lower than they were even a year ago.

Of all the makes badly affected by the late '80s hype and the recession which followed, Jaguar is making the fastest and most noticeable recovery. Aston Martins and the cheaper Ferraris are following but at a more moderate pace.

Interest among buyers still centre on two main categories; the sporting market and the luxury bespoke market. Family saloons from 1920s–60s, with no sporting pretensions, can now be bought very reasonably indeed. Prices vary from between £500–2,000 for the post-WWII models, and £3,000–6,000 for the pre-war ones – this area in particular has seen considerable auction activity.

A good Jaguar XK 120 drophead can be purchased for around £22,000–24,000, a Ferrari Dino for around £22,000–25,000, and Aston Martin saloons from the mid-seventies are making anything from £7,500–20,000 depending on condition, and with the early V8s generally doing less well than the six cylinder cars.

Rolls-Royce and Bentley saloons, are probably as cheap as they have ever been. A Silver Shadow in good condition could cost around £10,000–11,000 while one in poorer condition could go for as little as £4,000, demonstrating again that cars in good condition can command a premium. Good vintage examples, particularly open tops and those with pretty bodywork or good provenance, will still fetch £40,000–60,000, with good post-WWI Silver Ghosts averaging £40,000–60,000 in exceptional condition. Pre-war Ghosts will, however, make considerably more – anything from £180,000–500,000 depending on condition, coachwork, provenance and style. The same goes for Bentleys, with a good original 4½ litre blower making £350,000 upwards, although Blue Label 3 litres' can be bought for £45,000–60,000.

At the lower end of the market, the situation is still volatile, with confidence weak and those with money still unwilling to spend it on anything but the best quality. Buyers from overseas have also been discouraged by the introduction of vehicle registration tax in several EC countries (180% in Denmark on imported vehicles).

Provenance is still a very important aspect of a car, and this is particularly true in the case of interesting barn discoveries. The 1938 Jaguar SS 100 and 1923 Vauxhall 30/98 discovered by Sotheby's and offered in their September sale both came with full histories and sold for £55,000 and £62,000 respectively, despite their parlous condition.

To sum up, there is probably no better time to buy a collectors' car than now. The market is offering a unusually wide choice of high quality vehicles at early 1987 prices. As surplus cars are gradually sold, many of them to overseas buyers, the market will again level out. But remember, as always, quality has and still does command the highest prices and the keenest bidding.

Malcolm Barber

It's easy to spot who offers the premier classic car insurance.

For nearly a century, the three famous letters, RAC have been proudly borne by cars of quality. Founded by motoring enthusiasts in 1897, the RAC continues to work closely with Classic Car Owners Clubs to this day.

So, who better to trust with the insurance of your classic car than a company which has this enthusiasm, heritage and experience?

RAC Insurance Services has negotiated special discounts and benefits with the country's top insurers to offer you what you seek from classic car insurance.

It's called the RAC Classic Car Policy and it puts you on the road to better value motor insurance. You have the option of Comprehensive Cover which automatically includes a free expert valuation of your classic car. Alternatively, you can choose Fire and Theft plus Accidental Damage Cover. Either option includes cover for club events (excluding speed trials and racing) and free extension of cover into Europe.

Cover is available to low mileage drivers who own a pre-1985 standard production classic. The annual mileage should not exceed 7,500 miles but discounts are available if mileage is especially low.

Free with your policy: when you take out an RAC Classic Car Policy, you will receive your own **1995 RAC grille badge**, complimenting the full character and heritage of your classic car.

To find out how you can enjoy the best value cover call today for your free quotation on 0462 435 447. Make sure that your classic car carries the badge of one of the most prestigious names on the road.

RAC
INSURANCE
services

Call RAC Insurance Services on:

0462 435 447

even if your renewal is not yet due. Please quote ref: CLA3
(Lines open: 9.00am - 5.30pm Weekdays, 9.00am - 1.00pm Saturdays)

RAC Insurance Brokers Ltd are Lloyd's Brokers, Members of the British Insurance and Investment Brokers' Association and regulated in the conduct of investment business by the Insurance Brokers' Registration Council.
Registered Office: 10-12 Hunting Gate, Hitchin, Herts SG4 0TT.
Registered in England No.446043

AC

The first Autocarrier was produced in 1904 by John Portwine, a butcher, and John Weller, an engineer. It was a three-wheeled delivery van with two wheels at the front, and a single rear wheel being driven by a 5hp single cylinder engine.

A passenger version was soon produced and by the 1930s a range of sports cars and sports tourers was available laying the foundation for competition cars. This led to the Ace and, perhaps most famous of all, the Cobra.

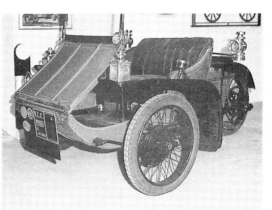

1910 AC Sociable 5/6hp 2 Seater, air-cooled engine, with flywheel driven fan, fold-flat mahogany framed windscreen, Rotax oil sidelamps, Lucas oil rear lamp, boa constrictor brass horn, brass fire extinguisher and luggage carrier, complete with hood.
£6,250–6,750 *S*

This car has been in a private collection for many years and has seen little use.

1911 AC Sociable 5/6hp 2 Seater, two front wheels and one rear wheel powered by 5hp single cylinder chain driven engine, good overall condition having been museum stored for many years.
£4,250–4,750 *S*

Entry to the open two seater is by lifting the hinged front. There is also a hinged front screen and access to the engine compartment is gained by lifting the rear luggage carrier.

1923 AC Royal 12hp 2 Seater with Dickey, 4 cylinders, 1496cc Anzani engine, quarter-elliptic springs, detachable steel disc wheels, leather upholstery, nickel fittings and CAV electrics, very original, museum stored for many years with only occasional use.
£7,800–8,200 *S*

This engine proved so successful that only slight modifications were made during its 30 years of production.

1935 AC Ace 16/56 4 Seater Sports Tourer, 2 litres, 6 cylinder engine, single overhead camshaft, light alloy block and crankcase with wet liners and 4 bearing crankshaft, to original specification in all major respects, museum displayed for many years, recommissioning required.
£18,000–20,000 *S*

c1950 AC 2 Litre 2 Door Saloon, Jaguar XK engine, re-imported from California, left hand drive, restoration project.
£1,000–1,200 *S*

Only 1,129 of these cars were built.

Cross Reference
Restoration Projects

AC Model	ENGINE cc/cyl	DATES	CONDITION 1	2	3
Sociable	636/1	1907-12	£9,500	£8,000	£4,000
12/24 (Anzani)	1498/4	1919-27	£14,000	£11,500	£7,500
16/40	1991/6	1920-28	£18,000	£15,000	£11,000
16/60 Drophead/Saloon	1991/6	1937-40	£24,000	£21,000	£15,500
16/70 Sports Tourer	1991/6	1937-40	£35,000	£26,000	£18,000
16/80 Competition 2 Seater	1991/6	1937-40	£55,000	£45,000	£35,000

1955 AC Ace Open Sports, 6 cylinders, 1991cc AC engine, original leather trim, good condition, original order throughout. **£24,000–26,000** *COYS*

AC Ace

- **Launched at the 1953 Earl's Court Motor Show.**
- **One of only two production cars to have independent suspension at that time.**
- **Straight 6 cylinder, 1991cc engine and 85bhp.**
- **Performance of 0–60mph in 11.4 seconds and top speed of about 103 mph.**

1985 AC 3000ME, Ford 3 litre V6 engine, fibreglass body, good condition throughout, low mileage. **£7,800–8,200** *ADT*

1959 AC Ace Open Sports, returned to UK from California in 1989, extensive renovation, including conversion to right hand drive, very good order throughout. **Est. £24,000–28,000** *COYS*

1962 AC Ace 2.6 Litre, 6 cylinders, 2553cc engine, excellent overall restored condition. **£38,000–40,000** *ADT*

Only a very few AC Aces were fitted with the Ford Zephyr 6 cylinder, 2.6 litre engine.

1955/68 AC Aceca, 8 cylinders, 302cu in engine, mechanically modified, Boss engine fully rebuilt and tuned, Nash 5 speed manual gearbox, Aceca body retained. **Est. £22,000–25,000** *ADT*

This car has been built up around chassis number CFX18 which belonged to an AC 428 and is now an original Aceca body fitted to the shortened original 428 frame.

AC Model	ENGINE cc/cyl	DATES	CONDITION		
			1	2	3
2 litre	1991/6	1947-55	£5,000	£2,500	£800
Buckland	1991/6	1949-54	£6,500	£4,500	£1,800
Ace	1991/6	1953-63	£27,000	£22,000	£15,000
Ace Bristol	1971/6	1954-63	£32,000	£28,000	£23,000
Ace 2.6	1553/6	1961-62	£35,000	£30,000	£29,000
Aceca	1991/6	1954-63	£24,000	£17,000	£12,000
Aceca Bristol	1971/6	1956-63	£28,000	£21,000	£16,000
Greyhound Bristol	1971/6	1961-63	£14,000	£10,500	£7,000
Cobra Mk II 289	4735/8	1963-64	£85,000	£80,000	£76,000
Cobra Mk III 427	6998/8	1965-67	£115,000	£100,000	£90,000
Cobra Mk IV	5340/8	1987-	£55,000	£40,000	£32,000
428 Frua	7014/8	1967-73	£19,000	£15,000	£11,000
428 Frua Convertible	7014/8	1967-73	£25,000	£20,000	£15,000
3000 ME	2994/6	1976-84	£13,000	£10,000	£8,000

ACME

Acme motor cars were built from about 1902 by James Reber, a bicycle manufacturer. The factory was located at Reading, Pennsylvania, but the company did not last long and consequently Acme vehicles are extremely rare.

1905 Acme 16hp 2 Seater Runabout, twin cylinder engine, independent foot brake added, re-upholstered in buttoned black leather, Lucas brass oil side lamps, brass horn and wooden wheels, generally good mechanical condition.
Est. £12,000–14,000 *S*

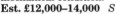

ALFA ROMEO

The ALFA Company was founded in 1910, and by 1918, following his acquisition of the business, Nicola Romeo added his name.

The Alfa Romeo reputation was founded on competition victories. The competition department was set up as Scuderia Ferrari – which was led and run by Enzo Ferrari, with engineer Luigi Bazzi and designer Vittorio Jano. The Jano-designed 6C model, in a series of racing and touring versions, is probably the most famous of the pre-war Alfas.

1930 Alfa Romeo 6C 1750 Gran Sport, Spider coachwork by Zagato, 6 cylinder, 1752cc engine, restored to concours winning standard.
Est. £160,000–180,000 *COYS*

1931 Alfa Romeo 6C 1750 Gran Sport, Spider coachwork by Zagato, excellent condition throughout.
£120,000–130,000 *COYS*

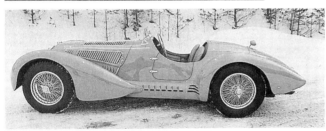

1939 Ex-works Alfa Romeo 6C 2500 SS (Tipo 256), 6 cylinder, 2443cc engine, Spider Corsa coachwork by Touring of Milan, totally restored, excellent condition.
£190,000–200,000 *COYS*

ALFA ROMEO Model	ENGINE cc/cyl	DATES	CONDITION 1	2	3
24HP	4084/4	1910-11	£21,000	£16,000	£12,000
12HP	2413/4	1910-11	£18,000	£11,000	£8,000
40-60	6028/4	1913-15	£32,000	£24,000	£14,000
RL	2916/6	1921-22	£30,000	£24,000	£14,000
RM	1944/4	1924-25	£28,000	£17,000	£13,000
6C 1500	1487/6	1927-28	£14,000	£10,000	£8,000
6C 1750	1752/6	1923-33	£85,000+	-	-
6C 1900	1917/6	1933	£18,000	£15,000	£12,000
6C 2300	2309/6	1934	£22,000	£18,000	£15,000
6C 2500 SS Cabriolet/Spider	2443/6	1939-45	£100,000	£50,000	£40,000
6C 2500 SS Coupé	2443/6	1939-45	£60,000	£40,000	£30,000
8C 2300 Monza/Short Chassis	2300/8	1931-34	£900,000	£400,000	£200,000
8C 2900	2900/8	1935-39	£000,000	£500,000	£300,000

Value is very dependent on sporting history, body style and engine type.

1947 Alfa Romeo 6C 2500 Freccia d'Oro,
6 cylinder, 2500cc engine, totally restored,
excellent condition.
£22,000–24,000 *COYS*

1950 Alfa Romeo 6C 2500SS Villa d'Este,
6 cylinder, 2443cc engine, coupé coachwork
by Touring of Milan.
£48,000–50,000 *COYS*

**1960 Alfa Romeo 1500 Spider 2 Seater
Sports Roadster,** left hand drive,
completely original, unrestored and rust-free,
excellent condition throughout.
Est. £11,500–13,500 *S*

1962 Alfa Romeo 1600 Giulia Spider,
twin Weber DCOE carburettors to Veloce
specification, original Solex downdraft
carburettor manifold and air cleaner
equipment available, imported into the
UK from California in 1989, very sound
original condition.
£8,500–9,500 *S*

1959 Alfa Romeo 2000 Spider, coachwork
by Touring of Milan, left hand drive, rebuilt
engine and bodywork, completely restored.
Est. £15,000–20,000 *BKS*

*According to the Alfa Romeo Owners' Club
there are no more than 8 examples of this
twin cam model known to exist in the
United Kingdom.*

1959 Alfa Romeo Guilietta Spider,
coachwork by Pininfarina, full restoration
with bare metal re-spray, interior
re-trimmed.
Est. £7,000–10,000 *BKS*

*Produced until 1962, the Giulietta Spider
was powered by a twin cam 4 cylinder engine
developing 80hp in standard form (against
53hp for the Giulietta sedan), with a top
speed of 103 mph and weighed less than
17 cwt dry. A total of 14,300 were built.*

**1962 Alfa Romeo Giulietta Spider
Veloce,** coachwork by Pininfarina, older
restoration, good condition throughout.
Est. £12,000–14,000 *S*

Alfa Romeo Giulia

- **Both the 4 cylinder 1600 and 6 cylinder
  2600 were derived from the Giulietta
  design by Orazio Satta.**
- **Introduced at the Monza Autodrome
  in 1962.**
- **Four cylinder 1600cc, twin overhead
  camshaft engine and 5 speed gearbox.**
- **Spider bodywork by Pininfarina,
  Sprint bodywork by Bertone.**

1964 Alfa Romeo Giulia Sprint GT 2+2 Coupé, Coachwork by Bertone, excellent condition throughout.
Est. £5,500–6,500 *S*

1964 Alfa Romeo Giulia Spider, coachwork by Pininfarina, 4 cylinder, 1570cc engine, complete restoration including a mechanical overhaul, new trim and bar metal re-spray, very good condition.
£8,500–9,500 *COYS*

1964 Alfa Romeo 2600 Spider, coachwork by Carrozzeria Touring, good overall condition.
£6,500–7,500 *S*

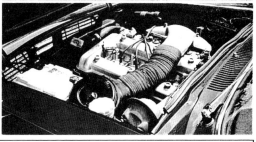

1965 Alfa Romeo Giulia GTC 1600, coachwork by Bertone/Touring, 4 cylinder, 1779cc engine, right hand drive, engine rebuilt, bare metal re-spray, good condition.
£11,500–12,500 *COYS*

ALFA ROMEO Model	ENGINE cc/cyl	DATES	CONDITION 1	2	3
2000 Spider	1974/4	1958-61	£11,000	£9,000	£5,000
2600 Sprint	2584/6	1962-66	£11,000	£7,500	£4,000
2600 Spider	2584/6	1962-65	£14,000	£12,000	£8,000
Giulietta Sprint	1290/4	1955-62	£10,000	£7,000	£4,000
Giulietta Spider	1290/4	1956-62	£10,000	£6,000	£4,500
Giulia Saloon	1570/4	1962-72	£4,000	£3,000	£1,000
Giulia Sprint (rhd)	1570/4	1962-68	£10,500	£6,000	£2,000
Giulia Spider (rhd)	1570/4	1962-65	£10,000	£7,000	£4,000
Giulia SS	1570/4	1962-66	£15,000	£13,000	£10,000
GT 1300 Junior	1290/4	1966-72	£7,000	£5,500	£4,000
1300GT Junior	1290/4	1973-75	£4,000	£2,000	£1,000
Giulia Sprint GT (105)	1570/4	1962-68	£7,500	£5,000	£3,000
1600GT Junior	1570/4	1972-75	£7,000	£4,000	£2,000
1750/2000 Berlina	1779/ 1962	1967-77	£3,500	£2,000	£1,000
1750GTV	1779/4	1967-72	£9,000	£7,000	£3,000
2000GTV	1962/4	1971-77	£8,000	£6,500	£3,000
1600/1750 (Duetto)	1570/ 1779/4	1966-67	£9,500	£8,000	£5,500
1750/2000 Spider (Kamm)	1779/ 1962/4	1967-78	£8,000	£6,000	£4,000
Montreal	2593/8	1970-77	£10,000	£8,000	£5,000
Junior Zagato 1300	1290/4	1968-74	£10,000	£8,000	£5,000
Junior Zagato 1600	1570/4	1968-74	£11,000	£9,000	£6,000
Alfetta GT/GTV (chrome)	1962/4	1974-84	£3,500	£2,500	£1,000
Alfasud	1186/ 1490/4	1972-83	£2,000	£1,000	£500
Alfasud ti	1186/ 1490/4	1974-81	£2,500	£1,200	£900
Alfasud Sprint	1284/ 1490/4	1976-85	£3,000	£2,000	£1,000
GTV6	2492/6	1981-	£4,000	£2,000	£1,000

1965 Alfa Romeo TZ1 Coupé,
coachwork by Zagato, 4 cylinder,
1570cc engine, not original,
but correct type and vintage,
original magnesium bellhousing
and sump, original Zagato seats,
continuous and 'known' history.
Est. £85,000–95,000 *COYS*

*This car is one of only 120
examples made.*

Miller's is a price GUIDE
not a price LIST

1967 Alfa Romeo 1600 Sprint GT,
4 cylinder, 1570cc engine, good
overall condition.
Est. £3,500–4,500 *ADT*

1969 Alfa Romeo 1300 Spider, very good
original condition throughout.
£6,200–6,800 *H&H*

1970 Alfa Romeo Giulia GT Junior Z,
coachwork by Zagato, 4 cylinder, 1799cc
engine, left hand drive, very good condition.
£8,000–8,500 *COYS*

**1972 Alfa Romeo GT Junior 2 Door
Coupé,** coachwork by Bertone, 1600cc engine
instead of original 1300cc unit, major
restoration, period radio.
Est. £4,000–6,000 *BKS*

1970 Alfa Romeo GT Junior Zagato,
non-standard 4 cylinder, 1750cc twin cam
engine, Chromodora wheels, excellent
overall condition.
£7,000–7,500 *ADT*

1972 Alfa Romeo 1750 Spider, 5 speed,
fuel injection, imported from USA, left hand
drive, new mohair soft top, new carpets, good
original condition.
£4,500–5,000 *CCTC*

1973 Alfa Romeo 1600 GT 4 Seater Coupé, excellent totally original condition.
£6,500–7,000 *S*

1973 Alfa Romeo Giulia 1600 Super, coachwork by Bertone, 4 cylinder, 1570cc engine, bodywork restored, very good condition.
£3,250–3,750 *COYS*

1976 Alfa Romeo 2 Litre Spider, restored condition.
£5,000–7,000 *VIC*

1975 Alfa Romeo Alfasud Sextet TTS Coupé, bodywork by Williams and Pritchard, 4 cylinder, 1588cc engine, staggered 6 seat arrangement, fair condition.
£1,600–1,800 *COYS*

1973 Alfa Romeo 2000 GT Veloce Sports Coupé, original factory specification, period radio, very good overall condition.
Est. £5,000–6,000 *S*

1973 Alfa Romeo Giulia 2000 GTV Coupé, coachwork by Bertone, 4 cylinder, 1962cc engine, restored including a full engine rebuild, re-trimmed interior and total body restoration, excellent condition.
£5,000–5,500 *COYS*

1974 Alfa Romeo 1600 Spider Junior 2 Seater Sports Convertible, original factory specification, very good overall condition throughout.
Est. £6,500–7,500 *S*

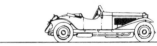

1975 Alfa Romeo 2000 GT, 4 cylinder, 1962cc engine, very good overall condition. **£2,500–2,750** *ADT*

1976 Alfa Romeo Spider Veloce, 4 cylinder, 1998cc engine, re-painted, good overall condition. **£6,500–7,000** *ADT*

1981 Alfa Romeo 2000 Spider Veloce, coachwork by Pininfarina, ex-Florida car, non-original Shelby Cobra wheels fitted, very good overall condition. **Est. £5,900–6,500** *S*

1982 Alfa Romeo GTV 2 Litre, 4 cylinder, 2000cc engine, good overall condition. **Est. £2,000–3,000** *ADT*

1983 Alfa Romeo GTV 2 Litre, 4 cylinder, 1962cc engine, re-sprayed, excellent condition. **£1,500–1,750** *ADT*

1988 Alfa Romeo Spider Veloce, coachwork by Pininfarina, American specification, fitted with air conditioning, alloy wheels. **£7,500–8,000** *CARS*

1989 Alfa Romeo Spider 2 Litre Series III, bodywork by Pininfarina, UK specification, pepperpot alloy wheels fitted. **£8,000–8,500** *CARS*

ALLARD

Although the Allard Motor Company Ltd., was not formed until 1945, Sidney Allard had produced a series of Ford powered Allard Specials from as early as 1937. Allard had ceased production by 1957, but continues to develop ideas and its involvement in motoring technology.

The K1 weighed 21cwt, was powered by a 3.6 litre Ford engine developing 85bhp, and produced 0–60mph in 13.6 seconds.

1948 Allard K1 2 Seater Sports, good condition and original specification in all major respects.
Est. £14,000–18,000 *S*

1954 Allard K3, Cadillac V8, 331cu in engine, 300bhp at 6000rpm, 3 speed automatic gearbox, 4 wheel hydraulic drum brakes, independent front suspension with coil springs, swinging half axles, radius arms, hydraulic shock absorbers, transverse leaf spring rear suspension, rigid axle, left hand drive, very low mileage, excellent original condition.
£28,000–30,000 *CNY*

ALLARD Model	ENGINE cc/cyl	DATES	CONDITION 1	2	3
K/K2/L/M/M2X	3622/8	1947-54	£17,000	£11,000	£7,500
K3	var/8	1953-54	£24,000	£15,000	£11,000
P1	3622/8	1949-52	£18,000	£12,000	£7,000
P2	3622/8	1952-54	£22,000	£18,000	£11,000
J2/J2X	var/8	1950-54	£60,000	£50,000	£35,000
Palm Beach	1508/4, 2262/6	1952-55	£10,000	£7,500	£4,500
Palm Beach II	2252/ 3442/6	1956-60	£22,500	£18,000	£11,000

ALLDAYS

1914 Alldays Midget 8.9hp 2 Seater, upholstery original and well preserved, a museum exhibit that requires recommissioning.
£9,000–9,500 *S*

Make the most of Miller's

Condition is absolutely vital when assessing the value of a vehicle. Top class vehicles on the whole appreciate much more than less perfect examples. Rare, desirable cars may command higher prices even when in need of restoration.

ALVIS

During the 1930s Alvis produced a series of useful sports cars as well as fast tourers of great refinement founded on the 12/50 model, which was produced between 1923 and 1932. A series of luxurious saloons was made after WWII, and the Alvis factory in Coventry still produces military armoured fighting vehicles.

1925 Alvis 12/50 TE Ducksback 3 Seater, short stroke engine with big port head, S-type 4 speed gearbox, polished aluminium coachwork, full weather equipment.
Est. £23,000–26,000 *S*

1934 Alvis Speed Twenty 4 Seater Tourer, sound car, good condition throughout, upholstery poor, ideal for restoration.
Est. £11,000–13,000 *S*

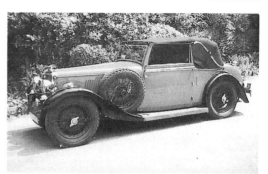

1934 Alvis Silver Eagle 3 Position Drophead Coupé, by Cross & Ellis, 6 cylinder, 2511cc engine, very good condition throughout.
£9,500–10,000 *ADT*

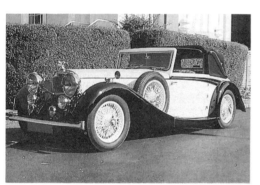

1936 Alvis Speed Twenty Type SD 3 Position Drophead Coupé, coachwork by Charlesworth, original engine, red leather interior, very good condition throughout.
£45,000–48,000 *S*

1938 Alvis 4.3 Litre 4 Door Sports Saloon, coachwork by Charlesworth, all synchromesh gearbox, transverse leaf independent front suspension, repainted, new leather upholstery and trim, new tyres, good condition throughout.
Est. £28,000–32,000 *S*

1938 Alvis 12/70 Sports, replica body, recent racing history, very good condition.
£13,000–14,000 *CGOC*

1954 Alvis TC 21/100 Grey Lady Saloon, coachwork by Mulliner, 6 cylinder, 2992cc pushrod overhead valve engine, good condition throughout.
£8,250–8,750 *S*

ALVIS Model	ENGINE cc/cyl	DATES	CONDITION 1	2	3
12/50	1496/4	1923-32	£16,000	£11,000	£7,000
Silver Eagle	2148	1929-37	£14,000	£10,000	£8,000
Silver Eagle DHC	2148	1929-37	£16,000	£11,000	£8,000
12/60	1645/4	1931-32	£15,000	£10,000	£7,000
Speed 20 (tourer)	2511/6	1932-36	£35,000	£28,000	£18,000
Speed 20 (closed)	2511/6	1932-36	£22,000	£15,000	£11,000
Crested Eagle	3571/6	1933-39	£10,000	£7,000	£4,000
Firefly (tourer)	1496/4	1932-34	£12,000	£10,000	£6,000
Firefly (closed)	1496/6	1932-34	£7,000	£5,000	£4,000
Firebird (tourer)	1842/4	1934-39	£13,000	£10,000	£6,000
Firebird (closed)	1842/4	1934-39	£7,000	£5,000	£4,000
Speed 25 (tourer)	3571/6	1936-40	£38,500	£30,000	£20,000
Speed 25 (closed)	3571/6	1936-40	£20,000	£15,000	£12,000
3.5 litre	3571/6	1935-36	£35,000	£25,000	£18,000
4.3 litre	4387/6	1936-40	£44,000	£30,000	£22,000
Silver Crest	2362/6	1936-40	£14,000	£10,000	£7,000
TA	3571/6	1936-39	£18,000	£12,000	£8,000
12/70	1842/4	1937-40	£14,000	£10,000	£7,000

1959 Alvis TD21 Drophead Coupé,
6 cylinder, 2993cc engine, 115bhp at
4000rpm, automatic gearbox, disc front
brakes, drum rear, independent coil front
suspension, semi-elliptic live axle rear, right
hand drive, very original generally good
condition, faded paintwork.
Est. £10,000–14,000 *C*

1959 Alvis TD21 Saloon, coachwork by
Park Ward, 3 litre engine, Borg Warner
automatic transmission, restored,
good condition.
Est. £10,000–11,000 *S*

**1962 Alvis TD21 MkII 3 Litre Sports
Saloon,** Webasto type sunroof, radio, wing
mirrors and twin auxiliary lights, as
standard on MkII, good overall condition,
comprehensive history.
Est. £6,500–8,000 *S*

1961 Alvis TD21 Drophead Coupé,
coachwork by Park Ward, 6 cylinder, 2993cc
engine, 115bhp at 4000rpm, automatic
gearbox, disc front brakes, drum rear,
independent coil front suspension,
semi-elliptic live axle rear, right hand drive,
good condition.
£7,500–8,000 *C*

> **Miller's is a price GUIDE
> not a price LIST**

**1961 Alvis TD21 3.0 Litre
2 Door Saloon,** coachwork
by Park Ward, very good
condition throughout.
£14,000–14,500 *BKS*

ALVIS Model	ENGINE cc/cyl	DATES	CONDITION 1	2	3
TA14	1892/4	1946-50	£9,000	£7,000	£4,000
TA14 DHC	1892/4	1946-50	£14,000	£12,000	£5,000
TB14 Roadster	1892/4	1949-50	£14,000	£9,000	£7,000
TB21 Roadster	2993/6	1951	£15,000	£9,000	£6,000
TA21/TC21	2993/6	1950-55	£12,000	£9,000	£5,000
TA21/TC21 DHC	2993/6	1950-55	£17,000	£13,000	£10,000
TC21/100 Grey Lady	2993/6	1953-56	£13,000	£11,000	£5,000
TC21/100 DHC	2993/6	1954-56	£21,000	£18,000	£14,000
TD21	2993/6	1956-62	£12,000	£9,000	£7,000
TD21 DHC	2993/6	1956-62	£22,000	£20,000	£12,000
TE21	2993/6	1963-67	£17,000	£13,000	£10,000
TE21 DHC	2993/6	1963-67	£25,000	£21,000	£15,000
TF21	2993/6	1966-67	£16,000	£12,000	£9,500
TF21 DIIC	2993/6	1966-67	£28,000	£18,000	£12,000

1965 Alvis TE21 Drophead Coupé, 6 cylinder, 2993cc engine, only 2 owners from new, stored for ten years, requires some cosmetic restoration.
£5,000–5,500 *ADT*

1966 Alvis TE21 Saloon, 6 cylinder, 2993cc engine, good overall condition.
Est. £10,000–12,000 *ADT*

ARMSTRONG-SIDDELEY

Armstrong-Siddeley was formed in 1919 when Armstrong Whitworth joined forces with the Siddeley-Deasy Motor Manufacturing Company. The Company produced a variety of cars, many under powered, but all well appointed and surmounted by the famous Armstrong-Siddeley sphinx mascot.

1952 Armstrong-Siddeley Whitley 4-Light Saloon, 6 cylinder, 2309cc engine, very good original condition throughout.
£3,800–4,200 *ADT*

1936 Armstrong-Siddeley 12hp Sports Coupé, 6 cylinder, 1434cc engine, original condition, requires restoration.
Est. £4,000–5,000 *ADT*

Cross Reference
Restoration Projects

Make the most of Miller's
Condition is absolutely vital when assessing the value of a vehicle. Top class vehicles on the whole appreciate much more than less perfect examples. Rare, desirable cars may command higher prices even when in need of restoration.

1960 Armstrong-Siddeley Star Sapphire, 6 cylinder, 3990cc engine, older restoration, very good overall condition.
Est. £6,000–7,000 *ADT*

ARMSTRONG-SIDDELEY Model	ENGINE cc/cyl	DATES	CONDITION 1	2	3
Hurricane	1991/6	1945-53	£10,000	£6,000	£3,000
Typhoon	1991/6	1946-50	£7,000	£3,000	£2,000
Lancaster/Whitley	1991/				
	2306/6	1945-53	£7,000	£5,000	£2,500
Sapphire 234/236	2290/4				
	2309/6	1955-58	£6,000	£4,000	£2,500
Sapphire 346	3440/6	1953-58	£8,000	£5,000	£3,000
Star Sapphire	3990/6	1958-60	£9,000	£6,000	£3,000

ASTON MARTIN

When David Brown (later Sir David) acquired Aston Martin the company used a first class chassis, the Atom, but the engines were under powered. To ensure a supply of 2.3 litre, 6 cylinder engines, Brown purchased the Lagonda Company. The engine was increased in size and performance, the result being the Aston Martin DB2. Race successes and a series of quality road cars in the 50s and 60s were not sufficient to enable the company to survive and, following a number of financial problems, it was bought by Ford in 1987.

1930 Aston Martin International 1½ Litre 4 Seater Sports Tourer, good condition throughout, no known modifications from maker's original specification.
Est. £32,000–38,000 *S*

1951 Aston Martin DB2 Vantage Coupé, 6 cylinder, 2580cc engine, excellent overall condition.
£36,000–38,000 *COYS*

Aston Martin DB2/4

- The DB2/4 was introduced in 1953 as an occasional 4 seater version of the 2 seater DB2.
- Engine size was increased to 2.9 litre developing about 140bhp.
- Top speed of approximately 120mph, with 100mph in third gear.

1953 Aston Martin DB2 Sports Coupé, rebuilt engine, restored, original leather interior.
Est. £19,000–20,000 *S*

1952 Aston Martin DB2, 6 cylinder, 2580cc engine, excellent original condition throughout.
Est. £32,000–34,000 *ADT*

ASTON MARTIN Model	ENGINE cc/cyl	DATES	CONDITION		
			1	2	3
Lionel Martin Cars	1486/4	1921-25	£26,000	£18,000	£16,000
International	1486/4	1927-32	£28,000	£18,000	£16,000
Le Mans	1486/4	1932-33	£52,000	£38,000	£32,000
Mk II	1486/4	1934-36	£40,000	£30,000	£25,000
Ulster	1486/4	1934-36	£65,000	£50,000	-
2 litre	1950/4	1936-40	£18,000	£14,000	£9,000

Value is dependent upon racing history, originality and completeness.
Add 40% if a competition winner.

1954 Aston Martin DB2/4 3 Litre 2 Door Drophead Coupé, original engine, good overall condition.
£29,000–31,000 *BKS*

1960 Aston Martin DB4 Sports Coupé, very good restored condition.
Est. £24,000–26,000 *S*

1961 Aston Martin DB4 Series II Superleggera Saloon, stainless steel exhaust system, resprayed, retrimmed, new carpet, good overall condition.
Est. £22,000–28,000 *BKS*

1960 Aston Martin DB4 Sports Coupé, major mechanical restoration, original car and leather interior.
£15,000–16,000 *S*

Aston Martin DB4

- Introduced in 1958 with a new 6 cylinder 3.7 litre engine designed by Tadek Marek producing about 240bhp.
- Bodywork by Touring of Milan.
- 0–60mph in about 9 seconds and a top speed of over 140mph.
- Only about 70 convertibles were produced between 1961 and 1963.

1961 Aston Martin DB4 Series II, extensively restored, very good condition.
£21,000–23,000 *H&H*

ASTON MARTIN Model	ENGINE cc/cyl	DATES	CONDITION		
			1	2	3
DB1	1970/4	1948-50	£18,000	£15,000	£11,000
DB2	2580/6	1950-53	£23,000+	£17,000	£13,000
DB2 Conv	2580/6	1951-53	£30,000	£20,000	£17,000
DB2/4 Mk I/II	2580/ 2922/6	1953-57	£30,000	£18,000	£12,000
DB2/4 Mk II Conv	2580/ 2922/6	1953-57	£28,000	£18,000	£14,000
DB2/4 Mk III	2580/ 2922/6	1957-59	£30,000	£18,000	£13,000
DB2/4 Mk III Conv	2580/ 2922/6	1957-59	£32,000	£19,000	£16,000
DB Mk III Conv	2922/6	1957-59	£33,000	£24,000	£20,000
DB Mk III	2922/6	1957-59	£30,000	£19,000	£16,000
DB4	3670/6	1959-63	£25,000	£18,000	£14,000
DB4 Conv	3670/6	1961-63	£45,000	£30,000	-
DB4 GT	3670/6	1961-63	£75,000+	£70,000	-
DB5	3995/6	1964-65	£32,000	£25,000	£18,000
DB5 Conv	3995/6	1964-65	£42,000	£30,000	-
DB6	3995/6	1965-69	£22,000	£17,000	£9,000
DB6 Mk I auto	3995/6	1965-69	£18,000	£13,000	£8,000
DB6 Mk I Volante	3995/6	1965-71	£35,000	£28,000	£22,000
DB6 Mk II Volante	3995/6	1969-70	£36,000	£30,000	£24,000
DBS	3995/6	1967-72	£11,000	£9,000	£6,500
AM Vantage	3995/6	1972-73	£14,000	£10,000	£7,000

1963 Aston Martin DB4 Series IV Convertible, coachwork by Touring of Milan, 6 cylinder, 3670cc engine, very good condition throughout. £50,000–52,000 *COYS*

1962 Aston Martin DB4 Series III, sports saloon coachwork by Touring, 6 cylinder, 3670cc engine, exceptionally sound original order throughout, complete restoration to concours standard. £42,000–44,000 *COYS*

1962 Aston Martin DB4 Convertible, 6 cylinder in line engine, twin overhead camshaft, 3670cc, 240bhp at 5500rpm, 4 speed gearbox with overdrive, 4 wheel disc brakes, all coil spring independent front suspension, good overall original condition. Est. £40,000–50,000 *C*

1964 Aston Martin DB5, 6 cylinder, 3995cc overhauled engine, professionally repainted and retrimmed, new chrome wire wheels and spinners, very good overall condition. Est. £27,000–30,000 *COYS*

1965 Aston Martin DB5 Coupé, coachwork by Touring, 6 cylinder, 3995cc rebuilt engine, to Vantage specification, gearbox overhauled. £19,000–22,000 *COYS*

1966 Aston Martin DB6 Vantage,
coachwork by Touring, 6 cylinder, 3995cc
rebuilt engine, rebuilt gearbox, excellent
condition throughout.
Est. £27,000–32,000 *COYS*

**Miller's is a price GUIDE
not a price LIST**

1966 Aston Martin DB6 MkI Sports Coupé,
chrome wire wheels, good all-round condition.
Est. £18,000–22,000 *S*

**1966 Aston Martin DB6
4 Litre MkI 2 Door Grand
Touring Coupé,** automatic
transmission, good original
overall condition.
Est. £17,000–20,000 *BKS*

1966 Aston Martin DB6, good condition.
£18,000–20,000 *BLE*

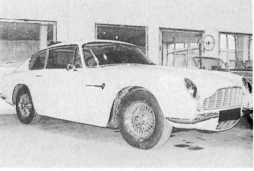

1967 Aston Martin DB6, only 29,000 miles
recorded, excellent original condition.
£26,000–28,000 *COYS*

1968 Aston Martin DB6 Sports Saloon,
automatic transmission, chrome wire wheels,
Webasto sunroof, good all-round condition.
Est. £18,000–22,000 *S*

1967 Aston Martin DB6, 6 cylinder, 3995cc engine, very good restored condition throughout.
£20,000–21,000 *ADT*

1969 Aston Martin DBS, 6 cylinder, 3995cc engine, wire wheels, leather interior, good condition.
£8,500–9,000 *ADT*

1970 Aston Martin DBS, fully restored to a very high standard.
£15,500–16,000 *ADT*

1971 Aston Martin DBS V8 4 Seater Sports Saloon, automatic transmission, generally very good condition.
£9,000–9,500 *S*

1971 Aston Martin DBS6 Grand Touring 4 Seater Coupé, 6 cylinder, twin overhead camshaft 3995cc engine, 282bhp at 5750rpm, Borg Warner automatic gearbox, 4 wheel servo disc brakes, independent front suspension, De Dion rear, very good overall condition.
£8,500–9,000 *C*

1973 Aston Martin AMV8 Coupé, V8 cylinder engine, twin overhead camshaft per bank, 5340cc, 5 speed manual gearbox, semi-platform type chassis, coil spring independent front suspension, De Dion rear, 4 wheel disc brakes, cast aluminium alloy wheels, 205 x 15 tyres, well maintained, good overall condition.
Est. £30,000–36,000 *C(A)*

1971 Aston Martin DBS V8, manual gearbox, 2 owners only, 41,000 miles recorded, leather interior.
£14,000–17,000 *VIC*

1973 Aston Martin AMV8 GT Coupé, very good condition overall.
Est. £46,000–53,000 *C(A)*

1973 Aston Martin AM Vantage, fully rebuilt, retrimmed, excellent condition.
£12,000–12,500 *ADT*

1973 Aston Martin AMV8, 8 cylinder, 5340cc engine, good original condition.
Est. £12,000–14,000 *ADT*

1974 Aston Martin V8 5.3 Litre Saloon, good restored condition.
£16,000–17,000 *BKS*

1975 Aston Martin V8 Sports Coupé, only 19,600 miles recorded, excellent condition throughout.
Est. £24,000–26,000 *S*

1974 Aston Martin V8 Saloon.
£16,000–20,000 *DJR*

1976 Aston Martin V8 Coupé,
BBS alloy wheels, bare metal respray,
very good condition throughout.
£20,000–22,000 *S*

1977 Aston Martin V8 Saloon, automatic
transmission, good overall condition.
Est. £14,500–15,500 *ADT*

**1977 Aston Martin
V8 Vantage Saloon,**
a well known car in
good original
condition throughout.
£22,000–23,000 *S*

1980 Aston Martin V8, bare metal respray,
rebuilt front and rear suspension, new rear
axle, rebuilt gearbox, brakes and new
steering rack, air conditioning, cruise control
and vantage driving lights.
£22,000–23,000 *H&H*

1985 Aston Martin Lagonda, V8, 5340cc
engine, only 46,000 miles recorded, good
condition, service history.
£16,000–17,000 *COYS*

1977 Aston Martin V8 Series I Vantage.
£25,000–35,000 *DJR*

1989 Aston Martin Virage.
£60,000+ *DJR*

AUBURN

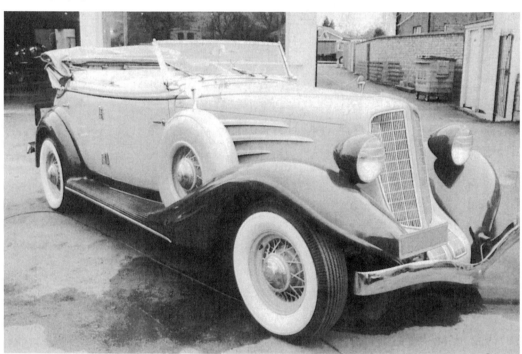

1934 Auburn 850Y Five Passenger Phæton, right hand drive, originally registered in South Africa, excellent restored condition throughout.
Est. £32,000–35,000 *S*

AUDI

The founder of Horch Cars, August Horch, left the Company in 1909 and by 1910 had started Audi. Both companies were in Zwickau in Germany. Due to contractual difficulties he was unable to use his own name on his cars so he adopted the Latin word Audi, which means listen, the same as Horch does in German.

1983 Audi Quattro 2 door Coupé,
excellent condition throughout.
Est. £5,300–5,800 *S*

AUSTIN

Following a growth period during WWI, the Austin Company was saved by the introduction of the ubiquitous Austin 7. Developed from an idea and design by Stanley Edge, the Austin 7 first appeared in 1922. A 7hp motor made it cheap to tax and was probably, and possibly still is, Britain's favourite motor car. A whole nation was introduced to motoring with the Austin 7, signalling the demise of the motorcycle combination.

It has been said that the Austin 7 is easy to drive badly and hard to drive well. Anyone who has driven one will concur that there is always scope for improvement in their personal driving skills.

c1928 Austin 7, coachwork by Mulliner, 4 cylinders, 750cc engine, wooden body frame, serviced and re-skinned in red leatherette, exceptionally well restored. Est. £4,000–6,000 *ADT*

Make the Most of Miller's

Veteran Cars are those manufactured up to 31 December 1918. Only vehicles built before 31 December 1904 are eligible for the London/Brighton Commemorative Run. Vintage Cars are vehicles that were manufactured between 1 January 1919 and 31 December 1930.

1911 Austin 7 Two Seater, with oil sidelamps, Rotax Clarion bulb horn, to original specification. £13,250–13,750 *S*

1927 Austin 7 Chummy, 4 cylinders, 747cc engine, completely restored, but due to protracted storage needs re-commissioning. £6,000–6,500 *ADT*

1930 Austin 7 Chummy Tourer, excellent overall condition. £5,250–5,750 *S*

1930 Austin 7hp Saloon, coachwork by The Swallow Coachbuilding Company, 4 speed gearbox and later carburettor, very good restored condition. £6,000–6,500 *S*

1930 Austin 7 Saloon, 4 cylinders, 747cc engine, good overall condition.
£3,250–3,750 *ADT*

1933 Austin 7 Long Door Saloon, 4 cylinder, 858cc engine, good overall condition.
£3,800–4,800 *ADT*

1931 Austin 7 Saloon, very good condition.
£3,000–3,750 *OMH*

1933 Austin 7 saloon, very good condition.
£3,750–4,250 *OMH*

1931 Austin 7 Saloon, coachwork by Swallow, complete but unrestored, museum stored, in good condition throughout.
£6,500–7,000 *BKS*

AUSTIN Model	ENGINE cc/cyl	DATES	CONDITION 1	2	3
25/30	4900/4	1906	£35,000	£25,000	£20,000
20	3600/4	1919-27	£18,000	£12,000	£6,000
12	1661/4	1922-26	£8,000	£5,000	£2,000
7	747/4	1924-39	£7,000	£4,000	£1,500
7 Coachbuilt	747/4	1924-39	£10,000	£9,000	£7,000
12/4	1861/4	1927-35	£5,500	£4,000	£2,000
16	2249/6	1928-36	£9,000	£7,000	£4,000
20/6	3400/6	1928-38	£12,500	£10,000	£8,000
12/6	1496/6	1932-37	£6,000	£4,000	£1,500
12/4	1535/4	1933-39	£5,000	£3,500	£1,500
10 and 10/4	1125/4	1932-47	£4,000	£3,000	£1,000
10 and 10/4 Conv	1125/4	1933-47	£5,000	£3,500	£1,000
18	2510/6	1934-39	£8,000	£5,000	£3,000
14	1711/6	1937-39	£6,000	£4,000	£2,000
Big Seven	900/4	1938-39	£4,000	£2,500	£1,500
8	900/4	1939-47	£3,000	£2,000	£1,000
28	4016/6	1939	£6,000	£4,000	£2,000

1933 Austin 7 Saloon, 4 cylinder, 748cc engine, good condition throughout.
Est. £3,800–4,800 *ADT*

This model was the last of the 'box' type saloon models to be produced before the introduction of the Ruby. The overall length was 119in (302cm) with a wheelbase of 81in (205.5cm).

1934 Austin 7 Box Saloon, 750cc engine, very good overall condition.
Est. £3,000–4,000 *LF*

1934 Austin 7 2 Door Saloon, 747cc engine, re-sprayed but very original, period tools, including a hand pump, very good condition.
£7,200–7,600 *BKS*

1934 Austin 7 Opal 2 Seater Tourer, in fair condition.
£4,000–4,500 *OMH*

1935 Austin 7hp Nippy Open Sports, chassis up restoration, very good condition throughout.
£7,250–7,500 *S*

Austin introduced the '65' Sports in June 1933, a 2 seater sports car with lower frame, reversed camber front springs, lowered front axle beam, high compression head, tulip valves, Zenith down-draught carburettor, cast aluminium ribbed sump and a radiator stoneguard. From 1934 onwards the car was marketed as the Nippy Sports.

1935 Austin 7 Ruby, 4 cylinders, 747cc engine, 33,000 miles recorded, 3 owners from new, exceptionally good unrestored condition.
£4,250–4,750 *COYS*

1935 Austin 7 Ruby, comprehensively restored to a very high standard.
£4,200–4,600 *H&H*

1936 Austin 7 Ruby, 34,000 miles recorded since new, very good original condition throughout.
£3,500–4,000 *ADT*

1936 Austin Ruby, very good overall condition.
Est. £4,500–5,000 *ADT*

1937 Austin 7 Ruby, excellent restored condition.
£3,500–4,750 *OMH*

1938 Austin 7 Ruby, good overall condition but requires some cosmetic restoration.
£1,500–1,750 *ADT*

1933 Austin 10/4, very good overall condition.
Est. £4,500–6,000 *ADT*

1932 Austin 10/4, an early example in good condition.
£5,500–5,750 *OMH*

1928 Austin 16/6 Doctor's Coupé, very good restored condition.
£8,200–8,600 *HOLL*

1933 Austin 16/6 Hearse, 6 cylinder, 2249cc engine, coachbuilt body from an original horse drawn hearse, large etched glass panels engraved with lilies of the valley, elaborate filigree decoration around the roof edges, silver plated interior fittings, engine re-built, good condition.
£6,500–7,000 *S*

1934 Austin 10 Clifton Drophead Coupé, 4 cylinders, 1141cc engine, quite good overall condition.
Est. £4,000–5,000 *ADT*

1934 Austin 10/4, very good condition.
£4,250–4,750 *OMH*

1935 Austin 10 Colwyn Cabriolet, very good original condition.
£5,200–5,750 *S*

1934 Austin 12/4 Harley, excellent condition.
£9,500–10,500 *OMH*

1935 Austin 12/4 Ascot, excellent condition.
£7,500–8,000 *OMH*

1937 Austin 12/4 New Ascot, 1535cc engine, older restoration.
£4,000–4,750 *OMH*

1937 Austin 12/4 New Ascot, very good condition.
£4,500–5,500 *OMH*

1939 Austin 10 Cambridge, very good condition throughout.
£3,750–4,250 *OMH*

AUSTIN Model	ENGINE cc/cyl	DATES	CONDITION 1	2	3
16	2199/4	1945-49	£3,000	£2,000	£1,000
A40 Devon	1200/4	1947-52	£2,000	£1,200	£750
A40 Sports	1200/4	1950-53	£6,000	£4,000	£2,000
A40 Somerset	1200/4	1952-54	£2,000	£1,500	£750
A40 Somerset DHC	1200/4	1954	£5,000	£4,000	£2,500
A40 Dorset 2 door	1200/4	1947-48	£2,000	£1,500	£1,000
A70 Hampshire	2199/4	1948-50	£2,000	£1,500	£1,000
A70 Hereford	2199/4	1950-54	£2,000	£1,500	£1,000
A90 Atlantic DHC	2660/4	1949-52	£8,000	£6,000	£4,000
A90 Atlantic	2660/4	1949-52	£6,000	£4,000	£3,000
A40/A50 Cambridge	1200/4	1954-57	£1,200	£750	£500
A55 Mk I Cambridge	1489/4	1957-59	£1,000	£750	£500
A55 Mk II	1489/4	1959-61	£1,000	£750	£500
A60 Cambridge	1622/4	1961-69	£1,000	£750	£500
A90/95 Westminster	2639/6	1954-59	£2,000	£1,500	£750
A99 Westminster	2912/6	1959-61	£1,500	£1,000	£500
A105 Westminster	2639/6	1956-59	£2,000	£1,500	£750
A110 Mk I/II	2912/6	1961-68	£2,000	£1,500	£750
Nash Metropolitan	1489/4	1957-61	£2,500	£1,500	£750
Nash Metropolitan DHC	1489/4	1957-61	£4,000	£3,000	£1,500
A30	803/4	1952-56	£1,000	£500	-
A30 Countryman	803/4	1954-56	£1,500	£1,000	-
A35	948/4	1956-59	£1,000	£500	-
A35 Countryman	948/4	1956-62	£1,500	£1,000	-
A40 Farina Mk I	948/4	1958-62	£1,250	£750	£200
A40 Mk I Countryman	948/4	1959-62	£1,500	£1,000	£400
A40 Farina Mk II	1098/4	1962-67	£1,000	£750	-
A40 Mk II Countryman	1098/4	1962-67	£1,200	£750	£300
1100	1098/4	1963-73	£1,000	£750	-
1300 Mk I/II	1275/4	1967-74	£750	£500	-
1300GT	1275/4	1969-74	£1,250	£1,000	£750
1800/2200		1964-75	£1,500	£900	£600
3 litre	2912/6	1968-71	£3,000	£1,500	£500

1939 Austin 8, 4 cylinder, 900cc engine, very low mileage, good original condition.
Est. £4,000–4,500 *ADT*

1939 Austin 8 Saloon, very good original condition.
£1,700–2,000 *S*

1953 Austin A40 Somerset, 1200cc engine, very good original condition.
£1,500–2,250 *OMH*

1951 Austin A40 Devon, very good original car.
£1,500–2,000 *OMH*

1952 Austin A90 Atlantic Sports Saloon, restored, very good condition throughout.
£5,250–5,750 *AAOC*

1949/51 Austin Atlantic Convertible, fully restored.
£13,000–15,000 *AAOC*

The air intakes on the front of the bonnet are not original.

1954 Austin A30 2 Door Saloon, 803cc engine, original condition.
£550–650 *H&H*

1955 Austin A40 Somerset 4 Door Saloon,
dry stored, running well, sound but requires
cosmetic attention.
£440–480 *S*

1955 Austin A30 4 Door Saloon,
excellent condition overall.
£2,750–3,000 *C*

1956 Austin A40 Cambridge,
excellent original condition.
£1,600–1,800 *OMH*

1959 Austin A40 2 Door Saloon,
original, good condition.
£770–840 *C*

1960 Austin A35 Saloon, following
a period of museum storage some
sympathetic restoration required.
£800–900 *S*

1963 Austin A60 Countryman,
low mileage, very good condition.
£1,500–2,000 *OMH*

Austin A40

- **Launched in 1958 as a part saloon/part estate car.**
- **Unusual hatch opening below the rear window to facilitate loading.**
- **Used mainly A35 components.**
- **Styled by Pininfarina of Italy.**

**1968 Austin Princess Vanden Plas
Saloon,** 1300cc engine, 39,900 miles
recorded, manual transmission, factory
sunroof, good original condition.
£1,250–1,500 *S*

1961 Austin A40 2 Door Saloon,
40,000 miles recorded, good
condition throughout.
£275–325 *C*

AUSTIN HEALEY

Donald Healey was one of the first British car producers to realise the enormous sales potential in America for British sports cars. He started his own company after WWII using standard components. However, it was the collaboration with Austin producing, most famously, the 100, 3000 and Sprite for which Donald Healey is best remembered.

1959 Austin Healey Sprite Mk I Roadster, left hand drive, meticulously restored retaining originality, very good overall condition.
£6,500–7,500 *S*

1959 Austin Healey Sprite MkI, very good original condition.
£7,000–7,500 *SJR*

1959 Austin Healey Sprite Mk I, good original condition.
£3,500–4,500 *OMH*

Austin Healey Sprite

- Used BMC A Series, 4 cylinder overhead valve engine from the Austin A35.
- In slightly modified form, including twin SU carburettors, the engine developed 43bhp and a top speed of about 80 mph.
- Over 50,000 Mk I 'frog-eyes' were produced during a 3 year at a price of £632 each.

> Miller's is a price GUIDE not a price LIST

1953 Austin Healey 100/4 Limited Edition 2 Seater Sports, totally stripped and restored from the ground up, concours condition.
£11,500–12,000 *S*

c1959 Austin Healey Sprite, fully restored.
£3,000–3,500 *CARS*

1954 Austin Healey 100/4, 4 cylinders, excellent condition throughout.
£14,000–15,000 *ADT*

1955 Austin Healey 100 BN1, imported from USA, excellent restored condition.
£14,250–14,750 *CCTC*

1955 Austin Healey 100/4 BN2, 4 cylinder, 2660cc engine, professionally converted to right hand drive, body-off restoration, excellent condition throughout.
Est. £13,000–14,000 *ADT*

1959 Austin Healey 3000 MkI,
6 cylinder, 2912cc engine, totally restored and mechanically overhauled, concours condition throughout.
£17,000–18,000 *COYS*

1959 Austin Healey 100/6, original right hand drive, excellent condition.
£10,750–11,500 *OMH*

1959 Austin Healey 100/6 2 Seater, overdrive, left hand drive, imported from USA, wire wheels, very low mileage, good condition.
£9,500–10,000 *CCTC*

1960 Austin Healey 3000 MkI, 6 cylinder, 3000cc engine, left hand drive, totally rebuilt, rust free, good condition.
Est. £12,000–14,000 *ADT*

1960 Austin Healey 3000 MkI, 6 cylinders, restored, very good condition.
£15,000–16,000 *ADT*

1960 Austin Healey 3000 MkI, 6 cylinder, 2912cc engine, original right hand drive, low recorded mileage of 28,000, good condition. **£11,500–12,000** *COYS*

1963 Austin Healey 3000 MkII BJ7, overdrive, restored. **£15,500–16,000** *SJR*

1962 Austin Healey 3000 MkII BT7 2+2 Seater, with aluminium head, triple Webers, side exhaust and wing vents, full concours rebuild. **£27,000–30,000** *SC*

Austin Healey 3000 MkI

- Developed from the 100/4 (4 cylinder) to the 100/6 (6 cylinder), the Austin Healey 3000 was launched in March 1959.
- The 2 seater was designated BN7.
- The 4 seater (or 2+2) was the BT7.
- The 2639cc engine from the 100/6 model was enlarged to 2912cc and produced 124bhp at 4600rpm.
- Four speed gearbox and could accelerate 0–60mph in 13.4 seconds with a top speed of about 116mph with overdrive.
- The bulk of approximately 42,000 cars made were exported to the USA.
- The last model, the MkIII BJ8, produced 148bhp and over 120mph.
- By December 1967 production had ceased.

1963 Austin Healey 3000 MkIIA, rebuilt to works specification, good condition. **£21,000–23,000** *CGOC*

> **Miller's is a price GUIDE not a price LIST**

1965 Austin Healey 3000 MkII 2+2 Sports Convertible, very good condition. **£14,000–14,500** *S*

1964 Austin Healey 3000 Mk III 2.9 Litre Sports 2 Seater, engine rebuilt, restored throughout, excellent condition. **Est. £24,000–28,000** *BKS*

1965 Austin Healey 3000 MkIII, 6 cylinder, 2912cc fully rebuilt engine, originally left hand drive, very good restored condition.
£17,000–17,500 *ADT*

1967 Austin Healey 3000 MkIII Phase II Roadster, 6 cylinder, 2912cc engine, excellent overall condition.
£12,000–12,500 *COYS*

AUSTIN HEALEY Model	ENGINE cc/cyl	DATES	CONDITION 1	2	3
100 BN 1/2	2660/4	1953-56	£20,000	£14,000	£8,000
100/6, BN4/BN6	2639/6	1956-59	£18,000	£13,500	£8,000
3000 Mk I	2912/6	1959-61	£20,000	£13,000	£8,500
3000 Mk II	2912/6	1961-62	£22,000	£15,000	£9,000
3000 Mk IIA	2912/6	1962-64	£23,000	£15,000	£11,000
3000 Mk III	2912/6	1964-68	£24,000	£17,000	£11,000
Sprite Mk I	948/4	1958-61	£5,000	£4,000	£2,000
Sprite Mk II	948/4	1961-64	£3,000	£2,000	£1,000
Sprite Mk III	1098/4	1964-66	£3,500	£2,000	£1,000
Sprite Mk IV	1275/4	1966-71	£3,500	£1,500	£1,000

AUSTIN NASH

1957 Austin Nash Metropolitan Convertible, sound running condition, poor interior.
£1,500–1,750 *C*

1957 Austin Nash Metropolitan, 4 cylinder, 1498cc engine, low mileage, very good original condition throughout.
£4,000–4,250 *ADT*

BAKER

c1904 Baker Electric Stanhope,
¾hp electric motor, requires
re-commissioning, sound condition.
£10,500–11,000 *S*

BEAN

1926 Bean 14hp Four Seater Tourer,
very good restored condition.
£14,200–14,600 *S*

1928 Hadfield Bean 14/45hp 5 Seater Tourer,
restored over 2 years, very good condition throughout.
£9,500–10,500 *S*

BELSIZE

**1912 Belsize Model K
10/12hp 2 Seater with
Dickey,** acetylene headlights,
Belsize oil sidelamps, BRC
oil rear lamp, acetylene
generator, very good overall
condition throughout.
£11,000–11,500 *S*

*The 10/12hp had a 1944cc
engine and was the most
popular model.*

BENTLEY

The motoring world can be divided into two – those who have tried a W. O. Bentley and those who have not. Walter Owen Bentley formed Bentley Motors in 1919 and in the next 12 years produced 3,024 cars starting with the 3 litre sports tourer and ending with the fabulous 8 litre supercar. Making the marque's name both on and off the track produced an enviable and discerning clientele, some of whom raced their own cars at venues such as Le Mans and Brooklands – their success on these tracks is now legendary. Many famous people flocked to buy these cars. In the end, unfortunately, the depression did for Bentleys what it did for a lot of other companies.

In 1931 the company was taken over by Rolls-Royce Motors and formed into Bentley Motors (1931) Ltd. This company continued to service the vintage Bentleys at London and introduced a new model built at their Derby plant. This 3½ litre car became known as the Derby Bentley and remained in production, albeit with the engine increased to 4¼ litres, virtually unchanged, until the events of 1939 caused production to cease.

1926 Bentley 3 Litre Speed Model Tourer, coachwork by Vanden Plas, in need of restoration, believed to be complete in all major respects.
£55,000–57,000 *S*

The Speed Model, introduced in 1924, is perhaps the most sought after of the 3 litre models with 118½in chassis, close ratio gearbox, distinctive 'Red Label' radiator and twin SU 'Sloper' carburettors. When fitted with Vanden Plas tourer coachwork it is perhaps to the ultimate specification.

> **Miller's is a price GUIDE not a price LIST**

1923 Bentley 3 litre Speed Model Vanden Plas Open Tourer, 4 cylinder, 2996cc rebuilt engine, restored, genuine excellent overall condition.
£60,000–63,000 *COYS*

1924 Bentley 3 litre Speed Model Boat Deck Tourer, coachwork by C. C. Haddow, Saltburn-by-Sea, good condition throughout.
Est. £50,000–60,000 *S*

This car was built in 1924 with Vanden Plas coachwork, but in 1935 was fitted with 2 door saloon coachwork believed to be by Barker. In 1972 the present 3 seater boat deck coachwork was fitted by Charles Haddow.

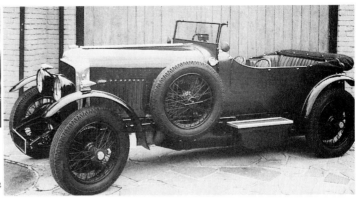

1928 Bentley 4½ Litre Open Tourer, excellent overall condition.
Est. £90,000–110,000 *COYS*

Originally built with 4 seater open coachwork by Vanden Plas, this car was re-bodied as a saloon in the 1950s, but has had a comprehensive mechanical re-build and reconstruction of the original Vanden Plas body.

1934 Bentley 3½ Litre Drophead, older restoration, excellent condition.
£43,000–45,000 *GAR*

1926 Bentley 6½ Litre Tourer, older restoration, as new condition throughout.
£188,000–190,000 *MAN*

1927 Bentley 4½ Litre Le Mans, very good condition throughout.
£158,000–160,000 *MAN*

1934 Bentley 3½ Litre Sports Saloon, coachwork by Freestone & Webb, restored in late 1980s, good condition throughout.
Est. £18,000–24,000 *S*

1934 The Bira Bentley, open sports tourer coachwork by Vanden Plas, excellent condition throughout.
£110,000–120,000 *COYS*

This car was delivered to Prince Bira in June 1934, and he used it to drive to motor races all-over Europe.

1935 Bentley 3½ Litre Top Hat Brougham, coachwork by Freestone & Webb, 6 cylinder in line engine, 4 speed gearbox, 4 wheel drum brakes, semi-elliptical front and rear suspension, fully restored to the highest standard.
£40,000–50,000 *CNY*

1935 Bentley 3½ Litre Drophead Coupé, coachwork by Park Ward, 6 cylinders, 3669cc engine, complete body restoration, good condition throughout.
Est. £34,000–38,000 *COYS*

Use the Index!
Because certain items might fit easily into any number of categories, the quickest and surest method of locating any entry is by reference to the index at the back of the book.

This index has been fully cross-referenced for absolute simplicity.

1937 Bentley 4¼ Litre Pillarless Saloon, coachwork by H. J. Mulliner, very good condition throughout.
£20,000–21,000 *S*

1938 Bentley 4¼ Litre Razor Edge Top Hat Sports Saloon, coachwork by Freestone & Webb, original condition.
Est. £20,000–25,000 *S*

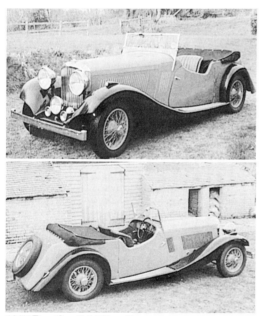

1937 Bentley 3.5 Litre Tourer, very good overall condition.
Est. £30,000–34,000 *S*

1937 Bentley 4¼ Litre Sports Saloon, original engine and coachwork, good condition generally, upholstery requires restoration.
Est. £18,000–19,000 *S*

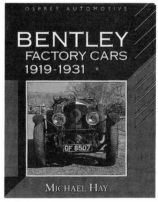

1939 Bentley MX 4¼ Litre Razor Edge Saloon, coachwork by Mann Egerton of Norwich, very good overall condition.
£26,000–28,000 *S*

From March 1936, the 4¼ litre engine rated at 29.4hp was available as an option in the 3½ litre 'Silent Sportscar' chassis. In total 1,241 4¼ litre chassis were built.

1946 Bentley MkVI Prototype 4¼ Litre Drophead Coupé with Hard Top, coachwork by Vanden Plas, almost complete restoration project.
£20,000–21,000 *S*

Cross Reference
Restoration Projects

1948 Bentley MkVI Standard Steel Saloon, good original condition, but some cosmetic attention required.
£6,000–6,500 *S*

1947 Bentley MkVI, 6 cylinder, 4250cc, 36,000 miles recorded from new, good original condition.
£11,000–12,000 *ADT*

1948/80 Bentley MkVI Sedanca De Ville Special, reconditioned chassis, engine rebuilt.
Est. £11,000–13,000 *ADT*

This unique Sedanca de Ville coachwork was commissioned in 1980 and built by Mallileau. The bodyshell was framed in ash and clad in hand-beaten aluminium.

BENTLEY Model	ENGINE cc/cyl	DATES	CONDITION 1	2	3
3 litre	2996/4	1920-27	£100,000	£75,000	£50,000
Speed Six	6597/6	1926-32	£400,000	£250,000	£160,000
4.5 litre	4398/4	1927-31	£175,000	£125,000	£80,000
4.5 litre Supercharged	4398/4	1929-32	£500,000	£300,000	£200,000
8 litre	7983/6	1930-32	£350,000	£250,000	£100,000
3.5 litre	3699/6	1934-37	£65,000	£30,000	£15,000
4.25 litre	4257/6	1937-39	£70,000	£35,000	£20,000
Mark V	4257/6	1939-41	£45,000	£25,000	£20,000

Prices are very dependent on engine type, body style and original extras like supercharger, gearbox ratio, history and originality.

1949 Bentley MkVI 4 Door Sports Saloon, coachwork by H. J. Mulliner, subject of an ongoing restoration, engine, electrics and transmission in excellent condition.
£7,000–7,500 *S*

Don't Forget!
If in doubt please refer to the 'How to Use' section at the beginning of this book.

1949 Bentley MkVI Standard Steel Saloon, totally re-built, very good condition throughout.
£21,000–23,000 *S*

1951 Bentley MkVI, 6 cylinder, 4257cc engine, good condition following a period of dry storage, would require some cosmetic refurbishment.
Est. £7,000–8,000 *ADT*

1951 Bentley MkVI 2 Door Drophead Coupé, coachwork by Leyshon-James, excellent concours-winning condition.
£29,000–30,000 *S*

1952 Bentley R Type, 4½ litres, manual gearbox, good overall condition.
£12,750–13,500 *Bro*

1952 Bentley MkVI Empress Saloon, coachwork by Hooper, upholstery renewed, chassis renovated, re-built engine and body, paintwork in excellent condition.
£18,000–19,000 *S*

1952 Bentley MkVI Lightweight Saloon, coachwork by H. J. Mulliner, manual 4 speed and reverse gearbox, gear lever on right, bodywork and interior restored.
£16,750–17,250 *S*

1952 Bentley MkVI Series P Standard Steel Saloon, bodywork slightly damaged, good original condition.
£12,500–13,000 *S*

1953 Bentley R Type Drophead Coupé, coachwork by Park Ward, very good original condition.
£31,000–33,000 *COYS*

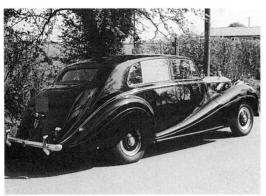

1953 Bentley R Type, coachwork by
H. J. Mulliner, excellent condition.
£28,000–30,000 *PJF*

**1953 Bentley R Type Standard Steel
Saloon,** 6 cylinder, 4257cc engine, automatic
transmission, optional sunroof, sound
original example, requires cosmetic attention.
£8,000–8,500 *COYS*

1954 Bentley R Type Drophead Coupé,
coachwork by Park Ward, very good
condition throughout.
Est. £40,000–45,000 *ADT*

*Drophead coupé bodies on R Type chassis are
extremely rare, and it is thought that this
Park Ward example is unique.*

**1953 Bentley R Type Standard Steel
Saloon,** 4 speed manual transmission
mechanically good, bodywork and paintwork
average, original upholstery, new carpets,
sunroof fitted.
£12,000–12,500 *S*

**1958 Bentley S1 Continental 2 Door
Saloon,** coachwork by Park Ward,
needs attention.
£31,000–32,000 *S*

**1956 Bentley S1 Continental Fastback
Saloon,** coachwork by H. J. Mulliner,
found in a barn and in need of restoration,
although engine and gearbox re-built.
£42,000–44,000 *S*

Cross Reference
Restoration Projects

**1958 Bentley S1
Continental Drophead
Coupé,** coachwork by
Park Ward, excellent
condition throughout.
£73,000–75,000 *PJF*

1959 Bentley S1 Continental Drophead
Coupé, coachwork by Park Ward,
excellent condition.
£90,000–95,000   *PJF*

1960 Bentley S2, good overall condition.
Est. £8,000–10,000   *ADT*

1960 Bentley S2 Saloon, 8 cylinder, 6230cc
engine, very good original condition.
£12,000–12,500   *ADT*

1961 Bentley S2 Standard Steel Saloon,
very good original condition.
£11,000–11,500   *S*

1960 Bentley S2 Continental Drophead
Coupé, coachwork by Park Ward, excellent
condition throughout.
Est. £29,000–33,000   *COYS*

1960 Bentley S2, subject of major restoration.
£16,750–17,250   *CGB*

1962 Bentley S2 Continental 2 Door Sports Saloon, coachwork by Mulliner Park Ward, good condition, requires minor cosmetic attention.
£40,000–42,000 *S*

1963 Bentley S3 Standard Steel Saloon, extensive bodywork restoration.
£16,500–17,000 *S*

1962 Bentley S2 Continental Flying Spur Saloon, coachwork by James Young, V8, 6230cc engine, comprehensively overhauled, bare metal re-spray, very good condition.
Est. £28,000–35,000 *COYS*

> *A rebuilt car is not necessarily more valuable than a car in good original condition, even if the restoration has been costly.*

1963 Bentley S2, 8 cylinder, 6230cc engine, good original condition throughout.
Est. £9,000–11,000 *ADT*

1963 Bentley S3, 8 cylinder, 6230cc engine, good original condition but some minor attention required.
Est. £9,000–11,000 *ADT*

1963 Bentley S3 Continental Coupé,
coachwork by Mulliner Park Ward, V8,
6230cc engine, mileage under 28,000,
very good original condition.
£18,000–19,000 COYS

1965 Bentley S3 Continental 2 Door
Saloon, coachwork by Mulliner Park Ward,
exceptional condition, paintwork and
bodywork unmarked.
Est. £28,000–32,000 S

1964 Bentley S2 Continental 2 Door
Saloon, coachwork by Mulliner Park Ward,
good paintwork and mechanical condition.
Est. £23,000–26,000 S

1964 Bentley S3 Flying Spur Continental
4 Door Saloon, coachwork by H. J. Mulliner,
good condition throughout.
Est. £33,000–36,000 S

BENTLEY Model	ENGINE cc/cyl	DATES	CONDITION 1	2	3
Abbreviations: HJM = H J Mulliner; PW = Park Ward; M/PW = Mulliner/Park Ward					
Mk VI Standard Steel	4257/ 4566/6	1946-52	£12,000	£10,000	£6,000
Mk VI Coachbuilt	4257/ 4566/6	1946-52	£25,000	£20,000	£12,000
Mk VI Coachbuilt DHC	4566/6	1946-52	£40,000	£30,000	£20,000
R Type Standard Steel	4566/6	1952-55	£12,000	£10,000	£7,000
R Type Coachbuilt	4566/6	1952-55	£25,000	£20,000	£15,000
R Type Coachbuilt DHC	4566/ 4887/6	1952-55	£50,000	£35,000	£25,000
R Type Cont (HJM)	4887/6	1952-55	£60,000	£40,000	£29,000
S1 Standard Steel	4887/6	1955-59	£15,000	£12,000	£7,000
S1 Cont 2 door (PW)	4877/6	1955-59	£30,000	£25,000	£20,000
S1 Cont Drophead	4877/6	1955-59	£80,000	£75,000	£50,000
S1 Cont F"back (HJM)	4877/6	1955-58	£45,000	£35,000	£25,000
S2 Standard Steel	6230/8	1959-62	£15,000	£9,000	£6,000
S2 Cont 2 door (HJM)	6230/8	1959-62	£60,000	£40,000	£30,000
S2 Flying Spur (HJM)	6230/8	1959-62	£45,000	£33,000	£22,000
S2 Conv (PW)	6230/8	1959-62	£60,000	£50,000	£35,000
S3 Standard Steel	6230/8	1962-65	£16,000	£11,000	£9,000
S3 Cont/Flying Spur	6230/8	1962-65	£45,000	£30,000	£25,000
S3 2 door (PW)	6230/8	1962-65	£30,000	£25,000	£18,000
S3 Conv (modern conversion - only made one original)	6230/8	1962-65	£40,000	£28,000	£20,000
T1	6230/6, 6750/8	1965-77	£10,000	£8,000	£4,000
T1 2 door (M/PW)	6230/6, 6750/8	1965-70	£15,000	£12,000	£9,000
T1 Drophead (M/PW)	6230/6, 6750/8	1965-70	£25,000	£18,000	£12,000

1966 Bentley T Type, good condition.
£5,750–6,250 *BLE*

> ### Don't Forget!
> *If in doubt please refer to the 'How to Use' section at the beginning of this book.*

1966 Bentley T Type 4 Door Saloon,
Harvey Bailey suspension, central locking,
intermittent wipers, Audio Line radio and
cassette, air conditioning and refrigeration,
excellent condition throughout.
Est. £8,500–10,000 *S*

1981 Bentley 8, very good condition throughout.
£10,000–10,500 *H&H*

1985 Bentley Mulsanne, very good
condition throughout.
£19,250–19,750 *CGOC*

> ### Did you know?
> *MILLER'S* Collectors
> Cars Price Guide *builds
> up year-by-year to form
> the most comprehensive
> photo-reference library
> system available.*

1987 Bentley Turbo R, long wheelbase,
electronic fuel injection, anti-lock braking
system, 66,000 miles, full service history.
£28,000–32,000 *VIC*

BENZ

1912 Benz 28/35 4 Seater Torpedo Open Tourer, mechanically good condition, museum stored for some years, requires checking before being re-commissioned for road use.
£24,000–26,000 *S*

BERLIET

1914 Berliet Type AI 10 22hp Shooting Brake, brass electric lighting, running board mounted klaxon, Smiths 0-60 mph speedometer, luggage rack, side facing bench seats to rear with 2 occasional seats, original black leather upholstery.
£12,000–14,000 *S*

BMW

Initially an aero engine manufacturer, the Bayerische Motoren Werke company was formed in 1917, but did not produce its first motor vehicle until about ten years later. BMW bought the Dixi works at Eisenach thus acquiring the licence to build Austin Sevens, although pre-war production was relatively low.

Following World War II, the Eisenach factory fell to the Russians, and pre-war BMW products were built by the East Germans bearing an EMW badge. BMW also lost its chief designer to Bristol, and it was several years before the Company recovered.

By the 1960s, their range of high performance sports saloon cars had become established and continues with great success today.

1938 BMW 328 2 Seater Sports, coachwork attributed to Weinberger, totally repainted, engine overhauled, restored to a very high standard. £72,000–74,000 *S*

1938 BMW 327 Sports 2 Door Cabriolet, restored to original specification. £37,000–38,000 *S*

1952 BMW 501 Saloon, left hand drive, dry stored for several years awaiting restoration. £600–700 *S*

> **Cross Reference**
> Restoration Projects

1972 BMW 3.0 CS 4 Seater Coupé, 3 speed automatic transmission, original velour interior, new eingine, good condition throughout. Est. £5,500–6,500 *S*

1972 BMW 2002 2 Door Saloon. £2,000–2,100 *DaD*

BMW

- In 1971 the 3.0 CS replaced the 2800 CS series.
- The 3.0 CSi featured fuel injection and all-round disc brakes and could achieve 0-60mph in 7.5 seconds, with a top speed of about 140mph.

1973 BMW 3 Litre CSi Sports Coupé, stored for 15 years, recorded mileage of 42,400, good to average condition throughout. £2,500–2,750 *S*

BMW Model	ENGINE cc/cyl	DATES	CONDITION 1	2	3
Dixi	747/4	1927-32	£6,000	£3,000	£2,000
303	1175/6	1934-36	£11,000	£8,000	£5,000
309	843/4	1933-34	£6,000	£4,000	£2,000
315	1490/6	1935-36	£9,000	£7,000	£5,000
319	1911/6	1935-37	£10,000	£9,000	£6,000
326	1971/6	1936-37	£12,000	£10,000	£8,000
320 series	1971/6	1937-38	£12,000	£10,000	£8,000
327/328	1971/6	1937-40	£30,000+	£18,000	£10,000
328	1971/6	1937-40	£60,000+	-	-

1973 BMW 2002 Touring, reconditioned manual gearbox, good condition.
Est. £1,500–2,000 *LF*

1973 BMW 3 Litre CS Coupé, repainted, good overall condition.
£1,100–1,300 *H&H*

1973 BMW 2 Litre 2000 Tii Touring Hatchback Coupé, good overall condition.
£1,750–2,000 *BKS*

The 2000 Tii is the rarest and most desirable of the Touring series.

1977 BMW 633 CSi 4 Seater Coupé, original bodywork and interior, good upholstery, recently re-sprayed.
£3,500–3,750 *S*

1984 BMW 323i 2 Door Saloon, sunroof, power steering, good overall condition.
£2,000–2,200 *S*

BMW Model	ENGINE cc/cyl	DATES	CONDITION 1	2	3
501	2077/6	1952-56	£9,000	£7,000	£3,500
501 V8/502	2580, 3168/8	1955-63	£10,000	£8,000	£4,500
503	3168/8	1956-59	£25,000	£20,000	£15,000
507	3168/8	1956-59	£85,000	£70,000	£50,000
Isetta (4 wheels)	247/1	1955-62	£3,000	£2,000	£1,000
Isetta (3 wheels)	298/1	1958-64	£4,000	£2,000	£1,000
Isetta 600	585/2	1958-59	£1,500	£1,000	£500
1500/1800/2000	var/4	1962-68	£1,100	£700	£200
2000CS	1990/4	1966-69	£5,500	£4,000	£1,500
1500/1600/1602	1499/ 1573/4	1966-75	£2,500	£1,500	£800
1600 Cabriolet	1573/4	1967-71	£6,000	£4,500	£2,000
2800CS	2788/6	1968-71	£5,000	£4,000	£1,500
1602	1990/4	1968-74	£2,000	£1,500	£1,000
2002	1990/4	1968-74	£3,000	£2,000	£750
2002 Tii	1990/4	1971-75	£4,500	£2,500	£800
2002 Touring	1990/4	1971-74	£3,000	£2,000	£500
2002 Cabriolet	1990/4	1971-75	£4,000	£3,000	£2,500
2002 Turbo	1990/4	1973-74	£9,000	£6,000	£4,000
3.0 CSa/CSi	2986/6	1972-75	£8,000	£6,000	£4,000
3.0 CSL	3003/ 3153/6	1972-75	£16,000	£12,000	£9,500
MI	3500/6	1978-85	£60,000	£45,000	£35,000
633/635 CS/CSI	3210/3453/6	1976-85	£6,500	£3,000	£2,000
M535i	3453/6	1979-81	£4,500	£3,000	£2,500

1980 BMW M1 2 Door Coupé, 6 cylinders, 3400cc, very good general condition throughout. **£44,000–48,000** *S*

BOND

The Bond company, founded by Laurie Bond, designed and produced a three-wheeler powered by a 2 stroke Villiers engine, chain driven to the single front wheel. The company was acquired by Reliant in the mid-1960s, and an all new 'Bug' was produced, powered by Reliant's 4 cylinder 700cc engine producing 29bhp.

1971 Bond Bug 700 ES, traditionally painted in orange with a black interior, good condition. **Est. £800–1,000** *ADT*

BRASIER

BRENNABOR

The Brandenbourg based manufacturer of the Brennabor, Gebr. Reichstein Brennabor-Werke, is recorded as a builder of motor vehicles as early as 1904. Brennabors were active in competition and produced in quite large numbers, although they were rare in England. Marketed in the UK as the Brenna, in 1911 the 4 seater 10hp model sold for £225.

1911 Brennabor 10hp 2 Seater Tourer, requires careful recommissioning. **Est. £12,000–14,000** *S*

This is the only Brennabor listed in the current Veteran Car Club of Great Britain.

1910 Brasier 12/18hp 5 Seater Tourer, 4 cylinder monobloc engine, 4 speed gearbox, brass fittings throughout with Phares Besnar acetylene headlamps, opera style oil sidelights, original leather upholstery, good original condition. **£12,500–13,500** *S*

1964 AC Cobra 289 4.7 Litre 2 Seater Sports Roadster, engine rebuilt, half-race cams, 4 barrel Holley carburettor, 6in painted wire wheels, right hand drive, only 46 made, excellent original condition. **£80,000–85,000** *BKS*

1958 Alfa Romeo Giulietta Spider Veloce, 5 year bare metal restoration, concours condition, a rare and genuine example. **£18,000–20,000** *COYS*

1960 Alfa Romeo Giulietta Sprint Speciale, bodywork by Bertone, excellent original overall condition, a very genuine example of one of the most desirable Giuliettas. **£12,000–13,000** *COYS*

1966 Alfa Romeo Giulia GTA 1600, alumium body panels, revised suspension, full race trim with twin plug head, 170bhp at 7500 rpm, very good condition. **£17,500–18,500** *COYS*

1960 Alfa Romeo Giulietta Sprint 1.3 Litre Sports Coupé, coachwork by Carrozzeria Bertone, a late example of the 750 Series, 80bhp engine rather than the 65bhp of the original Giuletta Sprint. **Est. £5,000–7,000** *BKS*

1963 Alfa Romeo Giulia Sprint GT, fully restored, excellent general condition. **£6,500–7,000** *COYS*

1974 Alfa Romeo Montreal, 200bhp engine with 137mph top speed, 6,000 miles recorded, excellent condition. **£6,000–6,500** *COYS*

1934 Alvis Crested Eagle, coachwork by Charlesworth, Type TD with 2511cc, 6 cylinder engine, SU carburettors, chassis length 123in. **Est. £13,000–16,000** *ADT*

1905 Alldays & Onions 10hp Swing Seat Tonneau, 4 seater body, brass acetylene headlamp, Lucas oil sidelamps. **£11,000–12,000** *S*

1934 Alvis Speed 20 Type SB 2 Door Coupé,
coachwork by Vanden Plas, 6 cylinders, 2511cc,
overhead valves, 87bhp at 4000rpm, 4 speed gearbox,
requires attention following museum storage.
£12,000–14,000 *CNY*

1964 Alvis TE21 Drophead Coupé, coachwork by
Graber/Park Ward, stored before complete
restoration, excellent condition.
£22,000–24,000 *COYS*

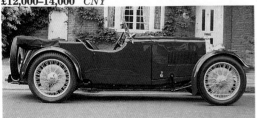

**1932 Aston Martin International 1½ Litre Open
Tourer,** coachwork by Bertelli, excellent restored
condition throughout.
Est. £38,000–42,000 *COYS*

**1930 Aston Martin 1½ Litre International
Open Tourer,** coachwork by Bertelli, Wolseley
bevel rear axle, new hood, sidescreens and tonneau
cover, excellent overall condition.
£32,000–34,000 *COYS*

**1935 Aston Martin MkII 1.5 Litre 4 Light
Saloon,** coachwork by Bertelli, stored for many
years, rare example of this model.
£40,000–42,000 *BKS*

**1964 Aston Martin
DB5 4 Litre 2 Door
Convertible,**
completely restored to
original specification.
Est. £50,000–55,000
BKS

1957 Aston Martin DB2/4 MkII 3 Litre Saloon,
coachwork by Tickford, completely rebuilt in the
1980s, top speed of 120mph.
£21,000–22,000 *BKS*

1953 Aston Martin DB2/4 Coupé, 6 cylinders,
twin camshaft, 2580cc, 125bhp at 5000rpm, 4 speed
manual gearbox, stainless steel exhaust.
Est. £17,000–20,000 *C*

**1965 Aston Martin DB5 Vantage 4 Litre 2 Door
Superleggera Saloon,** 5 speed and reverse gearbox
by ZF of Germany, excellent overall condition.
£28,000–29,000 *BKS*

1967 Aston Martin DB6 MkI Volante Drophead Coupé, automatic transmission, chrome wire wheels, very good condition.
Est. £40,000–50,000 *S*

1979 Aston Martin V8 Volante 5.3 Litre Drophead Coupé, 42,000 miles, concours condition throughout.
Est. £38,000–40,000 *BKS*

1974 Aston Martin V8 Vantage Coupé, 5340cc, converted to Series I specification, completely restored, excellent condition throughout.
£21,000–23,000 *COYS*

1936 Auburn Model 852 4.6 Litre Supercharged Speedster, stored, completely restored in USA, very good condition.
Est. £70,000–100,000 *BKS*

1929 Austin 7 'Top Hat' Saloon, 4 cylinders, 747cc, completely restored, very good condition.
£4,500–5,000 *ADT*

1926 Austin Heavy 12/4 Clifton Tourer, assembled in the Austin factory, exported to New Zealand until 1990, completely original, excellent condition.
£18,000–19,000 *CCK*

1934 Austin Eton Tourer with Dickey, 6 cylinders, 15.9hp, leather trim, good mechanics, restored.
£9,000–9,250 *Mot*

1955 Austin Healey 100/4 BN1 2 Seater Sports, museum stored for 9 years, very good condition.
£13,000–14,000 *S*

1957 Austin Healey 100/6 2+2 Seater Sports, 6 cylinders, 2639cc, left hand drive, good condition.
£11,000–12,000 *C*

1965 Austin Healey 3000 MkIII Open Sports, converted from left hand drive, bare metal re-spray, engine fully rebuilt, restored to a very high standard.
Est. £19,000–23,000 *ADT*

1958 Austin Healey 100/6 Open Sports, 6 cylinders, 2639cc, completely restored, left hand drive, excellent condition throughout.
£17,000–18,000 *COYS*

1964 Austin Healey 3000 MkIII Open Sports, total body restoration and mechanical overhaul, new trim, chrome and carpets, left hand drive.
£19,000–20,000 *COYS*

1966 Austin Healey 3000 MkIII Phase II 3 Litre Sports 2 Seater Convertible, fully documented restoration, wire wheels, adjustable steering column, overdrive, right hand drive, very good condition.
£34,000–36,000 *BKS*

1967 Austin Healey 3000 MkIII, fully restored, good condition.
£23,000–25,000 *SJR*

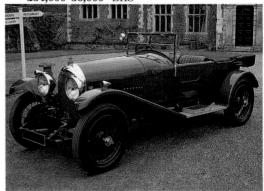

1925 Bentley Red Label 3 Litre Speed Model Replica, Vanden Plas Standard Sporting body by Robinson, originally with a tourer body, P100 headlamps, luggage box, completely restored.
£70,000–74,000 *BKS*

1922 Bentley 3 Litre, brakeless front axle, a rare early example, fully restored over 25 years.
£68,000–72,000 *MAN*

1927 Bentley Vanden Plas 4½ Litre Tourer, Bentley Drivers' Club concours champion 1965 and 1966, restored, excellent condition.
£150,000+ *MAN*

1923 Bentley 3 Litre Super Sports Barnato Racing Car Replica, very well restored, excellent condition.
£64,000–68,000 *MAN*

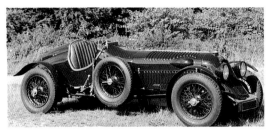

1928 Bentley 6½ Litre Racing Special, with 8 litre engine, excellent condition. **£250,000+** *MAN*

1928 Bentley 4½ Litre Le Mans, excellent restored condition throughout. **£160,000+** *MAN*

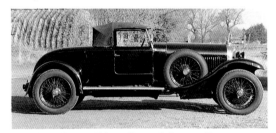

1928 Bentley 4½ Litre Open 2 Seater Tourer, original coachwork by Gill, excellent condition. **£130,000+** *MAN*

1930 Bentley 4½ Litre Supercharged Vanden Plas Tourer, gearbox rebuilt, control flow levers from a Tiger Moth, switched electric fan, 2 BTH CISE 12-S magnetos, 2 SU HGV5 carburettors, oil cooler, some aircraft instruments, unrestored original condition. **£390,000+** *S*

1929 Bentley 4½ Litre Sports Tourer, aluminium panelled body, 4 cylinder single overhead camshaft, 4398cc, 4 speed right hand change gearbox, right hand drive, restored and rebuilt, excellent condition throughout. **£270,000–280,000** *C(A)*

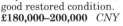

1931 Bentley 8 Litre Panelled Weymann Saloon, coachwork by H. J. Mulliner, 6 cylinders in line, 200bhp, 4 speed gearbox, 4 wheel drum brakes, semi-elliptical suspension, Bentley-Draper Duplex shock absorbers, right hand drive, very good restored condition. **£180,000–200,000** *CNY*

1931 Bentley 8 Litre Le Mans Tourer, 6 cylinders, excellent running condition throughout. **£290,000+** *MAN*

1931 Bentley 8 Litre Sports Saloon, rare short chassis, large sunroof, excellent condition. **£240,000+** *MAN*

This car was built for the Dupont family.

1931 Bentley 8 Litre Tourer, coachwork by Gurney Nutting, excellent original condition. **£465,000+** *MAN*

1934 Bentley 3½ Litre Drophead Coupé, coachwork by James Young of Bromley, complete mechanical and engine restoration, very good condition. **£55,000–58,000** *S*

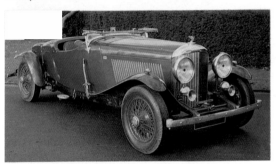

1934 Bentley 3½ Litre Special Roadster, originally a Sedenca Coupé by Gurney Nutting, very good condition. **Est. £23,000–27,000** *COYS*

1954 Bentley R Type Continental, very good condition. **£120,000–130,000** *PJF*

1937 Bentley 4¼ Litre Sedanca Coupé, coachwork by Gurney Nutting, excellent concours winning condition throughout. **Est. £60,000–80,000** *BKS*

1955 Bentley R Type Drophead Coupé, coachwork by Park Ward, very good condition. **£26,000–28,000** *PJF*

1956 Bentley S1 Continental Fastback, coachwork by H. J. Mulliner, very good condition. **£90,000–100,000** *PJF*

1954 Bentley R Type Continental Fastback, coachwork by H. J. Mulliner, very good condition throughout. **Est. £65,000–75,000** *S*

1957 Bentley S1, good original overall condition. **£8,000–9,000** *ADT*

1958 Bentley S1 4 Door Continental, coachwork by James Young, good condition. **£70,000–75,000** *PJF*

1964 Bentley S3, good overall condition.
£7,000–9,000 *BA*

1960 Bentley S2 Continental Drophead Coupé,
coachwork by Park Ward, extensively restored.
£36,000–38,000 *ADT*

*The basic price for a standard steel Rolls-Royce
Silver Cloud in 1960 was £3,995, whilst a Bentley
Continental was nearly £6,000.*

**1963 Bentley S3 2 Door Drophead Coupé
Conversion,** very good condition throughout.
Est. £30,000–35,000 *BKS*

1964 Bentley S3 Standard Steel Saloon,
very good condition.
£25,000–35,000 *PJF*

**1964 Bentley S3 Flying Spur 4 Door
Continental,** coachwork by H. J. Mulliner,
excellent condition.
£70,000–75,000 *PJF*

**1963 Bentley S3 6.2 Litre Standard Steel
Saloon,** very good condition throughout.
Est. £10,000–15,000 *BKS*

**1964 Bentley S3 Flying Spur Continental 4 Door
Saloon,** coachwork by H. J. Mulliner, bare metal
re-spray, 24,000 miles, good condition throughout.
£42,000–44,000 *S*

1965 Bentley Flying Spur Continental,
coachwork by H. J. Mulliner.
£70,000–75,000 *PJF*

1965 Bentley S3 Saloon, coachwork by James
Young, very good condition.
£30,000–35,000 *PJF*

1961 Bentley S2 Continental Coupé,
coachwork by H. J. Mulliner, very good condition.
£85,000–90,000 *PJF*

1965 Bristol 408 5.1 Litre 2 Door Sports Saloon, rebuilt Chrysler V8 engine, reconditioned TorqueFlite automatic transmission, excellent restored condition.
Est. £10,000–12,000 *BKS*

c1929 Bugatti Type 44 Cabriolet, 2 door convertible coachwork by Gangloff of Colmar, single overhead camshaft engine, driven from centre of crankshaft, 9 main bearings, very good condition.
£55,000–60,000 *S*

1967 Bristol 410 5.2 Litre 2 Door Coupé, interior original, 100mph in 23 seconds, top speed of 132mph, good overall condition.
Est. £5,000–8,000 *BKS*

1930 Bugatti Type 46 5.4 Litre 2 Door 'Coach', Carrosserie coachwork by Weymann, engine rebuilt, excellent condition after museum storage.
Est. £90,000–120,000 *BKS*

l. **1932 Bugatti 55/57 2 Seater Sports,** 8 cylinders, 3257cc, 3.3 litre double overhead camshaft, straight 8 engine, 4 rare Wingfield racing carburettors, excellent condition throughout.
Est. £80,000–100,000 *COYS*

1974 BMW 2002 Turbo 2 Door Coupé, engine completely rebuilt, original specification.
Est. £9,000–12,000 *S*

1939 Buick Model 60 Dual Cowl Phæton Saloon Tourer, coachwork by Maltby, 3 speed manual gearbox, left hand drive, concours winner.
£85,000–88,000 *CNY*

1960 Daimler SP250 A Series, with hood and hard top, average condition.
£7,500–8,000 *CGOC*

1961 Daimler SP250 B Series, with hard top, rare factory wire wheels, good original condition.
£13,500–14,500 *CGOC*

1961 Daimler SP250 B Series, chrome wire wheels, very good condition.
£14,000–16,000 *CGOC*

1954 Daimler Conquest 2.4 Litre Saloon, completely original condition.
£4,800–5,200 *BKS*

This car once belonged to Field Marshal Viscount Montgomery of Alamein.

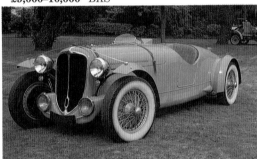

1966 Daimler DR450 4.6 Litre Majestic Major Limousine, servo-assisted Dunlop brakes, Hydrosteer power assisted steering, completely refurbished.
£9,000–10,000 *BKS*

c1935 Delahaye 135M Le Mans Style 2 Seater, rebodied with aluminium panelling over a steel frame, museum stored, requires completion for road or racing use.
£15,000–20,000 *S*

1923 Delage Type CO2 4.5 Litre 4 Seater Tourer, 40,000 miles, new hood and sidescreens, excellent restored condition throughout.
Est. £50,000–60,000 *S*

1938 Delahaye 135MS 2 Seater Roadster, non-original body, completely restored, excellent overall condition.
£82,000–84,000 *S*

1951 Ferrari 212 Inter Ghia Coupé, V12 engine, right hand drive, Borrani alloy rimmed wire wheels, in running order, requires mechanical attention.
Est. £50,000–60,000 *S*

1962 Ferrari 250GT Short Wheelbase Competitzione, V12, 60° engine, 2953cc, 280bhp at 7000rpm, 4 speed gearbox, 4 wheel disc brakes, matt black dashboard, perspex windscreen, top speed of over 160mph, good condition.
Est. £250,000–300,000 *CNY*

1962 Ferrari 250GT Lusso Berlinetta Coupé, 3 twin choke Weber carburettors, 250bhp, top speed of 150mph, interior well restored, finished to a very high standard, left hand drive.
Est. £110,000–125,000 *S*

1960 Ferrari 250GT Series II Cabriolet, coachwork by Pininfarina, V12 engine, 2953cc, 220bhp at 7000rpm, 4 speed synchromesh gearbox with overdrive, Dunlop disc brakes, Houdaille shock absorbers, left hand drive, excellent restored condition.
£62,000–65,000 *C*

1963 Ferrari 250GT Lusso 3 Litre Berlinetta coachwork by Carrozzeria Scaglietti, V12 engine, 240bhp at 7500rpm, bare metal re-spray, complete body restoration.
£90,000–94,000 *BKS*

r. **1962 Ferrari 400 Series 1 Superamerica Aerodynamica,** coachwork by Pininfarina, well restored, excellent condition.
Est. £150,000–180,000 *S*

1964 Ferarri 275 GTS, coachwork by Pininfarina, very good condition.
£90,000–130,000 *DKE*

1965 Ferrari 330GT 2+2 Coupé, coachwork by Pininfarina, V12 engine, 3967cc, 5 speed gearbox, Borrani wire wheels, left hand drive, good original condition.
£16,000–18,000 *COYS*

1963 Ferrari 250GTE 2+2 Coupé, coachwork by Pininfarina, engine fully rebuilt, excellent original condition throughout.
£31,000–33,000 *COYS*

1951 Ferrari 2.5 Litre Tipo 212 Barchetta, coachwork in the style of Carrozzeria Touring, restored to high standards, excellent condition.
£180,000–200,000 *BKS*

1977 Ferrari 400GT 4.8 Litre 2 Door Berlina, coachwork by Pininfarina, 53,000 miles, Blaupunkt stereo cassette, air conditioning, good original condition throughout.
£10,500–12,000 *BKS*

1969 Ferrari 365GT 4.4 Litre 2+2 Two Door Berlina, coachwork by Pininfarina/Scaglietti, manual gearbox, air conditioning, right hand drive, very good condition throughout.
£25,500–26,500 *BKS*

1966 Ferrari 275GTB, coachwork by Scaglietti, twin cam, very good condition.
£120,000–130,000 *DKE*

1972 Ferrari 246GT Dino, Berlinetta coachwork by Pininfarina, 5 speed gearbox, low mileage, good original overall condition.
£42,000–45,000 *COYS*

1969 Ferrari 365GTC 4.4 Litre 2 Door, Berlinetta coachwork by Pininfarina, 28,000 miles, rebuilt Borrani wire wheels, very good condition.
Est. £40,000–50,000 *BKS*

Only about 150 were built, of which fewer than 30 were right hand drive.

1969 Ferrari 365GTB 4 Daytona Berlinetta, 352bhp at 7500rpm, top speed of over 170mph, 0–60mph in 5.9 seconds, 0–100mph in 12 seconds, left hand drive.
Est. £100,000–110,000 *S*

1981 Ferrari 400i 4.8 Litre, Berlina coachwork by Pininfarina, front mounted V12 engine, 4823cc, manual transmission, one owner, only 30,000 miles, very good condition.
£23,000–25,000 *BKS*

1973 Ferrari 365 GTC/4 4.4 Litre, Berlinetta coachwork by Pininfarina, right hand drive, good overall condition.
Est. £35,000–45,000 *BKS*

1988 Fiat Bertone X19 Targa Roadster, 4 cylinders, 1500cc, 5 speed gearbox, only 160km, excellent condition.
Est. £12,500–15,000 *C(A)*

1973 Fiat Dino Spider 2.4 Litre, with factory hard top, Ferrari 65° V6 engine, 1987cc, very good condition.
Est. £20,000–25,000 *S*

1937 Ford Model Y 933cc Popular 2 Door Saloon, re-trimmed, restored, only 2 owners, excellent condition.
£8,500–9,500 *BKS*

1923 T IV 2 Ford Model T Hot Rod, V8, 454 cu in Big Block Chevrolet engine, completely rebuilt, excellent condition.
Est. £18,000–24,000 *CNY*

1935 Ford V8 Coupé, V8 side valve engine, 3622cc, 3 speed central change gearbox, 4 wheel drum type rod operated brakes, right hand drive, excellent and original condition.
£15,000–17,000 *C(A)*

1934 Ford Model 40 V8 Coupé De Luxe, ground-up restoration, only 51,000 miles, regular show winner, left hand drive, excellent overall condition.
Est. £16,000–20,000 *S*

1952 Ford Triple Spinner Sedan, V8 side valve engine, 3.6 litres, 3 speed manual gearbox with column change, box section chassis, drum type brakes, only one owner, right hand drive, original and well maintained.
£5,750–6,750 *C(A)*

1955 Ford Thunderbird 4.8 Litre 2 Seater, engine re-built, bodywork and chassis in good condition, optional removable wheel spats, electrically operated seats, restored.
£13,000–14,000 *BKS*

1933 Frazer-Nash Short Chassis TT Replica, coachwork by Elkington's, excellent original condition throughout.
£65,000–68,000 *S*

1938 Frazer-Nash BMW 328 2 Seater AFN Competition-Spec Sports Roadster, modified into a lightweight special, alloy body, original pattern alloy wheels, very good condition.
Est. £75,000–85,000 *BKS*

1927 Hispano-Suiza Type 49 Barcelona Weymann Saloon, lightweight Weymann fabric coachwork by H. J. Mulliner, original upholstery refurbished, original factory tools and handbook, La Cignogne Volante mascot, excellent condition.
£50,000–55,000 *S*

1950 Jaguar MkV 3.5 Litre Saloon,
3485cc, 4 speed central change gearbox, box section chassis, drum type brakes front and rear, right hand drive, fully restored, concours winning condition.
£15,000–17,000 *C(A)*

1951 Jaguar XK120 Roadster, rebuilt for concours events in Germany, featured at 1994 Essen Techno Classica.
£36,000–40,000 *SC*

1936 Jaguar SS100 2.5 Litre 2 Seater Sports, fully refurbished to original specification, excellent condition throughout.
£85,000–90,000 *BKS*

1950 Jaguar MkV 3.5 Litre Saloon, museum exhibited, very good original condition throughout.
£11,000–12,000 *BKS*

1953 Jaguar C-Type 3.4 Litre 2 Seater Competition Sports, excellent condition.
£255,000+ *BKS*
A very well-known historic motor car.

1949 Jaguar XK120 Super Sports 3.4 Litre 2 Seater Roadster, original power unit, aluminium body, converted to right hand drive, excellent condition.
Est. £50,000–60,000 *BKS*

1950 Jaguar XK120 Roadster, 3442cc twin cam engine, 160bhp, twin SU carburettors, 126mph, 0–60mph in 10 seconds, left hand drive, excellent condition.
Est. £24,000–28,000 *COYS*

1953 Jaguar XK120 3.4 Litre Special Equipment Roadster, totally restored, upholstery renewed, excellent concours winning standard throughout.
£42,000–45,000 *S*

1952 Jaguar XK120 Fixed Head Coupé, professionally re-sprayed, very well maintained, converted to left hand drive, excellent overall condition.
£22,000–25,000 *COYS*

1958 Jaguar XK150S 3.4 Litre 2 Seater Roadster, very well rebuilt, original fitted luggage, converted to right hand drive, excellent condition.
£41,000–44,000 *BKS*

1956 Jaguar XK140 Coupé, rebuilt C-Type engine with racing camshaft, light flywheel, all synchromesh gearbox with overdrive, louvred bonnet, disc brakes, converted to right hand drive, very good condition.
£14,000–16,000 *CCTC*

1956 Jaguar XK140 3.4 Litre Fixed Head Coupé, fully restored to highest standards, excellent condition.
£27,000–29,000 *BKS*

1958 Jaguar XK150S Roadster, 6 cylinders, 3781cc, 3.4 litre engine replaced with 3.8 litres, extensively restored, good condition throughout.
£29,000–32,000 *COYS*

1960 Jaguar XK150 3.4 Litre Drophead Coupé, only 2 owners, excellent original condition.
£27,000–30,000 *BKS*

**1954 Jaguar MkVII 3.4 Litre Saloon,
The Paladin Jaguar,** almost entirely hand-built
specifically for historic rallying, restored,
repainted, excellent condition.
Est. £8,000–10,000 *BKS*

1958 Jaguar MkI 3.4 Litre Sports Saloon,
extensively restored, excellent overall
condition throughout.
Est. £14,000–18,000 *BKS*

1961 Jaguar MkII 3.8 Litre Saloon,
lead free engine, XJS power steering, manual
gearbox with overdrive, tinted glass, air
conditioning, central locking, restored to
concours standard.
£52,500–55,000 *SC*

1963 Jaguar MkII 3.8 Saloon, originally with automatic
gearbox, now with 4 speed manual gearbox with overdrive,
completely rebuilt to a very high standard.
Est. £14,000–17,000 *ADT*

1964 Jaguar MkII Saloon, 6 cylinders, 3442cc, 37,000
miles, manual gearbox with overdrive, engine rebuilt,
chrome wire wheels, excellent original condition.
£17,000–17,500 *COYS*

1965 Jaguar S-Type 3.4 Litre Saloon,
excellent condition.
£17,000–20,000 *BKS*

*This is one of the finest examples of the Jaguar
S-Type in existence.*

**1962 Jaguar E-Type
Series I Two Seater
Roadster,** standard
trim apart from chrome
wire wheels, excellent
restored condition.
£38,000–42,000 *BKS*

**1962 Jaguar E-Type Series I 3.8 Litre
2 Seater Roadster,** very good restored
condition throughout.
£24,000–26,000 *BKS*

BRISTOL

The Bristol Aeroplane Company was one of the world's leading aircraft manufacturers, however, it was not until 1945 that the motor car division was formed. Using British versions of pre-war BMW models, Bristol developed their own style and by the early 1960s the Chrysler V8 engine was being used in a series of luxurious sports saloons. Bristol Cars Ltd., no longer has any direct links with the aircraft industry but still produces cars at Filton, near Bristol.

1947 Bristol 400, very good condition throughout.
£9,000–9,500 *H&H*

1948 Bristol 400, 6 cylinders, 1971cc, good mechanical order, excellent original condition.
Est. £15,000–20,000 *COYS*

Power was provided by Bristol's own version of the BMW 328 engine, a highly efficient 2 litre, 6 cylinder unit. Producing 80bhp at 4200rpm and driving through a 4 speed gearbox, the Bristol 400 could achieve 0-60mph in 19.1 seconds, and 94mph.

1950 Bristol 401 2 Litre 2 Door Sports Saloon, 6 cylinder engine, 85bhp, unpainted, unrestored example, lights and distributor missing, right hand drive.
£3,000–3,300 *C*

> **Cross Reference**
> Restoration Projects

1948 Bristol 400 Sports Saloon, excellent condition throughout.
Est. £18,000–22,000 *COYS*

1949 Bristol 400, 6 cylinder, 1971cc engine, very good condition throughout.
£15,000–15,500 *ADT*

> **Locate the source**
> *The source of each illustration in* Miller's Collectors Cars Price Guide *can be found by checking the code letters below each caption with the Key to Illustrations.*

1950 Bristol 402 Drophead Coupé, 6 cylinders, 1971cc, very good original condition.
£22,000–24,000 *COYS*

1951 Bristol 401, 6 cylinders, 1971cc engine, interior re-trimmed, very good overall condition.
Est. £9,500–10,500 *ADT*

1952 Bristol 401 2 Door Saloon, major restoration, paintwork needs attention, good condition throughout.
£7,750–8,250 *S*

1953 Bristol 401, excellent overall condition.
£7,250–7,750 *Bro*

1960 Bristol 406, good condition.
£9,750–10,000 *BLE*

1961 Bristol 406, very good restored condition throughout.
£9,750–10,000 *Bro*

Bristol 409

- **The Bristol 409 was very similar to its predecessor, the 408, but with a slightly more rounded grille and a faster top speed.**
- **Gears on automatic transmission could be manually held by a button on the dashboard.**
- **Powered by a V8, 5211cc Chrysler engine achieving a top speed of over 130mph.**

1964 Bristol 408, 8 cylinders, 5130cc, good condition.
Est. £8,500–9,500 *ADT*

The automatic gearbox on these models is operated by push buttons at the side of the steering column.

1966 Bristol 409 Sports Saloon, 78,000 miles, original specification throughout, excellent overall condition.
£7,750–8,250 *S*

1967 Bristol 410 5.2 Litre V8 Sports Saloon, completely restored, excellent condition throughout.
£8,000–8,500 *S*

1974 Bristol 411 MkIV, excellent overall condition.
£7,250–7,750 *BLE*

1975 Bristol 412 Convertible, basically sound but in need of cosmetic restoration.
£3,000–3,300 *S*

Bristol 412

- The Bristol 412 was launched in 1975, and cost £14,584.
- Designed by Zagato, it was the first Bristol convertible available for over 20 years.
- Powered by a Chrysler V8, 6556cc engine, with a torque-flite transmission.

1977 Bristol 603, 8 cylinders, 5200cc, good condition, some minor cosmetic restoration required.
Est. £11,000–13,000 *ADT*

A rebuilt car is not necessarily more valuable than a car in good original condition, even if the restoration has been costly.

1977 Bristol 411 MkII Sports Coupé, very good all-round condition.
£11,500–12,500 *S*

1977 Bristol 412 Convertible, 8 cylinder, 5898cc engine, good condition, requires cosmetic restoration.
£3,800–4,200 *ADT*

BRISTOL Model	ENGINE cc/cyl	DATES	CONDITION 1	2	3
400	1971/6	1947-50	£15,000	£12,000	£8,000
401	1971/6	1949-53	£15,000	£11,000	£7,000
402	1971/6	1949-50	£20,000	£18,000	£11,000
403	1971/6	1953-55	£18,000	£12,000	£8,000
404 Coupé	1971/6	1953-57	£19,000	£14,000	£10,000
405	1971/6	1954-58	£14,000	£11,000	£9,000
405 Drophead	1971/6	1954-56	£20,000	£18,000	£14,000
406	2216/6	1958-61	£10,000	£9,000	£5,000
407	5130/8	1962-63	£9,000	£7,000	£5,000
408	5130/8	1964-65	£10,000	£9,000	£5,000
409	5211/8	1966-67	£10,500	£9,500	£5,500
410	5211/8	1969	£12,000	£10,000	£5,500
411 Mk 1-3	6277/8	1970-73	£12,000	£9,000	£6,000
411 Mk 4-5	6556/8	1974-76	£12,500	£9,500	£7,000
412	5900/ 6556/8	1975-82	£14,500	£8,500	£5,500
603	5211/ 5900/8	1976-82	£12,000	£8,000	£5,000

BSA

1939 BSA Scout 2 Seater Sports,
newly re-trimmed interior, new hood,
sidescreens and tonneau cover, front
wheel drive.
£7,700–8,000 *Bro*

BUGATTI

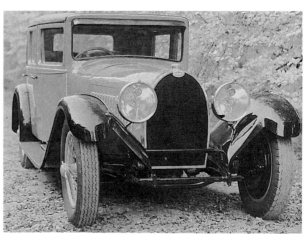

1930 Bugatti Type 46 Saloon, 4 door
coachwork, fabric covered top, wire wheels,
rear mounted fabric covered luggage trunk,
rear mounted spare wheel, re-upholstered,
new headlining, good restored condition.
£43,000–45,000 *S*

*This car was originally supplied in 1930 by
Etabliment André Mathon, exclusive agents
for Bugatti at Rue de Lille, Tourcoing.*

> **Cross Reference**
> Colour Review

BUICK

1910 Buick Model F Tourer,
flat horizontally opposed twin cylinder engine
under front seat, 22hp, 159cu in, 2 speed
planetary gearbox, rear drum brakes, full
elliptical spring suspension front and rear,
right hand drive, paint requires attention,
original upholstery, good condition.
£7,500–8,000 *CNY*

1940 Buick Series 40 Sport Coupé,
good overall condition.
£3,800–4,200 *S*

**1939 Buick Model 40 Straight Eight
4 Door Saloon,** left hand drive, Holback
Limousette patent roof, generally sound,
paintwork requires attention, museum
stored, needs careful recommissioning.
£4,700–5,000 *S*

**1948 Buick 8 Super Series 50 2 Door
Sedanette,** coachwork by Fisher, one owner,
right hand drive, very good overall condition.
£8,750–9,250 *S*

1948 Buick Series 50 Sedan, 8 cylinder,
4032cc engine, refurbished to original
specification, right hand drive.
£8,500–8,750 *ADT*

1966 Buick Riviera Coupé, 8 cylinder, 7631cc engine, standard specification included power steering, power brakes, automatic transmission, tilt steering wheel, dual exhausts, full carpeting and padded instrument panel, original interior equipment, excellent bodywork and overall condition.
Est. £7,000–8,000 *ADT*

1979 Buick Riviera Custom Super Stretch, mileage less than 30,000, good all-round condition.
Est. £5,000–6,000 *S*

The design of the stretch bodywork on this chassis is possibly unique, in that it has a chopped rear boot with a stretched front.

BUICK Model	ENGINE cc/cyl	DATES	CONDITION 1	2	3
Veteran	various	1903-09	£18,500	£12,000	£8,000
18/20	3881/6	1918-22	£12,000	£5,000	£2,000
Series 22	2587/4	1922-24	£9,000	£5,000	£3,000
Series 24/6	3393/6	1923-30	£9,000	£5,000	£3,000
Light 8	3616/8	1931	£18,000	£14,500	£11,000
Straight 8	4467/8	1931	£22,000	£18,000	£10,000
50 Series	3857/8	1931-39	£18,500	£15,000	£10,000
60 Series	5247/8	1936-39	£19,000	£15,000	£8,000
90 Series	5648/8	1934-35	£20,000	£15,500	£9,000
40 Series	4064/8	1936-39	£19,000	£14,000	£10,000
80/90	5247/8	1936-39	£25,000	£20,000	£15,000
McLaughlin	5247/8	1937-40	£22,000	£15,000	£10,000

Various chassis lengths and bodies will affect value. Buick chassis fitted with English bodies previous to 1916 were called Bedford-Buicks. Right hand drive can have an added premium of 25%.

Buick McLaughlin

Founded by Scotsman David Buick at the turn of the century, the Buick Motor Car Company of Flint, Michigan, was acquired by Durant for General Motors.Although the McLaughlin Motor Car Company Ltd., of Oshawa, Ontario, had been building cars since 1908, an arrangement was made to build McLaughlin cars with Buick engines. This continued until the outbreak of WWII. Today, General Motors, Canada, is still based at Oshawa.

1933 Buick McLaughlin 3.8 Litre Viceroy 4 Door Sedan, restored in North America to a high standard, requires minor cosmetic detailing to bring it up to concours standard, twin side mounted spare wheels, rear boot, spoked wheels, left hand drive.
Est. £11,000–13,000 *S*

1934 Buick McLaughlin Straight Eight 2 Door Coupé, imported into the UK at the end of WWII, right hand drive, good condition.
Est. £9,000–12,000 *S*

Miller's is a price GUIDE not a price LIST

Use the Index!
Because certain items might fit easily into any number of categories, the quickest and surest method of locating any entry is by reference to the index at the back of the book.

This index has been fully cross-referenced for absolute simplicity.

1936 Buick McLaughlin Straight Eight Limousine, coachwork by Fisher, supplied for the UK, very good condition throughout, with spare parts including another engine. Est. £10,000–12,000 *S*

1937 Buick McLaughlin 38hp Series 90 Limousine, coachwork by Thrupp & Maberley, straight 8 overhead valve, 5247cc engine, original right hand drive, good overall condition. £4,500–5,500 *S*

BUICK Model	ENGINE cu in/cyl	DATES	CONDITION 1	2	3
Special/Super 4 Door	248/ 364/8	1950-59	£6,000	£4,000	£2,000
Special/Super Riviera	263/ 332/8	1050-56	£8,000	£6,000	£3,000
Special/Super Convertible	263/ 332/8	1950-56	£7,500	£5,500	£3,000
Roadmaster 4 door	320/ 365/8	1950-58	£11,000	£8,000	£6,000
Roadmaster Riviera	320/ 364/8	1950-58	£9,000	£7,000	£5,000
Roadmaster Convertible	320/ 364/8	1950-58	£14,500	£11,000	£7,000
Special/Super Riviera	364/8	1957-59	£10,750	£7,500	£5,000
Special/Super Convertible	364/8	1957-58	£13,500	£11,000	£6,000

CADILLAC

Many firsts are attributed to Cadillac who pioneered the system which enabled parts to be interchangeable. The first electrically powered lighting system with electric starting and ignition resulted in the award of the Dewar Trophy in 1912. In 1930 Cadillac introduced the first production V16 engine amongst many other technical innovations.

Cadillac designer Harley Earl developed tail fins in the 1940s which were to influence American car design for nearly two decades. Cadillac was also the first American manufacturer to mass produce a luxury car, and it is often said that they did for the rich what Ford did for the poor.

1925 Cadillac V63 Eight 7 Passenger Sedan, left hand drive, fair paintwork, upholstery requires attention, engine, transmission, gearbox and chassis in good condition. Est. £12,000–15,000 *S*

1926 Cadillac Model 314 Victoria 4 Seater Coupé, V8, 5153cc engine, 35.1hp, drum headlights, Motor-Meter on radiator cap, 3 speed manual gearbox, wooden spoked hickory wheels, left hand drive, good condition throughout. Est. £20,000–24,000 *S*

1934 Cadillac Convertible Sedan V8, completely restored, concours standard, factory bi-plane bumper.
£45,000–50,000 *GAR*

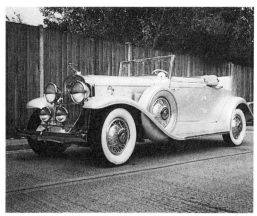

1931 Cadillac V8 Roadster, 3 speed transmission.
Est. £60,000–75,000 *H&H*

CADILLAC (pre-war) Model	ENGINE cc/cyl	DATES	CONDITION 1	2	3
Type 57-61	5153/8	1915-23	£20,000	£14,000	£6,000
Series 314	5153/8	1926-27	£22,000	£15,000	£6,000
Type V63	5153/8	1924-27	£20,000	£13,000	£5,000
Series 341	5578/8	1928-29	£22,000	£15,000	£6,000
Series 353-5	5289/8	1930-31	£32,500	£22,000	£12,000
V16	7406/16	1931-32	£40,000	£32,000	£18,000
V12	6030/12	1932-37	£42,000+	£25,000	£15,000
V8	5790/8	1935-36	£18,000+	£12,000	£6,000
V16	7034/16	1937-40	£45,000+	£30,000	£18,000

c1935 Cadillac Model 452D V16 Fleetwood Town Car, twin side-mounted spare wheels, rear bumper and windscreen wipers missing, requires cosmetic restoration.
£12,000–14,000 *S*

This car was at one time owned by Admiral Byrd, the famous Antarctic explorer.

1947 Cadillac Series 60 Special Fleetwood Sedan, chrome push button radio, under-seat heaters, Hydramatic transmission, single Carter carburettor with 'Climatic Control', the equivalent of an automatic choke unit, original specification, excellent overall condition.
Est. £24,000–26,000 *S*

1939 Cadillac Series 75 V8 Two Door 5 Passenger Convertible Coupé, coachwork by Fleetwood, 346cu in side valve engine, 3 speed gearbox, left hand drive, concours winning condition throughout.
Est. £32,000–40,000 *S*

1953 Cadillac Coupé De Ville V8, completely refurbished, new chrome and paintwork, new interior.
£5,000–6,000 *GAR*

1949 Cadillac Series 62 V8 Convertible Coupé, coachwork by Fisher, gearbox reconditioned, concours condition.
£35,000–38,000 *S*

This cars was best in class at the Louis Vuitton, Hurlingham Club concours.

1957 Cadillac Coupé De Ville, 8 cylinder, 6400cc engine, very good mechanical condition.
Est. £8,000–9,000 *ADT*

1957 Cadillac De Ville 4 Seater Fixed Head Coupé, left hand drive, very good condition throughout.
Est. £8,000–10,000 *S*

1958 Cadillac Series 62 Convertible, engine and brakes overhauled, new top, chrome trim very good.
Est. £14,000–18,000 *S*

CADILLAC Model	ENGINE cu in/cyl	DATES	CONDITION 1	2	3
4 door sedan	331/8	1949	£8,000	£4,500	£3,000
2 door fastback	331/8	1949	£10,000	£8,000	£5,000
Convertible coupé	331/8	1949	£22,000	£12,000	£10,000
Series 62 4 door	331/365/8	1950-55	£7,000	£5,500	£3,000
Sedan de Ville	365/8	1956-58	£8,000	£6,000	£4,000
Coupé de Ville	331/365/8	1950-58	£12,500	£9,500	£3,500
Convertible coupé	331/365/8	1950-58	£25,000	£20,000	£10,000
Eldorado	331/8	1953-55	£35,000	£30,000	£18,000
Eldorado Seville	365/8	1956-58	£11,500	£9,000	£5,500
Eldorado Biarritz	365/8	1956-58	£30,000	£20,000	£15,000
Sedan de Ville	390/8	1959	£12,000	£9,500	£5,000
Coupé de Ville	390/8	1959	£15,000	£9,000	£5,500
Convertible coupé	390/8	1959	£28,000	£20,000	£10,000
Eldorado Seville	390/8	1959	£13,000	£10,000	£6,000
Eldorado Biarritz	390/8	1959	£30,000	£20,000	£14,000
Sedan de Ville	390/8	1960	£10,000	£8,000	£4,500
Convertible coupé	390/8	1960	£27,000	£14,000	£7,500
Eldorado Biarritz	390/8	1960	£25,000	£17,000	£10,000
Sedan de Ville	390/429/8	1961-64	£7,000	£5,000	£3,000
Coupé de Ville	390/429/8	1961-64	£8,000	£6,000	£4,000
Convertible coupé	390/429/8	1961-64	£15,000	£9,000	£7,000
Eldorado Biarritz	390/429/8	1961-64	£19,500	£14,000	£9,000

1959 Cadillac 67 Imperial Fleetwood Limousine, V8 engine, 345bhp at 48000rpm, Hydramatic transmission, independent coil spring front suspension, good condition throughout.
Est. £7,000–9,000 *S*

> *A rebuilt car is not necessarily more valuable than a car in good original condition, even if the restoration has been costly.*

1961 Cadillac 'Jacqueline', V8, 390cu in engine, 345bhp at 4800rpm, 3 speed automatic gearbox, hydraulic drum brakes all round, independent coil spring front suspension, leaf springs rear, rigid axle, left hand drive.
Est. £33,500–43,500 *CNY*

This car was named after the most famous 'Jacqueline' of that era – Jacqueline Bouvier Kennedy, the wife of the young American President, inaugurated in that year.

CAESAR

CATERHAM

1987 Caterham Seven 1700 Super Sprint, 5 speed De Dion rear axle, British Racing Green wings and nose, polished aluminium body, alloy wheels.
£11,500–12,500 *KSC*

1929 Caesar Special 1056cc Boat-Tailed 2 Seater Sports, built in the early 1970s, based on 1929 Humber 9/28 components, recent engine re-build.
Est. £13,500–15,000 *S*

A competition car used for trials, hill climbs, sprints, rallies and races as well as road use.

Cross Reference
Humber

1989 Caterham Seven 1700 Super Sprint, 4 speed live axle, 150bhp uprated engine, alloy wheels.
£11,500–12,500 *KSC*

CHENARD-WALCKER

1912 Chenard-Walcker 2 Seater, wooden artillery wheels, brass acetylene headlights, oil powered side lights, 2 seater body, hood and instruments missing, fair condition but would benefit from a full restoration.
£5,750–6,500 *S*

1916 Chevrolet 4-90 4 Seater Tourer, renewed upholstery, good condition throughout, museum stored and would benefit from some restoration.
£5,500–6,000 *S*

1927 Chevrolet Capitol Series AA Four Sports Cabriolet, carefully restored, very good condition throughout.
£8,750–9,750 *S*

Over a million Chevrolets were built in 1927 and the Sports Cabriolet was a new model, accommodating two extra passengers in the rumble seat. This model cost $715 compared with $525 for the standard two seater, and the wooden spoke wheels fitted to this car were an optional extra.

1928 Chevrolet, 6 cylinder rebuilt engine, partially restored, original interior.
£4,000–5,000 *GAR*

CHEVROLET

After W. C. Durant lost control of his General Motors combine he teamed up with racing driver Louis Chevrolet to produce prototype vehicles. These were designed by Etienne Planche in Detroit but the company soon moved to Flint, Michigan, in 1913.

The Model 4-90 was so called because it sold for $490 and was introduced to compete with the Model T Ford. When the Model T ceased production in 1927 Chevrolet became America's best selling car manufacturer.

1920 Chevrolet 4-90 Tourer, excellent restored condition.
£8,000–10,000 *CGB*

1925 Chevrolet Superior Series K 2 Door Roadster, left hand drive, drum headlamps, wooden artillery wheels, two-piece opening windscreen, engine compartment original, no hood cover, some recommissioning required.
£4,800–5,400 *S*

> **Miller's is a price GUIDE not a price LIST**

1928 Chevrolet Model AB 'National'
4 Door Saloon, overhead valve, in line
4 cylinder, water-cooled monobloc engine,
3 speed and reverse gearbox, original
instrumentation and plush interior trim.
£3,500–4,500 S

1936 Chevrolet Series FC Roadster,
6 cylinder, 2600cc engine, right hand drive,
originally exported to Australia, excellent
restored condition.
£7,200–7,600 ADT

Chevrolet Aerosedan

- In 1948 eleven models of the
  Fleetmaster Six and Stylemaster
  Six were available.
- All models used the 6 cylinder
  overhead valve engine of 216.5cu in.
- The 2 door Aerosedan which could
  comfortably seat 5 people sold for
  $1,434 when new.
- 211,861 were built in 1948.

1948 Chevrolet Model 2144 Fleetline
Aerosedan, right hand drive, original
specification, recently restored.
Est. £7,500–9,000 S

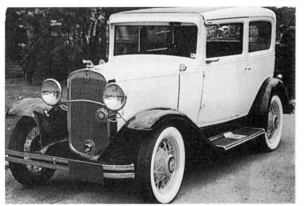

1931 Chevrolet AE Six 2 Door 5 Seater
Saloon, 6 cylinder engine, excellent
restored condition.
£8,750–9,000 Bro

1967 Chevrolet Camaro Sports
Convertible, V8, 5.7 litre engine, 295bhp,
automatic transmission, re-painted, good
condition throughout.
Est. £6,000–7,000 S

1969 Chevrolet Camaro Convertible 2-11
Pace Car, 5.7 litre engine, automatic gearbox,
original condition.
£11,500–12,500 COR

CHEVROLET Model	ENGINE cc/cyl	DATES	CONDITION		
			1	2	3
H4/H490 K Series	2801/4	1914-29	£9,000	£5,000	£2,000
FA5	2699/4	1918	£8,000	£5,000	£2,000
D5	5792/8	1918-19	£10,000	£6,000	£3,000
FB50	3660/4	1919-21	£7,000	£4,000	£2,000
AA	2801/4	1928-32	£5,000	£3,000	£1,000
AB/C	3180/6	1929-36	£6,000	£4,000	£2,000
Master	3358/6	1934-37	£9,000	£5,000	£2,000
Master De Luxe	3548/6	1938-41	£9,000	£6,000	£4,000

1973 Chevrolet Camaro 6.
£1,250–1,750 *CVPG*

1935 Chevrolet 2 Door 2 Seater Coupé,
left hand drive, boot mounted spare wheel,
good overall condition.
£4,000–4,500 *HOLL*

Chevrolet Corvette

First manufactured in 1953, Corvette
production now exceeds one million, making
it the best selling sports car of all time. Less
well known is the fact that this rugged V8
car is the world's best selling fibreglass
bodied car and is still in production today.
There have been four basic series with a fifth
expected for 1997.

The 1953–62 cars used a live axle chassis,
and from 1958 they had four headlamps.
Most collectable are probably the 1963–67
cars with independent rear suspension and
disc brakes, with big block engines available
from 1965.

A new body shape was launched in 1968
which ran until 1982, with soft bumpers
introduced in 1973–74, and a big fastback
window in 1978. The latest body has been
in production since 1984. The ZR–1 was
introduced in 1990 with 375bhp, 4 cam,
V8 engine designed by Lotus.

**1960 Chevrolet Corvette V8 2 Seater
Roadster,** manual gearbox, left hand drive,
good all-round condition.
£10,250–10,750 *S*

1965 Chevrolet Corvette Convertible,
5.4 litre engine, 4 speed gearbox, factory
side exhaust.
£15,000–17,000 *COR*

1961 Chevrolet Corvette Convertible,
with both hard and soft tops.
£19,000–21,000 *COR*

**1965 Chevrolet Corvette Sting Ray Sports
Coupé,** 327cu in engine, turbine wheels, left
hand drive, good condition throughout,
no air conditioning.
Est. £10,000–12,000 *S*

1966 Chevrolet Corvette Convertible,
5.4 litre automatic engine, factory side
exhaust, 'American Racing' wheels.
£17,500–18,500 *COR*

1971 Chevrolet Corvette LT-1, 5.7 litre engine, manual gearbox, very low mileage.
£21,500-22,500 *COR*

1973 Chevrolet Corvette, 5.7 litre automatic L82 engine.
£8,500-9,500 *COR*

1976 Chevrolet Corvette, 5.7 litre engine, manual gearbox, leather interior, air conditioning.
£8,500-9,500 *COR*

1978 Chevrolet Corvette 'Silver Anniversary', 5.7 litre automatic, low mileage.
£9,500-10,500 *COR*

1976 Chevrolet Corvette, 5.7 litre automatic, leather interior, air conditioning.
£8,500-9,500 *COR*

1979 Chevrolet Corvette, 8 cylinder, 5700cc L82 engine, 225bhp, 3 speed 350 turbo Hydramatic gearbox, power steering and brakes, limited slip differential, 40,000 miles recorded, correct radio/CB unit, cruise control, electric windows, central locking, telescopic leather steering wheel surround and correct front and rear spoilers, authentic throughout.
Est. £9,000-11,000 *ADT*

1981 Chevrolet Corvette, 5.7 litre automatic, leather interior, air conditioning, 12,000 miles recorded.
£13,500–14,500 *COR*

1985 Chevrolet Corvette, 5.7 litre automatic, low mileage, air conditioning.
£9,500–10,500 *COR*

CHEVROLET Model	ENGINE cu in/cyl	DATES	CONDITION 1	2	3
Stylemaster	216/6	1942-48	£8,000	£4,000	£1,000
Fleetmaster	216/6	1942-48	£8,000	£4,000	£1,000
Fleetline	216/6	1942-51	£8,000	£5,000	£2,000
Styleline	216/6	1949-52	£8,000	£6,000	£2,000
Bel Air 4 door	235/6	1953-54	£6,000	£4,000	£3,000
Bel Air sports coupé	235/6	1953-54	£7,000	£4,500	£3,500
Bel Air convertible	235/6	1953-54	£12,500	£9,500	£6,000
Bel Air 4 door	283/8	1955-57	£8,000	£4,000	£3,000
Bel Air sports coupé	283/8	1955-56	£11,000	£7,000	£4,000
Bel Air convertible	283/8	1955-56	£16,000	£11,000	£7,000
Bel Air sports coupé	283/8	1957	£11,000	£7,500	£4,500
Bel Air convertible	283/8	1957	£14,500	£10,500	£8,000
Impala sports sedan	235/6, 348/8	1958	£12,500	£9,000	£5,500
Impala convertible	235/6, 348/8	1958	£14,500	£11,000	£7,500
Impala sports sedan	235/6, 348/8	1959	£8,000	£5,000	£4,000
Impala convertible	235/6, 348/8	1959	£14,000	£10,000	£5,000
Corvette roadster	235/6	1953	£18,000	£14,000	£10,000
Corvette roadster	235/6, 283/8	1954-57	£16,500	£13,000	£9,000
Corvette roadster	283, 327/8	1958-62	£16,000	£12,000	£9,000
Corvette Stingray	327, 427/8	1963-67	£15,500	£12,000	£10,000
Corvette Stingray DHC	327, 427/8	1963-66	£20,000	£15,000	£8,000
Corvette Stingray DHC	427/8	1967	£16,000	£13,000	£10,000

Value will also be regulated by build options, rare coachbuilding options, and de luxe engine specifications etc.

CHRYSLER

1929 Chrysler 75 Roadster with Dickey Seat, 6 cylinder, 3500cc engine, right hand drive, good condition.
£7,500–8,000 *COYS*

The six cylinder, seven bearing, L-head engine produced 68bhp in 3.5 litre form.

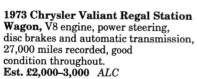

1973 Chrysler Valiant Regal Station Wagon, V8 engine, power steering, disc brakes and automatic transmission, 27,000 miles recorded, good condition throughout.
Est. £2,000–3,000 *ALC*

CITROËN

1926 Citroën Type B10 4 Door Saloon,
left hand drive, all steel 4 door saloon,
original specification in all major respects,
very good original example.
£3,500–4,000 *S*

1951 Citroën 11B, Paris built,
excellent all-round condition.
£6,500–7,500 *CR*

| Miller's is a price GUIDE |
| not a price LIST |

CITROËN Model	ENGINE cc/cyl	DATES	CONDITION 1	2	3
A	1300/4	1919	£4,000	£2,000	£1,000
5CV	856/4	1922-26	£7,000	£4,000	£2,000
11	1453/4	1922-28	£4,000	£2,000	£1,000
12/24	1538/4	1927-29	£5,000	£3,000	£1,000
2½litre	2442/6	1929-31	£5,000	£3,000	£1,500
13/30	1628/4	1929-31	£5,000	£3,000	£1,000
Big 12	1767/4	1932-35	£7,000	£5,000	£2,000
Twenty	2650/6	1932-35	£10,000	£5,000	£3,000
Ten CV	1452/4	1933-34	£5,000	£3,000	£1,000
Ten CV	1495/4	1935-36	£6,000	£3,000	£1,000
11B/Light 15/Big 15/7CV	1911/4	1934-57	£9,000	£5π,000	£2,000
Twelve	1628/4	1936-39	£5,000	£3,000	£1,000
F	1766/4	1937-38	£4,000	£2,000	£1,000
15/6 and Big Six	2866/6	1938-56	£7,000	£4,000	£2,000

1950 Citroën Light 15, small boot model,
very good condition.
£5,000–6,000 *OMH*

1953 Citroën 11BL, Paris built, recent
import, requires some restoration.
£2,500–2,750 *CR*

1954 Citroën Light 15, Slough built, recently restored, excellent all-round condition.
£10,500–11,000 *CR*

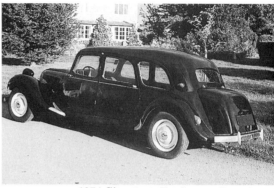

1954 Citroën 11F 8 Seater, Paris built, long wheelbase saloon, good condition.
£6,250–6,750 *CR*

1954 Citroën Big 15, French built, generally good condition.
£5,000–7,000 *OMH*

1954 Citroën 11B, Paris built, excellent all-round condition.
£7,000–7,500 *CR*

1955 Citroën Big 6, Slough built, mechanically sound.
£7,500–8,000 *CR*

1973 Citroën 2.4 Litre DS23 Pallas 4 Door Saloon, semi-automatic hydraulically controlled 4 speed transmission option, electric windows, generally good condition.
Est. £3,000–4,000 *BKS*

The Citroën Pallas was a de luxe variant of the DS series.

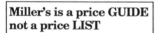

Miller's is a price GUIDE not a price LIST

CITROËN Model	ENGINE cc/cyl	DATES	CONDITION		
			1	2	3
2CV	375/2	1948-54	£1,000	£500	£250
2CV/Dyane/Bijou	425/2	1954-82	£1,000	£800	£500
DS19/ID19	1911/4	1955-69	£5,000	£3,000	£800
Sahara	900/4	1958-67	£5,000	£4,000	£3,000
2CV6	602/2	1963 on	£750	£500	£250
DS Safari	1985/4	1968-75	£5,000	£3,000	£1,000
DS21	1985/4	1969-75	£5,000	£3,000	£1,000
DS23	2347/4	1972-75	£5,000	£3,000	£1,000
SM	2670/ 2974/6	1970-75	£9,000	£6,000	£4,500

Imported (USA) SM models will be 15% less.

CLAN

1988 Clan Crusader Clover Sports Coupé, 4 cylinder, 1490cc Alfa Romeo engine, 5 speed manual gearbox, rigid glassfibre monocoque body, 978 miles recorded, only 22 built, virtually new.
£4,250–5,000 *ADT*

CLYNO

Clyno cars were produced as direct competition to the Morris car range. The factory was located at Wolverhampton, and was active between 1922 and 1929. The name derives from the inclined variable ratio belt pulley system developed by the founders Frank and Allwyn Smith.

1926 Clyno 11hp 2 Seater with Dickey, dashboard instrumentation original, upholstery restored, good weather equipment and sidescreens, CAV style torpedo sidelights, headlights converted for modern traffic conditions, engine re-built, restored.
£7,750–8,000 *S*

CLEMENT-BAYARD

It was not until 1899 that Clément-Bayard's car production commenced using a De Dion Bouton engine, while a Clément-Panhard was also produced to the design of Panhard et Levassor. Adolphe Clément began his industrial career manufacturing bicycles and he had also been actively involved in the development and manufacture of the pneumatic tyre.

1913 Clement-Bayard Type CB1 12hp Tourer, 3 speed gearbox, three-quarter elliptic rear suspension, Ducellier acetylene headlights with running board mounted generator, Securit oil sidelamps, double twist bulb horn, original black upholstery, original condition.
£9,000–10,000 *S*

1926 Clyno Tourer, 1100cc engine, full chassis-up restoration, excellent condition.
£8,000–9,000 *H&H*

COLUMBIA

1906 Columbia Mark XLVII 45hp 7 Passenger Touring, coachwork by C. P. Kimball, 4 cylinder F-head, 392cu in, 45hp engine, 4 speed gearbox, rear drum brakes, semi-elliptical leaf spring front suspension, full elliptical leaf springs rear, right hand drive, less than 5,000 miles recorded from new, excellent original condition.
£93,500–94,500 *CNY*

CORD

1937 Cord 812 Westchester Sedan,
8 cylinders, 4730cc engine, excellent fully
restored condition.
£14,500–15,000 *ADT*

*Designed by Gordon Behrig, the vehicle had
originally been intended as a small model
Duesenberg, also to be powered by the
Lycoming V8 engine but of slightly smaller
capacity. The 810 model was produced until
1937, followed by the 812 series.*

CUBITT

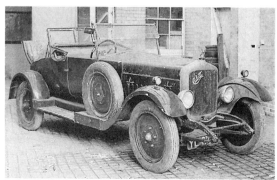

**1925 Cubitt Model K 15.9hp 2 Seater and
Dickey,** to original specification, unusual
features including leatherette covered
dashboard matching the upholstery, slatted
running boards, scuttle mounted horn, tool
locker in the spare wheel mounting, exhaust
outlet over the top of the petrol tank,
windscreen for the dickey seat, rare and
original but requires restoration.
£13,000–14,000 *S*

*The Cubitt car was built in Aylesbury and
production commenced in 1919 with a sturdy
16/20hp car, priced at a very competitive
£298, which rose to £398 by 1920.
S. F. Edge and John S. Napier were
appointed to direct the fortunes of the
company and update the car.*

Use the Index!
*Because certain items
might fit easily into any
number of categories, the
quickest and surest
method of locating any
entry is by reference to
the index at the back of
the book.*

*This index has been fully
cross-referenced for
absolute simplicity.*

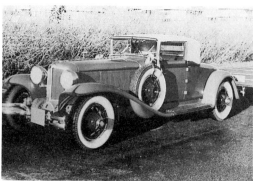

1931 Cord 4.9 Litre L-29 2 Seater Cabriolet,
coachwork by The Limousine Body Company,
restored maintaining originality, only two
owners from new.
Est. £60,000–90,000 *BKS*

CROSSLEY

**1909 Crossley 40hp Open Drive
Limousine,** mechanically complete and
original in all major respects although wheels
are slightly smaller than original, railway
carriage windows, passenger compartment
furnished with flower vases, bone handles,
floral light fittings, smoker's companion and
vanity case, silk blinds to doors and division,
8-day clock and a speaking tube to the driver.
£50,000–60,000 *S*

CUNNINGHAM

1953 Cunningham 5.4 Litre C3 Coupé,
coachwork by Carrozzeria Vignale, 331cu in,
220bhp V8 re-built engine, 4 speed manual
gearbox, only 30 miles recorded, good original
bodywork, original interior but driver's seat
torn, transmission, electrics and chassis
generally good condition, finished in red and
black duotone with black interior.
£35,000–37,000 *BKS*

*An example of the most famous of all post-
WWII specialised American car marques.*

DAIMLER

The Daimler engine patent rights were bought by F. R. Simms for the United Kingdom and the Colonies (excluding Canada) as early as 1891. It was nearly five years later that the first motor cars were offered for sale.

By 1910 they had merged with the Birmingham Small Arms Company but were already enjoying royal patronage. During WWI they produced a variety of products from staff cars and aeroplane engines to ammunition and armoured cars.

Between the wars continuing Royal orders enabled Daimler to flourish, including the acquisition of Lanchester. Jaguar took over Daimler in the 1960s and the Daimler badge still appears on a range of their current cars.

1924 Daimler 20hp C Type Landaulette, peaked V windscreen, diamond buttoned cloth upholstery, bone handles, newspaper nets, silk pulls and smoker's companion, Winkworth Electric Car Bell on the running board, museum displayed in recent years, requires careful recommissioning.
£16,000–17,000 *S*

1909 Daimler TB22 22.8hp Two Seater with Dickey, brass acetylene headlamps, electric sidelamps, brass horn, 2-person dickey seat, older restoration.
Est. £13,000–16,000 *S*

1938 Daimler DB18 2¼ Litre Drophead Coupé, very good condition throughout.
£13,000–13,500 *ADT*

c1897 Daimler 6hp Twin Cylinder 6 Seater Brake, original condition, requires restoring.
£40,000–42,000 *BKS*

1931 Daimler Double 6 Seven Seater Sedanca De Ville, coachwork by Thrupp & Maberley, V12 sleeve valve, 5296cc engine, Daimler fluid flywheel, 4-speed pre-selector gearbox, underslung worm final drive, mechanically good throughout, bodywork restored.
£23,000–25,000 *S*

> ## Don't Forget!
> *If in doubt please refer to the 'How to Use' section at the beginning of this book.*

1948 Daimler DB18 4 Door Saloon, very good restored condition.
£2,900–3,200 *H&H*

1952 Daimler DB18 Drophead Coupé, coachwork by Hooper, re-conditioned engine, totally original condition.
£4,000–5,000 *COYS*

Daimler DB18

- Two body styles were available between 1939 and 1950 and 3,365 chassis were built.
- The drophead coupé model was built by Tickford.
- The Consort was bodied by Mulliner.
- The 2522cc 6 cylinder engine produced 70bhp with a Wilson pre-selector gearbox.
- The Consort cost £2,075 when new in 1952.

1952 Daimler DB18 Consort Saloon, original upholstery, period radio, requires careful recommissioning.
£2,000–3,000 *S*

1953 Daimler Conquest Century 4 Door Saloon, running well and in good condition throughout.
£4,250–4,750 *S*

1955 Daimler DB18 Special Sports, coachwork by Barker, dry stored in recent years, good overall original condition.
Est. £8,000–9,000 *S*

1965 Daimler 2.5 Litre V8 Saloon, good condition throughout, requires recommissioning.
£3,250–3,500 *S*

1956 Daimler Special Series DB18 3½ Litre Empress Saloon, coachwork by Hooper, dry stored since 1989, very good condition throughout.
Est. £10,000–12,000 *S*

DAIMLER Model	ENGINE cc/cyl	DATES	CONDITION		
			1	2	3
Veteran (Coventry built)	var/4	1897-1904	£75,000	£60,000	£30,000
Veteran	var/4	1905-19	£35,000	£25,000	£15,000
30hp	4962/6	1919-25	£40,000	£25,000	£18,000
45hp	7413/6	1919-25	£45,000	£30,000	£20,000
Double Six 50	7136/12	1927-34	£40,000	£30,000	£20,000
20	2687/6	1934-35	£18,000	£14,000	£12,000
Straight 8	3421/8	1936-38	£20,000	£15,000	£12,000
Value is dependent on body style, coachbuilder and condition of the sleeve valve engine.					

1966 Daimler 2.5 Litre V8 4 Door Saloon,
engine rebuilt, body restored and re-sprayed,
original tool kit, handbook, maintenance
manual, parts list and some useful spares.
£2,750–3,000 *BKS*

1968 Daimler 2.5 Litre V8 Sports Saloon,
with stainless steel exhaust system,
brightwork re-chromed, carpets, door trim
and roof lining replaced, good overall
condition throughout.
£6,250–6,500 *S*

1968 Daimler 250 V8 Manual Saloon,
manual/overdrive gearbox, power steering,
good overall condition.
£2,750–3,000 *H&H*

1967 Daimler V8 2½ Litre, two owners
from new, very good overall condition.
Est. £6,000–7,000 *LF*

*This is a genuine 2½ litre model from the
Jaguar stable, rather than the later V8 250
from Leyland.*

1968 Daimler V8 250, 2548cc, recorded
mileage of 13,000, excellent original condition.
£9,500–10,500 *COYS*

1969 Daimler V8 250 Saloon,
excellent condition thoughout.
Est. £4,500–5,500 *S*

1969 Daimler V8 250 Saloon, requires
some attention, but generally good overall.
£1,400–1,600 *ADT*

1969 Daimler V8 250 Saloon,
very good overall condition.
£4,600–4,800 *ADT*

1967 Daimler Sovereign 4.2, automatic transmission, repainted, good original condition throughout.
Est. £2,500–3,500 *ADT*

1967 Daimler Sovereign 4.2 Litre Saloon, repainted, good original condition.
Est. £4,000–5,000 *ADT*

1969 Daimler Sovereign 420 Saloon, requires re-spray and general overhaul.
Est. £3,500–4,000 *S*

1969 Daimler Sovereign 4.2 Litre Saloon, engine rebuilt, original documentation.
£4,700–5,000 *Bro*

1973 Daimler Sovereign, good overall condition throughout.
Est. £2,000–3,000 *ADT*

1973 Daimler Double Six 4 Seater Saloon, automatic transmission, 2 additional rear stop lights, otherwise to maker's original specification, good condition throughout.
Est. £3,000–4,000 *S*

1976 Daimler Double Six 5.3 Litre 2 Door Coupé, re-imported from California, some work required to the bodywork.
Est. £1,500–2,000 *S*

DAIMLER Model	ENGINE cc/cyl	DATES	CONDITION 1	2	3
DB18	2522/6	1946-49	£7,500	£4,000	£1,000
DB18 Conv S/S	2522/6	1948-53	£11,000	£6,000	£2,000
Consort	2522/6	1949-53	£5,000	£3,000	£1,000
Conquest/Con.Century	2433/6	1953-58	£4,000	£2,000	£1,000
Conquest Roadster	2433/6	1953-56	£10,000	£6,000	£3,000
Majestic 3.8	3794/6	1958-62	£5,000	£2,000	£1,000
SP250	2547/8	1959-64	£12,000	£10,000	£4,500
Majestic Major	4561/8	1961-64	£6,000	£4,000	£1,000
2.5 V8	2547/8	1962-67	£7,000	£5,250	£2,500
V8 250	2547/8	1968-69	£6,000	£4,000	£2,000
Sovereign 420	4235/6	1966-69	£5,000	£3,500	£1,500

1977 Daimler 4.2 Litre Vanden Plas Saloon, very good original condition.
Est. £4,000–5,000 *S*

1961 Daimler SP250 B Series, 2547cc, 8 cylinders, bodywork needs attention.
£7,000–9,000 *OMH*

Daimler SP250

- The Daimler SP250, originally known as the Dart, had to drop the name due to legal action.
- The fibreglass bodied SP250 featured a 90° 2,548cc V8 engine designed by Edward Turner.
- This engine also powered the Daimler V8 250 Saloon series.
- Running gear very similar to the Triumph TR3A.

1963 Daimler SP250 C Series, hard top, with many factory extras and lights, good original condition.
£13,500–14,500 *CGOC*

1963 Daimler SP250 C Series, hard top, one owner, low mileage, good condition.
£16,000–17,000 *CGOC*

1964 Daimler SP250 Dart Sports 2 Seater, good condition but requires recommissioning.
£3,250–3,750 *S*

DARRACQ

1910 Darracq Type RRX 14/16hp Tourer, mechanically restored, but not fully re-assembled, substantially dismantled, upholstery and fittings entirely original and complete.
£15,000–16,000 *S*

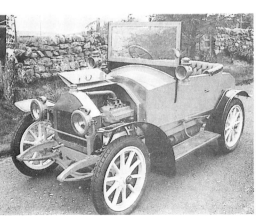

1910 Darracq, restored in 1978, good condition and running order.
£6,500–7,500 *COYS*

DATSUN

1969 Datsun Fairlady Convertible,
1600cc, rust free, good overall condition.
£5,250–5,650 *Bro*

1977 Datson 260Z, 40,000 miles,
very good condition.
£3,750–4,250 *Mot*

1981 Datsun 280 ZX Targa, chrome wire
wheels, recently fully restored.
£1,500–1,600 *H&H*

*The Datsun Z range of cars was introduced
in 1970.*

1983 Datsun 280 ZX Targa 4 Seater
Coupé, 6 cylinder, 2753cc engine, automatic
transmission, excellent all-round condition.
£2,500–2,700 *S*

DATSUN Model	ENGINE cc/cyl	DATES	CONDITION 1	2	3
240Z	2393/6	1970-71	£6,000	£4,000	£2,000
240Z	2393/6	1971-74	£4,500	£3,250	£1,500
260Z	2565/6	1974-79	£3,000	£2,250	£1,000
260Z 2+2	2565/6	1974-79	£2,250	£1,500	£800

DAYTON

1909 Dayton Reliable Surrey, rare
right hand drive, 2 forward gears and
reverse, pin chain drive from twin
cylinder engine.
£9,000–12,000 *ALC*

1906 De Dion Bouton Model AM, 9hp,
one cylinder, has been dry stored and
requires recommissioning, replica mudguards,
remainder of components original.
£9,500–11,000 *ADT*

DE DION BOUTON

The association between the Marquis Albert
de Dion and M. Georges Bouton was formed
in 1883. The De Dion company was the first
to manufacture cars on both sides of the
Atlantic, and by 1904 the company had
produced over 40,000 engines for other
manufacturers. One of the most important
features was the very successful De Dion axle
system which was designed by M. Trépardoux.

The last motor car was produced in 1932,
but a lightweight motorcycle was made in
the 1950s.

1901 De Dion Bouton Vis-a-Vis Model B1,
single cylinder, F-head, 3½hp, 393cc, 2 speed
gearbox, drum brakes on rear wheels, platform
front suspension, three-quarter elliptical
rear, in running order, fair overall condition.
£20,000–25,000   *CNY*

**1901 De Dion Bouton 4½hp Vis-a-Vis
Model G,** with Lucidus lamps, Larjo twin
trumpet brass horn and wooden wings,
professionally restored, very original condition.
Est. £16,000–20,000   *S*

**1904 De Dion Bouton Model Y 6hp Rear
Entrance Tonneau,** original body by
Philippon of Neuilly, with Stadium sight
lights and Lucas King of the Road rear lamp,
angle mounted dashboard clock and Desmo
horn, good condition.
£23,000–25,000   *S*

**1903 De Dion Bouton Model V 8hp Rear
Entrance Tonneau,** single cylinder engine,
with original 4 seat coachwork, good
overall condition.
£36,000–40,000   *S*

DELAGE

The famous one-eyed French motor pioneer,
Louis Delage, produced his first motor vehicle
in 1905 powered by a De Dion engine.
Following a period of racing and competition
success, Delage enjoyed an enviable
reputation similar to that of
Rolls-Royce and Hispano-Suiza.

Despite ever more racing victories, financial
problems led to the acquisiton of the company
by Delahaye in 1935. Production of Delage
ended in 1955 following the purchase of
Delahaye by Hotchkiss.

1928 Delage DR70 Park Ward Saloon,
right hand drive, very good condition
throughout.
Est. £14,000–16,000   *LF*

1937 Delage D8-120 4.3 Litre Deltasport Drophead Foursome Coupé, coachwork by Henri Chapron, a very rare and historic vehicle, excellent condition throughout.
£170,000–180,000 *BKS*

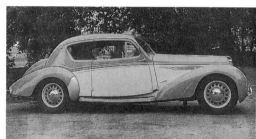

1940 Delage D6-75 Olympic Sports, 6 cylinder, 3000cc engine, 2 door pillarless coupé by Letourneau & Marchand, maintained to high standards, good overall condition.
Est. £18,000–22,000 *S*

DELAHAYE

1947 Delahaye Type 135M Three Position Drophead Coupé, coachwork by Chapron, although structurally very sound, requires full mechanical and electrical re-build.
Est. £20,000–27,000 *S*

1949 Delahaye 135M Cabriolet, coachwork by Chapron, 6 cylinder, 3557cc engine, excellent overall condition.
Est. £38,000–45,000 *COYS*

DE SOTO

1929 De Soto Series K 6 Cylinder Tourer, coachwork by Holden, Australia, little used, good mechanical condition,.
£7,250–7,750 *S*

1950 Delahaye 148L Saloon, rebuilt engine, original condition throughout and in running order.
£9,500–10,500 *C*

DODGE

1948 De Soto Custom Series 4 Door Sedan, right hand drive, extensively restored to a high standard.
Est. £6,500–7,500 *S*

1924 Dodge 35hp 5 Seater Tourer, right hand drive, new hood, very good condition.
£12,500–13,500 *Bro*

1933 Dodge KC Series (Australian) Customised Roadster, V8 replacement engine and automatic transmission, semi-elliptic front and rear suspension, left hand drive.
£30,000–32,000 *CNY*

This car was previously owned by Barbra Streisand.

1960 Dodge Phoenix 4 Door Saloon, right hand drive, push button automatic transmission, double headlights, good condition throughout.
Est. £6,000–7,000 *S*

1948 Dodge Kingsway 4 Door Sedan, right hand drive, very original, low mileage.
£4,500–5,500 *CGB*

DONNET-ZEDEL

Vinot et Deguingand had been building cars of high quality since the turn of the century. Their premises at Nanterre were taken over by Donnet who had taken over Zedel the previous year. Production of Donnet-Zedel cars commenced in 1924.

1927 Donnet-Zedel Type G 2 Seater Sports, possible third seat in the tail compartment, requires complete restoration.
£4,800–5,000 *S*

DUESENBERG

1933 Duesenberg Model J Convertible Victoria, coachwork by Rollston, straight 8 cylinders, double overhead camshaft, 420cu in, 265bhp at 4250rpm, 3 speed gearbox with freewheeling device, 4 wheel hydraulic drum brakes, semi-elliptical leaf spring suspension with hydraulic lever arm shock absorbers front and rear, left hand drive, requires restoration, some items missing, including dual tail lights and exhaust manifolds.
£245,000–255,000 *CNY*

> **Did you know?**
> *MILLER'S* **Collectors Cars Price Guide** *builds up year-by-year to form the most comprehensive photo-reference library system available.*

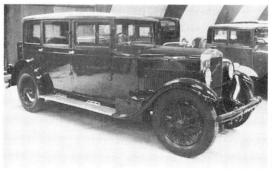

1928 Donnet-Zedel 12CV 4 Door 6 Light Saloon, right hand drive, wire spoked wheels, 2 occasional seats, rear mounted spare wheel, fitted trunk, restored, good condition throughout.
Est. £8,500–9,000 *S*

EDSEL

1959 Edsel Ranger 4 Door Saloon,
push button automatic transmission, left
hand drive, good overall condition including
original clear plastic seat covers.
Est. £6,000–8,000 *S*

ERSKINE

1928 Erskine Six Model 51 2 Door Sedan,
needs careful re-commissioning for road
use, original specification, very good
overall condition.
£3,300–3,500 *S*

ENFIELD

The Enfield Autocar Company Ltd., of
Hunt End Works, Redditch, was formed in
1906 to handle the car making activities of
the Enfield Cycle Company (makers of Royal
Enfield motorcycles). In 1908 they moved to
Fallows Road, Sparkbrook, Birmingham,
after being taken over by Alldays & Onions
Ltd. The latter company, who are still in
business today, was formed in 1650 and is
probably Britain's oldest engineering company.

**1975 Enfield Electric Model 8000
2 Seater Saloon,** stored for the past
5 years, requires new batteries.
£700–750 *S*

*A built-in charger enables the car to be
charged from a 240volt system, and charges
at 72 volts.*

> **Cross Reference**
> Micro Cars

1913 Enfield 14.3hp Open Tourer,
wire wheels, excellent condition throughout.
£14,500–15,500 *S*

> **Did you know?**
> *MILLER'S* Collectors
> Cars Price Guide *builds
> up year-by-year to form
> the most comprehensive
> photo-reference library
> system available.*

FACEL VEGA

1961 Facel Vega Facellia F2 Cabriolet,
4 cylinder, 1986cc engine, restored and
renovated with a Facel III Volvo 1.8 litre
overhead valve engine, re-sprayed, excellent
condition throughout.
£15,000–17,000 *ADT*

1961 Facel Vega HK500 Coupé, hardly
used since restoration.
£10,000–11,000 *S*

FERRARI

The famous prancing horse emblem, the Cavallino Rampante, was adopted as the Ferrari badge as soon as Enzo Ferrari started to produce motor cars. The badge was based on a trophy which had been presented to him after a famous racing victory in 1923. The trophy was presented by the Contessa Baracca, who was the mother of the WWI flying ace who featured the prancing horse motif on the fuselage of his aeroplane. At that time, Enzo Ferrari was based in Modena, before Italian post war legislation forced the factory move to Maranello, about 12 miles to the south.

1953 Ferrari 250 MM Coupé, coachwork by Pininfarina.
Est. £350,000–450,000 *DKE*

1954/5 Ferrari 500 Mondial Series 2, coachwork by Scaglietti .
£250–350,000 *DKE*

1956 Ferrari 250 GT Boano.
Est. £30,000–50,000 *DKE*

1959 Ferrari 250 Pininfarina Coupé.
£30,000–50,000 *DKE*

1960 Ferrari 250 GT Pininfarina Series 2 Convertible, V12, 2953cc engine, left hand drive, imported from America, retrimmed, restored and fully re-sprayed, carefully maintained.
£59,000–62,000 *COYS*

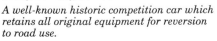
1963 Ferrari 250 GT SWB, 12 cylinder, 2953cc engine, Berlinetta coachwork by Pininfarina, engine completely rebuilt, excellent all-round condition.
£275,000–285,000 *COYS*

A well-known historic competition car which retains all original equipment for reversion to road use.

1961 Ferrari 250 GT Drogo, V12, 2953cc engine, Berlinetta coachwork by Piero Drogo, excellent condition.
Est. £65,000–75,000 *COYS*

Ferrari 275 GTB

- **Direct successor to the 250 GT SWB.**
- **Same 94⅗in wheelbase and short-block V12 engine.**
- **The 275 had independent rear suspension and 5 speed transaxle developed from the 250 LM.**
- **Arguably the finest of the front engined Ferraris.**

1965 Ferrari 275 GTB, 6 carburettor set-up on open air trumpets, 3 carburettors and air filter, comprehensively rebuilt, fully restored and retrimmed, excellent condition throughout.
£105,000–115,000 *COYS*

1969 Ferrari 365 GT 2+2 Coupé, V12, 4390cc engine, coachwork by Pininfarina, right hand drive, Borrani wire wheels, excellent condition.
Est. £32,000–35,000 *COYS*

1969 Ferrari 365 GT 2+2, resprayed, excellent condition.
£21,000–23,000 *ADT*

FERRARI Model	ENGINE cc/cyl	DATES	CONDITION 1	2	3
250 GT	2953/12	1959-63	£32,000	£22,000	£20,000
250 GT SWB (steel)	2953/12	1959-62	£235,000	£185,000	-
250 GT Lusso	2953/12	1962-64	£80,000	£65,000	£50,000
250 GT 2+2	2953/12	1961-64	£30,000	£21,000	£18,000
275 GTB	3286/12	1964-66	£100,000	£80,000	£70,000
275 GTS	3286/12	1965-67	£90,000	£70,000	£50,000
275 GTB 4-cam	3286/12	1966-68	£150,000	£110,000	£80,000
330 GT 2+2	3967/12	1964-67	£22,000	£18,000	£15,000
330 GTC	3967/12	1966-68	£55,000	£40,000	£25,000
330 GTS	3967/12	1966-68	£80,000	£70,000	£60,000
365 GT 2+2	4390/12	1967-71	£28,000	£20,000	£15,000
365 GTC	4390/12	1967-70	£40,000	£35,000	£30,000
365 GTS	4390/12	1968-69	£110,000	£80,000	£70,000
365 GTB (Daytona)	4390/12	1968-74	£90,000	£70,000	£50,000
365 GTC4	4390/12	1971-74	£45,000	£38,000	£30,000
365 GT4 2+2/400GT	4390/ 4823/12	1972-79	£20,000	£15,000	£10,000
365 BB	4390/12	1974-76	£55,000	£38,000	£30,000
512 BB/BBi	4942/12	1976-81	£50,000	£40,000	£30,000
246 GT Dino	2418/6	1969-74	£35,000	£25,000	£15,000
246 GTS Dino	2418/6	1972-74	£42,000	£28,000	£22,000
308 GT4 2+2	2926/8	1973-80	£15,000	£10,000	£8,000
308 GTB (fibreglass)	2926/8	1975-76	£25,000	£18,000	£15,000
308 GTB	2926/8	1977-81	£22,000	£16,000	£10,000
308 GTS	2926/8	1978-81	£26,000	£18,000	£11,000
308 GTBi/GTSi	2926/8	1981-82	£24,000	£17,000	£10,000
308 GTB/GTS QV	2926/6	1983-85	£21,500	£16,500	£9,500
400i manual	4823/12	1981-85	£15,000	£12,000	£10,000
400i auto	4823/12	1981-85	£13,000	£12,000	£8,000

1971 Ferrari 365 GTB/4 Daytona, V12, 4390cc engine, Berlinetta coachwork by Pininfarina, 33,500 miles from new, excellent original condition throughout. **Est. £70,000–85,000** *COYS*

> **Locate the source**
> *The source of each illustration in* Miller's Collectors Cars Price Guide *can be found by checking the code letters below each caption with the Key to Illustrations.*

Ferrari 246 GTS Dino

- The Ferrari 246 was so designated as it had a 2.4 litre, V6 engine.
- Only about 4,000 were built of which less than 1,200 had the detachable 'Spyder' roof.
- The bodywork was designed by Pininfarina over a tubular steel chassis.
- The car was named after Enzo Ferrari's son, Alfredino, who tragically died in 1956.
- The 4 camshaft, 2.4 litre, V6 engine produced 190 bhp and was transversely mounted above the 5 speed gearbox.

1972 Ferrari 246 GTS Dino, 6 cylinder, 2418cc engine, Spyder coachwork by Pininfarina, original and good condition throughout. **£32,000–34,000** *COYS*

1972 Ferrari 365 4.4 Litre GT4, 2+2 Berlina by Pininfarina, air conditioned, excellent condition. **Est. £15,000–20,000** *BKS*

1972 Ferrari 365 GTC/4 Coupé, 12 cylinders, 4390cc, coachwork by Pininfarina, excellent order throughout. **£29,000–30,000** *COYS*
Only 32 right hand drive examples were built.

1973 Ferrari 246 Dino 2 Seater Sports Coupé, excellent condition. **£25,000–27,000** *S*

1973 Ferrari 246 GT, low mileage, very good condition throughout. **Est. £38,000–42,000** *ADT*

1973 Ferrari 365 GTB/4 Daytona, 12 cylinder, 4390cc engine, Berlinetta coachwork by Pininfarina, engine and overall condition very good. **£62,000–65,000** *COYS*

**1974 Ferrari 365 4.4 Litre GT4 2+2
Coupé,** coachwork by Pininfarina, standard
power steering and air conditioning,
unmodified factory specification, good
condition, some cosmetic attention required.
Est. £13,000–15,000 *BKS*

1974 Ferrari 365 GT4 Berlinetta Boxer,
coachwork by Pininfarina, under 22,000
miles since new, regularly maintained,
excellent condition.
£45,000–55,000 *COYS*

1976 Ferrari 308 GT4 2 Door 2+2 Coupé,
coachwork by Bertone, good condition.
Est. £15,000–18,000 *S*

Ferrari 308 GT4

- **Introduced as the replacement for
  the Dino in 1974.**
- **Transverse mounted 2.9 litre, V8
  engine produced 255bhp.**
- **Manual 5 speed gearbox.**

1976 Ferrari 308 GTB, V8, 2927cc engine,
Berlinetta coachwork by Pininfarina,
fibreglass body, 51,000 miles from new,
excellent original condition.
£22,000–23,000 *COYS*

1981 Ferrari 400i, 12 cylinder, 4823cc
engine, automatic transmission, fuel
injection, good usable all-round condition.
Est. £16,000–18,000 *ADT*

1978 Ferrari 308 GT4 2+2 Coupé,
engine requires attention, otherwise in
fair condition.
£9,500–10,500 *S*

**1982 Ferrari 512i 4.9 Litre Berlinetta
Boxer,** coachwork by Pininfarina, 10,300
miles recorded, excellent condition throughout.
£55,000–57,000 *BKS*

**1985 Ferrari 308 GTS QV Berlinetta
Targa,** V8, 2927cc engine, coachwork by
Pininfarina, left hand drive, 37,000km from
new, virtually as new condition.
Est. £25,000–28,000 *COYS*

*308GTS Quattrovalvole models have a
4 valve per cylinder head as opposed to the
standard two.*

1984 Ferrari 308 GT Konig Spyder,
Konig body kit fitted, very good
condition throughout.
Est. £35,000–40,000 *S*

Miller's is a price GUIDE
not a price LIST

**1985 Ferrari Mondial Quattrovalvole
Sports Coupé.**
£12,000–15,000 *CARS*

1987 Ferrari Testarossa,
12 cylinder, 4942cc engine,
Berlinetta coachwork by
Pininfarina, left hand drive,
31,500km from new, excellent
condition throughout.
£40,000–46,000 *COYS*

FIAT

The FIAT Company, founded before the turn
of the century, is truly one of the giants of the
motor industry. As well as owning such
famous marques as Ferrari and Lancia, the
company's interests as a multi-national
industrial combine vary from aircraft,
railways, ship-building and machinery to
tourism and publishing. It operates over
200 factories including 35 car plants in over
20 countries. It has pioneered industrial
development in former eastern bloc countries
as well as the Third World.

1922 Fiat Tipo 501 2 Door Saloon, right
hand drive, original, requires refurbishing.
£4,000–5,000 *S*

1925 Fiat 501 4 Seater Tourer,
good condition.
£9,000–10,000 *OMH*

**1928 Fiat Tipo 520 Four Door 6 Light
Saloon,** recently repainted, sound and
original condition.
£4,000–5,000 *S*

FIAT Model	ENGINE cc/cyl	DATES	CONDITION		
			1	2	3
501	1460/4	1920-26	£6,000	£3,500	£1,500
519	4767/6	1923-29	£9,000	£7,000	£3,000
503	1473/4	1927-29	£8,000	£4,000	£2,000
507	2297/4	1927-28	£9,000	£5,500	£3,500
522/4	2516/6	1932-34	£10,000	£8,000	£3,500
508	994/4	1934-37	£5,000	£2,500	£1,500
527 Sports	2516/6	1935-36	£14,000	£8,000	£3,500
1.5 litre Balilla	1498/6	1936-39	£10,000	£7,000	£3,000
500	570/4	1937-55	£6,000	£2,500	£1,000
1100 Balilla	1089/4	1938-40	£4,500	£2,000	£1,000

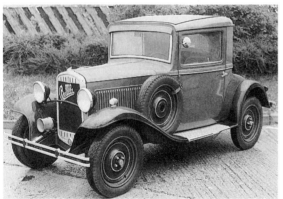

1933 Fiat Tipo 508 Balilla Fixed Head 2 Seater, 4 cylinders, 995cc, very good overall condition, requires re-commissioning.
£3,500–4,500 *COYS*

1939 Fiat Topolino, right hand drive, produced for the British market, requires restoration, fair condition throughout.
Est. £800–1,000 *LF*

1963 Fiat 1600 Twin-Cam 2+2 Coupé, coachwork by Fissore, twin choke Weber carburettors, 5 speed gearbox, all-round disc brakes, left hand drive, good overall condition.
£3,750–4,000 *S*

1938 Fiat Topolino Cabriolet, 4 cylinders, 569cc, ground-up restoration, very good condition.
£7,000–8,000 *COYS*

> **Miller's is a price GUIDE not a price LIST**

1954 Fiat 500 Giardiniera Estate, 4 cylinder, 596cc engine, very good condition throughout.
£2,500–3,500 *COYS*

1955 Fiat Belvedere 500B Station Wagon, 4 cylinder, 52 x 67mm, 570cc overhead valve engine, 4 speed gearbox with synchromesh on 3rd and 4th, 12 volt electrical equipment, unused for several years, only 24,800 miles, requires careful re-commissioning.
£3,500–4,000 *S*

This car produced a top speed of 56mph, with economical fuel consumption quoted at 52mpg.

1967 Fiat 600 Gamine Open Sports,
2 cylinder, 600cc engine, good original
condition throughout.
£3,750–4,000 *COYS*

1967 Fiat Dino 2 Litre Coupé, original
body, professionally repainted, upholstery
retrimmed, excellent condition.
Est. £6,000–7,000 *ADT*

1976 Fiat 126, very good condition.
£800–900 *H&H*

1967 Fiat Dino 2 Litre Coupé, stored for
5 years, original specification.
Est. £6,000–7,000 *S*

1970 Fiat 500 4 Seater Saloon, good
mechanical condition, excellent and
original upholstery.
£2,000–2,250 *S*

1972 Fiat 500L Saloon, restored, repainted,
original specification, excellent condition.
£3,000–3,250 *S*

1989 Fiat X1/9, 4 cylinder, 1499cc engine,
low mileage of 1,062, 'as new' condition.
Est. £6,500–7,500 *ADT*

FIAT Model	ENGINE cc/cyl	DATES	CONDITION 1	2	3
500B Topolino	569/4	1945-55	£3,000	£1,500	£750
500C	569/4	1948-54	£4,000	£1,700	£1,000
500 Nuova	479,499/2	1957-75	£3,000	£1,500	£750
600/600D	633, 767/4	1955-70	£3,000	£2,000	£1,000
500F Giardiniera	479, 499/2	1957-75	£3,000	£1,500	£1,000
2300S	2280/6	1961-68	£3,000	£1,700	£1,000
850	843/4	1964-71	£1,000	£750	-
850 Coupé	843, 903/4	1965-73	£1,500	£1,000	-
850 Spyder	843, 903/4	1965-73	£3,000	£2,000	£1,000
128 Sport Coupé 3P	1116/ 1290/4	1971-78	£2,500	£1,800	£1,000
130 Coupé	3235/6	1971-77	£5,500	£4,000	£2,000
131 Mirafiori Sport	1995/4	1974-84	£1,500	£1,000	£500
124 Sport Coupé	1438/ 1608/4	1966-72	£3,000	£2,000	£1,000
124 Sport Spyder	1438/ 1608/4	1966-72	£4,000	£2,500	£1,500
Dino Coupé	1987/ 2418/6	1967-73	£7,500	£5,500	£2,500
Dino Spyder	1987/ 2418/6	1967-73	£10,000	£7,000	£5,000
X1/9	1290/ 1498/4	1972-89	£3,500	£1,500	£1,000

FORD

Henry Ford enjoyed success with a series of best selling vehicles. The legendary Model T designed by Joseph Galamb to Henry Ford's specification and introduced in October 1908 surpassed all expectations. Between 1908 and 1927 over fifteen million were produced and it was the first car to be built on a moving production line. It is often said that the Model T put the world on wheels. By the early 1920s over half the cars in the world were Model T Fords. The Model T retained the same 2.9 litre engine and pedal-operated 2 speed epicyclic transmission throughout its production. Henry Ford was also a pioneer in expanding motor car production, setting up Ford factories throughout the world.

1906 Ford 15hp Model N 2 Seater Runabout, very early chassis number, totally restored, complete and original, very good condition throughout.
Est. £12,000–15,000 *S*

1912 Ford Model T 2 Seater Runabout, 2 E & J sidelights, and an E & J and a Radmore headlamp, fitted with Rushmore running board mounted generator, very good condition throughout.
£9,000–11,000 *S*

1914 Ford Model T Speedster, 2 seater runabout, monocle windscreen, 2 oil side lamps, acetylene gas headlamps, left hand drive, requires re-commissioning.
£3,500–4,500 *ADT*

1914 Ford Model T Raceabout, concours condition.
£20,000–22,000 *FHF*

1915 Ford Model T 2 Seater Roadster, fitted with 1926 electric starter engine, very good overall condition.
Est. £7,500–8,500 *S*

> *A rebuilt car is not necessarily more valuable than a car in good original condition, even if the restoration has been costly.*

1918 Ford Model T 4 Seater Open Tourer, wired for battery ignition, good condition throughout.
£7,750–8,000 *S*

1924 Ford Model T 2 Door, 4 Seater Saloon, epicyclic 2 speed gearbox, right hand drive, very good condition throughout.
£5,400–5,800 *ADT*

1924 Ford Model T 2 Door Tudor Saloon, new headlining, re-upholstered, original instrumentation, good condition throughout.
£5,000–6,000 *S*

Model A

- **Introduced in 1927 to replace the Model T.**
- **Produced to the same standards as the Model T using the best materials it was both robust and reliable.**
- **3 speed and reverse gearbox and a 4 cylinder side valve 3.3 litre engine, it cost about $500 when new.**

1928 Ford Model A 2 Door Doctor's Coupé with Dickey, restored to a very high overall standard.
Est. £8,000–10,000 *S*

1929 Ford Model A Roadster De Luxe with Dickey, to original factory specification apart from later dynamo and carburettor, good condition, requires re-commissioning.
£9,500–10,000 *S*

Cross Reference
Restoration Projects

c1930 Ford Model A 2 Door Fixed Head Coupé, distributor cap missing, engine otherwise complete, bodywork poor, unrestored condition.
£2,000–2,500 *S*

FORD Model	ENGINE cc/cyl	DATES	CONDITION 1	2	3
Model T	2892/4	1908-27	£10,000	£7,000	£4,000
Model A	3285/4	1928-32	£8,500	£6,000	£3,500
Models Y and 8	933/4	1933-40	£4,000	£3,000	£1,500
Model C	1172/4	1933-40	£4,000	£2,000	£1,000
Model AB	3285/4	1933-34	£10,000	£8,000	£4,500
Model ABF	2043/4	1933-34	£9,000	£6,000	£4,000
Model V8	3622/8	1932-40	£8,500	£6,000	£4,500
Model V8-60	2227/8	1936-40	£7,000	£5,000	£2,000
Model AF (UK only)	2033/4	1928-32	£9,000	£6,000	£3,500

A right hand drive vehicle will always command more interest than a left hand drive. Coachbuilt vehicles, and in particular drophead coupés, achieve a premium at auction. Veteran cars (i.e. manufactured before 1919) will often achieve a 20% premium.

1930 Ford Model A 2 Door Coupé with Dickey, very good restored condition.
£9,750–10,250 *S*

1932 Ford Model Y 8hp 2 Seater Open Tourer, coachwork by Kelsch of France, total body-off restoration, very good condition throughout.
£9,000–9,500 *S*

This car, carrying French coachwork, is considered to be unique.

Model Y Type

- The first entirely British Ford, the 8hp Y Type Popular, was produced at Dagenham from 1932 became a best-seller, prompting both Morris and Singer to produce similar vehicles.
- Most Y Types were saloons, with both 2 and 4 doors.
- The 2 door form became the first British saloon to sell for just £100.
- Commercial van variants were introduced in 1933.

1933 Ford Model B 4 Door Saloon, 24hp engine, excellent overall condition.
£10,000–12,000 *OMH*

1935 Ford Model Y 8hp Popular, 2 door Tudor version, excellent restored condition.
£5,000–5,250 *FYC*

Manufactured at Dagenham between 1932 and 1937.

1935 Ford Model Y 4 Door Saloon, dry stored for 30 years, restored, fitted with later wheels and better brakes, but with 5 original wheels, requires re-painting.
£2,000–2,500 *S*

1936 Ford Model Y 8hp Saloon, 4 cylinders, 933cc, dry stored, requires some re-commissioning before use.
£1,750–2,000 *ADT*

1936 Ford C Type Open Tourer, 4 cylinder, 1172cc engine, chassis-up mechanical re-build, upholstery refurbished, full mechanical overhaul, very good condition.
£3,500–3,750 *COYS*

One of only 6 known to still exist by the Ford 10 Register.

1936 Ford Model CX 10hp De Luxe Model C, 4 door version, very good condition. **£3,750–4,250** *FYC*

This model, without grille bars, was manufactured at Dagenham from September 1934–September 1935, and the Model CX from October 1935–March 1937.

1948 Ford Anglia Tourer, 4 cylinder side valve engine, 1172cc, 3 speed central change gearbox, box section chassis, beam axles mounted on semi-elliptic leaf springs, 4 wheel mechanical brakes, pressed steel wheels, right hand drive, generally original, good condition throughout. **£2,000–2,500** *C(A)*

1960 Ford Popular De Luxe, fair condition. **£400–500** *C*

1958 Ford Anglia, 4 cylinder, 1172cc engine, 3 speed manual gearbox, good original condition overall but bodywork requires attention. **£500–600** *ADT*

c1937 Ford Model 7Y 8hp 2 Door Saloon, running order, fair condition throughout. **£1,250–1,450** *S*

1939 Ford Prefect Tourer, replacement Ford engine, original in all other respects. **£5,500–6,000** *S*

The open cars were made in comparatively small numbers and the interruption of production by WWII makes surviving pre-war Prefect Tourers extremely rare.

1960 Ford Anglia 105E De Luxe Saloon,
oversquare 997cc engine, 4 speed gearbox,
two-tone paintwork, full width grille, period
accessories including fog lamp, wheel trims,
reversing lamp and exhaust deflector,
26,000 miles recorded, very good
condition throughout.
£1,300–1,400 *ALC*

1967 Ford Anglia Saloon, 997cc overhead
valve engine, 4 speed gearbox, very good
condition overall.
Est. £1,200–1,500 *LF*

1962 Ford Consul Capri 335 Coupé,
4 cylinder, 1340cc overhead valve engine,
4 speed transmission, original in all respects,
left hand drive, very good throughout.
Est. £3,250–4,000 *S*

1961 Ford Zephyr Zodiac Saloon,
very good original condition.
Est. £2,000–3,000 *ALC*

**1963 Ford Cortina Super 'Woody'
Estate,** original, rare.
£1,500–2,000 *OMH*

**1963 Ford Cortina 1500 Super 4 Door
Saloon,** very good condition throughout.
£1,250–1,500 *S*

**1965 Ford Lotus-Cortina MkI
Competition Saloon,** completely re-built
throughout, engine competition tuned,
contemporary magnesium Minilite wheels.
Est. £8,000–9,000 *S*

One of the earlier Lotus assembled cars.

1964 Ford Cortina MkI, 4 cylinder, 1498cc
engine, automatic gearbox, re-sprayed,
very good condition.
£900–1,000 *ADT*

Cross Reference
Competition Cars
Lotus

FORD (British built) Model	ENGINE cc/cyl	DATES	CONDITION 1	CONDITION 2	CONDITION 3
Anglia E494A	993/4	1948-53	£2,000	£850	£250
Prefect E93A	1172/4	1940-49	£3,500	£1,250	£900
Prefect E493A	1172/4	1948-53	£2,500	£1,000	£300
Popular 103E	1172/4	1953-59	£1,875	£825	£300
Anglia/Prefect 100E	1172/4	1953-59	£1,350	£625	£250
Prefect 107E	997/4	1959-62	£1,150	£600	£200
Escort/Squire 100E	1172/4	1955-61	£1,000	£850	£275
Popular 100E	1172/4	1959-62	£1,250	£600	£180
Anglia 105E	997/4	1959-67	£1,400	£500	£75
Anglia 123E	1198/4	1962-67	£1,550	£575	£150
V8 Pilot	3622/8	1947-51	£7,500	£4,000	£1,500
Consul Mk I	1508/4	1951-56	£2,250	£950	£400
Consul Mk I DHC	1508/4	1953-56	£4,750	£3,000	£1,250
Zephyr Mk I	2262/6	1951-56	£3,000	£1,250	£600
Zephyr Mk I DHC	2262/6	1953-56	£6,800	£3,250	£1,500
Zodiac Mk I	2262/6	1953-56	£3,300	£1,500	£700
Consul Mk II/Deluxe	1703/4	1956-62	£2,900	£1,500	£650
Consul Mk II DHC	1703/4	1956-62	£5,000	£3,300	£1,250
Zephyr Mk II	2553/6	1956-62	£3,800	£1,800	£750
Zephyr Mk II DHC	2553/6	1956-62	£8,000	£4,000	£1,500
Zodiac Mk II	2553/6	1956-62	£4,000	£2,250	£750
Zodiac Mk II DHC	2553/6	1956-62	£8,500	£4,250	£1,800
Zephyr 4 Mk III	1703/4	1962-66	£2,100	£1,200	£400
Zephyr 6 Mk III	2552/6	1962-66	£2,300	£1,300	£450
Zodiac Mk II	2553/6	1962-66	£2,500	£1,500	£500
Zephyr 4 Mk IV	1994/4	1966-72	£1,750	£600	£150
Zephyr 6 Mk IV	2553/6	1966-72	£1,800	£700	£150
Zodiac Mk IV	2994/6	1966-72	£2,000	£800	£150
Zodiac Mk IV Est.	2994/6	1966-72	£2,200	£950	£150
Zodiac Mk IV Exec.	2994/6	1966-72	£2,300	£950	£150
Classic 315	1340/ 1498/4	1961-63	£1,400	£800	£500
Consul Capri	1340/ 1498/4	1961-64	£2,100	£1,350	£400
Consul Capri GT	1498/4	1961-64	£2,600	£1,600	£800

1965 Ford Zodiac MkIII Saloon, 2555cc engine, 109bhp at 4800rpm, speed gearbox with a steering column gear change, front bench seat, wood effect dashboard and 4 sealed beam headlights, excellent original condition.
£2,000–2,500 *S*
The Ford Zodiac MkIII saloon sold for £1,017 when new.

1968 Ford Corsair 2000E De Luxe Saloon, manual gearbox, re-built, little used but requires careful re-commissioning.
£350–375 *S*

1967 Ford Cortina MkII 1600GT 2 Door Saloon, slightly lowered suspension and alloy wheels, good condition throughout.
Est. £4,000–4,500 *S*

1968 Ford Cortina Lotus MkII, 4 cylinder, 1558cc engine, chassis plate unavailable, very good overall condition.
£1,400–1,500 *ADT*

1970 Ford Cortina 1600E, 4 Door Saloon, full length sunroof, Rostyle wheels, black radiator grille, full instrumentation, original Motorola radio, cosmetically very good condition.
Est. £1,000–1,200 *S*

Ford Cortina MkII

- By 1967 the Ford Cortina was the best selling car in the UK.
- MkII was introduced in 1967 followed by the 1600E in 1968.
- 1600cc had Lotus designed suspension, crossflow engine, Rostyle wheels and wooden dashboard.
- It is a very collectable car today.

1969 Ford Cortina 1600E MkII 4 Door Saloon, good condition throughout.
Est. £1,500–2,000 *S*

1970 Ford Zephyr 4, low mileage.
£1,000–1,200 *OMH*

1972 Ford Capri 1600, 4 cylinders, 1599cc, later GL Sports wheels, good useable condition.
Est. £400–600 *ADT*

FORD (British built) Model	ENGINE cc/cyl	DATES	CONDITION 1	2	3
Cortina Mk I	1198/4	1963-66	£1,550	£600	£150
Cortina Crayford Mk I	1198/4	1963-66	£3,500	£1,800	£950
Cortina GT	1498/4	1963-66	£1,800	£1,000	£650
Lotus Cortina Mk I	1558/4	1963-66	£9,000	£7,500	£4,500
Cortina Mk II	1599/4	1966-70	£1,000	£500	£100
Cortina GT Mk II	1599/4	1966-70	£1,200	£650	£150
Cortina Crayford Mk II DHC	1599/4	1966-70	£4,000	£2,000	£1,500
Lotus Cortina Mk II	1558/4	1966-70	£5,500	£3,000	£1,800
Cortina 1600E	1599/4	1967-70	£2,800	£1,000	£450
Consul Corsair	1500/4	1963-65	£1,100	£500	£250
Consul Corsair GT	1500/4	1963-65	£1,200	£600	£250
Corsair V4	1664/4	1965-70	£1,150	£600	£250
Corsair V4 Est.	1664/4	1965-70	£1,400	£600	£250
Corsair V4GT	1994/4	1965-67	£1,300	£700	£250
Corsair V4GT Est.	1994/4	1965-67	£1,400	£700	£350
Corsair Convertible	1664/ 1994/4	1965-70	£4,300	£2,500	£1,000
Corsair 2000	1994/4	1967-70	£1,350	£500	£250
Corsair 2000E	1994/4	1967-70	£1,500	£800	£350
Escort 1300E	1298/4	1973-74	£1,900	£1,000	£250
Escort Twin Cam	1558/4	1968-71	£8,000	£5,000	£2,000
Escort GT	1298/4	1968-73	£3,000	£1,500	£350
Escort Sport	1298/4	1971-75	£1,750	£925	£250
Escort Mexico	1601/4	1970-74	£4,000	£2,000	£750
RS1600	1601/4	1970-74	£5,000	£2,500	£1,500
RS2000	1998/4	1973-74	£4,500	£2,200	£1,000
Escort RS Mexico	1593/4	1976-78	£3,500	£2,000	£850
Escort RS2000 Mk II	1993/4	1976-80	£6,000	£3,500	£2,000
Capri Mk I 1300/ 1600	1298/ 1599/4	1969-72	£1,500	£1,000	£550
Capri 2000/ 3000GT	1996/4 2994/6	1969-72	£2,000	£1,000	£500
Capri 3000E	2994/6	1970-72	£4,000	£2,000	£1,000
Capri RS3100	3093/6	1973-74	£6,500	£3,500	£2,000
Cortina 2000E	1993/4	1973-76	£2,500	£550	£225
Granada Ghia	1993/4 2994/6	1974-77	£4,000	£900	£350

1980 Ford Capri 2 Litre Ghia Coupé,
automatic transmission, 37,500 miles
recorded, service record, very good
original condition.
£1,600–1,700 *S*

1980 Ford Escort RS2000 Custom,
re-built, new interior, good condition.
£1,750–2,500 *Mot*

**1976 Ford Escort Ghia 1.6 Litre
Automatic 4 Door Saloon,** 1599cc engine,
3 speed automatic transmission, good
condition throughout.
£780–820 *S*

1979 Ford Granada 2.8 Sapphire.
£4,250–4,750 *GEC*

*One of 1,725 limited edition models produced
by Ford in 1979. There are less than 20 of
these cars registered with the Granada
Enthusiasts' Club.*

1955 Ford Thunderbird, hard and soft
tops, automatic, left hand drive.
£12,000–14,000 *CGB*

1984/85 Ford Granada 2.8 Ghia Estate,
stripped and re-built.
£6,000+ *GEC*

*This car has been a Granada Enthusiasts'
Club Overall Concours Winner.*

1956 Ford Fairlane Coupé Club Sedan,
very good overall condition.
£3,500–3,750 *ALC*

1956 Ford Thunderbird,
fully restored during 1987,
excellent condition throughout.
Est. £15,000–17,000 *ADT*

FORD (American built) Model	ENGINE cu in/cyl	DATES	CONDITION		
			1	2	3
Thunderbird	292/ 312/8	1955-57	£18,500	£13,500	£9,000
Edsel Citation	410/8	1958	£9,000	£4,500	£2,500
Edsel Ranger	223/6- 361/8	1959	£6,000	£3,500	£2,000
Edsel Citation convertible	410/8	1958	£12,000	£6,000	£4,000
Edsel Corsair convertible	332/ 361/8	1959	£10,500	£7,000	£4,500
Fairlane 2 door	223/6- 352/8	1957-59	£8,000	£4,500	£3,000
Fairlane 500 Sunliner	223/6- 352/8	1957-59	£12,000	£8,000	£6,500
Fairlane 500 Skyliner	223/6- 352/8	1957-59	£16,000	£10,000	£8,000
Mustang hardtop	170/6- 289/8	1965-66	£8,000	£5,000	£4,000
Mustang fastback	170/6- 289/8	1965-66	£9,000	£6,000	£5,000
Mustang convertible	170/6- 289/8	1965-66	£12,500	£8,500	£6,000
Mustang hardtop	260/6- 428/8	1967-68	£6,000	£4,000	£3,000
Mustang fastback	260/6- 428/8	1967-68	£6,000	£4,000	£3,000
Mustang convertible	260/6- 428/8	1967-68	£10,750	£6,000	£4,000

1957 Ford Fairlane, 8 cylinder, 6500cc engine, excellent re-built and restored condition. **£6,250–6,750** *ADT*

1956 Ford Thunderbird Convertible, excellent overall restored condition. **£14,000–14,500** *ALC*

1959 Ford Fairlane 500 Galaxie 2 Door Club Sedan, good running condition, fair condition throughout. **Est. £4,000–5,000** *S*

1963 Ford Thunderbird, automatic transmission, left hand drive, good condition throughout. **Est. £4,000–5,000** *LF*

1966 Ford Mustang Shelby GT350, 8 cylinder, 4736cc engine, restored, now an exact replica of a genuine GT350. **Est. £16,000–20,000** *ADT*

1965 Ford Mustang 289GT, 4 speed floor shift gearbox, disc brakes, left hand drive, rust free, good running order. **£4,000–4,500** *CCTC*

1966 Ford Mustang 289GT Hardtop Coupé, ground-up restoration throughout. Est. £6,000–8,000 *S*

1968 Ford Mustang 6.4 Litre Convertible, the V8 power unit of a later build date than the chassis, electrically powered hood, good overall condition. £5,000–5,500 *BKS*

Ford Mustang

- Introduced in May 1964, the Mustang was one of the most successful cars of the 1960s.
- A variety of engines was available from a 2786cc straight 6, several V8s and ultimately the 361cu in V8 Mach I.
- The racing 350GT was developed by Carol Shelby using Cobra components.

1969 Ford Mustang Mach I Sports Coupé, bare metal re-spray, engine re-built, restored order throughout. £7,400–7,800 *S*

1975 Ford Fairmont Estate, 5 litre, V8 engine, right hand drive, very low mileage. £2,000–2,750 *OMH*

Taunus

- The name Taunus was first applied to a German built Ford from the Cologne factory in 1939.
- Later the name was applied to all German built Fords, the 12M, 15M and 17M being fitted with 4 cylinder engines of 1.2 litre, 1.5 litre, etc.
- In 1964 a 20M with a 2 litre V6 engine was introduced.

1973 Ford Taunus 20M Saloon, original radio, service book, right hand drive, manual and original purchase invoice, excellent condition throughout. Est. £2,000–3,000 *S*

1959 Ford 10 Shirley Special, good condition. £1,500–2,000 *OMH*

FRANKLIN

Noted for their air-cooled engines, Franklins were produced from 1902 to 1934. The earliest models were very well advanced for their time, featuring a 4 cylinder transversely mounted air-cooled engine designed by John Wilkinson and financed by Herbert H. Franklin.

1924 Franklin 6 Cylinder Tourer, very good throughout. **£5,800–7,000** *S*

FRAZER-NASH

Archie Frazer-Nash founded the company that bore his name in 1924 with his partner F. N. Pickett, following the collapse of the GN company.

Very competitive and powerful in their time, the most famous Frazer-Nash cars are the chain driven sports cars. These 'Chain Gang' models were built to customer order and generally fitted with Meadows engines.

By 1934 Frazer-Nash were using the 2 litre BMW 328 engine. The most well-known post-WWII model was the Le Mans replica following their third place in 1949. One of these cars won the Targa Floria in 1951, the only British car ever to have won the gruelling Sicilian road race.

1952 Frazer-Nash Le Mans Open 2 Seater Replica by Crosthwaite & Gardner, 6 cylinder, 1971cc re-built engine, excellent condition. **Est. £33,000–40,000** *COYS*

One of 4 or 5 replicas built in the late 1970s using factory drawings.

1928 Franklin Airman 46hp Sedan, coachwork by Rauling Automobile Bodies of Cleveland, Ohio, air-cooled, 6 cylinder overhead valve engine, left hand drive, original in all major respects. **£8,000–9,000** *S*

c1934 Frazer-Nash Special TT Replica Two Seater, 4 cylinder, 1496cc Meadows 4ED engine completely stripped and re-assembled, re-built in 1989/90, new chassis based on the 1934 model, re-built carburettors and magnetos, immaculate condition. **Est. £34,000–38,000** *COYS*

The body is a replica of the factory-designed 2 seater, with an aluminium skin over an ash frame, aluminium wings and flooring, new black Connolly trim and tonneau cover.

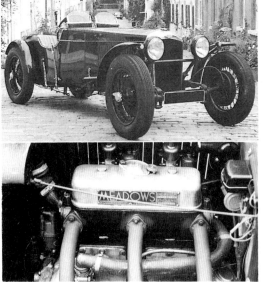

1935/36 Frazer-Nash Emeryson TT Replica, 4 cylinders, 1465cc, built on early Frazer-Nash chassis, now with Meadows engine, HRG front axle and brakes, good condition throughout. **Est. £25,000–35,000** *COYS*

Instead of a gearbox, 4 chains running on different sized sprockets were mounted on the rear axle, the latter a solid steel bar without differential and located by radius arms.

1954 Frazer-Nash Le Mans GT Coupé,
Bristol BMW 328 engine, completely re-built,
excellent condition.
£42,000–44,000 *COYS*

*The Le Mans Coupé was the first closed car
the company made, and this is one of only
9 examples.*

1955 Frazer-Nash Le Mans 2 Litre Coupé,
competed at Le Mans 1959, a very historic
sports car, in generally fine order.
Est. £45,000–55,000 *BKS*

GILBERN

FULLER

**1910 Fuller Model B Four Passenger High
Wheeler,** 2 cylinder horizontally opposed
L-head, 173cu in engine, 2 speed epicyclic
gearbox, rear drum brakes, full elliptical
spring front and rear suspension, right hand
drive, requires some cosmetic restoration.
£4,500–5,500 *CNY*

*The Fuller Co. was one of the oldest and
largest manufacturers of horse-drawn
vehicles before they branched out into
making cars.*

> **Don't Forget!**
> *If in doubt please refer
> to the 'How to Use'
> section at the beginning
> of this book.*

1968 Gilbern Genie 3 Litre, Ford engine,
gearbox with overdrive, new sunroof,
chrome, interior trim, re-sprayed.
£3,800–4,400 *CCTC*

1970 Gilbern Genie, fully restored to a very high standard. **Est. £4,500–5,500** *ADT*

1913 GN Grand Prix 2 Seater Sports Cyclecar, good condition throughout, Dating Certificate and VSCC Blue Form. **Est. £13,500–15,000** *S*

GOLIATH

1955 Goliath GP900E Roll Top Cabriolet, left hand drive specification, roll-back top, broken windscreen, to original specification, one instrument missing otherwise complete, requires restoration. **£250–350** *S*

> **Cross Reference**
> Restoration Projects

GORDON KEEBLE

The Gordon Keeble was the brainchild of a collaboration between John Gordon, earlier of Peerless, and Jim Keeble. Its combination of an advanced multi-tubular steel frame chassis, a Chevrolet V8 engine and body designed by Bertone attracted a good deal of attention when it was launched in 1961.

1971 Gordon Keeble GK1 Sports Saloon, excellent concours winning condition. **Est. £15,000–18,000** *S*

GN

H. R. Godfrey and Archie Frazer-Nash made their first cyclecar in 1910 at the Etna Works, Bell Lane, Hendon. Early cars featured JAP and Antoine V-twin engines, but by 1911 GN were producing their own engine units.

In post war years production was about 50 cars per week and GN cars enjoyed some considerable successes in the long distance Exeter and Land's End trials and in the 200 Mile Race at Brooklands. The car proved to be a lively performer, with an engine capacity of 1087cc and overall car weight of approximately 6½cwt .

1921 GN 10hp 2 Seater Sports, museum stored for many years, running order, should be recommissioned before road use. **£7,800–8,200** *S*

GRAY

The Gray Motor Corporation was founded in 1922 in Detroit by former Ford employees, with F. L. Klingensmith as President. The cars, based closely on the Model T Ford, sold well initially but production had ceased by 1926 when the firm collapsed.

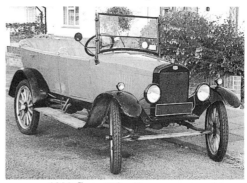

1922 Gray 21hp Tourer, restored to roadworthy condition, some spare parts, mechanically good condition, the interior needs attention. **£3,750–4,000** *LF*

GORDON KEEBLE Model	ENGINE cc/cyl	DATES	CONDITION		
			1	2	3
GKI/GKIT	5395/8	1964-67	£11,000	£8,000	£5,000

HEALEY

1952 Healey Tickford 2.4 Litre Sports Saloon, coachwork restored and repainted, original specification in all major respects.
£8,500–9,000 *S*

1953 Healey F Type Silverstone 2 Seater, engine rebuilt to competition standards, only 2,000 miles since rebuild, excellent condition throughout.
£16,000–16,500 *S*

Cross Reference
Austin Healey

HILLMAN

The first Hillman, designed by Louis Coatalen, was a 24hp 4 cylinder model to be used in the 1907 Tourist Trophy race. Bicycle manufacturer William Hillman was producing a range of successful motor vehicles by the outbreak of WWI and between the wars Hillman's good fortune was ensured by the introduction of the Minx. The 1935 version was the first small British car to feature a 4 speed synchromesh gearbox.

By the 1960s Hillman was in financial trouble and the company, owned by the Rootes Group since 1928, was acquired by the Chrysler Corporation in 1964. The Hillman name had disappeared by 1976.

1937 Hillman Minx 4 Door Tourer, 4 cylinder, 1124cc engine, good condition.
Est. £6,000–7,000 *ADT*

It is believed that this car is the only known example on the Hillman Register.

1946 Hillman Minx 4 Door Saloon, 42,000 miles, very good condition throughout.
Est. £2,500–3,000 *HOLL*

1950 Hillman Minx 4 Door Saloon, dry stored, condition generally good, bodywork and paintwork fair.
£450–480 *S*

1962 Hillman Super Minx 1600.
£1,450–1,550 *CVPG*

1955 Hillman Minx Saloon, good original overall condition.
£1,300–1,500 *ALC*

1963 Hillman Imp Saloon, in running order, partially restored.
Est. £600–900 *LF*

1967 Hillman Imp Californian, 4 cylinders, 875cc, one registered owner since new, 22,600 miles recorded, good condition.
£1,000–1,100 *ADT*

HILLMAN Model	ENGINE cc/cyl	DATES	CONDITION		
			1	2	3
Minx Mk I-II	1184/4	1946-48	£1,750	£800	£250
Minx Mk I-II DHC	1184/4	1946-48	£3,500	£1,500	£250
Minx Mk III-VIIIA	1184/4	1948-56	£1,750	£700	£350
Minx Mk III-VIIIA DHC	1184/4	1948-56	£3,750	£1,500	£350
Californian	1390/4	1953-56	£2,000	£750	£200
Minx SI/II	1390/4	1956-58	£1,250	£450	£200
Minx SI/II DHC	1390/4	1956-58	£3,500	£1,500	£500
Minx Ser III	1494/4	1958-59	£1,000	£500	£200
Minx Ser III DHC	1494/4	1958-59	£3,750	£1,500	£400
Minx Ser IIIA/B	1494/4	1959-61	£1,250	£500	£200
Minx Ser IIIA/B DHC	1494/4	1959-61	£3,750	£1,250	£500
Minx Ser IIIC	1592/4	1961-62	£900	£500	£200
Minx Ser IIIC DHC	1592/4	1961-62	£3,000	£1,500	£500
Minx Ser V	1592/4	1962-63	£1,250	£350	£150
Minx Ser VI	1725/4	1964-67	£1,500	£375	£100
Husky Mk I	1265/4	1954-57	£1,000	£600	£200
Husky SI/II/III	1390/4	1958-65	£1,000	£550	£150
Super Minx	1592/4	1961-66	£1,500	£500	£100
Super Minx DHC	1592/4	1962-64	£3,500	£1,250	£450
Imp	875/4	1963-73	£800	£300	£70
Husky	875/4	1966-71	£800	£450	£100
Avenger	var/4	1970-76	£550	£250	£60
Avenger GT	1500/4	1971-76	£950	£500	£100
Tiger	1600/4	1972-73	£1,250	£650	£200

HISPANO-SUIZA

1928 Hispano-Suiza H6 B Sedanca Landaulette, coachwork by Henri Chapron, wood framing sound but may need some replacement, door handles, some engine parts and part of the windscreen surround missing, the car has spent time in the open, restoration project.
£34,000–36,000 *S*

HOTCHKISS

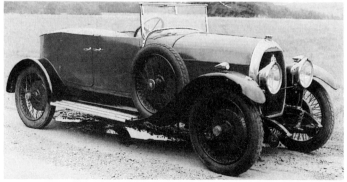

c1926 Model AM2 Boat Tailed Open Tourer, bodywork rebuilt in 1948 from the original, to maker's original specification, engine rebuilt later, many engine spares, good overall condition.
Est. £12,000–14,000 *S*

HUDSON

J. L. Hudson from Detroit financed
R. D. Chapin enabling him to start the
Hudson Company in 1909. A famous Hudson
was the 'Step Down' model of 1948 in which
the floor level was below the sills, hence the
name.

Hudson merged with Nash in 1954 to form
the American Motors Corporation and
Hudsons were produced at Kenosha in
Wisconsin, USA for two more seasons.
The Hudson name had disappeared by
the end of 1957.

1952 Hudson Hornet 4 Door Saloon,
imported from California, 55,000 miles from
new, good condition throughout.
Est. £11,000–13,000 *S*

HUMBER

Thomas Humber was making bicycles as
early as 1868. Early products consisted of
tricycles and quadricycles but the first real
success, however, was the production of a car
called the Humberette of 1903. Humber
were soon producing cars at two locations,
Coventry and Beeston, with the latter
factory's cars enjoying a reputation for a
higher standard of finish.

A member of the Rootes Group, the
company was acquired by Chrysler in 1964
and by the end of the 1970s the Humber
name had disappeared.

1927 Humber 9/20hp 3 Door Saloon,
original buttoned cord upholstery, has not
been in regular use but runs well.
£6,800–7,200 *S*

**c1913 Hudson Model 37 Open 4/5 Seater
Tourer,** no rear lights, canvas hood requires
replacement, right hand drive.
£9,000–10,000 *S*

1954 Hudson Hornet 4 Door Sedan,
6 cylinder, 4 speed automatic gearbox,
original interior, left hand drive, very
good condition.
£8,000–9,500 *CGB*

1914 Humberette 8hp 2 Seater, brass
acetylene scuttle-mounted headlamps, brass
bulb horn and Stepney wheel, museum
stored, requires re-commissioning.
Est. £6,000–8,000 *S*

**1930 Humber 16/50 2.2 Litre 6 Cylinder
Saloon,** bodywork good condition, original
interior, mechanics need some attention.
£8,250–8,750 *Mot*

1929 Humber 9/28 Tourer, 3 speed and
reverse, direct drive gearbox with gate
change at the right hand side, very good
restored condition.
£8,500–9,000 *ADT*

HUMBER Model	ENGINE cc/cyl	DATES	CONDITION 1	2	3
Veteran	var	1898			
		1918	£25,000	£20,000	£14,000
10	1592/4	1919	£7,000	£5,000	£3,000
14	2474/4	1919	£8,000	£6,000	£4,000
15.9-5/40	2815/4	1920-27	£9,500	£7,000	£4,000
8	985/4	1923-25	£7,000	£5,000	£2,500
9/20-9/28	1057/4	1926	£7,000	£5,000	£4,000
14/40	2050/4	1927-28	£10,000	£8,000	£5,000
Snipe	3498/6	1930-35	£8,000	£6,000	£4,000
Pullman	3498/6	1930-35	£8,000	£6,000	£4,000
16/50	2110/6	1930-32	£9,000	£7,000	£5,000
12	1669/4	1933-37	£7,000	£5,000	£3,000
Snipe/Pullman	4086/6	1936-40	£7,000	£5,000	£3,000
16	2576/6	1938-40	£7,000	£5,000	£3,000

Pre-1905 or Brighton Run cars are very popular.

1946 Humber Hawk, 4 cylinder, 1900cc engine, requires some restoration before regular use.
£1,400–1,600 *ADT*

1952 Humber Pullman Limousine, coachwork by Thrupp & Maberly, 6 cylinders, 4086cc, very good and original throughout.
£5,000–5,400 *ADT*

1957 Humber Hawk Saloon, original specification in all major respects, recently museum exhibited.
£2,800–3,200 *S*

1966 Humber Super Snipe Series 6A 5/6 Seater Saloon, 6 cylinder, 2960cc engine, automatic transmission, mechanically very good, bodywork excellent, power-assisted steering, well maintained.
£2,800–3,200 *S*

HUMBER Model	ENGINE cc/cyl	DATES	CONDITION 1	2	3
Hawk Mk I-IV	1944/4	1945-52	£2,750	£1,500	£600
Hawk Mk V-VII	2267/4	1952-57	£2,500	£1,500	£400
Hawk Ser I-IVA	2267/4	1957-67	£2,500	£850	£325
Snipe	2731/6	1945-48	£5,000	£2,600	£850
Super Snipe Mk I-III	4086/6	1948-52	£4,700	£2,400	£600
Super Snipe Mk IV-IVA	4138/6	1952-56	£5,500	£2,300	£550
Super Snipe Ser I-II	2651/6	1958-60	£3,800	£1,800	£475
Super Snipe SIII VA	2965/6	1961-67	£3,500	£1,800	£400
Super Snipe S.III-VA Est.	2965/6	1961-67	£3,950	£1,850	£525
Pullman	4086/6	1946-51	£4,500	£2,350	£800
Pullman Mk IV	4086/6	1952-54	£6,000	£2,850	£1,200
Imperial	2965/6	1965-67	£3,900	£1,600	£450
Sceptre Mk I-II	1592/4	1963-67	£2,050	£900	£300
Sceptre Mk III	1725/4	1967-76	£1,600	£600	£200

HUPMOBILE

Robert Craig Hupp and his brother, Louis, founded the Hupp Motor Car Corporation in Detroit in 1908. The Model 20 was exhibited at The Detroit Automobile Show in February 1909. The first cars were conventional runabouts with two bucket seats, a drum-shaped fuel tank at the rear, and powered by a conventional water-cooled 4 cylinder engine developing 16.9hp.

1912 Hupmobile Model 32 Roadster, chassis detail and engine compartment restored to concours standard.
£14,000–15,000 *S*

In 1912 the more powerful Model 32 was announced for the 1913 season, with 4 cylinders, 106in wheelbase and developing 32hp.

1925 Hupmobile Model E Straight 8 4/5 Seater Tourer, right hand drive, good condition throughout.
£14,000–15,000 *S*

INNOCENTI

1980 Innocenti Mini, 998cc, left hand drive, good original order.
£700–800 *EP*

1969 Innocenti Sports Coupé, coachwork by Ghia, 1098cc Sprite engine, to maker's specification and fully restored, good roadworthy condition.
Est. £6,500–7,500 *S*

The Societa Generale per L'Industria Metalurgica e Mecanica of Milan were already well-known as makers of the Lambretta motor scooter when, in 1961, they extended their activities to car manufacture. They produced the 948cc Austin A40 under licence, and their subsequent models were all variations on themes by the British Motor Corporation.

ISO

1972 Iso Grifo Series II Coupé, coachwork by Bertone, excellent condition throughout.
Est. £30,000–40,000 *COYS*

Designed by Bizzarini, the Grifo (meaning Griffin in Italian) is the legendary bird which preys on horses, an allusion of Iso's desire to conquer Ferrari. One of only 6 right hand examples built.

INVICTA

1929 Invicta 3/4½ Litre Large Chassis Tourer, saloon body replaced with Le Mans-style 4 seater, very good overall condition.
Est. £25,000–35,000 *BKS*

1976 Iso Lele 5.7 Litre V8 Sports Coupé, stored for the last 10 years, low mileage, excellent condition.
Est. £10,000–12,000 *S*

JAGUAR

When the Jaguar E-Type was announced in 1961, it was a sensation. With a steel monocoque body, directly attributed to the highly successful and desirable D-Type, it could reach a top speed of around 150mph.

By 1965 the original 3.8 litre engine had been replaced with a 4.2 litre, still a straight 6 cylinder unit with twin overhead camshaft, producing over 265bhp. The second series included a 2+2 version, and automatic transmission was introduced as an optional extra.

By 1971 the third series was available incorporating the strict American emission control equipment. The 5.3 litre V12 was also introduced. By 1974 the Coupé and 2+2 had been phased out and by 1975 the last E-Type had been produced.

1938 Jaguar SS 2½ Litre Saloon, original factory specification, very good condition throughout.
£11,000–12,000 *S*

1949 Jaguar MkV 3½ Litre Sports Saloon, prolonged period of storage, some re-commissioning will be required.
£4,500–4,750 *S*

Only 3,124 examples were produced for the home market, a further 4,690 being exported, and the car achieved considerable success in competitions.

1936 Jaguar SS100 Roadster, 6 cylinders, 2663cc, dry stored for 30 years, complete and original condition, recent full restoration, excellent condition throughout.
Est. £65,000–75,000 *COYS*

1938 Jaguar SS100 Roadster, completely restored to highest standards, excellent condition throughout.
Est. £68,000–78,000 *COYS*

1939 Jaguar SS 3½ Litre Saloon, dry stored, original paintwork, rust free, excellent original condition.
£13,000–13,500 *BKS*

Although some 1,065 3½ litre saloons were built pre-war, the survival rate is low. Not to be confused with the more common post-war cars, this example is thought to be one of perhaps 30 pre-war SS 3½ litre saloons existing worldwide.

JAGUAR Model	ENGINE cc/cyl	DATES	CONDITION		
			1	2	3
SSI	2054/6	1932-33	£20,000	£16,000	£12,000
SSI	2252/6	1932-33	£22,000	£17,000	£13,500
SSII	1052/4	1932-33	£18,000	£15,000	£11,000
SSI	2663/6	1934	£26,000	£22,000	£15,000
SSII	1608/4	1934	£18,000	£15,000	£12,000
SS90	2663/6	1935	£60,000+		
SS100 (3.4)	3485/6	1938-39	£70,000+		
SS100 (2.6)	2663/6	1936-39	£60,000+		

Very dependent on body styles, completeness and originality, particularly original chassis to body.

1948 Jaguar MkV 3½ Litre Sports Saloon, fully restored, good overall condition.
£12,000–12,500 *S*

1948 Jaguar 2½ Litre 3 Position Drophead Coupé, completely overhauled, original upholstery.
£16,000–16,500 *S*

Jaguar

- The William Lyons styled roadster was powered by the new 3442cc twin cam XK engine producing 160bhp via twin SU carburettors, and could achieve 126mph and 0–60mph in 10 seconds.
- In October 1948, with an aeroscreen and aluminium undershield the only modifications, an XK120 recorded 132.6mph for the flying mile in Jabekke, Belgium, making it the fastest off-the-shelf car in the world at that time.

1950 Jaguar XK120 Roadster, 6 cylinders, 3442cc, original right hand drive, mechanical and cosmetic overhaul, front servo disc brakes, excellent condition.
£27,000–28,000 *COYS*

1951 Jaguar XK120 3.8 Litre Competition Roadster, rack-and-pinion steering, rebuilt transmission with Powr-Lok limited slip differential, engine rebuilt, bodywork restored, interior retrimmed.
Est. £18,000–20,000 *BKS*

1952 Jaguar XK120 2 Seater Sports Roadster, imported from USA, right hand drive, fully restored, very good condition.
Est. £22,000–23,000 *S*

This car was one of the last to have chrome sidelights.

1953 Jaguar XK120 Drophead Coupé,
6 cylinders, 3442cc, right hand drive, very
good original condition.
£13,500–14,500 *COYS*

**1953 Jaguar XK120M 3.4 Litre Fixed
Head Coupé,** excellent condition.
Est. £28,000–34,000 *BKS*

*The 'Special Equipment Model' had high-lift
camshafts, knock-off wire wheels, and 1in
diameter torsion bars, to which could be
added a series of engine and transmission
modifications at extra cost. In basic form the
XK120 Coupé cost £1,140, to which the
'Special Equipment' modification added an
extra £115.*

**1953 Jaguar XK120 3.8 Litre Fixed Head
Coupé,** fully restored, good overall condition.
£15,500–16,000 *BKS*

*Jaguar built only 195 right hand drive
XK120 fixed head coupés, less than 8% of
total production, and according to Jaguar
records, fewer than half of those right hand
drive coupés still survive.*

1954 Jaguar XK120 Roadster, left hand
drive, good condition overall.
£21,500–22,000 *S*

**1955 Jaguar XK140 3.4 Litre
Drophead Coupé,** right hand drive,
superb restored condition.
£47,000–48,000 *BKS*

**1955 Jaguar XK140 SE Fixed Head
Coupé,** sympathetic restoration, good
overall condition.
£19,750–18,250 *ADT*

*The XK140 was introduced in 1954 and was
basically the same car as the XK120, except
that it had a 190bhp engine fitted as standard.
Rack-and-pinion steering and different trim
and decoration were also revised.*

1956 Jaguar XK150 Drophead Coupé,
6 cylinder in line engine, twin overhead
camshaft, twin SU carburettors, 3442cc,
210bhp at 5750rpm, 4 speed manual gearbox,
disc brakes all round, double wishbone front
suspension, torsion bars, anti-roll bar, rear
live axle, semi-elliptic leaf springs, right
hand drive, originally left hand drive, new
wire wheels.
£23,000–24,000 *C*

1955 Jaguar XK140SE Drophead Coupé,
6 cylinders, 3442cc, original right hand drive,
complete restoration to highest standards.
£38,000–39,000 *COYS*

**1956 Jaguar XK140 3.4 Litre Fixed Head
Coupé,** imported from Belgium but right
hand drive, good sound example.
£14,500–15,000 *BKS*

**1956 Jaguar XK140 SE Fixed Head
Coupé,** 6 cylinders, 3442cc, rare right hand
drive, original 'Special Equipment' example
with C-Type cylinder head, overdrive gearbox
and wire wheels, very good overall condition.
£18,000–18,500 *COYS*

**1958 Jaguar XK150 3.4 Litre Drophead
Coupé,** 6 cylinders, 3442cc, excellent
all-round condition.
Est. £32,000–34,000 *ADT*

1958 Jaguar XK150S Roadster, good
original condition.
Est. £19,000–24,000 *COYS*

JAGUAR Model	ENGINE cc/cyl	DATES	CONDITION 1	2	3
XK120 roadster aluminum	3442/6	1948-49	£35,000	£20,000	£15,000
XK120 roadster	3442/6	1949-54	£22,000	£18,000	£14,000
XK120 DHC	3442/6	1953-54	£20,000	£15,000	£11,000
XK120 Coupé	3442/6	1951-55	£16,000	£10,000	£8,000
C-type	3442/6	1951	£110,000	+	
D-type	3442/6	1955-56	£300,000	+	
XKSS (original)	3442/6	1955-57	£320,000	+	
XK140 roadster	3442/6	1955-58	£28,000	£23,000	£15,500
XK140 DHC	3442/6	1955-58	£25,000	£20,500	£15,000
XK140 Coupé	3442/6	1955-58	£14,000	£9,000	£5,500
XK150 roadster	3442/6	1958-60	£24,000	£20,500	£14,000
XK150 DHC	3442/6	1957-61	£22,000	£15,000	£5,000
XK150 Coupé	3442/6	1957-60	£14,000	£9,000	£6,000
XK150S roadster	3442/ 3781/6	1958-60	£35,000	£22,000	£17,000
XK150S DHC	3442/ 3781/6	1958-60	£34,000	£22,000	£16,500
XK150S Coupé	3442/ 3781/6	1958-61	£22,000	£17,000	£11,500

1958 Jaguar XK150 Drophead Coupé,
original trim, sound original example.
Est. £23,000–26,000 *S*

1960 Jaguar XK150S Fixed Head Coupé,
6 cylinders, 3781cc, excellent condition
throughout.
£18,000–19,000 *ADT*

**1960 Jaguar XK150S 3.8 Litre Drophead
Coupé,** engine rebuilt, stainless steel
exhaust and Kenlowe fan, original right
hand drive, good condition.
£31,000–33,000 *BKS*

1957 Jaguar MkVIII, 6 cylinders, 3442cc,
right hand drive, automatic transmission,
bare metal respray, very good overall condition.
Est. £5,750–6,750 *ADT*

**1960 Jaguar XK150 3.8 Litre Drophead
Coupé,** right hand drive, optional overdrive,
original leather, excellent overall condition.
Est. £25,000–30,000 *BKS*

*Only 264 3.8 litre drophead coupés were
manufactured and of these only 87 were
fitted with right hand drive.*

**1960 Jaguar XK150S 3.8 Litre Fixed
Head Coupé,** renewed upholstery and trim,
wire wheels, good condition throughout.
Est. £20,000–22,000 *S*

1961 Jaguar MkII 3.4 Litre Automatic,
original condition, only 2 owners, unused
for 6 years, right hand drive, upholstery and
chrome in good condition, in running order
but needs attention.
£3,250–3,750 *CCTC*

1961 Jaguar MkII 3.4 Litre Saloon,
6 cylinders, 3442cc, interior trim complete,
but requires refurbishment.
Est. £4,000–5,000 *ADT*

1961 Jaguar MkII 3.4 Litre Saloon,
6 cylinders, 3442cc, re-sprayed, new wire
wheels, engine in excellent condition, manual
gearbox with overdrive.
£4,750–5,000 *ADT*

1961 Jaguar MkII 3.4 LitreSports Saloon,
paintwork and chrome requires restoration,
dashboard veneer requires refinishing,
automatic transmission, electrics and chassis
in good condition.
Est. £4,000–6,000 *BKS*

1964 Jaguar MkII 2.4 Litre Saloon,
6 cylinders, 2483cc, automatic gearbox,
very good original condition.
£5,750–6,000 *ADT*

**1965 Jaguar S-Type 3.8 Litre 4 Door
Saloon,** restored, good condition throughout.
£6,500–7,000 *S*

*Bridging the gap between the compact MkII
and the MkX saloons, the S-Type Jaguar was
introduced in 1964 in both 3.4 litre and 3.8
litre form.*

1962 Jaguar MkII 3.8 Litre Saloon,
6 cylinders, 3781cc, very good, original and
rust free condition.
£11,000–12,000 *COYS*

JAGUAR Model	ENGINE cc/cyl	DATES	CONDITION 1	2	3
1½ Litre	1775/4	1945-49	£8,500	£5,500	£2,000
2½ Litre	2663/6	1946-49	£10,000	£7,500	£2,000
2½ Litre DHC	2663/6	1947-48	£17,000	£11,000	£8,000
3½ Litre	3485/6	1947-49	£12,000	£6,000	£4,000
3½ Litre DHC	3485/6	1947-49	£19,000	£13,500	£5,500
Mk V 2½ Litre	2663/6	1949-51	£8,000	£5,000	£1,500
Mk V 3½ Litre	3485/6	1949-51	£11,000	£7,000	£1,800
Mk V 3½ Litre DHC	3485/6	1949-51	£20,000	£17,000	£8,500
Mk VII	3442/6	1951-57	£10,000	£7,500	£2,500
Mk VIIM	3442/6	1951-57	£12,000	£8,500	£2,500
Mk VIII	3442/6	1956-59	£8,500	£5,500	£2,000
Mk IX	3781/6	1958-61	£9,000	£7,000	£2,500
Mk X 3.8/4.2	3781/6	1961-64	£7,500	£3,500	£1,500
Mk X 420G	4235/6	1964-70	£5,000	£3,000	£1,200
Mk I 2.4	2438/6	1955-59	£7,000	£5,500	£2,000
Mk I 3.4	3442/6	1957-59	£9,000	£6,000	£2,500
Mk II 2.4	2483/6	1959-67	£6,000	£5,000	£2,000
Mk II 3.4	3442/6	1959-67	£9,000	£6,500	£3,000
Mk II 3.8	3781/6	1959-67	£9,850	£6,000	£4,000
S-Type 3.4	3442/6	1963-68	£9,000	£6,500	£2,000
S-Type 3.8	3781/6	1963-68	£10,000	£6,500	£2,000
240	2438/6	1967-68	£7,000	£5,000	£2,500
340	3442/6	1967-68	£8,000	£7,000	£3,000
420	4235/6	1966-68	£6,000	£3,000	£2,000

Manual gearboxes with overdrive are at a premium.

1966 Jaguar MkII 3.4 Litre Saloon,
6 cylinders, double overhead camshaft,
3442cc, 220bhp at 5500rpm, 4 speed manual
gearbox with overdrive, Dunlop servo
assisted disc brakes, independent coil front
suspension, cantilever rear, right hand drive,
engine and gearbox completely rebuilt,
restored to immaculate condition.
£18,000–19,000 *C*

1966 Jaguar MkII 3.8 Litre Saloon,
USA imported, left hand drive, manual
gearbox with overdrive, rust free bodywork,
good running order.
£7,000–7,250 *CCTC*

1967 Jaguar MkII 3.8 Litre Saloon,
manual gearbox with synchromesh and
overdrive, original right hand drive,
repainted, chrome wire wheels, very good
original condition.
£9,000–9,250 *CCTC*

1966 Jaguar S-Type 3.8 Litre Saloon,
manual gearbox with overdrive, excellent
restored condition throughout.
£10,750–11,250 *Mot*

1966 Jaguar MkII 3.4 Litre Saloon,
manual gearbox with overdrive, 38,000
recorded miles, good original trim, excellent
restored condition.
£8,750–9,250 *Mot*

1967 Jaguar 240 4 Door Saloon, to MkII
3.8 Litre specification, converted to right
hand drive, reconditioned 3.8 litre engine,
rust free body, good condition.
£16,000–16,500 *BKS*

1967 Jaguar MkII 3.8 Litre 4 Door Saloon
manual transmission, recent bare metal
respray, original upholstery, very good condition
£11,000–11,500 *BKS*

1968 Jaguar 240 Saloon, 6 cylinders,
2483cc, manual gearbox with overdrive,
very good original condition.
£3,800–4,200 *ADT*

1968 Jaguar 240 Saloon, engine rebuilt, bare metal repaint, brakes overhauled, good condition throughout.
Est. £5,000–7,000 *S*

Fitted with a 2483cc version of Jaguar's famous 6 cylinder overhead camshaft engine, the 240 model was basically a continuation of the MkII 2.4 litre saloon.

1968 Jaguar 240 Saloon, 6 cylinders, 2483cc, wire wheels, doors require attention, good condition throughout.
£2,750–3,000 *ADT*

1962 Jaguar E-Type 3.8 Lightweight Replica, new aluminium panelwork, fully repainted, new chassis framework and floorpan, engine with 4.2 pre-engaged starter motor, flywheel and clutch assembly, 4 speed manual gearbox, interior re-trimmed, aluminium hardtop, vented boot lid, excellent workmanship and condition.
Est. £25,000–30,000 *ADT*

1962 Jaguar E-Type Series I Roadster, 6 cylinders, 3781cc, paintwork renewed, original working radio, very good condition throughout.
Est. £20,000–25,000 *COYS*

> **Cross Reference**
> Replica Cars

1962 Jaguar E-Type 3.8 Series I Roadster, 6 cylinders, 3781cc, left hand drive, flat floor model, ground-up restoration, excellent condition throughout.
£26,000–28,000 *COYS*

1963 Jaguar E-Type Series I 3.8 Litre Fixed Head Coupé, right hand drive, completely rebuilt, bare metal respray, brightwork re-chromed, 35,000 miles, Koni shock absorbers, excellent overall condition.
Est. £17,000–20,000 *BKS*

1963 Jaguar E-Type 3.8 Fixed Head Coupé,
6 cylinders, 3781cc, professionally restored,
excellent condition.
Est. £2,000-22,000 *ADT*

1964 Jaguar E-Type 4.2 Roadster,
6 cylinders, 4235cc, chrome wire wheels,
fully retrimmed, only 155 miles since the
rebuild, excellent condition.
Est. £25,000–27,000 *ADT*

**1965 Jaguar E-Type 4.2 Series I Fixed
Head Coupé,** refurbished, chrome wire
wheels, very good condition.
£16,500–17,000 *SJR*

1963 Jaguar E Type 3.8 Coupé, major
mechanical and body restoration to prize
winning standards.
Est. £20,000–25,000 *S*

1964 Jaguar E-Type Series I Roadster,
6 cylinder in line engine, double overhead
camshaft, 3781cc, 265bhp, 5400rpm, 4 speed
manual gearbox, disc brakes all-round,
independent torsion bar front suspension,
independent coil rear, left hand drive, very
good condition throughout.
£22,000–25,000 *CNY*

**1964 Jaguar E-Type 3.8 Fixed Head
Coupé,** standard manual gearbox, fair to
good overall condition.
Est. £17,000–18,000 *ADT*

**1966 Jaguar E-Type 4.2 Litre Series I
2+2 Coupé,** all synchromesh gearbox, good
condition throughout.
Est. £12,000–16,000 *BKS*

**1965 Jaguar E-Type 4.2 Litre Series I
2 Seater Roadster,** original leather seats,
comprehensive engine rebuild, very good
condition throughout.
Est. £18,000–25,000 *BKS*

1967 Jaguar E-Type 4.2 Litre 2+2 Fixed Head Coupé, restored, excellent condition throughout.
Est. £12,000–16,000 *BKS*

1967 Jaguar E-Type 4.2 Litre Roadster, well used, paintwork and upholstery in poor condition, chassis fair, gearbox and transmission in working condition, requires total restoration.
£5,500–6,000 *S*

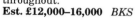

1969 Jaguar E-Type 4.2 Litre Series II 2+2 Sports Coupé, 6 cylinders, twin overhead camshaft, 4235cc, 265bhp at 5500rpm, 4 speed manual gearbox, 4 wheel disc brakes, independent suspension all round, right hand drive, resprayed, very good original condition.
Est. £11,000–14,000 *C*

1969 Jaguar E-Type 4.2 Roadster, restored, very good condition.
£20,000–21,000 *CCTC*

1970 Jaguar E-Type 4.2 Series II 2 Seater Roadster, engine restored, good overall condition.
£18,500–19,500 *BKS*

1969 Jaguar E-Type Roadster Series II, original UK right hand drive, restored, many new parts.
£17,500–18,000 *CCTC*

JAGUAR Model	ENGINE cc/cyl	DATES	CONDITION 1	2	3
E-type 3.8 flat floor roadster (RHD)		1961	£40,000	£30,000	£21,500
E-type SI 3.8 roadster	3781/6	1961-64	£28,000	£18,000	£13,000
E-type 3.8 FHC	3781/6	1961-64	£18,000	£13,000	£9,000
E-type SI 4.2 roadster	4235/6	1964-67	£22,000	£18,000	£12,000
E-type 2+2 manual FHC	4235/6	1966-67	£15,000	£10,000	£8,000
E-type SI 2+2 auto FHC	4235/6	1966-68	£13,000	£9,000	£7,000
E-type SII roadster	4235/6	1968-70	£22,000	£18,000	£12,000
E-type SII FHC	4235/6	1968-70	£18,000	£12,000	£8,000
E-type SII 2+2 manual FHC	4235/6	1968-70	£15,000	£10,000	£8,000
E-type SIII roadster	5343/12	1971-75	£35,000	£24,000	£15,000
E-type SIII 2+2 manual FHC	5343/12	1971-75	£19,000	£14,000	£10,000
E-type SIII 2+2 auto FHC	5343/12	1971-75	£17,000	£12,000	£9,000
XJ6 2.8 Ser I	2793/6	1968-73	£2,600	£1,500	£1,000
XJ6 4.2 Ser I	4235/6	1968-73	£3,000	£2,000	£1,000
XJ6 Coupé	4235/6	1974-78	£7,000	£3,000	£2,000
XJ6 Ser II	4235/6	1973-79	£3,500	£2,000	£750
XJ12 Ser I	5343/12	1972-73	£3,500	£2,250	£1,500
XJ12 Coupé	5343/12	1973-77	£8,000	£4,000	£2,000
XJ12 Ser II	5343/12	1973-79	£2,000	£1,500	-
XJS manual	5343/12	1975-78	£6,000	£4,500	£2,500
XJS auto	5343/12	1975-81	£4,000	£2,200	£1,500

1971 Jaguar E-Type Series III Fixed Head Coupé, 12 cylinders, 5343cc, Webasto sliding sunroof, wire wheels, good original condition.
£10,000–10,500 *ADT*

1971 Jaguar E-Type Series III Fixed Head Coupé, 12 cylinders, 5343cc, right hand drive, good overall condition.
£11,000–12,000 *ADT*

1972 Jaguar E-Type 5.3 Litre V12 Series III 2+2 Coupé, original in every respect, maintained in first class condition, overall mileage 26,000.
£16,000–17,000 *BKS*

1972 Jaguar E-Type V12 Series III Roadster, original right hand drive, restored to factory specification, concours condition.
Est. £38,000–42,000 *S*

1973 Jaguar E-Type Series III Fixed Head Coupé, 12 cylinders, 5300cc, converted to right hand drive, engine refurbished, bodywork re-sprayed, very good condition.
Est. £20,000–22,000 *ADT*

1973 Jaguar E-Type 5.2 Litre V12 Series III 2 Seater Roadster, restored, excellent condition.
£48,000–50,000 *BKS*

1973 Jaguar E-Type Series III Fixed Head Coupé, 12 cylinders, 5343cc, good overall condition.
Est. £11,000–13,000 *ADT*

1973 Jaguar E-Type V12 Series III, manual gearbox.
£11,000–15,000 *VIC*

1964 Jaguar E-Type 3.8 Litre Roadster,
triple Weber carburettors, Le Mans exhaust,
uprated brakes, suspension, wheels and tyres,
completely rebuilt to concours standard.
£45,000–48,000 *SC*

**1969 Jaguar E-Type 4.2 Litre Series II
Roadster,** engine completely rebuilt, original
trim, bodywork in good condition, one owner
for 21 years.
£22,000–23,000 *Mot*

**1971 Jaguar E-Type Series III V12
Roadster,** reconditioned engine, new Gertrag
5 speed gearbox, re-upholstered, fully restored,
excellent condition.
£44,000–46,000 *S*

1963 Jaguar MkX 3.8 Litre Saloon, re-painted,
otherwise totally original, very good condition.
£11,000–12,000 *BKS*

1976 Jensen Interceptor Convertible,
bare shell rebuild, fully overhauled.
£32,000–35,000 *SC*

1973 Jaguar E-Type Series III V12,
manual gearbox, one owner, excellent condition.
£28,000–32,000 *VIC*

**1974 Jensen Interceptor 7.2 Litre 2 Door
Grand Touring Coupé,** coachwork by Vignale,
poor condition, some restoration work required.
£4,000–5,000 *BKS*

1934 Lagonda M45 ST 34 Pillarless Saloon, only 4 owners, very good original condition throughout. **Est. £27,500–32,500** *S*

1935 Lagonda M45 Rapide T7 Style Tourer, Smiths 'Jackall' jacking system, freewheel option, fully restored to a very high standard, excellent condition throughout. **Est. £48,000–55,000** *COYS*

1936 Lagonda LG45 Drophead Coupé, 4½ litre, 6 cylinder in line engine, 4 speed manual gearbox, rebuilt and refurbished, very good condition. **Est. £35,000–40,000** *CNY*

c1967 Lamborghini Miura P400, V12 engine, 3992cc, 370bhp at 7700rpm, 5 speed gearbox, left hand drive, very good restored condition. **£43,000–46,000** *CNY*

1973 Lamborghini Espada 2+2 Coupé, coachwork by Carrozzeria Bertone, front mounted, V12, 4 litre engine, 350bhp, 5 speed transmission, well maintained. **£11,000–12,000** *BKS*

1971 Lamborghini Miura P400 SV, V12 engine, 9in rear wheels, low profile tyres, 25,000 miles, excellent condition. **Est. £80,000–110,000** *BKS*

1925 Lancia Lambda 4 Seater Tourer, short V4 engine, 50bhp at 3000rpm, aluminium cylinder block, good running order. **£34,000–36,000** *S*

1992 Lamborghini Diablo, V12 engine, 5.7 litres, 0–60mph in under 4 seconds, 3,000 recorded miles, right hand drive, very good condition. **£70,000–72,000** *ADT*

1961 Lancia Appia, Berlinetta coachwork by Zagato, V4 engine, 1089cc, 85–90bhp, repainted, period Facetti components including special inlet manifold, good condition. **£16,000–16,500** *COYS*

1962 Lancia Flaminia GT 2.5 3C Coupé, coachwork by Touring, V6 engine, 2458cc, new Koni dampers, 15in diam. wheels, converted to right hand drive, requires cosmetic attention. **£5,000–6,000** *COYS*

1908 Locomobile Type I Tonneau, 4 cylinder, T-head engine, 4 speed gearbox, electric lighting, generator, high tension magneto, excellent condition. **£128,000–130,000** *CNY*

1959 Lotus Elite 1.2 Litre Sports Coupé, modified to semi-lightweight racing specification, Stage Five prepared Coventry-Climax engine, close-ratio MG gearbox, bodywork rebuilt and trimmed, good condition. **£19,500–20,500** *BKS*

1967 Lotus Elan S3/SE Fixed Head Coupé, excellent restored condition. **£12,500–13,500** *KSC*

1966 Lotus Elan S3 Drophead Coupé, with some S2 features including a wood rimmed steering wheel, good condition. **£11,500–12,500** *KSC*

1969 Lotus Europa S2 Type 54, alloy wheels, good condition. **£6,000–6,500** *KSC*

1970 Lotus Europa Series II 1.5 Litre Sports Coupé, Renault 16 engine mounted at the end Elan-type frame, all-round independent coil suspension, front wheel disc brakes, good condition throughout. **£6,500–7,000** *BKS*

1969 Lotus Elan S4 Drophead Coupé, totally rebuilt on a Spyder chassis and running gear, Stromberg carburettors, very good condition. **£10,500–11,500** *KSC*

1972 Lotus Elan Sprint Drophead Coupé, rebuilt big valve engine, excellent condition. **£13,500–14,500** *KSC*

1973 Lotus Europa Twin Cam Special, 5 speed gearbox, completely restored. **£12,000–15,000** *KSC*

1973 Lotus Elan Sprint Drophead Coupé, only 26,000 miles from new, excellent original conditon throughout. **£13,500–14,500** *KSC*

1986 Lotus Esprit S3, only 19,000 miles, factory fitted removable roof, very good condition. **£10,000–10,500** *KSC*

1990 Lotus Excel SA, full leather upholstery, air conditioning, cruise control, excellent condition. **£10,500–11,500** *KSC*

1990 Lotus Esprit Turbo SE, only 16,000 miles, air conditioning, sunroof, excellent condition. **£22,000–24,000** *KSC*

1934 Maserati 4CS 1½ Litre Supercharged Sports 2 Seater, vertical 4 cylinder engine, dual overhead camshafts, 115bhp at 6000rpm, 4 speed gearbox with reverse, excellent restored condition. **£112,000–115,000** *S*

1963 Maserati 3500GTi Sebring Coupé, coachwork by Touring, rebuilt, engine overhauled, stainless steel exhaust, retrimmed interior, less than 5,000 miles, excellent condition. **£27,000–28,000** *COYS*

This is one of just 348 Sebrings built.

1962 Maserati 3500GTi Coupé, coachwork by Touring, converted to triple Webers, excellent condition throughout.
Est. £15,000–20,000 *COYS*

1975 Maserati Bora, Berlinetta coachwork by Ital Design, V8 engine, 4719cc, 350bhp, re-sprayed, under 26,000 miles, excellent overall condition.
£17,500–18,500 *COYS*

1929 Mercedes-Benz 630K Fully Convertible Town Car, coachwork by Erdmann & Rossi, Berlin, museum displayed, excellent condition.
£82,000–85,000 *S*

1954 Mercedes-Benz 220A Cabriolet, 6 cylinders, 80bhp at 4600rpm, 4 speed manual gearbox, under 18,000 miles, left hand drive, excellent original condition.
Est. £35,000–40,000 *CNY*

1971 Mercedes-Benz 300SEL 6.3 Litre Automatic, completely overhauled, good overall condition.
£6,000–6,500 *C*

1970 Maserati Ghibli Coupé, coachwork by Ghia, V8 engine, 4719cc, professionally stored, left hand drive, good overall condition.
£13,250–14,000 *COYS*

1929 Mercedes-Benz Nurburg 460 Limousine, 2 rear occasional seats, courtesy lights, wind-down divison, very good original condition.
£32,000–42,000 *S*

c1914 Mercedes-Benz Roadster, 4 cylinders, 2 litres, 4 speed gearbox, engine partly dismantled.
£12,800–13,400 *C(A)*

1953 Mercedes-Benz 300S Convertible, 6 cylinders, excellent restored condition.
Est. £125,000–135,000 *CNY*
This car was first owned by Bing Crosby.

1960 Mercedes-Benz 300D Saloon, 6 cylinders, 2996cc, 160bhp at 5700rpm, automatic transmission, power steering, Becker Mexico radio, sunroof, good condition throughout.
£12,000–13,000 *COYS*

1972 Mercedes-Benz 280CE 2.8 Litre 2 Door Coupé, only 43,000 miles, right hand drive, very good original condition throughout.
£4,250–4,750 *BKS*

1985 Mercedes-Benz 230E 4 Door Saloon, automatic transmission, one owner, 50,000 miles recorded, well maintained.
£5,000–5,500 *C*

1957 Mercedes-Benz 300SL Roadster, 215bhp, fuel injection, 0–60mph in 7 seconds, top speed of 135mph, very good condition throughout.
Est. £110,000–120,000 *S*

1978 Mercedes-Benz 350SL V8 Sports, 16,000 miles, hard and soft tops, very good condition.
£18,500–19,000 *Mot*

1971 Mini Cooper 'S' Saloon, 1.3 litres, engine rebuilt, general condition poor, requires attention.
£1,000–1,250 *BKS*

1980 Mercedes-Benz 450SEL 6.9 Litre 4 Door Saloon, V8 engine, poor condition.
£5,000–5,500 *BKS*

This car was the property of the late James Hunt.

1956 Mercedes-Benz 300SL Gullwing Coupé, 0–60mph in 8.8 seconds, top speed of 129mph, museum stored, restored, excellent restored condition.
£125,000–130,000 *S*

1960 Mercedes-Benz 190SL Roadster, coachwork by Sindelfingen, 4 cylinders, 1897cc, requires mechanical attention, good condition.
£10,000–10,500 *COYS*

1971 Morris Mini Cooper 1275 'S' 2 Door Sports Saloon, 1.3 litres, very good original condition throughout.
£3,750–4,250 *BKS*

1937 MG TA Open Sports, 4 cylinders, 1298cc, engine and gearbox fully rebuilt, completely restored. **£11,000–11,500** *COYS*

1951 MG TD Open Sports, 4 cylinders, 1250cc, original right hand drive, very well restored, excellent condition. **Est. £11,500–13,500** *COYS*

1952 MG TD 2 Seater Sports Roadster, 1¼ litres, original right hand drive, excellent overall condition. **£14,000–14,500** *BKS*

1952 MG Midget TD Series 2 Series Sports, fully restored to concours condition. **£12,500–13,000** *S*

1957 MGA 1.9 Litre Fixed Head Coupé, with MGB engine, original engine available, original right hand drive, restored, good condition. **£5,750–6,250** *BKS*

1959 MGA Twin Cam 1.5 Litre Fixed Head Coupé, left hand drive, good condition. **£10,000–11,000** *BKS*

1956 MGA Roadster, 4 cylinders, 1489cc, 68bhp at 5500rpm, 0–60mph in 15 seconds, restored to concours winning standard. **£11,000–11,500** *COYS*

1966 MG Midget Mk2, completely original, only 25,000 miles, good condition. **£5,250–5,750** *KSC*

1962 MGA 1600 MkII Roadster, imported, wire wheels, restored, good condition. **£14,500–15,000** *SJR*

1973 MG Midget, round wheel arches, wire wheels, new top, good condition.
£1,800–2,200 *CCTC*

1968 MGB Roadster, 4 cylinders, 1948cc, full bare metal re-spray, new chrome, upholstery, trim and dashboard, good condition.
£8,000–8,500 *COYS*

1972 MGB Roadster, body and interior restored, good condition.
£4,000–4,500 *Mot*

r. **1972 MGB GT,** original bodywork, re-sprayed, some replacements, good mechanical condition.
Est. £1,200–1,800 *ADT*

1973 MGB 1.8 Litre Roadster, one owner, well maintained, very good original condition.
£7,250–7,750 *BKS*

1974 MGB Roadster, body completely restored, re-sprayed, new trim, carpets and soft top, overdrive, RoStyle wheels, rubber bumper, excellent condition.
£3,500–4,000 *CCTC*

1973 MGB Roadster, bodywork repainted, good condition throughout.
£5,500–5,750 *ADT*

1965 MG Berlinette Coupé, coachwork by Coune, wide wire wheels, low profile tyres, stainless steel exhaust, very good condition.
£6,500–7,000 *COYS*

56 examples were built, of which only 12 are known to exist.

1980 MGB GT, good condition.
£1,500–2,500 *VIC*

1953 MG Arnolt Supercharged Convertible, coachwork by Bertone, 4 cylinders, 1200cc, knock-off wire wheels, good condition.
Est. £18,000–22,000 *COYS*

c1961 Morgan 4/4 Series IV, 1340cc, 62bhp, 4 speed gearbox, bench seats, good condition. **£11,500–12,500** *FHD*

Only 206 models were built between 1961 and 1963.

1976 Morgan 4/4 Four Seater, Ford 1600GT engine, 4 speed Ford Cortina gearbox. **£12,000–13,000** *FHD*

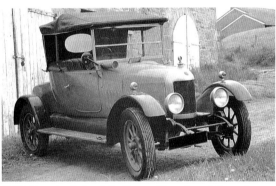

1922 Morris Oxford Bullnose Drophead Coupé, very good original condition. **£7,500–8,000** *COYS*

1925 Morris Oxford Bullnose 2 Seater with Dickey, very good condition throughout. **£12,000–13,000** *OMH*

1939 Morris 8 Series E, very good condition throughout. **£2,750–3,500** *OMH*

1970 Morgan 4/4 Open Sports, 4 cylinders, 1599cc, low mileage, completely restored, excellent condition. **£9,000–10,000** *COYS*

c1954 Morgan +4 Four Seater, Vanguard engine, 0–60mph in 14.1 seconds, 25mpg. **£20,000–25,000** *FHD*

Only 51 cars of this design were made, and the majority were exported to America.

1923 Morris Cowley Sports, replica body, very good condition. **£7,500–8,000** *CGOC*

1932 Morris Minor 2 Seater Tourer, restored, good condition. **£5,000–5,500** *OMH*

1966 Morris Minor Traveller Estate, interior re-trimmed, woodwork replaced, requires cosmetic attention, very original condition. **Est. £800–1,500** *ALC*

1915 Packard 3-38 Seven Passenger Touring,
6 cylinder L-head engine, 3 speed progressive gearbox,
left hand drive, restored, good condition.
Est. £46,000–54,000 *CNY*

1938 Packard Opera 1600 Coupé 2+2,
6 cylinders, left hand drive, completely restored.
£8,000–9,500 *CGB*

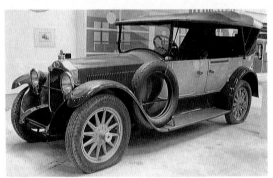

1918 Packard Twin-Six 43.2hp Tourer, V12 side
valve engine, Waltham instrumentation, 2 occasional
rear seats, museum displayed, good condition.
£19,000–21,000 *S*

1914 Peugeot 'Bebe' 856cc Open 2 Seater,
replica coachwork in the style of Henri Gauthier,
4 cylinders, very good original condition.
£20,000–21,000 *BKS*

1959 Peerless 2 Litre GT, Triumph TR3 engine,
overdrive, wire wheels, fibreglass bodywork.
£3,000–3,300 *CCTC*

Only 294 of this model were made.

c1980 Peugeot 504 Cabriolet, styled and
manufactured by Pininfarina, left hand drive,
good original overall condition.
£6,000–8,000 *CLP*

c1980 Peugeot 504 Coupé, V6 fuel injected
engine, left hand drive, poor condition.
£2,000–2,500 *CLP*

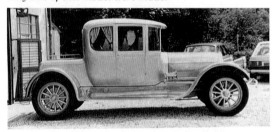

1920 Pierce-Arrow 48hp Opera Coupé, chassis
and engine 23ct gold and nickel plated, completely
restored, right hand drive, excellent condition.
£22,000–25,000 *S*

1959 Pontiac Bonneville 2 Door Hard Top,
automatic transmission, 17,000 miles, original
interior, left hand drive, very good condition.
£8,000–9,000 *CGB*

**1961 Pontiac Monte Carlo Prototype Convertible
'Dream Car',** coachwork by Fisher Body Company,
V8 engine, 4 speed manual gearbox, left hand drive,
minor surface rust, fair overall condition.
£42,000–44,000 *CNY*

1956 Porsche 356A Speedster, coachwork by Reutter, 4 cylinders, 1582cc, ground-up restoration, concours condition.
£38,000–40,000 *COYS*

1963 Porsche 356B 1600 Super Cabriolet, 75bhp, factory fitted removable hard top, well maintained condition throughout.
£14,000–15,000 *COYS*

1969 Porsche 911S Sports Coupé, 6 cylinders, 1991cc, left hand drive, very good original condition.
£6,000–8,000 *COYS*

1972 Porsche 911E 2.4 Coupé, 6 cylinders, 2431cc, electric windows, tinted windows, very good and original condition throughout.
£7,000–8,000 *COYS*

1973 Porsche 911 Carrera RS 2.7 Coupé, 6 cylinders, 2687cc, built to Touring specifications, well maintained, excellent condition throughout.
£22,000–23,000 *COYS*

1973 Porsche 911 Carrera RS 2.8 Litre Lightweight Coupé, converted to RSR specification, rebuilt to excellent condition.
Est. £40,000–50,000 *BKS*

1981 Porsche Carrera GTS Coupé, 4 cylinders, 2000cc, 245bhp, top speed 155mph, 0–60mph in 6.2 seconds, excellent original condition throughout.
£19,000–21,000 *COYS*

c1902 Renault Type G8 CV Series B Folding Seat Tonneau with Canopy, single cylinder engine, requires restoration.
£18,000–19,000 *S*

1907 Renault Type V 4.4 Litre Roi des Belges Tourer, replacement body built in 1960s, restored, very good overall condition.
Est. £28,000–35,000 *BKS*

1934 Riley Lynx 9hp 4 Door 4 Seater, engine, steering and suspension overhauled, new chrome work, good restored condition.
£14,500–15,500 *Mot*

1951 Riley RMB 2.5 Litre 4 Door Saloon, engine re-built, reconditioned transmission and gearbox, bodywork restored, good condition.
£6,000–6,500 *BKS*

1952 Riley RMB 2.5 Litre, body-off restoration timber framing, mechanics, chrome, upholstery, trim and dashboard restored.
£8,500–9,500 *Mot*

1923 Rolls-Royce 40/50 Silver Ghost 2 Door Coupé with Dickey, coachwork by Park Ward Ltd., very good condition throughout.
£50,000–54,000 *S*

1914 Rolls-Royce 40/50 Silver Ghost London to Edinburgh Tourer, factory rebuilt in early 1920s, excellent condition.
£175,000–225,000 *MCh*

This car once belonged to Lawrence of Arabia.

1923 Rolls-Royce 20hp 2 Seater with Dickey, original Barker landaulette coachwork replaced now fitted with coachwork in the style of Hamilton of Aberdeen, centre gearchange, good overall condition.
£20,000–22,000 *S*

1921 Rolls-Royce 40/50 Silver Ghost Barker Torpedo Styled Open Tourer, excellent condition throughout.
£90,000–120,000 *MCh*

1925 Rolls-Royce 40/50 Silver Ghost Phæton, coachwork by Brewster & Co., New York, excellent condition.
£62,000–65,000 *S*

1926 Rolls-Royce Silver Ghost 4 Door Sports Sedan, coachwork by Brewster, 6 cylinders, 7428cc, 453 cu in, 3 speed gearbox with reverse, very good condition throughout. **£38,000–40,000** *CNY*

1925 Rolls-Royce Springfield Silver Ghost 40/50 Suburban Limousine, good overall condition. **Est. £30,000–35,000** *S*

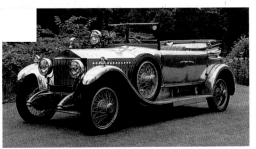

1926 Rolls-Royce Phantom I Series V 40/50 Allweather Cabriolet, polished aluminium coachwork by H. J. Mulliner, divided and opening windscreen, excellent condition. **£78,000–80,000** *S*

1926 Rolls-Royce Phantom I 40/50 Coupé Cabriolet with Dickey, coachwork by Barker, excellent condition throughout. **£80,000–85,000** *S*

1928 Rolls-Royce 20hp Sedanca de Ville, coachwork by Barker, occasional seats, cocktail cabinet, rear courtesy blind, museum stored, engine rebuilt, very good condition. **Est. £30,000–38,000** *S*

1929 Rolls-Royce 40/50 Phantom I Sedanca de Ville, coachwork by Le Baron, excellent original condition. **Est. £60,000–70,000** *S*

Rolls-Royce introduced the New Phantom in 1925 as a replacement for the Silver Ghost. It retained many of the features of its predecessor but the engine was significantly different. The capacity was 7668cc with detachable cylinder heads and pushrod operated overhead valves.

This car was one of the last New Phantoms to be produced. It was tested on 27th February 1929 and delivered to The Car Mart Ltd., Park Lane, London who shipped the chassis to New York for Le Baron to add the coachwork. The quality of work executed by Le Baron can be seen by the condition of the body 65 years on with all doors fitting perfectly and no detectable rattles or shakes when driven.

The interior of this car is also of interest with its Art Deco fittings and green and black lacquered cabinet work.

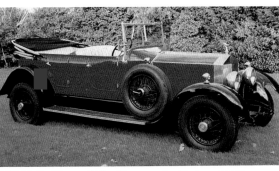

1929 Rolls-Royce 20hp Tourer, 6 cylinders, 3257cc, Barker type opening windscreen, Grebel style headlamps, modern coils in ignition system, engine refurbished, very good condition. **£24,000–28,000** *ADT*

1930 Rolls-Royce Phantom II Sedanca de Ville, very good condition.
£80,000–82,000 *BLE*

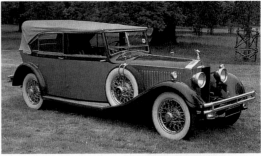

1930 Rolls-Royce Phantom II 40/50 Tourer, coachwork by Hooper, twin side mounted spare wheels, later auxiliary driving lights, good condition.
£35,000–37,000 *S*

1933 Rolls-Royce 20/25 Close Coupled 4 Door Sports Saloon, coachwork by Freestone & Webb, sunroof, spare wheels, good condition.
£25,000–30,000 *S*

1933 Rolls-Royce 20/25 3.7 Litre 4 Seater Fixed Head Coupé, coachwork by Park Ward, engine re-built, re-wired, very good general condition.
£26,000–28,000 *BKS*

1933 Rolls-Royce Phantom II 7.7 Litre Continental Sports Owner-Driver Sunroof Saloon, coachwork by Freestone & Webb, completely restored, excellent condition.
£75,000–80,000 *BKS*

1934 Rolls-Royce 20/25 Close Coupled Sports Saloon, coachwork by Freestone & Webb, no known modifications, good condition throughout.
Est. £26,000–30,000 *S*

1934 Rolls-Royce Phantom II 7.7 Litre Fixed Head Coupé, 2 seater coachwork by Hooper, body restored, re-painted, excellent condition throughout.
£55,000–58,000 *BKS*

1935 Rolls-Royce 20/25 4¼ Litre Special Touring Saloon, coachwork by Park Ward, re-painted, restored, good condition throughout.
£24,000–26,000 *BKS*

1934 Rolls-Royce 20/25 Gurney Nutting Owen Sedanca Coupé, twin trumpet horns, centre driving light, rear mounted spare wheel and wheel discs, very good condition.
£52,000–55,000 *S*

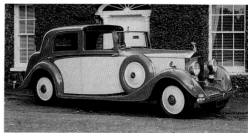

1935 Rolls-Royce 20/25 Continental 2 Door Sports Saloon, coachwork by Barker, Carl Zeiss headlamps, Butlers Atlantic spotlight, mirror, centre auxiliary driving lamp, excellent restored condition. **£43,000–46,000** *S*

1936 Rolls-Royce 25/30 4¼ Litre Sedanca de Ville, by J. Gurney Nutting, 4257cc, straight 6 engine, reconditioned gearbox and final drive, restored, good condition throughout. **Est. £28,000–34,000** *BKS*

1936 Rolls-Royce 25/30 Owner Driver Saloon by Barker, 6 cylinders, 4257cc, restored, excellent condition throughout. **£24,000–25,000** *ADT*

1937 Rolls-Royce Phantom III 5.6 Litre 4 Light Sports Saloon, coachwork by J. Gurney Nutting, B80 straight 8 engine, completely re-built, good condition throughout. **£32,000–35,000** *BKS*

1954 Rolls-Royce Silver Dawn, automatic transmission, 35,000 miles, good restored condition. **Est. £30,000–35,000** *S*

1957 Rolls-Royce Silver Cloud, 6 cylinders, 4887cc, Hydramatic automatic transmission, good original condition. **Est. £13,500–15,000** *ADT*

1937 Rolls-Royce 25/30 Enclosed Limousine, coachwork by Thrupp & Maberly, 6 cylinder engine, 4257cc, 4 speed manual gearbox, sliding sunroof, restored, fair overall condition. **£22,000–25,000** *CNY*

1960 Rolls-Royce Phantom V 7 Seater Limousine, coachwork by Park Ward, power assisted steering, cocktail cabinet, mechanically good condition. **£32,000–35,000** *S*

1963 Rolls-Royce Silver Cloud III, good condition throughout. **£18,000–19,000** *BA*

**1964 Rolls-Royce Silver Cloud III Series B
2 Door Saloon,** coachwork by Mulliner Park
Ward, restored, good condition throughout.
Est. £24,000–26,000 *S*

1973 Rolls-Royce Corniche Convertible,
6750cc, compliant suspension, power hood,
76,000 miles, full service history.
£25,000–28,000 *VIC*

1976 Rolls-Royce Silver Shadow Series I,
full service history, excellent condition.
£9,000–11,000 *VIC*

**1972 Rolls-Royce Silver
Shadow,** coachwork by
Hooper & Co., long wheelbase,
electrically operated
division, air conditioning,
good condition.
£11,000–12,000 *ADT*

1976 Rolls-Royce Camargue, very good
condition throughout.
£20,000–21,000 *Bro*

1978 Rolls-Royce Corniche Convertible,
excellent condition throughout.
£32,000–34,000 *BLE*

1978 Rolls-Royce Silver Shadow II,
20,000 miles, very well maintained,
excellent condition throughout.
£18,000–19,000 *JNic*

1981 Rolls-Royce Silver Spirit, full service
history, very good condition throughout.
£12,000–15,000 *VIC*

1989/91 Rolls-Royce Emperor State Landaulette,
coachwork by Hooper & Co., right hand drive, little
used, excellent condition throughout.
£82,000–85,000 *S*
*Only 16 Landaulettes were built between 1961 and 1986
for ceremonial use by heads of state and Royalty.*

1973 Jaguar E-Type V12 2+2,
very good condition.
£13,000–15,000 *BA*

**1973 Jaguar E-Type V12 Series III
Roadster,** 60° overhead cam V12 engine,
5343cc, 241bhp at 4750rpm, 4 speed manual
gearbox, disc brakes all-round, wishbone
front suspension, torsion bars and anti-roll
bar, rear independent with lower wishbones,
radius arms, coil springs and anti-roll bar,
left hand drive, original special equipment
including wire wheels, air conditioning and
luggage rack, very good overall.
Est. £30,000–35,000 *CNY*

1974 Jaguar E-Type Series III Roadster,
12 cylinders, 5343cc, original right hand
drive, automatic transmission, chrome wire
wheels, original condition throughout.
Est. £22,000–25,000 *COYS*

1962 Jaguar MkX, 6 cylinders, 3781cc,
excellent condition.
Est. £2,500–3,500 *ADT*

**1962 Jaguar MkX 3.8 Litre 4 Door
Saloon,** very good condition throughout.
£9,000–9,500 *BKS*

1966 Jaguar MkX Saloon, interior
refurbished, good usable overall condition.
Est. £5,000–8,000 *ADT*

1968 Jaguar 420 Saloon, 6 cylinders,
4235cc, excellent fully restored condition.
Est. £9,000–12,000 *ADT*

1967 Jaguar 420G, automatic, 4.2 litre
engine, low mileage, triple carburettors,
excellent condition.
£4,600–4,800 *CCTC*

1968 Jaguar XJ6 Series I, 6 cylinders, 4235cc, replaced engine and automatic gearbox, good overall condition.
Est. £1,000–1,200 *ADT*

1968 Jaguar 420G, 6 cylinders, 4235cc, fully refurbished to a good standard.
Est. £2,500–3,500 *ADT*

1969 Jaguar 420G, 6 cylinders, 4235cc, fair condition throughout.
Est. £3,000–3,500 *ADT*

1973 Jaguar XJ12L 5.3 Litre Sports Saloon, maintained to a high standard, original manufacturer's specification throughout.
£2,500–2,800 *S*

The Jaguar XJ6 and XJ12 won the major international 'car of the year' awards in 1969 and 1972 respectively. The first series of 6 cylinder saloons was introduced in 1968, the engine was the XK unit having now been developed with a capacity of 4.2 litres, although a 2.8 litre version was also available.

1973 Jaguar XJ6 4.2 Litre Series I 4 Door Saloon, rare manual transmission, very good condition.
£4,500–4,750 *BKS*

1973 Jaguar XJ6, left hand drive, good condition throughout.
£2,000–3,000 *BA*

1975 Jaguar XJ12 Series II, 12 cylinders, 5343cc, repainted after poor storage, no known major faults, upholstery and Vinyl trim in good condition, original condition throughout.
£3,500–3,800 *ADT*

1976 Jaguar XJ6C 4.2 Litre 2 Door Coupé, extremely good condition throughout.
£6,000–6,500 *BKS*

1977 Jaguar XJ6 3.4 Litre, 6 cylinders,
3442cc, automatic gearbox, very good
original condition.
Est. £2,000–3,000 *ADT*

1978 Jaguar XJ12C 5.3 Litre 2 Door Coupé,
very good condition throughout.
Est. £4,000–6,000 *BKS*

1980 Jaguar XJ12 5.3 Litre 4 Door Saloon,
condition generally reflects careful use.
£2,500–2,800 *S*

*Jaguar's range of XJ12 cars was announced
in 1972, adopting the basic body design of the
XJ6 cars, but using 5.3 litre V12 engine and
with automatic transmission as standard.*

**1984 Jaguar XJ12 Sovereign HE
Saloon,** low mileage, very good
original mechanical condition.
£6,000–6,400 *S*

Jaguar XJS

- Using the V12 engine developing about
  285bhp, the XJS had a top speed of
  around 150mph.
- The HE (high efficiency) cylinder
  head, developed by Michael May,
  cut fuel consumption by nearly
  20 per cent.

1985 Jaguar XJS 3.6 Cabriolet, with hard
top, excellent original condition, 23,000 miles
from new.
£9,000–9,500 *S*

Don't Forget!

*If in doubt please refer
to the 'How to Use'
section at the beginning
of this book.*

1985 Jaguar XJS 5.3 Litre HE Coupé,
automatic transmission, less than 30,000
miles from new, excellent original condition.
£5,500–5,750 *BKS*

**1979 Jaguar XJS
Drophead Coupé,**
very good condition.
£6,000–6,500 *BLE*

JENSEN

Founded in 1934 by the Jensen brothers, Alan and Richard, the factory at West Bromwich produced coachbuilt bodies for specialised vehicles. The first car to bear the Jensen name was a 3.6 litre Ford V8 engined S-Type. Wartime production was geared to commercial vehicles and the first model launched in 1946 was designated PW (post-war).

In 1957 Jensen was one of the first British manufacturers to employ disc brakes all round. The Jensen brothers retired during the 1960s, when the company was acquired by the Norcross Group. The V8 engined CV8 was launched in 1963, and the fibreglass bodied 541 appeared in 1964.

1954 Jensen Interceptor Cabriolet, fair condition.
£2,500–2,750 *CBG*

Cross Reference
Restoration Projects

1937 Jensen S-Type Dual Cowl Tourer, V8 engine, 6546cc, excellent restored condition.
£42,000–44,000 *COYS*

1956 Jensen 541 Sports Saloon, 6 cylinder overhead valve engine, 3993cc, 125bhp, 4 speed manual gearbox with overdrive, servo assisted 4 wheel drum brakes, independent front suspension, leaf spring live axle rear, right hand drive, extensive service history, extremely original example, requires attention to its original interior and exterior paintwork, usable condition.
£4,000–4,400 *C*

1957 Jensen 541R, very good condition.
£15,000–15,500 *CBG*

1960 Jensen 541R, manual gearbox with overdrive, unrestored condition.
£9,750–10,500 *Bro*

1964 Jensen CV8 MkII, very good condition.
£14,000–14,500 *CBG*

1963 Jensen CV8 MkI, re-painted fibreglass body, excellent condition throughout.
£13,200–13,600 *ADT*

1965 Jensen CV8 MkII, 8 cylinders, 6276cc, good original overall condition.
Est. £9,000–11,000 *ADT*

1966 Jensen CV8 MkIII Sports Coupé, very good all-round condition.
Est. £12,000–13,000 *S*

1966 Jensen CV8 MkIII, very good condition.
£14,000–14,500 *CBG*

1966 Jensen CV8 MkIII, manual gearbox.
£16,500–17,000 *CBG*
This was the last of ten CV8 manuals built.

1967 Jensen FFI, concours condition.
£35,000–36,000 *CBG*

1968 Jensen Interceptor MkI, Chrysler V8 engine, 6276cc, power steering, re-painted, very good condition throughout.
Est. £4,000–5,000 *ADT*

Jensen Interceptor MkI

- The MkI Jensen Interceptor featured the Chrysler 6276cc V8 engine and Torqueflite transmission.
- Acceleration was tested at 0–60mph in 7.3 seconds and 0–100mph in 19 seconds.
- Introduced in 1966, it was produced for 3 years.
- The MkI was the most powerful of the range, producing 325bhp at 4600rpm, and 425lb of torque at 2800rpm.

1968 Jensen Interceptor MkI 6.3 Litre 2 Door Sports Coupé, low mileage, completely original condition.
£18,000–19,000 *BKS*

1968 Jensen Interceptor Coupé,
coachwork by Vignale, V8 engine, 6276cc,
substantial restoration and maintenance,
suspension and gearbox rebuilt.
£6,500–6,800 *COYS*

1969 Jensen Interceptor MkI, factory
restored, excellent condition throughout.
£9,500–9,750 *Mot*

JENSEN Model	ENGINE cc/cyl	DATES	CONDITION		
			1	**2**	**3**
541/541R/541S	3993/6	1954-63	£10,000	£6,000	£3,500
CV8 Mk I-III	5916/ 6276/8	1962-66	£12,000	£6,000	£4,000
Interceptor SI-SIII	6276/8	1967-76	£10,000	£5,000	£4,500
Interceptor DHC	6276/8	1973-76	£20,000	£12,000	£9,000
Interceptor SP	7212/8	1971-76	£10,000	£8,000	£6,500
FF	6766/8	1967-71	£13,000	£10,000	£9,000
Healey	1973/4	1972-76	£5,000	£3,000	£1,500
Healey GT	1973/4	1975-76	£6,000	£3,000	£2,000

1972 Jensen FF MkIII, excellent condition.
£25,000–26,000 *CBG*

1973 Jensen Interceptor MkIII,
excellent condition.
£12,000–15,000 *VIC*

1973 Jensen Interceptor MkIII Saloon,
new torque converter, louvred bonnet,
windscreen, air conditioning, carburettor,
core plugs and starter motor, ignition system,
tyres and gaskets, good condition throughout.
Est. £8,000–9,000 *S*

1973 Jensen Interceptor MkIII Coupé,
coachwork by Vignale, V8 engine, 7212cc,
excellent condition throughout.
£11,000–11,500 *COYS*

**1973 Jensen Interceptor MkIII 7.2 Litre
Sports Coupé,** very good original condition.
Est. £5,000–6,000 *S*

1976 Jensen Coupé, excellent condition
throughout.
£20,000–22,000 *CBG*

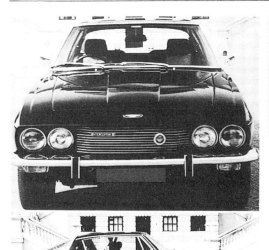

1976 Jensen Coupé, excellent overall condition.
£14,000–15,000 *CBG*

This was one of only 20 right hand drive models produced.

JENSEN-HEALEY

1974 Jensen Interceptor MkIII J Series, 1990s concours winner.
£20,000–22,000 *CBG*

1973 Jensen-Healey, 4 cylinders, 1973cc, 4 speed transmission, fully re-painted, fair paintwork, some engine work completed.
Est. £2,200–2,600 *ADT*

1976 Jensen GT Hatchback, good overall condition.
£3,000–3,300 *S*

1975 Jensen-Healey MkII, 5 speed gearbox, excellent condition throughout.
£7,500–8,000 *CBG*

1976 Jensen-Healey MkII, 5 speed gearbox, concours condition.
£10,000–11,000 *CBG*

JOWETT

1974 Jensen-Healey MkII, 4 speed gearbox, excellent condition throughout.
£9,500–10,000 *CBG*

1925 Jowett Long Four 7hp 4 Seater Tourer, engine re-built, good condition throughout.
Est. £5,000–7,000 *S*

LAGONDA

Lagonda was purchased by solicitor, Mr Alan Good, for £67,000 in 1935. This was the year that Lagonda joined Bentley on the list of pre-war winners of the famous 24 hours race at Le Mans. A three-car team was entered, all of which survive today, powered by the 4½ litre Meadows engine. The winning car, driven by Hindmarsh and Fontes, attained an average speed of 77mph.

After the war, David Brown acquired Lagonda for £55,000, mainly to ensure a supply of engines for the Aston Martin DB2. The Lagonda name still features on some Aston Martin products today.

1906 Lagonda 10hp Twin-Cylinder Fore Car, original condition, requires lighting equipment and some re-commissioning before use.
£5,000–5,500 *S*

1923 Lagonda Model K 11.9hp Coupé, re-painted, re-trimmed, requires re-commissioning after storage.
£5,500–6,500 *ADT*

This Model K Coupé is identifiable by the wing mounted headlamps, folding hood and two-seater coachwork.

1929 Lagonda 3 Litre Tourer, very good overall cosmetic appearance, full weather equipment, twin rear mounted spare wheels.
Est. £28,000–32,000 *S*

1930 Lagonda 3 Litre Special Low Chassis Weymann Saloon, remarkably original condition, requires complete refurbishment and re-commissioning.
Est. £15,000–20,000 *S*

1939 Lagonda V12 4 Door Sports Saloon, coachwork by Lagonda, meticulous restoration, potential concours d'élégance winner.
£58,000–60,000 *S*

1932 Lagonda 16/80, 6 cylinders, 2 litres, body by Abbott, leather re-trimmed, new weather equipment and chrome.
£23,000-23,500 *Mot*

1932 Lagonda 2 Litre Continental 4 Seater Open Sports Tourer, always maintained in good running order, completely original condition.
Est. £22,000–28,000 *COYS*

The Continental was a special variant of Lagonda's 2 litre Speed Model, which was made in small numbers between 1930 and 1933. It was derived from the Lagonda 14/60 which was introduced in 1926.

LAGONDA Model	ENGINE cc/cyl	DATES	CONDITION 1	2	3
12/24	1421/4	1923-26	£14,000	£10,000	£8,000
2 litre	1954/4	1928-32	£28,000	£25,000	£19,000
3 litre	2931/6	1928-34	£35,000	£30,000	£22,000
Rapier	1104/4	1934-35	£13,000	£6,500	£5,000
M45	4429/6	1934-36	£35,000	£26,000	£18,000
LG45	4429/6	1936-37	£40,000	£30,000	£20,000
LG6	4453/6	1937-39	£40,000	£28,000	£20,000
V12	4480/V12	1937-39	£75,000	£50,000	£40,000

Prices are very dependent upon body type, originality and competition history.

Miller's is a price GUIDE not a price LIST

1936 Lagonda LG45 Rapide Style Sports Tourer, excellent concours prize-winning condition throughout.
£50,000–52,000 *COYS*

1939 Lagonda LG6 Short Chassis Sports Saloon, well maintained, excellent original condition.
Est. £17,000–22,000 *COYS*

1936 Lagonda LG45 Pillarless Saloon, factory coachwork, Alvis synchromesh gearbox, original G9 box available, good original condition.
£18,000–18,500 *COYS*

1939 Lagonda V12 Le Mans, recently restored to highest standard.
£129,000+ *MAN*

Cross Reference
Restoration Projects

1940 Lagonda V12 Rapide 4½ Litre 3 Seater Roadster, completely original, requires restoration.
£110,000+ *BKS*

In 1940 the Lagonda V12 Rapide, at £1,600, was one of the most expensive cars on the British market, when a similar aged Ford Anglia cost £125.

LAGONDA (post-war) Model	ENGINE cc/cyl	DATES	CONDITION		
			1	2	3
3 litre	2922/6	1953-58	£10,500	£7,000	£4,500
3 litre DHC	2922/6	1953-56	£14,000	£10,000	£8,500
Rapide	3995/6	1961-64	£11,000	£7,000	£4,500

1955 Lagonda MkI 3 Litre Drophead Coupé, coachwork by Tickford, 6 cylinders, 2922cc, restored to the highest standards throughout.
£23,000–24,000 *COYS*

1956 Lagonda MkII 3 Litre Sports Saloon, good condition throughout.
£9,500–10,000 *S*

1984 Lagonda 5.3 Litre Saloon, good condition throughout.
Est. £14,000–16,000 *S*

LAMBORGHINI

Tractor manufacturer, Ferrucio Lamborghini, started motor car production in 1963, allegedly because he was not happy about his treatment by Enzo Ferrari. He engaged some of the best Italian designers and engineers, including Bizzarini and Dallara.

By 1966 the Miura appeared with a V12 3929cc engine, and with its astonishing good looks Lamborghini had established itself amongst the top manufacturers of the world's supercars.

1969 Lamborghini Miura S, Berlinetta coachwork by Bertone, V12 engine, 3929cc, rare right hand drive, excellent overall condition.
£47,000–49,000 *COYS*

1974 Lamborghini Espada Series 3 Coupé, coachwork by Bertone, 12 cylinders, 3929cc, excellent all-round condition.
£12,000–13,000 *COYS*

The 3rd Series had ZF power steering, re-jigged spring and shock rates, altered rear suspension arms, and a 'wraparound' dashboard.

1974 Lamborghini Urraco P250, 8 cylinders, 2463cc, re-painted, right hand drive, original and fair condition.
Est. £10,500–11,500 *ADT*

LAMBORGHINI Model	ENGINE cc/cyl	DATES	CONDITION 1	2	3
350 GT fhc	3500/12	1964-67	£80,000	£50,000	£30,000
400 GT	4000/12	1966-68	£60,000	£50,000	£30,000
Miura LP400	4000/12	1966-69	£60,000	£50,000	£30,000
Miura S	4000/12	1969-71	£80,000	£60,000	£40,000
Espada	4000/12	1969-78	£18,000	£14,000	£10,000
Jarama	4000/12	1970-78	£22,000	£15,000	£13,000
Urraco	2500/8	1972-76	£18,000	£11,000	£8,000
Countach	4000/12	1974-82	£60,000	£40,000	£30,000

1974 Lamborghini P250S Urraco 2+2 Coupé, coachwork by Bertone, 5 speed gearbox, right hand drive, very good condition throughout.
Est. £10,000–12,000 *S*

1975 Lamborghini Urraco P300, 8 cylinders, 2997cc, left hand drive, good mechanical condition.
£12,000–12,500 *ADT*

1982 Lamborghini Countach 5000S, 12 cylinders, 4754cc, right hand drive, very good overall condition, some slight cosmetic attention needed throughout.
£68,000–72,000 *ADT*

Lamborghini Urraco

- **The Urraco was powered by a 2483cc V8 engine, producing 220bhp at 7500rpm.**
- **This engine was a development of the V8 fitted in the Miura, and could achieve over 143mph and 0–60mph in 8.5 seconds.**
- **Introduced in 1971, the Urraco had McPherson strut suspension, replacing the wishbone/coil system in earlier models.**

LANCHESTER

Founded by Frederick Lanchester in Coventry, the first Lanchester vehicle appeared as early as 1895. It was the first car to be fitted with Dunlop pneumatic tyres.

By 1931 Lanchester had been taken over by Daimler. At that time Lanchester cars were only 'badge engineered' Daimlers, and by 1956 the Lanchester name had disappeared.

1937 Lanchester Eleven 10.8hp 4 Door Saloon, original sliding sunroof has been sealed, trafficators fitted, engine and electrics not working, paintwork fair, straightforward restoration project.
£2,000–2,300 *S*

1950 Lanchester D10 4 Door Saloon, very good restored condition.
£2,300-2,600 *S*

LANCHESTER Model	ENGINE cc/cyl	DATES	CONDITION 1	2	3
LD10	1287/4	1946-49	£2,500	£1,500	£750
LD10 (Barker bodies)	1287/4	1950-51	£2,800	£1,500	£700

LANCIA

Lancia's famous Lambda model was produced from 1923 until 1931. Made in nine series it had a narrow V4 engine and excellent road holding ability. The engine was a little over 2 litres with an aluminium cylinder block and cast iron head and 2 overhead valves per cylinder, developing about 50bhp at 3000rpm. The chassis was a skeleton framework of flanged pressed steel members rivetted together. Cross bracing for side members was provided by scuttle and bulkhead panels and a rigid backbone, which included the propeller shaft tunnel.

1927 Lancia Lambda 7th Series Tourer, narrow angle V4 engine, 2570cc, 4 speed central change non-synchromesh gearbox, platform type chassis with integral tail section, independent front suspension by sliding pillars and coil springs, beam rear axle with semi-elliptic leaf springs, 4 wheel mechanical drum brakes, centre lock wire type wheels, 6.00 x 22 tyres, right hand drive, very original vehicle, good overall condition throughout.
£43,000–45,000   *C(A)*

1926 Lancia Lambda 7th Series 2.4 Litre Short Chassis 4 Seater Torpedo, completely original, 4 speed gearbox, only 1,000 miles since complete overhaul.
Est. £30,000–45,000   *BKS*

1927 Lancia Lambda 7th Series 4 Seater Tourer, original specification, subject of older restoration, in good condition throughout.
£20,000–21,000   *S*

1959 Lancia Aurelia B24 Convertible, coachwork by Pininfarina, V6 engine, 2451cc, very good original condition.
£35,000–38,000   *COYS*

1955 Lancia Aurelia B24 Spyder, coachwork by Pininfarina, restored as closely as possible to original specification, past concours d'élégance winner, good mechanical condition.
Est. £40,000–60,000   *S*

1962 Lancia Flaminia 2500 Coupé, coachwork by Pininfarina, good overall condition, dry stored in recent years.
£3,000–3,250   *S*

LANCIA Model	ENGINE cc/cyl	DATES	CONDITION 1	2	3
Theta	4940/4	1913-19	£24,000	£16,500	£8,000
Kappa	4940/4	1919-22	£24,000	£16,000	£8,000
Dikappa	4940/4	1921-22	£24,000	£16,000	£8,000
Trikappa	4590/4	1922-26	£25,000	£18,000	£10,000
Lambda	2120/4	1923-28	£35,000	£20,000	£10,000
Dilambda	3960/8	1928-32	£24,000	£16,000	£8,000
Astura	2604/8	1931-39	£25,000	£18,000	£9,000
Artena	1925/4	1931-36	£9,000	£5,000	£2,000
Augusta	1196/4	1933-36	£9,000	£4,000	£2,000
Aprilia 238	1352/4	1937-39	£10,000	£5,000	£3,000

LANCIA Model	ENGINE cc/cyl	DATES	CONDITION		
			1	2	3
Aprilia 438	1486/4	1939-50	£11,000	£6,000	£3,000
Ardea	903/4	1939-53	£10,000	£5,000	£3,000
Aurelia B10	1754/6	1950-53	£7,000	£5,000	£2,000
Aurelia B15-20-22	1991/6	1951-53	£10,000	£5,000	£2,500
Aurelia B24-B24S	2451/6	1955-58	£30,000	£15,000	£10,000
Aurelia GT	2451/6	1953-59	£15,000	£10,000	£7,000
Appia C10-C105	1090/4	1953-62	£6,000	£3,000	£2,000
Aurelia Ser II	2266/6	1954-59	£10,000	£5,000	£3,000
Flaminia Zagato	2458/6	1957-63	£18,000	£10,000	£7,000
Flaminia Ser	2458/6	1957-63	£12,000	£7,000	£5,000
Flavia 1500	1500/4	1960-75	£6,000	£4,000	£2,000
Fulvia	1091/4	1963-70	£3,000	£2,000	£1,000
Fulvia S	1216/4	1964-70	£3,500	£2,500	£1,500
Fulvia 1.3	1298/4	1967-75	£3,000	£2,000	£1,000
Stratos	2418/6	1969-71	£30,000	£18,000	£10,000
Flavia 2000	1991/4	1969-75	£3,000	£1,500	£500
Fulvia HF/1.6	1584/4	1969-75	£5,000	£2,000	£1,000
Beta HPE	1585/4	1976-82	£3,000	£1,500	£500
Beta Spyder	1995/4	1977-82	£4,000	£1,500	£800
Monte Carlo	1995/4	1976-81	£6,000	£3,000	£1,000

Competition history could cause prices to vary.

1964 Lancia Flavia Vignale Drophead 4 Seater Convertible, 1.8 litre engine, front wheel drive, 4 wheel disc brakes, hard and soft tops, good running order.
£5,500–6,000 *RT*

1969 Lancia Fulvia Fanalone 1.6 Litre HF Rallye 2 Door Sports Coupé, fully restored, stripped and rebuilt to the highest standards, original factory parts, Campagnolo wheels.
Est. £18,000–24,000 *BKS*

Lancia Flavia

- Introduced in 1960, the Lancia Flavia was the first front wheel drive car produced in Italy.
- The flat 4 cylinder engine could exceed 113mph with 0–60mph in 11.9 seconds.
- Bodies were available from Zagato, Vignale and Pininfarina.

Miller's is a price GUIDE not a price LIST

1965 Lancia Flavia 1.8 Litre Zagato Sport, coachwork by Zagato, original specification, floor mounted gear change, left hand drive.
Est. £10,000–12,000 *S*

1970 Lancia Fulvia Zagato S1 Sports Coupé, original specification, good condition throughout.
£4,400–4,800 *S*

1971 Lancia Fulvia Zagato Sports Coupé, re-painted, mechanically good, bodywork in excellent condition.
Est. £5,000–6,000 *S*

1972 Lancia Fulvia Zagato, 4 cylinders, 1231cc, standard V4 engine, 5 speed manual gearbox, right hand drive, very good condition.
Est. £4,500–5,500 *ADT*

1973 Lancia Fulvia Series II Coupé, right hand drive, very good overall condition.
£2,400–2,800 *C*

1982 Lancia Gamma Coupé, 4 cylinders, 2484cc, 5 speed manual gearbox, all-round disc brakes, air conditioning, electric windows, left hand drive.
£900–1,000 *ADT*

LAND ROVER

1975 Lancia Stratos Berlinetta, coachwork by Bertone, 6 cylinders, 2418cc, never been restored, regularly maintained, excellent condition throughout.
Est. £34,000–40,000 *COYS*

1956 Land Rover Short Wheel Base Utility, original with no significant modifications, freewheel front hubs.
Est. £900–1,250 *ALC*

LAND ROVER Model	ENGINE cc/cyl	DATES	CONDITION 1	2	3
Ser 1	1595/4	1948-51	£2,200	£1,000	£500
Ser 1	1995/4	1951-53	£2,000	£1,000	£300
Ser 1	1995/4	1953-58	£2,000	£1,000	£300
Ser 1	1995/4	1953-58	£2,800	£1,500	£750
Ser 2	1995/4	1958-59	£2,000	£950	£500
Ser 2	1995/4	1958-59	£2,800	£1,200	£500
Ser 2	2286/4	1959-71	£2,000	£950	£500
Ser 2	2286/4	1959-71	£2,500	£1,200	£500
Range Rover	3528/V8	1970-	£5,000	£1,200	£600

LA SALLE

1937 La Salle Touring Sedan, 8 cylinders, 4950cc, good running order throughout. **Est. £12,000–14,000** *ADT*

The Series 37-50 La Salle for 1937 was available in 5 different styles, from 2 door touring sedan through to sports coupé.

LEA-FRANCIS

1926 Lea-Francis Model J 12/22hp 4 Seater Coupé, coachwork by Cross & Ellis, chassis-up restoration, later carburettor and cooling fan, excellent condition throughout. **£7,500–8,000** *S*

The J Type was introduced for the 1926 season and first produced in 1925. It featured the 1496cc Meadows engine, a 4 speed gearbox and front wheel brakes were standard.

LEA-FRANCIS Model	ENGINE cc/cyl	DATES	CONDITION		
			1	2	3
12HP	1944/4	1923-24	£10,000	£5,000	£3,000
14HP	2297/4	1923-24	£10,000	£5,000	£3,000
9HP	1074/4	1923-24	£7,000	£4,000	£2,000
10HP	1247/4	1947-54	£10,000	£5,500	£3,000
12HP	1496/4	1926-34	£11,000	£6,000	£4,000
Various 6 cylinder models	1696/6	1927-29	£13,500	£9,500	£5,000
Various 6 cylinder models	1991/6	1928-36	£10,500	£8,750	£5,000
14HP	1767/4	1946-54	£6,000	£4,000	£2,000
1.5 litre	1499/4	1949-51	£10,000	£5,000	£2,500
2.5 litre	2496/4	1950-52	£12,000	£8,000	£4,000

Lea-Francis

- **The Lea-Francis 1.8 Sports had a 4 cylinder 1767cc engine with twin SU carburettors and twin fuel pumps.**
- **It could produce 70bhp at 4700rpm.**
- **Equipped with a 4 speed synchromesh gearbox, Hydro-mechanical brakes and 16in wheels.**

Cross Reference Restoration Projects

LÉON BOLLÉE

Built at Le Mans in France, most Léon Bollées were imported in chassis form and fitted with Connaught coachwork.

1948 Lea-Francis 14hp MkIII Saloon, coachwork by Coachcraft A.P.A. Ltd., very good original condition following a period of museum storage. **£2,500–2,700** *S*

Did you know? *MILLER'S Collectors Cars Price Guide builds up year-by-year to form the most comprehensive photo-reference library system available.*

1914 Léon Bollée 18hp Tourer, 4 cylinder side valve engine, 2.7 litres, 4 speed gearbox, hide upholstery, nickel fittings, electric lighting, detachable Rudge Whitworth wire wheels, good overall condition. **£14,000–18,000** *S*

LINCOLN

After Henry Leland left Cadillac in 1917, he designed another large, side valve V8 engined car and formed the Lincoln Motor Company in Detroit in 1920. The first Lincoln V8 was marketed in 1921, and featured a 5.8 litre engine which developed 81bhp. The cars were advanced for the period, with detachable cylinder heads and full pressure lubrication. President Coolidge purchased a Lincoln in 1924, and the link between the marque and the White House has endured to this day.

1926 Lincoln Model 8 Four Door 6 Light Saloon, drum headlights, all original instrumentation, forward opening screen, leather roof, good overall condition.
£10,000–11,000 *S*

1939 Lincoln Zephyr V12 4 Door Sedan, fully refurbished, excellent condition.
£10,000–11,000 *GAR*

1968 Lincoln Continental Long Wheelbase Limousine, coachwork by Lehman-Peterson of Chicago, 7.5 litre engine, power steering, air conditioning, upholstery unmarked, restored over a 2 year period, excellent condition throughout.
£4,250–4,500 *S*

Between 200 and 300 examples of this model were built on an extended Lincoln Continental chassis over a 3 year period.

1969 Lincoln Continental MkIII 4 Door Sedan, standard factory specification, in running order.
£1,250–1,450 *S*

LINCOLN Model	ENGINE cu in/cyl	DATES	CONDITION 1	2	3
Première Coupé	368/8	1956-57	£6,000	£4,000	£2,000
Première Convertible	368/8	1956-57	£14,000	£8,000	£5,000
Continental Mk II	368/8	1956-57	£10,000	£6,000	£4,000
Continental 2 door	430/8	1958-60	£6,000	£4,000	£2,000
Continental Convertible	430/8	1958-60	£18,000	£10,000	£6,000

LION-PEUGEOT

The Lion-Peugeot commenced as an independent venture by Robert Peugeot in the motorcycle factory at Beaulieu-Valentigney, which had been used for car manufacture until the establishment of the SA des Automobiles Peugeot in 1897.

> **Cross Reference**
> Peugeot

1906 Lion-Peugeot Type VC 9hp 2 Seater, very original, museum stored, requires re-commissioning before use, generally good condition.
£11,000–13,000 *S*

LLOYD ALEXANDER

Although Lloyd cars were in production in the Edwardian era, it was not until 1957, when in the hands of Borgward, that Lloyd announced the Alexander. It was a substantial vehicle with steel coachwork and powered by a 600cc engine. The collapse of Borgward in 1961 signalled the end of Lloyd.

c1960 Lloyd Alexander 600cc Saloon, museum stored, complete and original in all major respects, restoration project.
£550–700 *S*

1901 Locomobile 5½hp 4 Seater Spindleback Steam Surrey, hidden brake on transmission added for safety, good condition throughout.
£16,250–16,500 *S*

c1914 Locomobile 2 Seater with Single Dickey Seat, replica body, outside handbrake, dual ignition, 2 Lucas coils under dashboard, correct Locomobile oil pressure gauge, Westinghouse voltmeter, non-original Hanomag speedometer, headlamps and radiator in polished brass, left hand drive.
£16,500–17,000 *S*

LOCOMOBILE

By 1901 Locomobile, founded by Lorenzo Barber and John Walker, was reputed to be the largest vehicle manufacturer of its kind in America. When over 5,400 locomobile 'steamers' had been produced they sold the production rights back to Stanley's, the steam vehicle pioneers who had sold the design originally to Locomobile. The Stanley brothers were consultants to both companies.

Despite this marvellous start, steam driven vehicles were soon outsold by petrol driven machines, mainly for safety reasons, but also because it took at least thirty minutes to get enough steam up!

1899 Locomobile Steam Runabout, 2 cylinder engine, full elliptic leaf spring transversally mounted front suspension, full elliptical leaf springs rear, centre tiller drive, restored, not run since mid-1980s, requires mechanical examination.
£23,000–25,000 *CNY*

> **Don't Forget!**
> *If in doubt please refer to the 'How to Use' section at the beginning of this book.*

LORRAINE-DIETRICH

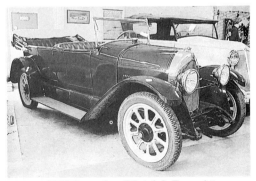

1923 Lorraine-Dietrich Type A4 4/5 Seater Torpedo Tourer, 12CV 4 cylinder model, rear wheel braking only, steel artillery wheels, opening windscreen, wood capping to the door trims, a rear mounted spare wheel, Lucas sports coil, left hand drive.
£9,000–12,000 *S*

LOTUS

The first real road-going car produced by Colin Chapman at the Lotus works at Cheshunt was the Elite. Arguably one of the prettiest British sports cars every produced, it was powered by a 4 cylinder Coventry-Climax engine of 1216cc, which provided astonishing performance for a small engine. The Elite featured an innovative construction consisting of a three-piece glass fibre monocoque reinforced with steel sections. This was very light and efficient, but extremely expensive to produce. As a result, the Elite's successor, the Elan, featured a steel 'backbone' which was much easier and cheaper to make.

The Elite had many track successes, but production had ceased by 1963 after slightly less than 1,000 had been built during its four year run. By comparison, over 12,000 Elans were built between 1962 and 1973.

1954 Lotus Six, 4 cylinders, 1275cc, excellent restored and rebuilt condition.
Est. £12,500–13,500 *ADT*

Lotus Elan

- Launched in 1962, the Lotus Elan initially had a 1499cc engine producing about 105bhp.
- The S2 and S3 introduced in 1964 and 1965 produced 115bhp and 126bhp respectively from the Ford based twin cam engine.
- Very popular in team Gold Leaf colours of red, gold and white.

1965 Lotus Elan S2 Drophead Coupé, restored, on genuine Lotus galvanised chassis, black factory hard-top.
£14,000–14,500 *KSC*

1963 Lotus Elan S1, fitted with factory hard top, completely restored to concours standard.
£20,000–21,000 *KSC*

This car was a Club Lotus Festival winner for best Elan.

1967 Lotus Elan S3 Drophead Coupé, renovated over 9 years, engine re-built, paintwork restored in Gold Leaf colours, brakes overhauled, original interior trim, chassis replaced.
Est. £8,000–9,000 *S*

LOTUS Model	ENGINE cc/cyl	DATES	CONDITION		
			1	2	3
Six		1953-56	£10,000	£7,000	£4,500
Seven S1 Sports	1172/4	1957-64	£12,000	£9,000	£4,000
Seven S2 Sports	1498/4	1961-66	£9,000	£7,000	£4,000
Seven S3 Sports	1558/4	1961-66	£9,000	£7,000	£4,000
Seven S4	1598/4	1969-72	£6,000	£4,500	£2,500
Elan S1 Convertible	1558/4	1962-64	£10,000+	£8,000	£4,500
Elan S2 Convertible	1558/4	1964-66	£9,000+	£6,500	£4,000
Elan S3 Convertible	1558/4	1966-69	£11,000+	£7,250	£5,000
Elan S3 FHC	1558/4	1966-69	£11,000	£6,000	£4,000
Elan S4 Convertible	1558/4	1968-71	£11,000+	£8,000	£5,000
Elan S4 FHC	1558/4	1968-71	£9,000	£6,250	£4,150
Elan Sprint Convertible	1558/4	1971-73	£10,000+	£7,500	£5,000
Elan Sprint FHC	1558/4	1971-73	£9,000	£6,250	£4,500
Europa S1 FHC	1470/4	1966-69	£3,500	£2,000	£1,500
Europa S2 FHC	1470/4	1969-71	£4,000	£2,500	£1,500
Europa Twin Cam	1558/4	1971-75	£7,000	£5,000	£3,250
Elan +2S 130	1558/4	1971-74	£7,000	£4,500	£3,000
Elite S1 FHC	1261/4	1974-80	£3,000	£2,500	£1,500
Eclat S1	1973/4	1975-82	£3,500	£3,000	£1,500
Esprit 1	1973/4	1977-81	£6,500	£5,000	£3,000
Esprit 2	1973/4	1976-81	£7,000	£5,000	£3,000
Esprit S2.2	2174/4	1980-81	£6,500	£5,500	£3,000
Esprit Turbo	2174/4	1980-90	£10,000	£6,500	£3,500

Prices vary with some limited edition Lotus models.

1967 Lotus Elan S3/SE Drophead Coupé,
very good condition.
£12,000–13,000 *KSC*

1967 Lotus Elan 2+2, very good
re-built condition.
£4,000–5,000 *ADT*

1969 Lotus Europa S2 Type 54,
re-trimmed interior, good condition.
£5,500–5,750 *KSC*

1970 Lotus Europa S2, fitted with Renault
1600cc engine, very good condition.
£4,600–4,800 *CGOC*

**1971 Lotus Elan Sprint Fixed Head
Coupé,** Lotus galvanised chassis,
excellent condition throughout.
£12,500–13,000 *KSC*

1970 Lotus Elan S4 Drophead Coupé,
engine uprated to sprint specification,
re-painted, good condition throughout.
£8,000–9,000 *ADT*

1972 Lotus Elan Sprint Drophead Coupé,
excellent restored condition.
£11,000–11,500 *Mot*

1973 Lotus Europa Twin Cam Special,
5 speed gearbox, 40,000 miles from new,
excellent original condition.
£14,000–14,500 *KSC*

1972 Lotus Europa Twin Cam, race
prepared, very good condition.
£8,000–8,500 *CGOC*

**1973 Lotus Elan Sprint Fixed Head
Coupé,** Gold Leaf colours, excellent
condition throughout.
£12,000–12,500 *KSC*

1974 Lotus Elite 2 Litre Coupé, optional
air conditioning, well maintained, good
overall condition.
Est. £4,000–6,000 *BKS*

*This car was owned by the late Ronnie
Peterson during his most successful season as
number one driver with Team Lotus.*

1974 Lotus Elan +2S 130/5, 4 cylinders,
1558cc, good condition.
£4,750–5,000 *ADT*

1985 Lotus Esprit Turbo, leather interior,
air conditioning, glass sunroof.
£9,000–9,500 *KSC*

1973 Lotus Europa Twin Cam Special,
5 speed gearbox, finished in JPS black with
gold coach lines, excellent condition.
£12,000–14,000 *KSC*

1989 Lotus Esprit Turbo SE, leather
interior, air conditioning, glass sunroof.
£18,000–18,500 *KSC*

1973 Lotus Elan Sprint Drophead Coupé,
only 13,000 miles from new, hard top,
excellent unrestored condition.
£20,000–21,000 *KSC*

1990 Lotus Esprit, non-turbo version of the
new shaped model, air conditioning, glass
sunroof, only 22,000 miles recorded, with
full history.
£15,000–15,500 *KSC*

1989 Lotus Esprit Turbo SE,
air conditioning, glass sunroof,
only 14,000 miles recorded.
£19,000–19,500 *KSC*

MARCOS

Created by Jem Marsh and Frank Costin, the Marcos Gullwing soon established an enviable racing record. The 1172cc side valve Ford engined Gullwing could accelerate to 60mph in about 7 seconds, and exceed 120mph.

The Marcos Coupé designed in 1964 by Dennis Adams was, like the Gullwing, based on a wooden aircraft-type construction. This was superceded by a steel framed chassis with a variety of engines available. Despite several financial crises, Marcos survived and the company still produce a V8 engined wholly updated version of the Coupé which is as stunning as the original built over 30 years ago.

1967 Marcos 1600GT, Ford 1600 engine, race prepared, very good condition.
£7,500–7,750 *CGOC*

> **Cross Reference**
> Racing Cars

> **Miller's is a price GUIDE not a price LIST**

1968 Marcos 1600GT Sports Coupé, body off rebuild, marine ply replaced where necessary, re-sprayed.
£4,500–5,000 *BKS*

MARCOS Model	ENGINE cc/cyl	DATES	CONDITION 1	2	3
1500/1600/1800	1500/1600/1800/4	1964-69	£7,000	£5,000	£2,500
Mini-Marcos	848/4	1965-74	£3,500	£2,500	£1,500
Marcos 3 litre	3000/6	1969-71	£7,000	£5,000	£4,000

MASERATI

The Maserati legend was almost entirely based on its racing heritage, with awesome pre-war racing cars, winning many Grand Prix. There were 6 Maserati brothers, one of whom, Alfieri, won the 1926 Targa Florio in a 1.5 litre Diatto racer.

Following several changes, Maserati continued to produce world-beating racing cars and, driven by such drivers as Moss, Hawthorn and Fangio, many Grand Prix victories were gained. Maserati still produce highly desirable road-going sports super cars which bear the famous Maserati Trident badge, the badge of Bologna, the city in which the brothers started production.

1964 Maserati Mistral 2 Seater Sports Coupé, 5 speed manual gearbox, engine, gearbox, electrics and chassis in excellent condition, aluminium bodywork good.
£9,500–10,000 *S*

1957 Maserati A6G/54 Spyder, coachwork by Frua, excellent condition.
£75,000–78,000 *COYS*

1966 Maserati Quattroporte 4.7 Litre Sports Saloon, coachwork by Frua, original interior, manual gearbox, left hand drive, braking system requires attention.
£6,500–7,500 *S*

1967 Maserati Mistral 4 Litre GT Coupé,
very well finished, excellent condition.
£13,000–13,500 *S*

Maserati Mistral

- **Launched in 1964, the Mistral was designed by Frua.**
- **Originally powered by a 3500cc engine, it was upgraded to 3700cc with a 4 litre engine option for the coupé version.**
- **The fuel injected 6 cylinder engine of 4014cc could produce 255bhp at 5500rpm.**
- **The Mistral is very sought-after by Maserati enthusiasts.**

1971 Maserati Mexico 2 Door Coupé,
very good condition throughout.
£14,000–15,000 *S*

1972 Maserati Indy 4.7 Litre ZF, 5 speed
manual gearbox, excellent restored condition
throughout.
£19,500–20,000 *Mot*

1970 Maserati 115 Ghibli Coupé,
V8 engine, twin overhead camshaft, 4709cc,
330bhp at 5500rpm, 5 speed manual
synchromesh gearbox, servo assisted
ventilated disc brakes, upper and lower
A-Arms front suspension, coil springs, anti-
roll bar, live axle, radius arms, semi-elliptic
leaf springs rear, left hand drive,
extensively renovated, original interior,
very good condition.
£9,000–9,500 *C*

**1971 Maserati Indy 4.2 Litre Sports
Coupé,** 23,000 miles from new, stored for
7 years, original right hand drive.
Est. £16,000–18,000 *S*

1972 Maserati Mexico Coupé, coachwork
by Vignale, V8, 4719cc 4 cam engine, 290bhp
at 5500rpm, quadruple Weber carburettors,
5 speed ZF gearbox, automatic transmission,
excellent condition throughout.
£12,000–13,000 *COYS*

MASERATI Model	**ENGINE** cc/cyl	**DATES**	**CONDITION**		
			1	2	3
AG-1500	1488/6	1946-50	£30,000	£20,000	£10,000
A6G	1954/6	1951-53	£50,000	£35,000	£22,000
A6G-2000	1985/6	1954-57	£45,000	£35,000	£20,000
3500GT	3485/6	1957-64	£25,000	£15,000	£9,000
5000GT	4935/8	1960-65	£40,000	£20,000	£10,000
Sebring	3694/6	1962-66	£25,000	£18,000	£10,000
Quattroporte	4136/8	1963-74	£15,000	£10,000	£8,000
Mistral	4014/6	1964-70	£15,000	£10,000	£7,500
Mexico	4719/8	1965-68	£18,000	£14,000	£9,000
Ghibli	4719/8	1967-73	£25,000	£20,000	£12,000
Ghibli-spyder	4136/8	1969-74	£50,000	£40,000	£25,000
Indy	4136/8	1969-74	£18,000	£14,000	£9,000
Bora	4719/8	1971-80	£25,000	£18,000	£11,000
Merak	2965/6	1972-81	£18,000	£14,000	£9,000
Khamsin	4930/8	1974-81	£16,000	£10,000	£8,000

1972 Maserati Ghibli SS 4.9 Litre Sports Coupé, only 15,000 miles recorded, very good original condition overall.
£17,000–18,000 *S*

1975 Maserati Merak 3 Litre V6 Sports Coupé, engine fully rebuilt, transmission and gearbox overhauled, interior re-conditioned.
Est. £12,000–14,000 *S*

1977 Maserati Merak SS, 6 cylinders, 2965cc, left hand drive, good general condition, requires some attention.
Est. £8,000–9,000 *ADT*

1986 Maserati Bi-turbo, 6 cylinders, 2500cc, manual gearbox, air conditioning, left hand drive, generally good condition.
Est. £5,000–6,000 *ADT*

MATHIS

1924 Mathis 10hp Cloverleaf 3 Seater Tourer, two-piece opening brass windscreen, requires restoration.
£2,500–3,500 *S*

1973 Maserati Indy 4.9 Litre Sports Coupé, coachwork by Vignale, requires some minor attention, good condition overall.
£10,500–12,000 *S*

Maserati Ghibli

- Styled by Giugiaro at the Ghia studio, the Ghibli was introduced in 1967.
- Featuring the Maserati V8 engine, it could exceed 160mph.
- One of the last great front engined super cars.

1977 Maserati Khamsin 4.9 Litre Sports Saloon, manual 5 speed ZF gearbox, right hand drive, unused for 3 years, requires re-commissioning before use.
Est. £10,000–12,000 *S*

1979 Maserati Merak SS, 6 cylinders, 2965cc, engine and hydraulics re-built, new clutch, very good condition overall.
£10,000–11,000 *ADT*

MATRA

1983 Matra Murena, Chrysler 4 cylinder, 2.2 litre engine, 5 speed gearbox, steel body, good condition throughout.
Est. £3,500–4,500 *ADT*

McLAREN

1969 McLaren M6GT V8 6 Litre Sports Coupé, Chassis No. 02, mid-engined Chevrolet V8, 550bhp, Hewland L. G. 5 speed gearbox, full aluminium monocoque with bonded steel bulkheads, side mounted fuel bags, polyester fibreglass bodywork.
Est. £55,000–60,000 *S*

Chassis No. 02 was the only road car built as a project by Bruce McLaren and was later owned by Denny Hulme and Phil Kerr in New Zealand before finding its way to the United States.

MERCEDES-BENZ

Mercedes-Benz was formed in 1926 with the amalgamation of Mercedes and Benz. This new company based at Stuttgart included three famous names from the Daimler-Benz board, Nibel, Nallinger and, most famous of all, Ferdinand Porsche.

Although Mercedes had made very successful racing cars before WWI, the sports and racing cars produced between the wars were unparalleled. They also manufactured a wide range of saloon cars, all superbly built, from the 170 Series to the 500s. This trend continues today with Mercedes-Benz being one of the world's largest and most successful motor manufacturers.

MAXWELL

The first Maxwell Model L Tourabout was in production by 1905 using a simple water-cooled 2 cylinder engine and within 3 years a full range of 2 and 4 cylinder cars was available, ranging from 14–40hp. Sales were so good that by 1910 Maxwell was the largest automobile manufacturer in America.

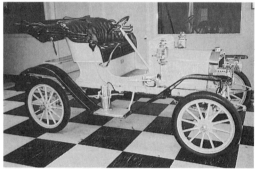

1909 Maxwell Model A, 2 cylinder horizontally opposed 10hp engine, 2 speed planetary gearbox, rear drum brakes, right hand drive, very good restored condition.
Est. £12,000–15,000 *CNY*

1929 Mercedes-Benz Nurburg 460 31.7hp 32/90 Rolling Chassis, part restored to a high standard, requires completing.
£16,500–18,000 *S*

1937 Mercedes-Benz 230 Cabriolet A 2 Seater, coachwork by Sindelfingen, straight 6 side valve, 2229cc engine producing 55bhp at 3000rpm via a single Solex carburettor, 4 speed manual gearbox, 73mph maximum speed, in need of full restoration.
£29,000–30,000 *COYS*

1937 Mercedes-Benz 230 Cabriolet B, coachwork by Sindelfingen, 6 cylinders, 2229cc, original condition, requires total restoration.
£7,000–7,500 *COYS*

1937 Mercedes-Benz 200/230 Cabriolet A, coachwork by Sindelfingen, 6 cylinders, 2229cc, complete but requires restoration.
£13,000–13,500 *COYS*

c1938 Mercedes-Benz 170H Cabriolet,
original specification in all major respects,
Marchal headlamps, museum stored,
paintwork poor, requires restoration.
£6,500–7,500 *S*

1953 Mercedes-Benz 300 Cabriolet D,
coachwork renovated, good original condition
to maker's specification.
Est. £53,000–63,000 *S*

1953 Mercedes-Benz 170S Cabriolet A,
coachwork by Sindelfingen, 4 cylinders,
1697cc, full history, restored to a high
standard, excellent condition.
£28,000–29,000 *COYS*

*During the 1920s Mercedes-Benz concentrated
production on its 6 cylinder machines, such
as the SS/SSK models, together with more
mundane side valve, 6 cylinder models for the
mass market. These were followed in 1930 by
the Type 170 which, with a 1.7 litre,
4 cylinder engine, was the smallest
Mercedes-Benz model yet made.*

1951 Mercedes-Benz 170S Cabriolet A,
original Stuttgart fitted suitcases, original
radio, restored.
Est. £32,000–42,000 *S*

*It was not until 1948 that Mercedes-Benz
production recommenced, and was based on
the successful pre-WWII 170 four cylinder
model. The basic design was laid down in
1931 by the Hungarian Dr. Josef Ganz, a
consulting engineer to Mercedes-Benz, but the
post-war 170s owed more to the 170V
developed in 1935.*

1953 Mercedes-Benz 300B Convertible,
6 cylinder in line engine, 2996cc, 4600rpm,
4 speed manual gearbox, hydraulic drum
brakes all-round, independent coil spring
suspension front and rear, excellent overall
condition, left hand drive.
Est. £40,000–47,000 *CNY*

1954 Mercedes-Benz 300B Saloon,
original interior, running order, requires
cosmetic attention.
£9,800–10,200 *S*

1955 Mercedes-Benz Gullwing, finished
in silver, red interior, totally restored,
good condition.
£125,000+ *BLE*

MERCEDES-BENZ Model	ENGINE cc/cyl	DATES	CONDITION 1	2	3
300AD	2996/6	1951-62	£12,000	£10,000	£8,000
220A/S/SE Ponton	2195/6	1952-60	£7,500	£3,500	£1,800
220S/SEB Coupé	2915/6	1956-59	£9,000	£5,000	£3,500
220S/SEB Cabriolet	2195/6	1958-59	£22,000	£18,000	£7,000
190SL	1897/4	1955-63	£15,000	£12,000	£9,000
300SL 'Gullwing'	2996/6	1954-57	£120,000	£100,000	£70,000
300SL Roadster	2996/6	1957-63	£110,000	£90,000	£70,000
230/250SL	2306/2496/6	1963-68	£13,000	£9,000	£7,000
280SL	2778/6	1961-71	£14,000	£10,000	£8,000
220/250SE	2195/2496/6	1960-68	£8,000	£6,000	£3,000
300SE	2996/6	1961-65	£10,000	£8,000	£5,000
280SE Convertible	2778/6	1965-69	£20,000	£16,000	£12,000
280SE V8 Convertible	3499/8	1969-71	£25,000	£18,000	£15,000
280SE Coupé	2496/6	1965-72	£7,000	£4,000	£3,000
300SEL 6.3	6330/8	1968-72	£12,000	£7,000	£3,500
600 & 600 Pullman	6332/8	1964-81	£25,000	£10,000	£8,000

1963 Mercedes-Benz 300SE, 6 cylinders, 2996cc, very good condition.
£4,000–4,400 *ADT*

1964 Mercedes-Benz 220SE Saloon, original specification, good general condition.
Est. £8,000–9,000 *S*

The 220 engine, with Bosch fuel injection, developed 134bhp at 5000rpm, giving a top speed of about 105mph.

1966 Mercedes-Benz 200 4 Door Saloon, very good original condition.
£1,800–2,000 *S*

1966 Mercedes-Benz 250SE 2.5 Litre 2 Door Coupé, very good overall condition.
£14,000–14,500 *BKS*

1966 Mercedes-Benz 250SE Coupé, 6 cylinders, 2496cc, body fully restored, engine, gearbox and fuel injection system rebuilt, reconditioned radiator, new exhaust system, brakes overhauled, left hand drive, excellent condition.
£18,000–19,000 *COYS*

1966 Mercedes-Benz 250SE Cabriolet, bare metal respray, engine replaced, good overall condition.
Est. £12,000–15,000 *ALC*

1968 Mercedes-Benz 280SE Saloon, low mileage of 56,000, automatic 4 speed gearbox, power assisted steering, good condition.
Est. £7,000–8,000 *S*

1967 Mercedes-Benz 300SE Coupé, fully restored in 1989, very good overall condition.
£15,000-16,000 *S*

1968 Mercedes-Benz 280SE Saloon, right hand drive, good overall condition.
£1,250–1,500 *LF*

1970 Mercedes-Benz 280SE 3.5 Litre 2 Door Coupé, very good restored condition throughout.
Est. £8,000–12,000 *BKS*

Between 1969 and 1971 4,502 right hand drive 280SE 3.5 coupés and convertibles were built with floor mounted automatic transmission and power steering.

1970 Mercedes-Benz 300SEL Long Wheelbase Saloon, excellent restored condition.
Est. £5,000–7,000 *S*

Mercedes-Benz 280SE

- The 280SE 3.5 litre was introduced in 1969 as both a coupé and convertible.
- It was the ultimate in luxury with wood and leather work trim reminiscent of the earlier hand-built cars.
- Performance was remarkable for a 4 or 5 seater car, with 0–60mph in under 10 seconds, and a top speed of 125mph.
- It had an iron block aluminium head V8 engine used in the 350SL range.

1972 Mercedes-Benz 280SE 3.5 Litre Coupé, right hand drive, exterior in good conditon, interior requires restoration.
£1,000–1,100 *C*

1977 Mercedes-Benz 450SEL 6.9 Litre 4 Door Saloon, maintained to a high standard throughout.
£10,000–10,500 *S*

1973 Mercedes-Benz 280CE Coupé, 6 cylinders, 2746cc, excellent condition, full service history, right hand drive.
£2,500–2,800 *COYS*

1977 Mercedes-Benz 450SEL 6.9 Litre, right hand drive, excellent condition throughout.
£7,000–7,500 *COYS*

1978 Mercedes-Benz 280SE Saloon,
sunroof, right hand drive, body
requires attention.
£700–800 *S*

**1979 Mercedes-Benz 450SEL 6.9 Litre
Sports Saloon,** good original condition
throughout.
£10,500–11,000 *S*

1981 Mercedes-Benz 380SEL Saloon,
lowered suspension, dealer-fitted Forenzer
body kit, sports performance wheels and
tyres, overhauled gearbox.
£4,800–5,200 *S*

> ## Locate the source
> *The source of each
> illustration in* Miller's
> Collectors Cars Price
> Guide *can be found by
> checking the code letters
> below each caption with
> the Key to Illustrations.*

1961 Mercedes-Benz 190SL,
good condition.
£17,000–17,500 *ADT*

1960 Mercedes-Benz 190SL Roadster,
body repaired and repainted, mechanically
excellent, good interior condition.
£9,000–9,500 *COYS*

1967 Mercedes-Benz 250SL, hard and soft
tops, good restored condition.
£13,000–13,500 *Mot*

1961 Mercedes-Benz 300SL Roadster,
6 cylinder in line engine, 2996cc, 215bhp,
4 speed manual gearbox, hydraulic disc
brakes all-round, independent coil spring
front suspension, independent swing axle,
coil spring rear, left hand drive, hard top and
fitted luggage, excellent restored condition.
£135,000–140,000 *CNY*

1969 Mercedes-Benz 280SL Roadster,
mileage 45,000, good original interior, left
hand drive.
£9,500–10,000 *S*

1969 Mercedes-Benz 280SL Roadster,
very good restored condition.
Est. £16,500–17,000 *S*

1972 Mercedes-Benz 350SL, 8 cylinders,
3499cc, good mechanical condition.
Est. £13,000–14,000 *ADT*

1972 Mercedes-Benz 350SL, good original
condition, full service history.
£13,500–14,000 *SJR*

1973 Mercedes-Benz 380SL Sports, 66,000
miles, full service history, excellent condition.
£12,000–15,000 *VIC*

1973 Mercedes-Benz 380SL, ABS brakes,
rear seat, hard and soft tops.
£12,000–15,000 *VIC*

**1973 Mercedes-Benz 450SL 2 Seater
Convertible,** recent body-off restoration, soft
and hard tops, hard top damaged, very good
overall condition.
Est. £5,500–6,000 *S*

1984 Mercedes-Benz 280SL,
full service history, 66,000 miles,
excellent condition.
£15,500–16,000 *SJR*

MERCEDES-KNIGHT

1913 Mercedes-Knight 16/45 Tourer,
by Daimler Motoren Gesellschaft, Stuttgart-
Unterturkheim, Germany, 4 cylinder double
sleeve valve, 4086cc, 4 speed right hand
change gearbox, channel section chassis with
beam axles and semi-elliptic leaf springs
front and rear, drum type brakes on rear
wheels, foot operated transmission brake
behind gearbox, centre lock wire type wheels
with 5.00 x 24 tyres, original fittings and
equipment, in running condition.
£28,000–30,000 *C(A)*

*The American designed Knight double sleeve
valve engine became very popular during the
period from 1910 to the late 1920s, due to its
smooth and silent running.*

MG

Cecil Kimber sold tuned versions of William Morris's cars when he was manager of Morris Garages in Oxford, hence the name MG. The first MG produced is open to some discussion, though it is certain that the initial success for MG came with the 847cc MG Midget, based on the Morris Minor. A series of 6 cylinder sports cars was produced alongside the 4 cylinder J-Types, P-Types and, perhaps most famous, the T series. The T series continued into the 1950s with the TF, which was superceded by the MGA series. MG always produced affordable sports cars, and the badge still continues today.

1929 MG M-Type Midget Open Sports, 4 cylinders, 847cc, extensively restored to concours condition, only 53 miles recorded since restoration.
£11,000–12,000 *COYS*

MG Midget

- Based on the 847cc Morris Minor, single overhead camshaft, 4 cylinder engine producing 20bhp.
- With lowered leaf spring suspension, the fabric-bodied boat tail 2 seater was capable of 65mph.
- The Midget, or M-Type, was to become the first British sports car for the masses.

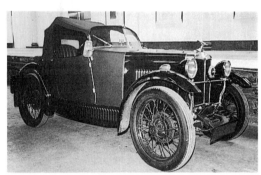

1931 MG M-Type Midget Roadster, older restoration, but very good condition throughout.
Est. £8,000–10,000 *ALC*

c1932 MG K2/L-Type Magna 2 Seater, replica body built in 1960s, fishtail exhaust, quick release filler caps.
£13,500–15,000 *S*

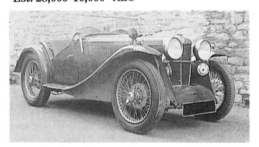

1933 MG J2 Sports 2 Seater, original upholstery, very straightforward and rewarding restoration project.
£5,800–6,200 *S*

Announced in August 1932 and developed from the M-Type and Montlhéry Midgets, the J2 was attractively priced to leave 'ten bob' change out of £200.

1936 MG TA 2 Seater Sports, very good condition throughout.
£9,000–9,500 *S*

MG Model	ENGINE cc/cyl	DATES	CONDITION		
			1	2	3
14/28	1802/4	1924-27	£26,000	£18,000	£10,000
14/40	1802/4	1927-29	£25,000	£18,000	£10,000
18/80 Mk I/Mk II/Mk III	2468/6	1927-33	£40,000	£28,000	£20,000
M-Type Midget	847/4	1928-32	£11,000	£9,000	£7,000
J-Type Midget	847/4	1932-34	£14,000	£12,000	£10,000
J3 Midget	847/4	1932-33	£18,000	£14,000	£12,000
PA Midget	847/4	1934-36	£13,000	£10,000	£8,000
PB Midget	936/4	1935-36	£14,000	£10,000	£8,000
F-Type Magna	1271/6	1931-33	£22,000	£18,000	£12,000
L-Type Magna	1087/6	1933-34	£22,000	£16,000	£12,000
K1/K2 Magnette	1087/6	1932-33	£45,000	£40,000	£35,000
N Series Magnette	1271/6	1934-36	£35,000	£30,000	£20,000
TA Midget	1292/4	1936-39	£13,000	£12,000	£9,000
SA 2 litre	2288/6	1936-39	£22,000	£18,000	£15,000
VA	1548/4	1936-39	£12,000	£8,000	£5,000
TB	1250/4	1939-40	£15,000	£11,000	£9,000

Value will depend on body style, history, completeness, racing history, the addition of a supercharger and originality.

1947 MG Y-Type Safety Saloon,
unrestored, requires attention, dry stored.
Est. £3,000–4,000 *N*

1938 MG TA, 4 cylinders,
1588cc, chassis-up
rebuild, re-sprayed,
excellent condition.
£9,000–10,000 *ADT*

1946 MG TC, full chassis-up rebuild, original
engine and gearbox, very good condition.
£14,000–14,500 *H&H*

*The TC was in production from 1945-49 for
British buyers, initially at the basic price of
£375. The TC had risen in price to £412 by
mid-1946.*

1953 MG TF, some
minor attention
required, very good
condition throughout.
£10,500–11,000 *ADT*

1951 MG TD 1250cc Sports 2 Seater,
excellent condition throughout.
£14,000–14,500 *S*

*The T Series began in 1936 with the TA,
followed by the TC which proved to be
immensely popular in the USA. Both had
1250cc engines and synchromesh gearboxes.*

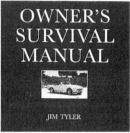
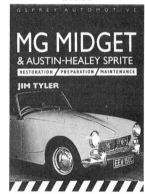

1958 MGA 1500 Roadster, older restoration, standard wheels. £13,000–13,500 *SJR*

1958 MGA Twin-Cam 2 Seater Sports Roadster, rebuilt to the highest standard, excellent condition throughout. **Est. £25,000–28,000** *S*

The twin-cam MGA is a rare car, only 2,111 having been produced between 1958 and 1960. This is a well known concours winning vehicle.

1959 MGA 1500 Roadster, wire wheels, fully restored. £15,000–15,500 *SJR*

1957 MGA 1500, 4 cylinders, 1489cc, restored, good condition. **Est. £11,500–12,500** *ADT*

1958 MGA 1500 Roadster, 4 cylinder, 1498cc rebuilt engine, 4 speed manual gearbox also rebuilt, right hand drive. £8,400–8,800 *ADT*

1960 MGA 1600 Roadster MkI, fully restored USA import, left hand drive, all new chrome and leather trim, new tops and chrome wire wheels. £9,500–10,000 *CCTC*

1971 Rolls-Royce Silver Shadow Long Wheelbase Saloon, V8 engine, 6750cc, automatic gearbox, recently resprayed.
£11,000–12,000 *S*

1973 Rolls-Royce Corniche Fixed Head Coupé, 8 cylinders, 6750cc, automatic gearbox, magnolia leather interior, air conditioning, slight damage to rear bumper, good condition throughout.
Est. £17,000–23,000 *ADT*

1975 Rolls-Royce Camargue Coupé, coachwork by Pininfarina, 8 cylinder, 6750cc engine, cream leather upholstery, front headlamp wipers.
Est. £18,000–20,000 *ADT*

1975 Rolls-Royce Camargue 2 Door Saloon, coachwork by Mulliner Park Ward, extensively restored, excellent condition throughout.
£24,000–28,000 *S*

1975 Rolls-Royce Silver Shadow I Long Wheelbase Saloon, rear window reduced, Everflex roof, cream leather upholstery, very good condition.
£9,500–10,500 *S*

1975 Rolls-Royce Silver Shadow Long Wheelbase Saloon, 8 cylinder, 6750cc engine, air conditioning, good condition throughout.
£14,000–15,000 *ADT*

1976 Rolls-Royce Camargue 2 Door Saloon, coachwork by Mulliner Park Ward, 6.7 litres, V8 engine, leather upholstery, only 20,000 miles recorded.
£40,000–43,000 *S*

1976 Rolls-Royce Silver Shadow, 8 cylinder, 6750cc engine, automatic gearbox, beige leather interior, repainted, good condition.
£8,000–9,000 *ADT*

1976 Rolls-Royce Silver Shadow, 8 cylinders, Shadow II style front spoiler, excellent mechanical condition.
Est. £9,000–10,000 *ADT*

1977 Rolls-Royce Silver Shadow II Saloon, V8 engine, steel monocoque chassis, new exhaust, air conditioning, good condition.
Est. £11,500–13,000 *S*

1968 Rover P6 2000 TC Series 1 Saloon,
2 Litres, 39,000 miles recorded from new,
excellent original condition.
£3,800–4,200 *BKS*

1984 Rover Vitesse, 3.9 litres, 5 speed manual
gearbox, excellent restored body.
£3,000–3,250 *Mot*

1933 Singer Fourteen 1.7 Litre Saloon, Startix
automatic electric engine, Singer clutchless gear
change, self-cancelling indicators, good condition.
£5,000–6,000 *BKS*

*A dashboard control enables the freewheel
mechanism to be operated.*

1932 SS II Fixed Head Coupé, 4 cylinder, 1006cc
engine, 3 speed transmission, unrestored but
complete, an excellent restoration project.
£6,250–6,750 *BKS*
*Just 549 examples of this coupé were produced in
1932–33, at a cost of £210 each.*

**1936 SS 100 2½ Litre
2 Seater Roadster,**
completely restored,
excellent condition.
Est. £70,000–80,000 *BKS*

*Total production of the
SS 100 was 314 in both
engine variants.*

1936 SS II 1.3 Litre 2 Door Saloon, 21,000 miles
recorded from new, original leather upholstery
cracked, very good overall condition.
£14,000–15,000 *BKS*

Less than 90 examples of this luxury car were produced.

**1948 Standard Flying Eight 1 Litre 4 Seater
Tourer,** smooth running engine, older well
maintained restoration.
£5,000–5,500 *BKS*

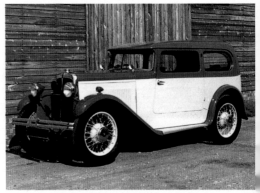

1931 Standard Big Nine 2 Door Saloon,
coachwork by Swallow, very good restored condition.
£13,250–13,750 *BKS*

1927 Sunbeam 16hp Tourer, 6 cylinder, 2035cc rebuilt engine, all brightwork in good condition, very good condition throughout.
Est. £19,000–22,000 *ADT*

1954 Sunbeam Alpine Special, 4 cylinders, 2267cc, twin choke downdraught Solex carburettor with double manifold, 97bhp at 4500rpm, 0–60mph in under 17 seconds, excellent restored condition.
£15,000–16,000 *COYS*

1950 Talbot-Lago T26 GS 'Grand Sport' Coupé, coachwork by Saoutchik, 6 cylinder in-line, 4482cc engine, 190bhp at 4200rpm, 4 speed Cotal pre-selector gearbox, hydraulic drum brakes, good condition.
£62,000–65,000 *CNY*

1921 Talbot Type 4SW 25/50hp Saloon, 4 cylinders side valve, 4520cc, 4 speed gearbox, totally restored, good all-round condition.
£18,000–20,000 *S*

1959 Triumph TR3A, 4 cylinder, 1991cc engine, disc brakes on front wheels, left hand drive, 84,000 miles recorded, recent rebuild, excellent condition.
Est. £9,000–12,000 *COYS*

1959 Triumph TR3A Open Sports, 4 cylinder, 1991cc engine, TR4 gearbox with syncromesh 1st gear and overdrive, recent gound-up restoration, superb example.
£11,000–12,000 *COYS*

1954 Triumph TR2 Roadster, 2000cc engine, long door, completely restored, very good condition.
£6,500–8,500 *ALC*
This is a good example of a classic sports car.

1965 Triumph TR4A, fitted with wire wheels, very sound unrestored condition, left hand drive.
£6,250–6,750 *NTC*

1968 Triumph TR5, chrome wire wheels, rebuilt to a high standard.
£9,500–10,500 *NTC*

1969 Triumph TR6, 2498cc engine, complete chassis-up rebuild, chrome wire wheels, overdrive, 85,000 miles recorded from new.
£5,500–6,500 *H&H*

1969 Triumph TR6, 150bhp, right hand drive original, fair condition.
£3,500–4,000 *CCTC*

1973 Triumph TR6, 150bhp, totally restored, excellent condition.
£10,000–10,500 *BLE*

1972 Triumph TR6, 150bhp, original body and chassis, right hand drive, excellent condition.
£6,500–6,750 *CCTC*

1974 Triumph TR6, original right hand drive, overdrive, good condition throughout.
£7,000–10,000 *VIC*

1973 Triumph TR6, rebuilt, finished in original colour with black trim, concours condition.
£9,250–9,750 *NTC*

1973 Triumph Stag 3 Litre Sports 2+2 Seater, manual transmission, good condition throughout.
Est. £4,000–6,000 *BKS*

1973 Triumph Stag 3 Litre Sports 2+2 Seater, automatic transmission, excellent black interior trim, very good overall condition.
£5,750–6,250 *BKS*

1973 Triumph Stag Mk II, original V8 engine, automatic transmission, good original condition, hard and soft tops.
£3,500–3,750 *CCTC*

1975 Triumph Stag, rebuilt engine, automatic transmission, very good condition throughout.
£5,500–6,000 *LF*

1970 TVR Tuscan V6 Coupé, well maintained, very good condition.
£3,000–4,000 *COYS*

This car was displayed by TVR at the 1970 Motor Show.

1923 Vauxhall OD 23/60 Tourer, coachwork by Kington, 4 cylinder, 3963cc engine, extensively restored, excellent condition.
Est. £38,000–45,000 *COYS*

1934 Vauxhall 14/6 Four Door Saloon, good restored condition.
£5,750–6,500 *OMH*

1924 Vauxhall 30/98 OE Wensum Style Tourer, recently the subject of extensive restoration.
Est. £55,000–65,000 *S*

1962 Vauxhall VX/490 Saloon, dry stored since 1974, very good original condition.
£2,500–2,800 *ALC*

1950 Volkswagen Beetle, 4 cylinder air-cooled, 1131cc engine, 25bhp at 3300rpm, 4 speed gearbox, 4 wheel drum brakes, left hand drive, in sound condition.
£4,000–4,500 *CNY*
This car was one of the first Beetles to be exported to USA.

1963 Volvo P1800 1.8 Litre Sports Coupé, coachwork by Pressed Steel/Jensen, engine in good condition, bodywork completely rebuilt.
£4,000–4,400 *BKS*

r. **1932 Wolseley Hornet 1.2 Litre 4 Seater Sports Tourer,** coachwork by Swallow, good overall condition.
£12,000–13,000 *BKS*

1970 Austin 6cwt Van, 1098cc engine, fitted with new wings, good condition throughout.
£2,100–2,300 *LF*

1954 Fordson 8cwt Pick-Up Conversion, good overall condition.
£1,200–1,300 *LF*
Converted from a Fordson 5cwt van.

c1895 Shand Mason Horsedrawn Fire Engine with Steam Pump, spoon braking on rear wheels, sympathetically restored, retaining originality in all major respects, complete with hoses, seating for five.
£12,400–12,800 *S*

1927 Ford Model TT Fire Truck, 4 cylinder, L-head, 176.7cu in engine, 20bhp at 1600rpm, planetary gearbox, rear drum brakes, left hand drive, good condition following a period of museum display.
£8,500–9,500 *CNY*

1948 Austin K2 3.5 Litre 2 Ton Dropside Truck, well restored historic commercial vehicle, good condition throughout.
£4,000–4,400 *BKS*

1965 Morris FGR40 Dropside Lorry, has been in continuous use since new, well maintained, in entirely original and excellent condition.
Est. £2,000–4,000 *ALC*

1961 Ford Thames 7cwt Utility, side windows are a later addition, good condition overall.
£1,400–1,600 *LF*
These vehicles were once common, but are now rare.

1910 Panhard et Levassor Wine Truck, 4 cylinder in-line engine, 2440cc, 16hp, 4 speed in line manual gearbox, drum brakes, solid suspension.
Est. £30,000–36,000 *CNY*

1944 Ford Jeep 2.2 Litre Open Utility, less than 30,000 miles recorded from new, restored for display at Chudleigh Motor Museum.
Est. £4,000–6,000 *BKS*
One of 290,000 built by Ford during WWII.

**1957–58 Aston Martin DBR2 4.2 Litre
2 Seater Sports Racer,** a well known and
historic race car in superb restored condition.
£800,000+ *BKS*
The ex-works Stirling Moss/George Constantine.

c1937 The Attenborough Special, VSCC eligible,
by Harliss and Stokes, based on a 1926 GP Frazer
Nash chassis, dry sump 2 litre Aston Martin engine,
supercharged by a Godfrey blower.
£35,000–45,000 *S*

1936 Austin Seven Monoposto, built by Wragg,
VSCC registered, excellent condition.
£12,500–13,000 *Car*

**1980–90 Austin Seven 750cc Single Seater
Racer,** by Sherwood Restorations, recently rebuilt
engine, VSCC racing potential.
Est. £8,000–12,000 *BKS*

Chassis stamped 'works 011' from a series of 12.

1959 Austin Healey 3000 Mk I Competition,
modified to full works competition specification in
the 1960s, excellent restored condition.
Est. £20,000–26,000 *COYS*

1948 Bardon-Turner-JAP Formula Junior,
single cylinder, 500cc engine, complete but in need
of race preparation.
£3,000–3,400 *COYS*

1980 BMW M1 Mid-Engined Competition Coupé,
March Engines Ex-Le Mans 'IMSA Category', restored to
1980 Le Mans form, 3.5 litre fuel-injected race engine.
£52,000–54,000 *BKS*

1967 Brabham BT 21B, 4 cylinder, 1038cc rebuilt
Cosworth SCA engine, excellent condition.
£16,000–18,000 *COYS*

1991 Caterham Super Seven 1700 BDA,
4 speed live axle, adjustable seats, competition
exhaust and oil cooler.
£12,000–12,500 *KSC*

1957 Arnott Le Mans Gullwing Coupé,
FWA engine, Triumph 4 speed gearbox,
top speed 135mph, restored to exact
original specification, excellent condition.
Est. £22,000–27,000 *COYS*

1971 Chevron B19, prepared for racing, good condition.
£40,000–42,000 *COYS*

This was the works car driven by Chris Craft, and due to the successes of Chevron 35 of these cars were sold.

1969 Alexis MK15, restored by Jester Racing.
£10,000+ *Car*

An ideal 'budget' historic Formula Ford.

1968 Chevron B8 BMW, original and race ready.
£39,000–40,000 *Car*

Although this car has been prepared ready to race, it has not done so for several years.

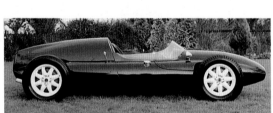

**1957 Cooper-Climax T43 Formula 2 1.5 Litre
Single Seater,** very good overall condition,
excellent chassis and transmission.
Est. £28,000–34,000 *BKS*

1953 Cooper Mk7A JAP 500cc F3,
recently fully restored.
£15,000–16,000 *Car*

This car was the last 500 driven by Stirling Moss.

**1928 Dixon's Graphite Special 3.5 Litre Single Seater
Racing Car,** bodywork by Dreyer of Indianapolis, VSCC
blue form, very good condition throughout.
Est. £18,000–20,000 *S*

1972 Elden Mk10C Formula Ford, very
competitive pre-1974 Championship contender.
£7,500–8,000 *Car*

1967 Ford Cortina GT 1.5 Litre 2 Door Saloon, to competition specification, with roll cage, racing seats with full safety harness, plumbed in fire extinguisher system, very good restored condition. **Est. £6,000–8,000** *BKS*

1959 Gemini BMC MkII Formula Junior, polished alloy, restored, with FIA papers, excellent condition. **£15,000–16,000** *Car*

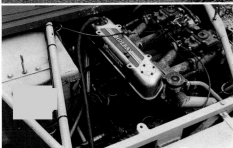

1964 Ginetta G4R, 1500cc Holbay racing engine, a rare model R with independent rear suspension. **£20,000+** *Car*

1986 Ford Sierra Cosworth, built to the highest standard by Roger Dowson Engineering. **Est. £6,000–7,000** *H&H*

This car won the 1990 Firestone Production Saloon Car Championship, driven by Andy Middlehurst.

1963 Ford Anglia, prepared for historic rallying, excellent condition throughout. **£5,750–6,250** *Car*

This car finished in the 1994 Historic Monte Carlo Rally.

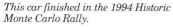

1987 Harrier LR7, 4.2 litre Rovercraft V8 engine, 320bhp, Weber carburettors, with dry sump system, Hewland FT200 5 speed gearbox, monocoque tub with unequal length wishbone front suspension, blade type anti-roll bar. **Est. £12,000–16,000** *COYS*

The original Spyder bodywork is also available with this car.

1953 Jaguar C-Type 3.4 Litre 2 Seater Competition Sports, a well known and historic racing car with provenance and history. **Est. £230,000–260,000** *BKS*

1962 Jaguar E-Type 3.8 Litre, coachwork in the style of E2A, Weber carburettors, restored to road race specification, converted from an early right hand drive fixed head coupé, re-panelled in aluminium. **£26,000–28,000** *BKS*

l. **1961 Jaguar E-Type 3.8 Litre Competition Roadster,** 6 cylinders, 3781cc original engine, 9:1 compression ratio, lightened flywheel, competition clutch springs, close ratio gearbox, restored to near original specification. **£45,000–50,000** *COYS*

1955 Jaguar XK140 C-Type Coupé, 3.8 litre engine, straight port cylinder head, 2in carburettors, disc brakes and 72-spoke chrome wire wheels, original right hand drive. **£14,000–14,500** *HRR*

1964 Jaguar MkII 3.8 Litre Coombs Modified 4 Door Saloon, 0–60mph in 7 seconds, lightened and balanced clutch and flywheel, compression ratio of 9 or 10:1, twin 2in carburettors, Koni shock absorbers. **Est. £35,000–45,000** *BKS*

1976 Jaguar XJ12C 5.3 Litre 2 Door Coupé Group 2 Broadspeed 'Big Cat' Racing Replica, V12 engine, prepared to full competition specification. **Est. £12,000–16,000** *BKS*

This car is not prepared to full competition specification, being more a visual replica of the original racing design.

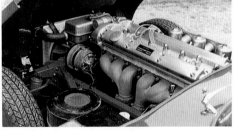

r. **1966 Jaguar E-Type,** in excellent condition. **£29,500+** *Car*

This car has successfully completed several Historic Rallies.

1989 Ex-Works Jaguar XJR-11 Sports-Racing Coupé , 6 cylinder, 3000cc engine, rebuilt by TWR with a 3 litre IMSA engine, excellent condition throughout.
£62,000–66,000 *COYS*

One of only 6 Jaguar XJR-11s produced.

1966 Lola T70 Spyder, in ready to race condition.
£150,000+ *Car*

This is a very famous Can-Am car driven by Denny Hulme to many wins including the TT.

1961 Lotus 20 Formula Junior, updated to Lotus 22 specification, restored, excellent condition.
£22,000–24,000 *Car*

This car was the winner in 5 class races in 1994.

1968 Lotus 51 Formula Ford, original Renault gearbox, restored, excellent condition, very collectable.
£19,500–20,000 *Car*

1954 Kurtis-Lincoln Model 500 2 Seater Sports Roadster, 7 litre Lincoln V8 engine, Holley carburettors, 3-into-1 exhaust headers, adjustable Rose jointed suspension and vented front brakes, period safety harness and roll bar.
Est. £20,000–25,000 *BKS*

1958 Lotus 7 Series 1, 998cc BMC engine
all alloy body, fully restored.
£15,000–16,000 *Car*

**1961 Lotus 20 Formula Junior Ex-Works Team
Lotus Car,** updated to Lotus 22 specification,
fully restored.
£25,000–26,000 *Car*
This car is currently competing in Historic events.

1964 Lotus Elan Series 1, 185bhp racing Lotus twin
cam engine, prepared to full race specification.
£25,000–27,000 *Car*
*This car holds an excellent record as a competitor in
Historic GT events.*

1964 Lotus Elan Series 1, in full FIA, GTS
racing trim.
£22,500–23,000 *CAR*
*An ideal vehicle for Historic events both at home
and abroad.*

1969 Lotus 61 Formula Ford, restored to
excellent ready to race condition.
£15,000–15,500 *Car*
*A fine example of the 'Flying Wedge'. A very
collectable car.*

1969 Merlyn Mk11A, restored in 1993, lap record
holder at Spa.
£17,500–18,500 *Car*
*This car holds 6 class wins from 9 months of
Historic racing.*

1971 Merlyn Mk20 Formula Ford, restored.
£15,000–15,500 *Car*

A very competitive car in pre-1971 Historic Formula Ford Series events.

1966 MGB Roadster, mildly tuned engine, overdrive, up-rated suspension, bucket seats, wire wheels, hard top, fire extinguisher.
£8,000–8,500 *HRR*

Prepared to competition standard in Historic Rallies.

1933 Dixon Riley, all the unique Dixon Riley components are still on this car including a button-type throttle pedal and a steering column mounted hand throttle to facilitate downshifting, the most original and successful of the pair of Dixon Rileys still in existence, actively campaigned in VSCC.
Est. £130,000–150,000 *S*

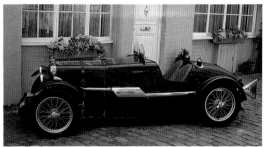

1934 MG Midget Q-Type Replica, 4 cylinders, 965cc, Phoenix crankshaft, Cosworth pistons, Marshall K100 supercharger, 8.39 rear axle, close ratio gearbox, maximum speed 100mph, concours condition.
Est. £28,000–33,000 *COYS*

1989 Porsche RLR 962/201 Group C Competition Car, built by Richard Lloyd Racing from a 956, raced at Le Mans and WSPC, used for display purposes.
Est. £60,000–70,000 *S*

1972 Renault Alpine A110 1600S, in Group 4 rally trim, very good condition.
£18,000–18,500 *Car*

This car has competed in Historic rally events.

r. **1967 Ex-Works MGC GTS,** 6 cylinder, 2968cc engine, re-discovered in 1986 on its return to the UK, in original condition, comprehensively restored throughout.
£46,000–48,000 *COYS*

1905 Star 70hp 10 Litre 4 Cylinder Gordon Bennett Racing 2 Seater, 10,168cc engine, restored to full 100mph racing condition, magnificent and historically important car. **£155,000+** *BKS*

1933 White Riley, this unique and great car is in perfect working order. **Est. £180,000–210,000** *S*

One of the finest racing/sports cars of the 1930s with a continuous history.

1978 Triumph TR7, V8 engine, 5 speed gearbox, prepared ready to race standard with all safety equipment. **£4,250–4,750** *HRR*

1977 Toyota Technic TT773 Formula Three, restored, in perfect ready to race condition. **£12,500–13,500** *Car*

1963 Volvo PV544. **£8,500–9,500** *Car*

This car finished 2nd in the 1994 Monte Carlo Historic Rally, driven by Roger Eland.

1992 Ferrari 196S Replica, 6 cylinder, 1987cc engine, made in Italy. **Est. £35,000–40,000** *COYS*
This is such a perfect copy that it is virtually impossible to detect that it is not an original car.

1981 Auburn 851 Speedster Replica, Chevrolet V8 engine, automatic transmission, fibreglass body, 2 seater, left hand drive. **£15,000–15,500** *Mot*

1994 EG Autokraft Ferrari 365GTB/4 LM 5.3 Litre Daytona Replica, a jig-built space frame similar to original, mechanics based on Jaguar XJS, 265bhp V12 engine, 4 speed gearbox to a limited-slip differential unit. **Est. £15,000–18,000** *BKS*

1994 Ford GTD40 MkIIA, V8, 5200cc engine,
all other components selected to respect the spirit
of the original.
£25,000–30,000 *COYS*

1991 Dax GT40 5 Litre Coupé, 300bhp,
302cu in Ford V8 engine, 0–60mph
in under 5 seconds.
Est. £17,000–20,000 *BKS*
*Genuine GT40s are rarely sold at auction, the last
one reached a price of £250,000.*

**1990 Jaguar D-Type 3.8 Litre Replica 2 Seater
Sports Roadster,** by L & R Roadsters, XK Series
6 cylinder engine, 4 speed gearbox.
£20,000–21,000 *BKS*

**1964 Jaguar E-Type 3.8 Litre Reproduction
'Lightweight' Coupé.**
£60,000–62,000 *BKS*

This car is a well detailed reproduction.

1987/90 Transformer HF2000 Stratos, aluminium
2.3 litre, 230bhp Dino engine, Ferrari 5 speed transaxle,
1,250 miles recorded.
£15,000–16,000 *COYS*

**1989 Kougar Sports Mk2 4.2 Litre 2 Seater
Roadster,** 4.2 litre Jaguar 6 engine, high lift
cams, triple SU carburettors, 5 speed gearbox.
£17,000–19,000 *BKS*

c1988 Maserati 450S Replica, V8, 4200cc twin plug
head engine, excellent overall condition.
£23,000–25,000 *COYS*

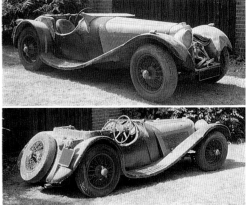

1929 Rolls-Royce 20/25 Saloon with Division,
coachwork by Victor Broom (1928) Ltd., recently
discovered, the aluminium bonnet is pitted but
original, requires general attention and recommissioning.
£7,500–9,000 *S*

1937 Jaguar SS100 2½ Litre Sports 2 Seater,
one of the most original SS100 Jaguars, an exciting
discovery and interesting restoration project.
£65,000–68,000 *S*

The Savage Replica Agricultural Engine, requires careful recommissioning.
Est. £10,000–15,000 *S*

1921 Clayton Steam Wagon with Box Van, 'The Fenland Princess', has not been steamed in recent years and requires careful recommissioning.
Est. £25,000–30,000 *S*

1927 Foden D Type Showman's Steam Tractor 'Angelina', requires recommissioning with the usual safety checks.
£34,000–36,000 *S*

1923 Horsedrawn Bow-Top Living Wagon, by Fred Hill of Swinefleet, well restored example.
Est. £20,000–30,000 *S*

1908 Horsedrawn Reading Wagon, by Dunton & Sons, unusually decorated waist panels, the subject of a 4 year restoration.
Est. £30,000–40,000 *S*

1915 Horsedrawn Ledge Wagon, by Dunton & Sons, Reading, restored over a 4 year period, with extensive external gilded carving of 400 doves and acanthus leaves, excellent condition.
Est. £30,000–40,000 *S*

1908 Horsedrawn Bow-Top Living Wagon, by William Wright of Rothwell Haigh, Leeds, restored over 2 years, excellent overall condition.
Est. £20,000–30,000 *S*

1960 MGA MkI Roadster, disc brakes, rebuilt, excellent condition.
£9,000–11,000 *VIC*

1960 MGA 1600 MkII, completely restored.
£11,750–12,500 *BLE*

1978 MG Midget 1500, 4 cylinders, 1491cc, reconditioned engine, good condition throughout.
£2,500–2,800 *ADT*

1964 Ex-Works MGB Roadster, 4 cylinders, 1801cc, excellent condition.
£25,000–27,000 *COYS*

This historically important MGB was MG's penultimate works entry at Le Mans, and one of just 3 lightweight MGBs built.

> **Cross Reference**
> Racing Cars

1966 MGB Roadster, 4 cylinders, 1798cc, very good condition throughout.
£3,500–3,800 *ADT*

1968 MGC GT, 6 cylinder, 2912cc engine, stainless steel exhaust, re-upholstered, reconditioned engine, good condition throughout.
Est. £5,600–6,600 *ADT*

Although visually similar to the MGB, the MGC model featured a 3 litre straight six engine which produced 145bhp at 5250rpm.

1969 MGB GT, 4 cylinders, 1797cc, wire wheels, very good all-round condition.
Est. £2,000–2,500 *ADT*

1971 MGB 2 Seater Sports, rebored engine only 826 miles recorded since, overhauled gearbox, new upholstery, stainless steel exhaust.
£8,500–8,800 *S*

Introduced in 1962 as a new replacement for the MGA, the B featured unit construction, 95bhp, a 1795cc overhead valve engine and was available as an open 2 seater or as a GT coupé.

1959 MG Magnette, good original condition.
£1,500–1,750 *OMH*

1986 MG Metro 6R4 3 Litre Sports Competition Coupé, Goodman 3 litre 350bhp engine, only 350 miles from new.
Est. £15,000–18,000 *S*

The MG Metro 6R4 was a mid-engined 2 seater with 4 wheel drive and a turbocharged V6 2.6 litre twin-cam engine. In standard form it gave 250bhp but many examples, including the works cars, sometimes gave nearly twice that power.

1958 MG Magnette ZB Varitone, good original condition.
£2,750–3,250 *OMH*

Cross Reference
Racing Cars

MG Model	ENGINE cc/cyl	DATES	CONDITION 1	2	3
TC	1250/4	1946-49	£13,000	£11,000	£7,000
TD	1250/4	1950-52	£13,000	£9,000	£5,000
TF	1250/4	1953-55	£15,000	£13,000	£8,000
TF 1500	1466/4	1954-55	£16,000	£14,000	£9,000
YA/YB	1250/4	1947-53	£5,500	£2,750	£1,500
Magnette ZA/ZB	1489/4	1953-58	£3,000	£2,000	£500
Magnette Mk III/IV	1489/4	1958-68	£2,500	£850	£350
MGA 1500	1489/4	1955-59	£9,000	£6,500	£3,500
MGA 1500 FHC	1489/4	1956-59	£7,000	£5,000	£3,000
MGA 1600	1588/4	1959-61	£11,000	£9,000	£4,500
MGA 1600 FHC	1588/4	1959-61	£7,000	£5,000	£3,000
MGA Twin Cam	1588/4	1958-60	£17,000	£12,000	£9,000
MGA Twin Cam FHC	1588/4	1958-60	£14,000	£9,000	£7,000
MGA 1600 Mk II	1622/4	1961-62	£12,000	£10,000	£4,000
MGA 1600 Mk II FHC	1622/4	1961-62	£9,000	£7,000	£3,000
MGB Mk I	1798/4	1962-67	£7,000	£4,000	£1,200
MGB GT Mk I	1798/4	1965-67	£5,000	£3,500	£1,000
MGB Mk II	1798/4	1967-69	£7,500	£4,000	£1,500
MGB GT Mk II	1798/4	1969	£4,500	£2,500	£850
MGB Mk III	1798/4	1969-74	£6,500	£4,000	£1,100
MGB GT Mk III	1798/4	1969-74	£4,500	£2,500	£1,000
MGB Roadster (rubber bumper)	1798/4	1975-80	£6,000	£4,500	£1,200
MGB GT	1798/4	1975-80	£4,000	£3,000	£1,000
MGB Jubilee	1798/4	1975	£6,000	£3,000	£1,200
MGB LE	1798/4	1980	£8,500	£4,750	£2,250
MGB GT LE	1798/4	1980	£6,000	£3,750	£2,000
MGC	2912/6	1967-69	£8,000	£6,500	£4,000
MGC GT	2912/6	1967-69	£6,000	£4,500	£2,000
MGB GT V8	3528/8	1973-76	£8,250	£6,000	£3,000
Midget Mk I	948/4	1961-62	£4,000	£2,000	£850
Midget Mk II	1098/4	1962-66	£3,000	£2,000	£850
Midget Mk III	1275/4	1966-74	£3,200	£2,000	£850
Midget 1500	1491/4	1975-79	£3,000	£2,000	£850

All prices are for British right hand drive cars. Deduct 10-15% for left hand drive varieties, even if converted to right hand drive.

MINERVA

Between the two World Wars, Minerva Motors SA was a most highly respected Belgian marque, developed from a bicycle business founded by Sylvain de Jong in Antwerp. Minerva became a serious and highly regarded motor manufacturer, and one which counted C. S. Rolls amongst its early overseas dealers.

1927 Minerva Model AC 5.3 Litre 4 Door Sports Limousine, with division, coachwork by Hibbard et Darrin, excellent condition throughout.
Est. £40,000–60,000 *BKS*

1984 Mini Monaco 1000cc Cabriolet, only 22,000 miles, excellent condition throughout.
£4,000–4,500 *S*

The Mini Monaco was commissioned by British Leyland and sold through their dealers. Only a few were made, the name Monaco being sanctioned by HRH Prince Rainier of Monaco.

MINI

Project ADO15 was given the approval of Leonard Lord to go into production in 1958, and by August 1959 the Mini was introduced. Designed by Alec Issigonis, the Mini became a cult car, a symbol of the swinging sixties, with front wheel drive, transverse engine and a compact body style. It was produced at Longbridge and Cowley as the Austin and Morris versions, and soon appeared as the Riley Elf and Wolseley Hornet, with increased engine capacity and minor alterations.

1964 Morris Mini 1275cc Cooper S, restored, concours condition.
£9,000–10,000 *S*

The Mini Cooper S was announced in 1963 following work by John Cooper and Issigonis who produced the first 998cc Mini Cooper in July 1961. This second version was to initially feature the 970cc engine and a 1275cc version. The former unit was dropped by 1965. Designed primarily for competition work, the Cooper version was an instant success.

1969 Austin Mini Cooper, 4 cylinders, 998cc, re-sprayed, stainless steel exhaust and manifold, excellent condition.
£4,400–4,800 *ADT*

1965 Morris Mini Saloon, 850cc, good original condition.
£840–880 *LF*

MINI Model	ENGINE cc/cyl	DATES	CONDITION 1	2	3
Mini	848/4	1959-67	£2,000	£900	-
Mini Countryman	848/4	1961-67	£1,800	£900	-
Cooper Mk I	997/4	1961-67	£5,000	£3,000	£1,500
Cooper Mk II	998/4	1967-69	£3,500	£3,000	£1,500
Cooper S Mk I	var/4	1963-67	£6,000	£4,000	£2,000
Cooper S Mk II	1275/4	1967-71	£5,000	£4,000	£2,000
Innocenti Mini Cooper	998/4	1966-75	£3,000	£1,500	-

MMC

The Motor Manufacturing Co. Ltd., of 95 New Bond Street, London, rescued MMC after the collapse of Lawson's Great Horseless Carriage Company. Production of the marque continued at the The Motor Mills, Coventry.

1903 MMC 20hp Rear Entrance Tonneau with Wagonette Body Alternative.
Est. £130,000–150,000 *S*

MORETTI

The Moretti Company took great pride in hand building small stylish sports cars from 1926 until 1960. Unlike many small Italian manufacturers such as Siata, Cisitalia, Abarth and Nardi, Moretti built almost the entire car themselves.

1960 Moretti Tour de Monde Coupé,
4 cylinders, 750cc, single overhead camshaft, extensively restored, requires finishing, very original condition with matching engine and chassis numbers.
£2,600–3,000 *COYS*

1938 Morgan 4/4 Drophead Coupé,
4 cylinders, 1122cc, fully restored, very good condition throughout.
Est. £10,000–15,000 *COYS*

This is one of the extremely rare and very desirable drophead coupé models.

MOON

c1916 Moon 6-30 Touring, 6 cylinder, 224cu in Continental engine, 24½hp, 3 speed gearbox, rear wheel drum brakes, semi-elliptical leaf spring front and rear suspension, left hand drive, fair to good overall condition.
£4,500–5,000 *CNY*

MORGAN

The Morgan Motor Company was founded in 1910 by H. F. S. Morgan, with great encouragement from his father, the Reverend H. G. Morgan, and is still being run by direct descendants. The first cars were three-wheelers, and Morgans remained faithful to this layout until 1939.

1948 Morgan F4 3 Wheeler 4 Seater Tourer, Ford 10hp SV engine, with spare engine.
£5,200–5,600 *HOLL*

1967 Morgan 4/4 2 Seater Sports, chassis-up restoration, engine fully reconditioned, Ford Sierra 4 speed gearbox.
£10,000–10,500 *S*

1973 Morgan 4/4, 1600cc Fiat twin-cam engine, 5 speed gearbox, fully restored.
£10,800–11,200 *H&H*

c1990 Morgan 4/4, Ford 1600cc engine,
5 speed Sierra gearbox.
£16,000–18,000 *FHD*

1964 Morgan +4, excellent condition.
£15,000–20,000 *FHD*

*The Morgan +4 was introduced in 1950 and
finished in 1969. It was originally fitted with
a 2088cc Vanguard engine, but after 1953 a
Triumph TR2 engine was used. The +4 was
re-introduced in 1988.*

1948 Morgan +4 2 Seater, originally built
as the prototype +4 with 1760cc engine,
very rare, excellent restored condition.
£17,000–20,000 *PC*

MORGAN Model	ENGINE cc/cyl	DATES	CONDITION 1	2	3
4/4 Series I	1098/4	1936-50	£9,000	£7,000	£6,000
Plus 4	2088/4	1950-53	£12,000	£9,000	£7,000
Plus 4	1991/4	1954-68	£11,000	£9,000	£7,000
4/4 Series II/III/IV	997/4	1954-68	£8,000+	£6,000	£3,000
4/4 1600	1599/4	1960 on	£11,000	£9,000	£6,000
Plus 8	3528/8	1969 on	£17,000	£13,500	£10,000

1969 Morgan +8, Rover V8, 3.5 litre engine,
Moss gearbox.
£23,000–25,000 *FHD*

*This is now a very collectable Morgan, and
highly sought after.*

1983 Morgan +8, 3.5 litre engine,
very good condition.
£16,000–18,000 *FHD*

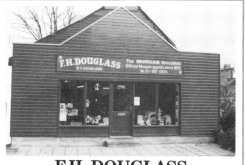

MORRIS

William Morris was firstly a bicycle manufacturer in 1894, and moved on to motorcycles around 1901. The motorcycle business did not prove too successful, and by 1908 he sold his interest to concentrate on his expanding garage business.

By 1910 he operated under the name The Morris Garage. Deciding that he too would manufacture cars, he made car assembly his main line of business in order to produce a high volume of vehicles at a reasonable price.

1921 Morris Cowley 11.9hp Bullnose Tourer, requires restoration and servicing following museum display.
£9,000–10,000 *S*

1923 Morris Cowley 11.9hp Bullnose 2 Seater with Dickey, rebodied, good running order with no major known modifications, excellent restored condition.
£10,000–10,500 *S*

The Bullnose Morris, so called on account of its distinctive radiator, was a remarkable car, designed and built by William Morris. It was assembled from components supplied by outside manufacturers.

1913 Morris Bullnose Oxford, 4 cylinder 1017.8cc in line engine, 16.4bhp at 2400rpm, 3 speed manual gearbox, rear wheel brakes only, semi elliptic front suspension, three-quarter elliptic rear, right hand drive, very good original condition.
£14,000–15,000 *C*

This car is fitted with a Zenith carburettor rather than a White & Poppe, and it is known that the brakes have linings rather than being cast iron.

> *A rebuilt car is not necessarily more valuable than a car in good original condition, even if the restoration has been costly.*

1929 Morris Oxford 14/28 Coupé, 4 cylinders, 1802cc, good all-round condition.
£6,400–6,800 *ADT*

This car has Duralumin connecting rods and aluminium pistons, a 3 bearing crankshaft, with white metal bearings in bronze shells, a 3 speed gearbox, a 5 stud rear axle and 18in artillery wheels. 4 wheel brakes were fitted as standard, with 12in diameter brake drums and half-elliptic springs front and rear.

1927 Morris Cowley Fixed Head Coupé with Dickey, fair condition.
£7,750–8,250 *Bro*

1928 Morris Cowley, 4 cylinders, 1498cc,
good condition overall.
£5,500–6,500 *ADT*

1934 Morris Oxford 16hp, excellent
condition throughout.
£11,500–12,500 *OMH*

MORRIS Model	ENGINE cc/cyl	DATES	CONDITION 1	2	3
Prices given are for saloons					
Cowley (Bullnose)	1550/4	1913-26	£10,000	£8,000	£6,000
Cowley	1550/4	1927-39	£8,000	£6,000	£4,000
Oxford (Bullnose)	1803/4	1924-27	£14,000	£10,000	£6,000
Oxford	1803/4	1927-33	£10,000	£8,000	£6,000
16/40	2513/4	1928-33	£8,000	£7,000	£6,000
18	2468/6	1928-35	£9,000	£7,000	£5,000
8 Minor	847/4	1929-34	£5,500	£4,000	£2,000
10/4	1292/4	1933-35	£5,000	£3,000	£1,500
25	3485/6	1933-39	£10,000	£8,000	£5,000
Eight	918/4	1935-39	£4,000	£3,000	£1,500
10HP	1140/4	1939-47	£4,500	£3,000	£1,500
16HP	2062/6	1936-38	£5,000	£3,500	£2,000
18HP	2288/6	1935-37	£5,000	£3,500	£2,500
21HP	2916/6	1935-36	£6,000	£4,000	£2,500

A touring version of the above is worth approximately 30% more and value is very dependent on body
type and has an increased value if coachbuilt.

1932 Morris Minor Saloon, fully restored.
£4,500–5,000 *OMH*

1933 Morris Minor, 4 cylinders, 1056cc,
correct calorimeter, very good condition.
£4,000–5,000 *ADT*

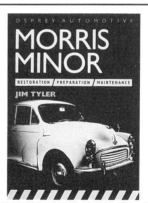

1931 Morris Minor Folding Head Saloon,
4 cylinders, 885cc, little used over five years,
requires re-commissioning, good condition
throughout.
£3,500–4,500 *ADT*

*William Morris's answer to the Austin Seven
was first shown to the public at the London
Motor Show in 1928. It was an immediate hit
and various coachbuilders used the efficient
78in wheelbase to sell to the mass market.
A new side valve version of the car, launched
in 1931, made history as being the first £100
automobile, although it only offered 2 seats.*

1936 Morris 8 Series I Tourer,
good usable condition.
£4,500–5,500 *OMH*

1935 Morris 8 Series I, only 1,000 miles
since overhaul, retrimmed and well restored.
£4,000–4,500 *Bro*

1939 Morris 10 Series M, 4 cylinders,
1140cc, good original condition.
£1,500–1,700 *ADT*

*This car was purchased in 1939 and has
been owned by the same family since.*

**1949 Morris Minor Series MM 2 Door
Saloon,** very good original condition.
£2,200–2,500 *S*

This car featured in the TV series Heartbeat.

MORRIS Model	ENGINE cc/cyl	DATES	CONDITION		
			1	2	3
Minor Series MM	918/4	1948-52	£1,800	£1,000	£300
Minor Series MM Conv	918/4	1948-52	£3,250	£1,500	£650
Minor Series II	803/4	1953-56	£1,500	£850	£300
Minor Series II Conv	803/4	1953-56	£3,000	£2,000	£650
Minor Series II Est	803/4	1953-56	£2,500	£1,000	£350
Minor 1000	948/4	1956-63	£1,750	£925	£250
Minor 1000 Conv	948/4	1956-63	£3,000	£2,000	£750
Minor 1000 Est	948/4	1956-63	£2,000	£1,200	£350
Minor 1000	1098/4	1963-71	£2,000	£950	£250
Minor 1000 Conv	1098/4	1963-71	£3,500	£2,250	£750
Minor 1000 Est	1098/4	1963-71	£3,000	£1,200	£400
Cowley 1200	1200/4	1954-56	£1,675	£1,000	£300
Cowley 1500	1489/4	1956-59	£1,750	£950	£350
Oxford MO	1476/4	1948-54	£2,000	£850	£250
Oxford MO Est	1476/4	1952-54	£3,000	£1,500	£350
Series II/III	1489/4	1954-59	£2,000	£1,200	£300
Series II/III/IV Est	1489/4	1954-60	£2,250	£1,350	£250
Oxford Series V Farina	1489/4	1959-61	£1,800	£800	£250
Oxford Series VI Farina	1622/4	1961-71	£1,750	£750	£200
Six Series MS	2215/6	1948-54	£2,500	£1,500	£500
Isis Series I/II	2639/6	1955-58	£2,500	£1,300	£450
Isis Series I/II Est	2639/6	1956-57	£2,600	£1,350	£500

1954 Morris Minor, 4 cylinders, 803cc, reconditioned engine, new clutch, restored bodywork.
Est. £2,000–2,500 *ADT*

1962 Morris Minor 1000 4 Door Saloon, very good condition throughout.
£2,600–2,800 *S*

1959 Morris Minor Convertible, 4 cylinders, 1098cc, good condition.
£3,300-3,600 *ADT*

1966 Morris Minor 1000 2 Door Deluxe, good condition throughout.
Est. £1,500–2,000 *S*

1968 Morris Oxford, 4 cylinders, 1622cc, stored for a long period.
£100–120 *ADT*

1969 Morris 1300 4 Door Saloon, very good original condition.
£1,100–1,200 *S*

Developed from the 1100, and continuing the front wheel drive theme of the Issigonis Mini, the 1300 proved to be a best seller in the 1960s until 1971, when Morris-badged versions were discontinued.

1966 Morris Mini Moke, 4 cylinders, 848cc, restored.
Est. £2,000-2,200 *ADT*

Cross Reference
Mini

NAPIER

1912 Napier Colonial 15hp Tourer, requires re-commissioning after long period of museum exhibition.
£10,000–13,000 *S*

The 15hp Napier was introduced in 1909, a 4 cylinder car, with engine cast in pairs and produced alongside the 6 cylinder cars. The front mounted flywheel and worm drive rear axle were specifically designed to give the car extra ground clearance for Colonial use, the target market place for this model.

NASH-HEALEY

1950 Nash-Healey Roadster, 6 cylinders, 3827cc, a rare example, excellent condition.
£10,000–11,000 *COYS*

NSU

Felix Wankel spent many years developing the rotary engine concept, and eventually sold his design to NSU in West Germany. The twin rotor powered unit, called the Ro80, was an incredible machine, revving up to 7000rpm.

1975 NSU Ro80 Sports Saloon, very good overall condition.
£1,400–1,500 *S*

NASH

1919 Nash Model 681 5 Seater Tourer, 4 litre, 6 cylinder engine with pushrod overhead valves, in running order, some cosmetic attention required.
£9,500–11,500 *S*

NEUSTADT-PERRY

The Neustadt-Perry was built by the Neustadt Motor Car Company of St Louis, Missouri, from 1902 until 1907. The company made both steam and petrol types.

1903 Neustadt-Perry 5hp 2 Seater Runabout, single cylinder water-cooled 1500cc engine, 2 forward speeds and reverse, single chain final drive, restored, good condition throughout.
£9,000–10,000 *S*

OLDSMOBILE

1903 Oldsmobile Curved Dash 5hp Runabout, excellent condition throughout.
Est. £12,000–13,000 *S*

OLDSMOBILE Model	ENGINE cc/cyl	DATES	CONDITION 1	2	3
Curved Dash	1600/1	1901-04	£14,000	£13,000	£11,000
30	2771/6	1925-26	£9,000	£7,000	£4,000
Straight Eight	4213/8	1937-38	£12,000	£8,000	£6,000

1936 Oldsmobile Series L Eight 2 Door Convertible, not used for many years, requires attention, right hand drive.
£4,800–6,000 *S*

OPEL

1956 Opel Rekord L 1500cc 2 Door Saloon, to original factory specification, left hand drive, good condition.
£500–600 *S*

ORIENT

Produced by the Waltham Manufacturing Company of Waltham, Massachusetts, the Orient Buckboard was marketed in the UK by the National Motor Company, Manchester. Priced at 90 guineas, the company offered a 60 day guarantee on the car. The design was simple but effective and the car had a claimed top speed of 35mph and would climb a 1:12 hill in top gear.

OWEN

1974 Owen Sedanca 4.2 Litre Coupé, by Williams & Pritchard/Panther Westwinds, extremely rare, good condition throughout.
£4,000–4,400 *BKS*

Exact production figures of these rare cars are unknown, but it is thought that only 4 were completed.

1904 Orient Motor Buckboard 4hp 2 Seater, engine rebuilt, good restored overall condition.
Est. £6,500–7,000 *S*

A single cylinder vertical engine powered the buckboard, with friction drive variable gears and chain drive, and a hickory and ash frame mounted on elliptical front springs and helical rear springs.

PACKARD

1912 Packard Model 30 Seven Passenger Touring, 4 cylinder, T-head 432cu in engine, 3 speed gearbox, rear drum brakes, semi-elliptical leaf spring suspension front and rear, right hand drive, completely restored, correct finish, original colours.
Est. £100,000–113,000 *CNY*

1934 Packard Eight 11th Series Sedan, well maintained throughout.
£16,000–18,000 *S*

PACKARD Model	ENGINE cc/cyl	DATES	CONDITION 1	2	3
Twin Six	6946/12	1916-23	£25,000	£20,000	£13,000
6	3973/6	1921-24	£20,000	£15,000	£12,000
6, 7, 8 Series	5231/8	1929-39	£35,000	£25,000	£14,000
12	7300/12	1936-39	£35,000	£30,000	£18,000

**1929 Packard Standard Eight 6th Series
Sedan,** major restoration, drives well, very
good condition throughout.
£14,000–14,500 *S*

1949 Packard Clipper Saloon,
5.4 litres, imported from America, very
good condition throughout.
£2,100–2,300 *H&H*

PAIGE

**1917 Paige Model 640 7 Passenger
Touring,** 6 cylinders, older restoration.
£12,000–12,500 *GAR*

**1923 Paige Series 670 5 Passenger Sport
Phæton,** frame-off restoration in 1971,
not driven since restoration .
£15,000–16,000 *GAR*

PANHARD ET LEVASSOR

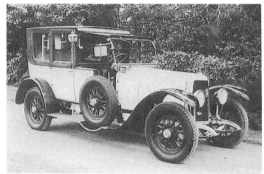

**1920 Panhard et Levassor Open Drive
Coupé Chauffeur,** coachwork by Henri
Binder, Paris, museum stored, engine seized,
requires attention, very good condition.
£32,000–34,000 *S*

PANTHER

Modelled after the original Jaguar SS100,
the Panther J72 was built to a very high
standard and had Jaguar running gear.
In 1974 the company uprated the engine
option to include a V12, 5.3 litre unit.
Production was at the company's factory
in Byfleet, Surrey, and other models in the
range include the DeVille convertible, Lima
and Solo.

1978 Panther J72, 12 cylinders, 5340cc,
very good condition throughout.
Est. £15,000–17,00 *ADT*

PEERLESS

Built between 1957 and 1960 at their Slough
factory, Peerless had been servicing and
repairing American Peerless commercial
vehicles for many years. Initially called the
Warwick, the Peerless GT was based on the
Triumph TR3 and competed at Le Mans in
1958. Only about 300 were built and probably
less than ten survive today.

1959 Peerless GT2 Four Seater Coupé,
good restored condition.
£5,000–5,200 *Bro*

PEUGEOT

1904 Peugeot 5hp Single, VCC dated, restored in 1980s, running well.
£18,500–19,000 *Mot*

1923 Peugeot Type 174 20/30hp Limousine, museum displayed, left hand drive, basically sound condition, requires re-commissioning.
£7,500–8,500 *S*

PEUGEOT Model	ENGINE cc/cyl	DATES	CONDITION 1	2	3
153	2951/4	1913-26	£5,000	£4,000	£2,000
163	1490/4	1920-24	£5,000	£4,000	£2,000
Bebe	676/4	1920-25	£7,000	£6,000	£3,000
156	5700/6	1922-24	£7,000	£5,000	£3,000
174	3828/4	1922-28	£6,000	£4,000	£2,000
172	714/4	1926-28	£4,000	£3,000	£1,500
183	1990/6	1929-30	£4,000	£3,000	£1,500
201	996/4	1930-36	£4,000	£3,000	£1,500
402	2140/4	1938-40	£4,000	£3,000	£1,000

Right hand drive cars will always achieve more interest than left hand drive. Good solid cars.

1956 Peugeot 203 4 Door Saloon, re-upholstered, left hand drive, good original condition.
Est. £1,500–2,000 *S*

The 203 was a compact 4 seater 4 door saloon with 'airline' styling, and sold in the UK for £634 plus £265 purchase tax.

1974 Peugeot 304 S Cabriolet, later type 304 engine, bodywork fair, good mechanical condition, new hood, re-trimmed leather seats.
£2,750–3,250 *CLP*

1974 Peugeot 504 Convertible, good overall condition.
£1,300–1,500 *S*

The cars started life as left hand drive models, although the majority of conversions to right hand drive for the UK market, such as this one, were carried out by Hodec Engineering of Byfleet, Surrey.

1985 Peugeot 205 Turbo 16 Evolution I, 4 cylinder, twin overhead camshaft, 16 valve with Turbo KKK engine, 340bhp at 7600rpm (mid-engined), 5 speed manual gearbox with permanent 4 wheel drive, disc brakes all round (dual circuit), independent suspension, anti-roll bar, left hand drive, excellent restored condition.
£20,000–22,000 *C*

The 205 Turbo 16 was conceived by Peugeot from scratch in 1983 and designed to win the World Rally Championship in Group B which it succeeded in doing in 1985 and '86.

PHOENIX

J. van Hooydonk was a member of the
Phoenix Cycling Club and British importer
and concessionaire for Minerva motorcycles
and engines. In 1903 he founded the Phoenix
Motor Company and commenced production
of motorcycles and three-wheelers in London.

1906 Phoenix 5/6hp Trimo Forecar,
Miller Excelite acetylene lighting, museum
displayed for many years, older restoration,
requires re-commissioning.
£7,000–7,500 *S*

PIPER

The Piper GT was constructed by ex-racing
driver George Henrotte, and featured a
tubular steel backbone frame. It was initially
available with various one litre engines, but
after 1968, ownership of the firm changed
and the so-called GTT featured a bigger
engine, front disc brakes and improved
suspension. Only about 150 Pipers were
ever made.

PIERCE-ARROW

**1917 Pierce-Arrow A 4-66 Seven
Passenger Touring Car,** 6 cylinders,
T-head, 825cu in, 13½ litres, 92bhp at
1800rpm, 4 speed gearbox, rear drum brakes,
front semi-elliptical leaf spring suspension,
three-quarter elliptical rear, right hand
drive, excellent condition throughout.
£120,000–122,000 *CNY*

*According to records, this car was produced
in the second half of 1917 and was delivered
from the factory to the White House on
September 20th 1917 for President Woodrow
Wilson's personal use. Letters from the White
House confirm its history.*
   *As a genuine touring bodied 66 with an
incredible history, it is indeed one of the most
significant cars of this period in existence.*

**1932 Pierce-Arrow Club V8
Brougham,** older restoration,
good condition.
£22,000–22,500 *GAR*

**1969 Piper GTT Fixed
Head Coupé,** body off
restoration in 1985, good
working condition.
£4,000–6,000 *ALC*

PLYMOUTH

1941 Plymouth Coupé,
recently imported from USA,
good running order.
£4,200–4,600 *H&H*

PONTIAC

1950 Pontiac Silver Streak Streamliner Sedan, superb concours winning condition.
£5,500–5,800 *S*

An electronic fuel pump on this car is the only minor modification from the original specification.
The Streamliner Six was offered in 3 styles in 1950, Sedan, Sedan Coupé and Station Wagon, and was available with Hydra-Matic or synchromesh gearbox. The L-head engine displaced some 239 cu in and developed 90bhp at 3400rpm.

PONTIAC Model	ENGINE cc/cyl	DATES	CONDITION 1	2	3
Six-27	3048/6	1926-29	£9,000	£7,000	£4,000
Silver Streak	3654/8	1935-37	£12,000	£9,000	£5,500
6	3638/6	1937-49	£7,000	£4,000	£3,500
8	4078/8	1937-49	£7,000	£4,000	£3,500

PORSCHE

1958 Porsche 356A Super, 4 cylinders, 1600cc, very good condition throughout.
£6,500–7,500 *ADT*

1959 Porsche 356B 1600cc Sports Coupé, original specification, excellent condition throughout.
Est. £10,000–12,000 *S*

1973 Porsche RS 2.7 Litre Touring, only 2 previous owners, very good original condition.
£26,000–28,000 *BKS*

1969 Porsche 911E, 6 cylinders, 1991cc, 5 speed manual gearbox, excellent condition throughout.
Est. £6,000–7,000 *ADT*

Porsche 911

- 911 Carrera first appeared in 1972 and was based on a lightened 911S with a distinctive rear spoiler.
- The air-cooled, flat, 6 cylinder, 2687cc engine produced about 210bhp.
- RS stands for Rennsport (German).
- Top speed of over 150mph and 0–60mph in less than 5 seconds.

1973 Porsche Carrera RS 2.7 Litre, 6 cylinders, 2687cc, electric windows, restored to concours condition, original right hand drive Touring specification.
£27,000–29,000 *COYS*

PORSCHE Model	ENGINE cc/cyl	DATES	CONDITION 1	2	3
356	var/4	1949-53	£12,000	£8,000	£4,000
356 Cabriolet	var/4	1951-53	£20,000	£14,000	£10,000
356A	1582/4	1955-59	£11,500	£7,000	£3,000
356A Cabriolet	1582/4	1956-59	£15,000	£9,000	£7,000
356A Speedster	1582/4	1955-58	£23,000	£19,000	£14,000
356 Carrera	1582/ 1966/4	1960-65	£24,000	£20,000	£15,000
356C	1582/4	1963-65	£11,000	£8,000	£4,000
356C Cabriolet	1582/4	1963-64	£15,000	£12,000	£7,000
911/911L/T/E	1991/6	1964-68	£8,500	£5,500	£3,500
912	1582/4	1965-68	£6,500	£5,000	£2,000
911S	1991/6	1966-69	£11,000	£8,000	£5,500
911S	2195/6	1969-71	£11,000	£8,000	£6,000
911T	2341/6	1971-73	£8,000	£6,000	£4,000
911E	2341/6	1971-73	£9,000	£7,000	£5,000
914/4	1679/4	1969-75	£4,000	£3,000	£1,000
914/6	1991/6	1969-71	£5,000	£3,500	£1,500
911S	2341/6	1971-73	£14,000	£9,000	£7,500
Carrera RS lightweight	2687/6	1973	£32,000	£28,000	£16,000
Carrera RS Touring	2687/6	1973	£30,000	£26,000	£18,000
Carrera 3	2994/6	1976-77	£14,000	£9,000	£7,000
924 Turbo	1984/4	1978-83	£4,500	£3,000	£1,500

Sportmatic cars are less desirable.

1974 Porsche 911 Carrera Targa, excellent condition.
£16,000–17,000 *ADT*

1977 Porsche 911 Carrera 3 Litre Sportmatic, 100,000 miles recorded, electric sunroof, service history, very good condition.
£9,000–12,000 *VIC*

1988 Porsche 911 Club Sport, 6 cylinders, 3165cc, race prepared, now in good condition throughout.
£13,500–14,500 *ADT*

1979 Porsche 928 Coupé, excellent overall condition.
£4,400–4,800 *S*

A departure from all Porsche's traditions, the new 928 of 1977 was powered by a water-cooled V8 cylinder engine of 4474cc capacity, conventionally mounted at the front of the car and driving through the rear wheels. The single overhead camshaft (per bank) engine developed 240bhp at 5500rpm, and the 928 had a maximum speed of 142mph.

PUNGS-FINCH

W. A. Pungs and E. E. Finch, father and son-in-law, went into partnership in 1904. Finch was the engineer, having made his first car in 1902, while Pungs provided the finance and the factory site. Their first productions were the D and F models, several hundred of which were built, but none seem to have survived.

1906 Pungs-Finch Limited Prototype, 4 cylinders, overhead camshaft, 684cu in, 50hp, 3 speed gearbox, rear drum brakes, semi-elliptical leaf spring suspension front and rear, right hand drive, some re-commissioning required following a period of storage.
£46,000–48,000 *CNY*

RAMBLER

The Rambler name was first used on a bicycle made by Thomas B. Jeffery and R. Philip Gormully in Chicago, the second largest bicycle factory in the USA. Prototype cars were built in 1897 and 1898, and in 1900 were displayed at the Chicago and New York automobile shows. These early Ramblers, with front mounted engines, were advanced for an American car of that period.

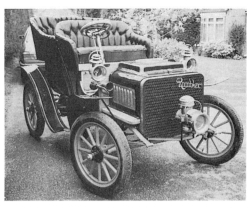

1904 Rambler Model K 16hp 4 Seater Rear Entrance Tonneau, very good overall condition.
Est. £23,000–25,000 *S*

1966 Rambler Classic Sedan, V8 cylinder, 327cu in engine, automatic 3 speed gearbox, monocoque chassis, independent front suspension, beam rear axle, right hand drive, disc front brakes, drum rear, American Motors bolt on wire type wheels, 215 x 15 tyres, Australian assembled, fully restored, excellent original condition.
Est. £7,500–10,000 *C(A)*

RELIANT

1967 Rambler Rogue American Convertible, unused for some time, requires attention.
Est. £800–1,250 *ALC*

1966 Reliant Scimitar, 6 cylinders, 2553cc, Raymond Mays head and triple SU carburettors, comprehensively restored.
Est. £8,000–9,000 *ADT*

Don't Forget!
If in doubt please refer to the 'How to Use' section at the beginning of this book.

1972 Reliant Scimitar GTE, 6 cylinders, 2994cc, fair condition, requires some attention.
£250–300 *ADT*

RELIANT Model	ENGINE cc/cyl	DATES	CONDITION		
			1	2	3
Sabre 4 Coupé & Drophead	1703/4	1961-63	£4,500	£2,750	£1,000
Sabre 6 " "	2553/6	1962-64	£5,000	£3,250	£1,000
Scimitar GT Coupé SE4	2553/6, 2994 V6	1964-70	£4,500	£2,500	£1,000
Scimitar GTE Sports Estate SE5/5A	2994/V6	1968-75	£4,500	£2,000	£750
Scimitar GTE Sports Estate SE6/6A	2994/V6	1976-80	£6,000	£3,500	£1,250
Scimitar GTE Sports Estate SE6B	2792/V6	1980-86	£8,000	£5,000	£2,000
Scimitar GTC Convertible SE8B	2792/V6	1980-86	£10,000	£8,000	£5,500

1973 Reliant Scimitar GTE, 6 cylinders, 2994cc, reconditioned automatic gearbox, replacement original front seat covers, sliding factory fitted sunroof, very good condition. **£1,600–1,800** *ADT*

1909 Renault AX 8hp 2 Seater with Dickey, restored 16 years ago, Salsbury Dietz oil sidelamps, Stepney wheel, double twist brass bulb horn, very good condition throughout. **£13,500–14,000** *S*

RENAULT

Louis Renault built his first car in 1898, mounting a De Dion engine on the front of a primitive tubular frame. The remarkable feature of the car was the sprung live rear axle, a feature soon to be copied by his contemporaries. Initially using engines of 1¾hp and 3hp, 4½hp cars appeared in 1900 and by 1902 the single cylinder cars were produced in 6hp and 8hp versions alongside a 10hp twin.

1914 Renault Coupé Chauffeur, coachwork by Arthur Boulogne, excellent original fittings, including occasional fold-down rear seats, buttoned cord upholstery, veneers and inlay work, lace trimmings to the rear, drop-down division to chauffeur's compartment, railway carriage pulls and similar railway carriage windows, blinds and bone handles to rear doors, electric headlights by Ouvrard & Villars of Paris with Grey and Davis electric sidelights, copper speaking tube, Jones speedometer, 8-day clock, electric klaxon, excellent condition. **£28,000–30,000** *S*

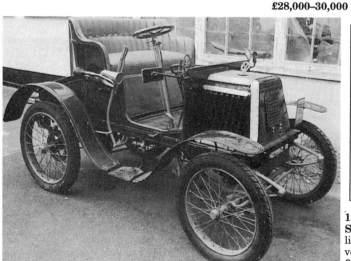

> **Use the Index!**
> *Because certain items might fit easily into any number of categories, the quickest and surest method of locating any entry is by reference to the index at the back of the book.*
>
> *This index has been fully cross-referenced for absolute simplicity.*

1901 Renault Type D Series E 4½hp 2 Seater, little used in recent years, very good overall condition. **£15,500–16,000** *S*

RENAULT Model	ENGINE cc/cyl	DATES	CONDITION		
			1	2	3
40hp	7540/6	1919-21	£30,000	£20,000	£10,000
SR	4537/4	1919-22	£10,000	£7,000	£5,000
EU-15.8HP	2815/4	1919-23	£5,000	£3,000	£2,000
GS-IG	2121/4	1920-23	£5,000	£3,000	£2,000
JP	9123/6	1922-29	£25,000	£20,000	£15,000
KJ	951/4	1923-29	£6,000	£4,000	£2,000
Mona Six	1474/6	1928-31	£7,000	£5,000	£3,000
Reinastella	7128/8	1929-32	£25,000	£20,000	£15,000
Viva Six	3181/6	1929-34	£10,000	£7,000	£3,000
14/45	2120/4	1929-35	£7,000	£5,000	£2,000
Nervahuit	4240/8	1931	£12,000	£10,000	£7,000
UY	1300/4	1932-34	£7,000	£5,000	£2,000
ZC/ZD2	4825/8	1934-35	£12,000	£10,000	£7,000
YN2	1463/4	1934-39	£7,000	£5,000	£2,000
Airline Super and Big 6	3620/6	1935	£10,000	£8,000	£5,000
18	2383/4	1936-39	£9,000	£5,000	£3,000
26	4085/6	1936-39	£12,000	£8,000	£5,000

Veteran pre-war models like the 2 cylinder AX, AG and BB are very popular, with values ranging between £6,000 and £15,000. The larger 4 cylinder cars like the AM, AZ, XB and VB are very reliable and coachbuilt examples command £25,000+.

1964 Renault 8 Saloon, completely original condition, only 35,900 miles from new, manual gearbox, excellent overall condition. **£550-600** *LF*

1968 Renault Caravelle Convertible, 4 cylinders, 1108cc, usable condition. **Est. £4,000-5,000** *ADT*

RENAULT Model	ENGINE cc/cyl	DATES	CONDITION		
			1	2	3
4CV	747/ 760/4	1947-61	£3,500	£2,000	£850
Fregate	1997/4	1952-60	£3,000	£2,000	£1,000
Dauphine	845/4	1956-66	£1,500	£1,000	£350
Dauphine Gordini	845/4	1961-66	£2,000	£1,000	£450
Floride	845/4	1959-62	£3,000	£2,000	£600
Caravelle	956/ 1108/4	1962-68	£4,500	£2,800	£750
R4	747/ 845/4	1961-86	£2,000	£1,500	£350
R8/R10	1108/4	1962-71	£1,800	£750	£200
R8 Gordini	1108/4	1965-66	£8,000	£5,000	£2,000
R8 Gordini	1255/4	1966-70	£8,000	£5,500	£2,500
R8S	1108/4	1968-71	£2,000	£1,200	£400

REXETTE

The Rex Motor Manufacturing Co. Ltd., of Coventry produced the Rexette with a car type frame, and the water-cooled 5hp single cylinder engine and was started by a handle. It had a 2 speed gearbox with brakes on all 3 wheels and sold for 100 guineas.

1904 Rexette 5hp Forecar, full set of gas lighting, excellent overall condition. **Est. £12,000-15,000** *BKS*

According to records, this car is one of 4 currently dated prior to 1905, and only 5 are known to exist.

RILEY

1931 Riley 9 Four Seater Drophead Coupé, coachwork by Hoyal Body Corporation (1928) Ltd., excellent restored condition.
£11,500–12,000 *S*

This is one of just 2 Hoyal bodied Rileys known to survive, and was the subject of a ground-up restoration some 4 years ago, including an engine rebuild.

1931 Riley 9 Special Tourer, originally a Monaco saloon built on a Plus Ultra chassis, engine rebuilt, good overall condition.
Est. £7,500–10,000 *ALC*

1935 Riley 12/4 Open Tourer, 4 cylinders, 1496cc, originally a Falcon saloon, rebodied with 2 door, 4 seater sports tourer coachwork, very good condition.
£11,750–12,500 *COYS*

1934 Riley Lynx 4 Door Tourer, 4 cylinders, 1087cc, twin SU carburettors, Riley 9hp chassis with Rudge Whitworth centre lock wheels and 13in brake drums, very good condition throughout.
£12,500–13,000 *ADT*

1950 Riley RMA 1½ Litre Saloon, very good condition throughout.
£5,000–5,500 *S*

1937 Riley Lynx 1½ Litre 4 Door 4 Seater Tourer, reconditioned engine, original upholstery, good condition throughout.
Est. £16,500–17,500 *S*

In 1936, the 1½ litre range consisted of the Adelphi, Kestrel and Falcon saloons and the Lynx tourer. These models continued until the take-over of the company in 1938, and featured 4 cylinder overhead valve engines, 4 speed gearboxes with a variety of coachwork options available.

RILEY Model	ENGINE cc/cyl	DATES	CONDITION		
			1	2	3
9hp	1034/2	1906-07	£9,000	£6,000	£3,000
Speed 10	1390/2	1909-10	£10,000	£6,000	£3,000
11	1498/4	1922-27	£7,000	£4,000	£2,000
9	1075/4	1927-32	£10,000	£7,000	£4,000
9 Gamecock	1098/4	1932-33	£14,000	£10,000	£6,000
Lincock 12hp	1458/6	1933-36	£9,000	£7,000	£5,000
Imp 9hp	1089/4	1934-35	£35,000	£28,000	£20,000
Kestrel 12hp	1496/4	1936-38	£8,000	£5,000	£2,000
Sprite 12hp	1496/4	1936-38	£40,000	£35,000	£20,000

RILEY Model	ENGINE cc/cyl	DATES	CONDITION 1	2	3
1½ litre RMA	1496/4	1945-52	£5,000	£3,500	£1,500
1½ litre RME	1496/4	1952-55	£5,000	£3,500	£1,500
2½ litre RMB/F	2443/4	1946-53	£9,000	£7,000	£3,000
2½ litre Roadster	2443/4	1948-50	£13,000	£11,000	£9,000
2½ litre Drophead	2443/4	1948-51	£20,000	£18,000	£10,000
Pathfinder	2443/4	1953-57	£3,500	£2,000	£750
2.6	2639/6	1957-59	£3,000	£1,800	£750
1.5	1489/4	1957-65	£4,000	£2,000	£850
4/68	1489/4	1959-61	£1,500	£700	£300
4/72	1622/4	1961-69	£1,600	£800	£300
Elf I/II/III	848/4	1961-66	£1,500	£850	£400
Kestrel I/II	1098/4	1965-67	£1,500	£850	£400

1950 Riley 2½ Litre Saloon, 4 cylinders, 2443cc, 4 speed manual gearbox, very good condition overall.
£3,300–3,600 *ADT*

1962 Riley One-Point-Five MkIII 4 Door Saloon, average mechanical condition, bodywork below average, replacement fibreglass front wing, requires cosmetic work.
£240–280 *BKS*

In Riley terms, the One-Point-Five proved a great sales success. Over 40,500 were built, making it the most popular model in the marque's 70 year history, outselling even the Nine.

1955 Riley RME 1½ Litre Saloon, 4 cylinders, 1496cc, very good condition throughout.
Est. £8,000–10,000 *ADT*

ROCHET-SCHNEIDER

Edouard Rochet of Lyon, France, began building bicycles in his father's garage in the 1880s. He joined Théophile Schneider in 1894 and they built their first automobile. The first Rochet-Schneiders were a derivative of the Benz Vélos. By 1901, they were building 4 cylinder automobiles.

1966 Riley Elf MkII, 4 cylinders, 998cc, very good original condition.
£1,000–1,200 *ADT*

1907 Rochet–Schneider 40/50 Double Chain Drive Flyabout, 4 cylinder T-head engine, bore and stroke 5½ x 7in, 674cu in, 50hp, 4 speed gearbox, rear drum brakes and on transaxle, semi-elliptical leaf spring front suspension, 3 semi-elliptical leaf springs rear, one transversally mounted, right hand drive, restored to almost new condition.
£140,000–160,000 *CNY*

Although the body is light, sliding drawer tool boxes and removable rear doors are built in to it, and for real racing the whole rear portion of the body can be removed to make a 2 seater.

1966 Riley 4/72 Saloon, 4 cylinders, 1622cc, low mileage, fair condition.
£800–900 *ADT*

ROLLS-ROYCE

1921 Rolls-Royce Silver Ghost,
very good condition.
£80,000–82,000 *BLE*

**1923 Rolls-Royce 20hp 2 Seater with
Dickey,** coachwork by Park Ward, good
condition throughout.
Est. £22,000-25,000 *S*

1923 Rolls-Royce Silver Ghost Tourer,
6 cylinders, 7428cc, very good condition.
£65,000–68,000 *COYS*

*The 40/50 used twin iron blocks with an
alloy crankcase, and the 7046cc, 6 cylinder,
side valve engine had a 7 bearing crankshaft,
integral cylinder heads, roller cam followers,
full pressure lubrication, twin plugs per
cylinder and dual magneto and coil ignition.
Breathing through Royce's own carburettor,
it produced 50hp at 1500rpm allied to
tremendous torque.*

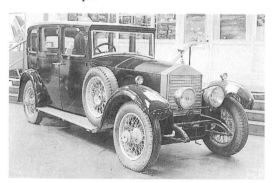

1923 Rolls-Royce 20hp 4 Door Saloon,
coachwork by Litchfields Motor Body
Builders, upholstery in good condition,
original instrumentation, occasional rear
seats, general refurbishment required.
£9,500–12,000 *S*

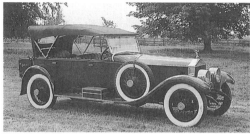

**1921 Rolls-Royce Silver Ghost Pall Mall
Open Tourer,** 6 cylinders, 7428cc, correct
American Bosch magneto, 4 speed gearbox,
excellent original condition.
£60,000–63,000 *COYS*

*In 1920 Rolls-Royce announced that the
40/50 Silver Ghost was to be manufactured
at their factory in Springfield, Massachusetts,
in order to avoid the duty charged on imported
cars. Almost every part of the chassis was
made in the USA to the same exacting
standards of the English cars. Production
ceased in 1926, by which time 1,703 chassis
had been made.*

Make the Most of Miller's

*Veteran Cars are those manufactured
up to 31 December 1918. Only vehicles
built before 31 December 1904 are
eligible for the London/Brighton
Commemorative Run. Vintage Cars are
vehicles that were manufactured
between 1 January 1919 and 31
December 1930.*

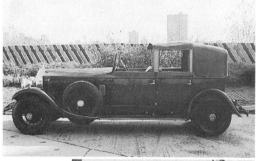

1925 Rolls-Royce Phantom I, Salamanca
coachwork by Galle, 6 cylinders, 7668cc,
requires restoration, original condition.
£27,000–28,000 *COYS*

*The new Phantom took over from the Silver
Ghost in 1925, and was the shortest lived of
all Rolls-Royce models. Some 2,200 chassis
were built in this country between 1925 and
1929 and the model was also produced at
the American factory in Springfield,
Massachusetts, where 1,140 were made.*
 *This chassis carries a desirable and
ingenious Salamanca body, offering the style
of a formal classical limousine and when
'fully collapsed' an open tourer, with the
options of Landaulette and Sedanca de Ville
in between.*

1926 Rolls-Royce Silver Ghost, Playboy
Roadster coachwork by Brewster, 6 cylinder,
7428cc engine, excellent restored condition.
£76,000–80,000 *COYS*

*The Brewster Playboy was one of the most
attractive of all the body designs evolved by
Rolls-Royce of America. Only 28 examples
were built on both the Silver Ghost and the
Phantom I chassis.*

1928 Rolls-Royce Phantom I, 6 cylinders,
7668cc, originally fitted with a fixed cabriolet
body by Thrupp and Maberly, now fitted with
Grosvenor-style 4 seater tourer coachwork,
good overall condition.
£25,000–26,000 *COYS*

**1928 Rolls-Royce Phantom I Dual Cowl
Open Tourer,** extensive restoration.
£42,000–44,000 *COYS*

1929 Rolls-Royce 20/25 Town Car,
coachwork by Hibbard & Darrin of Paris,
6 cylinders, 224cu in, overhead valve, 4 speed
manual gearbox, 4 wheel drum brakes, semi-
elliptical spring suspension, right hand drive,
requires attention but good general condition.
£17,000–20,000 *CNY*

1929 Rolls-Royce 20hp Open Tourer,
6 cylinders, 3127cc, excellent running condition.
£22,000–24,000 *COYS*

**1930 Rolls-Royce Phantom II 40/50
Limousine,** twin side mounted spare wheels,
rear luggage trunk, MCL centre spotlight,
very good condition throughout.
Est. £19,000–21,000 *S*

ROLLS-ROYCE Model	ENGINE cc/cyl	DATES	CONDITION 1	2	3
Silver Ghost 40/50	7035/6	pre-WWI	£350,000	£120,000	£50,000
Silver Ghost 40/50	7428/6	post-WWI	£110,000	£70,000	£35,000
20hp (3 speed)	3127/6	1922-25	£29,000	£23,000	£15,000
20hp	3127/6	1925-29	£30,000	£24,000	£15,000
Phantom I	7668/6	1925-29	£50,000	£28,000	£22,000
20/25	3669/6	1925-26	£30,000	£18,000	£13,000
Phantom II	7668/6	1929-35	£40,000	£30,000	£20,000
Phantom II Continental	7668/6	1930-35	£60,000	£40,000	£28,000
25/30	4257/6	1936-38	£24,000	£18,000	£12,000
Phantom III	7340/12	1936-39	£38,000	£28,000	£14,000
Wraith	4257/6	1938-39	£38,000	£32,000	£25,000

Prices will vary depending on heritage, originality, coachbuilder, completeness and body
style. A poor reproduction body can often mean the value is dependent only upon a rolling chassis
and engine.

1930 Rolls-Royce 20/25 Saloon, coachwork
by Thrupp & Maberly, good running order,
good original condition.
£15,500–16,000 *COYS*

**1932 Rolls-Royce 20/25 Three Position
Drophead Coupé,** coachwork by
Gurney Nutting, 6 cylinders, 3699cc,
extensively refurbished.
Est. £70,000–85,000 *COYS*

*This is probably one of the finest examples
of this model available.*

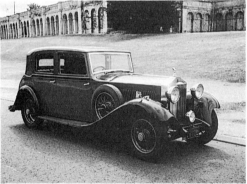

1934 Rolls-Royce 20/25 Sports Saloon,
coachwork by Hooper, very good condition.
£19,250–20,000 *BA*

1934 Rolls-Royce 20/25 Shooting Brake,
coachwork by Joseph Cockshoot, good
condition cosmetically, engine rebuilt, new
interior, completely rewired, new exhaust,
suspension overhauled, new tyres.
Est. £24,000–27,000 *S*

1932 Rolls-Royce 20/25 Sports Saloon,
coachwork by Freestone & Webb, requires
re-trimming, mechanically sound.
Est. £20,000–25,000 *S*

*Freestone & Webb were formed in 1923, based
at Willesden, London, and concentrated on
motor bodies for private orders mainly on
Rolls-Royce and Bentley chassis. They
exhibited regularly at the London Motor
Shows and for 9 years took the coveted Gold
Medal in the Private Coachbuilders competition.*

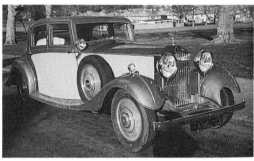

1934 Rolls-Royce 20/25 Sports Saloon,
coachwork by William Arnold, good
general condition.
£19,750–20,000 *BA*

**1934 Rolls-Royce 20/25 Four Door Sports
Saloon,** coachwork by Thrupp & Maberly,
good overhauled condition throughout.
Est. £20,000–23,000 *S*

1934 Rolls-Royce 20/25 Sports Saloon,
coachwork by Thrupp & Maberly, good
all-round condition.
£16,000–17,000 *BA*

1934 Rolls-Royce 20/25 Sports Saloon,
coachwork by Hooper, very good
restored condition.
Est. £22,000–25,000 *COYS*

*The Rolls-Royce 20 had been a very successful
model, but by 1929 coachwork was becoming
heavier and more elaborate, so the 20/25 was
introduced. The engine was increased from
3.1 to 3.7 litres, with a corresponding
improvement in top speed and acceleration.*

**1936 Rolls-Royce Phantom II
Continental Touring Saloon,** coachwork
by Barker, 6 cylinders, 7668cc, excellent
restored condition.
£34,000–36,000 *COYS*

*Between 1929 and 1935 a total of 1,681
Phantom IIs were produced, of which just 281
were the Continental version.*

1936 Rolls-Royce 20/25, coachwork by
H. J. Mulliner, 3128cc, well restored.
£12,000–13,000 *H&H*

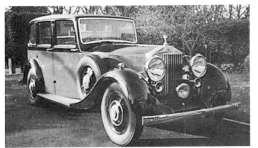

1937 Rolls-Royce 25/30 Limousine,
coachwork by Park Ward, original condition
with no modifications from maker's
specification, good bodywork, chassis and
mechanical condition, good original leather,
passenger compartment re-trimmed in cloth.
£16,000–17,000 *S*

**1935 Rolls-Royce 20/25 Long Wheelbase
4 Door Saloon with Division,** coachwork
by H. J. Mulliner of Chiswick, good
condition throughout.
Est. £17,000-18,000 *S*

> **Miller's is a price GUIDE
> not a price LIST**

**1935 Rolls-Royce 20/25 4 Door Sports
Sedan,** aluminium coachwork by William
Arnold, nearly new black leather interior,
wood and mechanics in excellent condition.
£13,000–15,000 *CGB*

1937 Rolls-Royce Wraith Saloon,
coachwork by Park Ward, upholstery and
trim renewed, good condition throughout.
£23,000–25,000 *S*

**1951 Rolls-Royce Silver Wraith
7 Passenger Limousine,** coachwork by
Park Ward, used mainly for wedding hire,
original interior reflects careful usage,
excellent mechanical condition.
£15,500–16,500 *S*

1952 Rolls-Royce Silver Dawn,
6 cylinders, 4500cc, recently dry
stored, requires some re-commissioning,
very good restored condition.
£18,000–18,500 *ADT*

*During the first two years of production
only 170 Silver Dawn cars were
manufactured and these early cars
were fitted with the 4¼ litre engine.
From July 1951 a 4½ litre engine
was installed.*

1937 Rolls-Royce Phantom III Sedanca,
coachwork by Hooper, extensively
refurbished, potential concours winner,
excllent condition.
£50,000–52,000 *COYS*

1954 Rolls-Royce Silver Wraith, coachwork
by H. J. Mulliner, very good condition.
£33,000–35,000 *PJF*

1955 Rolls-Royce Silver Dawn,
ery good condition.
£36,000–38,000 *PJF*

> **Miller's is a price GUIDE
> not a price LIST**

1956 Rolls-Royce Silver Cloud, 6 cylinders,
4887cc, excellent condition throughout.
Est. £14,000–16,000 *ADT*

1958 Rolls-Royce Silver Cloud I,
very good condition.
£20,000–22,000 *BA*

**1958 Rolls-Royce Silver Cloud I Standard
Steel Saloon,** bodywork in good condition,
standard power steering, 52,000 miles from
new, excellent original condition throughout.
£13,000–14,000 *COYS*

1959 Rolls-Royce Silver Cloud I Standard Steel Saloon, 6 cylinders, very good condition.
£33,000–35,000 *PJF*

1959 Rolls-Royce Silver Cloud I Standard Steel Saloon, electrics, chassis, tyres and mechanics in good condition, paintwork, bodywork and upholstery fair.
£7,500–8,000 *S*

1959 Rolls-Royce Silver Cloud I Convertible, adapted by H. J. Mulliner, very good condition.
£120,000–130,000 *PJF*

1960 Rolls-Royce Phantom V Touring Limousine, coachwork by James Young, V8 cylinders, 6230cc, single headlamps, full air conditioning, drinks cabinet with Stuart Crystal decanters and glasses, one owner, 40,000 miles from new, excellent condition throughout.
£40,000–42,000 *COYS*

The Phantom V was the most expensive and largest car on the home market, if not in the world, at the time.

1963 Rolls-Royce Silver Cloud III Touring Limousine, coachwork by James Young of Bromley, picnic trays, air conditioning, electric windows and central division, reading lights, excellent condition.
£26,000–28,000 *S*

ROLLS-ROYCE Model	ENGINE cc/cyl	DATES	CONDITION 1	2	3
Silver Wraith LWB	4566/ 4887/6	1951-59	£22,000	£15,000	£9,000
Silver Wraith SWB	4257/ 4566/6	1947-59	£20,000	£12,000	£9,000
Mark VI	4257/6	1946-54	£20,000	£12,000	£7,000
Mark VI Coachbuilt	4257/6	1946-54	£22,000	£13,000	£6,000
Silver Wraith Drophead	4257/ 4566/6	1947-59	£50,000	£35,000	£25,000
Silver Dawn St'd Steel	4257/ 4566/6	1949-52	£25,000	£15,000	£10,000
Silver Dawn St'd Steel	4257/ 4566/6	1952-55	£30,000	£20,000	£15,000
Silver Dawn Coachbuilt	4257/ 4566/6	1949-55	£35,000	£25,000	£18,000
Silver Dawn Drophead	4257/ 4566/6	1949-55	£60,000	£50,000	£30,000
Silver Cloud I	4887/6	1955-59	£18,000	£10,000	£8,000
SCI Coupé Coachbuilt	4887/6	1955-59	£30,000	£20,000	£15,000
SCI Conv (HJM)	4887/6	1955-59	£80,000	£60,000	£40,000
Silver Cloud II	6230/8	1959-62	£19,000	£10,000	£8,000
SCII Conv (HJM)	6230/8	1959-62	£80,000	£75,000	£40,000
SCII Conv (MPW)	6230/8	1959-62	£60,000	£40,000	£32,000
Silver Cloud III	6230/8	1962-65	£25,000	£12,000	£10,000
SCIII Conv (MPW)	6230/8	1962-65	£70,000	£45,000	£35,000
Silver Shadow	6230/ 6750/8	1965-76	£11,000	£8,000	£6,000
S Shadow I Coupé (MPW)	6230/ 6750/8	1965-70	£15,000	£10,000	£8,000
SSI Drophead (MPW)	6230/ 6750/8	1965-70	£33,000	£25,000	£18,000
Corniche fhc	6750/8	1971-77	£15,000	£11,000	£8,000
Corniche Convertible	6750/8	1971-77	£28,000	£22,000	£18,000
Camargue	6750/8	1975-85	£35,000	£25,000	£18,000

1962 Rolls-Royce Phantom V 7 Seater Limousine, coachwork by James Young of Bromley, engine overhauled, good condition throughout.
£43,000–44,000 *S*

Current from 1959 until 1968, the Phantom V was built in limited numbers, a total of 832 examples leaving the factory during this period.

1963 Rolls-Royce Silver Cloud III Standard Steel Saloon, good condition throughout.
£9,250–9,750 *S*

Introduced in 1962 together with the Bentley S3, the final development of the Silver Cloud featured the 6230cc, V8 engine and automatic transmission with hypoid final drive.

1964 Rolls-Royce Silver Cloud III, good all-round condition.
£16,750–17,250 *BA*

1964 Rolls-Royce Silver Cloud III Drophead Coupé, very good condition.
£40,000–42,000 *BLE*

1964 Rolls-Royce Silver Cloud III Saloon, requires servicing and attention to braking system, fair condition throughout.
£10,500–11,000 *S*

1964 Rolls-Royce Silver Cloud III, good all-round condition.
£15,000–16,000 *BA*

1965 Rolls-Royce Silver Cloud III Drophead Coupé, coachwork by Mulliner Park Ward, left hand drive, virtually unused since restoration, excellent condition throughout.
£47,000–50,000 *S*

1965 Rolls-Royce Phantom V, coachwork by James Young, very good condition.
£88,000–90,000 *PJF*

1965 Rolls-Royce Silver Cloud III Drophead Coupé Continental, coachwork by Mulliner Park Ward, very good condition.
£78,000–80,000 *PJF*

1968 Rolls-Royce Silver Shadow,
8 cylinders, 6250cc, very good
condition throughout.
£7,500–8,000 *ADT*

**1968 Rolls-Royce Convertible Drophead
Coupé,** coachwork by Mulliner Park Ward,
hide interior, wood veneer dashboard, knee-
roll and door cappings, very good condition.
£18,500–20,000 *CARS*

1970 Rolls-Royce Coupé, coachwork
by Mulliner Park Ward, good paintwork,
original interior, full history and
Rolls-Royce service.
£14,000–15,000 *CGOC*

**1975 Rolls-Royce Silver Shadow Long
Wheelbase Saloon,** stainless steel exhaust,
excellent condition throughout.
£19,000–20,000 *S*

*This car was once the property of Her Royal
Highness the Princess Margaret, Countess
of Snowdon from 1975 until 1979.*

**1970 Rolls-Royce Silver Shadow 2 Door
Coupé,** coachwork by Mulliner Park Ward,
8 cylinders, 6230cc, re-painted, requires a
little attention.
£13,000–13,500 *ADT*

*The Pressed Steel Company at Cowley, near
Oxford, manufactured the standard steel
bodies, and it was not until 1969, after the
introduction of the drophead coupé, that the
2 door fixed head coupé was produced by
H. J. Mulliner and Park Ward.*

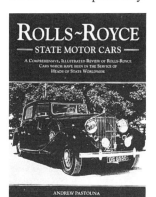

1972 Rolls-Royce Corniche, 6 cylinders,
6745cc, good overall condition.
£12,500–13,000 *ADT*

1975 Rolls-Royce Corniche Convertible,
very good condition.
£36,000–38,000 *PJF*

ROVER

Owen Clegg joined Rover from Wolseley in September 1910 and in his short period with the company, ending in 1912, his impact on the company's fortunes was enormous. The Rover 12 was his brainchild, a car designed for volume production and similar in many respects to the Wolseley 12/16. The monobloc 75 x 130mm engine was efficient and reliable and gave a comfortable touring speed of around 40–45mph.

1912 Rover 12hp 2 Seater with Dickey, Rotax electric lighting, Lucas oil sidelamps, brass bulb horn, hand operated windscreen wiper, brass speedo, 8-day clock, exhaust whistle, little recent use, requires re-commissioning.
£14,500–15,000 *S*

By 1912 the engine of the 12hp car had been developed to produce 28bhp, and was priced at £315 for a 5 seater.

1906 Rover 6hp 2 Seater, P & M acetylene headlamps, oil sidelamps, and a brass horn, good overall condition.
£7,400–7,800 *S*

1929 Rover 10/25hp Weymann Sunshine Saloon, original condition, concours d'élégance winner in recent years, requires re-commissioning following museum display.
£5,000–5,500 *S*

Beside the contemporary Austin 12 and Morris Cowley the Rover 10/25hp looked expensive at £250 in 1929.

1932 Rover 10hp Ten Special 4 Door Saloon, mechanically good condition, running order.
£10,000–10,500 *S*

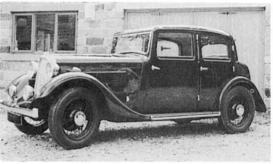

1935 Rover 12 Sportsman Saloon, 4 cylinders, 1496cc, body-off restoration, excellent condition.
£8,800–9,200 *ADT*

Other features of the car include the Rover free-wheel, opening windscreen and the continuous chassis lubrication system with the reservoir situated on the bulkhead.

1932 Rover 12hp Pilot Weymann Saloon, horn set in the radiator stoneguard and rear door spats, which keep the rear mudguard clean for the rear seat passengers, original specification, requires careful re-commissioning.
£4,500–5,500 *S*

The 12hp Pilot with Weymann saloon coachwork, sliding roof, radiator stoneguard and wire wheels, was priced complete at £230. It was powered by a 1410cc, 6 cylinder engine with a 4 speed gearbox with silent third speed.

> *A rebuilt car is not necessarily more valuable than a car in good original condition, even if the restoration has been costly.*

1937 Rover 10 Saloon, 4 cylinders, 1389cc, original semaphore arm indicators, rear luggage rack, spoke wheels, very good original condition.
£6,600–7,000 *ADT*

1947 Rover 14 Four Door Saloon, drives well, had careful use, unused since 1992, requires careful re-commissioning.
£4,000–4,500 *S*

This car was used by Siegfried Farnon (Robert Hardy) in the original series of All Creatures Great and Small.

1947 Rover P3 12hp, 4 cylinders, 1389cc, re-sprayed, very good condition throughout.
£2,800–3,000 *ADT*

1948 Rover P3 75, 6 cylinders, 2103cc, sympathetic restoration, professional re-spray, 4 speed manual gearbox, excellent condition throughout.
£5,500–6,000 *ADT*

1961 Rover 100 P4 Saloon, body, interior and mechanics very good.
Est. £1,500–2,500 *LF*

The Rover 100 is one of the most desirable of the P4 range of Rovers, with the new 7 bearing, pump-cooled, 2625cc engine introduced in 1960.

1964 Rover P4 95, show standard throughout.
£3,400–3,800 *H&H*

1955 Rover 75 P4, 2230cc, very good condition throughout.
£900–1,100 *H&H*

The P4 Series of Rovers date back to 1949, and the basic shape remained virtually unchanged until 1964 by which time more than 130,000 cars had been made.

ROVER Model	ENGINE cc/cyl	DATES	CONDITION 1	2	3
10hp	998/2	1920-25	£5,000	£3,000	£1,500
9/20	1074/4	1925-27	£6,000	£4,000	£2,000
10/25	1185/4	1928-33	£6,000	£4,000	£2,500
14hp	1577/6	1933-39	£6,000	£4,250	£2,000
12	1496/4	1934-37	£5,000	£3,000	£1,000
20 Sports	2512/6	1937-39	£6,000	£4,000	£2,500

1967 Rover 2000 Saloon, 43,000 miles, good general condition, not used recently, requires re-commissioning.
£500–550 *S*

1963 Rover 110 Saloon, manual transmission, original leather upholstery.
£1,400–1,500 *S*

The Rover 110 was the final development of the P4 Series of Rovers which had made their mark in the 1950s and continued in production until May 1964. The 110 followed the basic design of the earlier cars but its introduction in 1962 saw the compression ratio raised to 8.8:1 and a corresponding increase in performance. In 1963 the 110 was produced alongside the 95 and the P5 3 litre cars and sold for £1,534, compared with a Humber Super Snipe at £1,541 and a Jaguar MkII at £1,596.

1969 Rover 2000 SC Automatic, 1978cc, well maintained, very good original condition.
£2,000–2,200 *H&H*

1967 Rover 2000 Saloon, automatic transmission, very good condition.
£1,400-1,600 *LF*

ROVER Model	ENGINE cc/cyl	DATES	CONDITION 1	2	3
P2 10	1389/4	1946-47	£2,900	£2,000	£500
P2 12	1496/4	1946-47	£3,200	£2,300	£600
P2 12 Tour	1496/4	1947	£6,500	£3,000	£1,000
P2 14/16	1901/6	1946-47	£4,000	£2,800	£700
P2 14/16 Sal	1901/6	1946-47	£3,700	£2,500	£700
P3 60	1595/4	1948-49	£3,000	£2,000	£800
P3 75	2103/6	1948-49	£3,800	£2,700	£800
P4 75	2103/6	1950-51	£2,800	£1,000	£800
P4 75	2103/6	1952-64	£2,500	£900	£800
P4 60	1997/4	1954-59	£2,300	£750	£800
P4 90	2638/6	1954-59	£2,900	£1,100	£500
P4 75	2230/6	1955-59	£2,500	£900	£400
P4 105R	2638/6	1957-58	£3,000	£1,600	£500
P4 105S	2638/6	1957-59	£3,000	£1,600	£250
P4 80	2286/4	1960-62	£2,500	£900	£500
P4 95	2625/6	1963-64	£2,800	£1,600	£500
P4 100	2625/6	1960-62	£3,200	£1,500	£500
P4 110	2625/6	1963-64	£3,250	£1,600	£500
P5 3 litre	2995/6	1959-67	£3,500	£2,000	£550
P5 3 litre Coupé	2995/6	1959-67	£5,000	£3,500	£750
P5B (V8)	3528/8	1967-74	£6,000	£4,000	£900
P5B (V8) Coupé	3528/8	1967-73	£6,000	£4,250	£1,250
P6 2000 SC Series 1	1980/4	1963-65	£2,200	£800	-
P6 2000 SC Series 1	1980/4	1966-70	£2,000	£800	-
P6 2000 SC Auto Series 1	1980/4	1966-70	£1,500	£600	-
P6 2000 TC Series 1	1980/4	1966-70	£2,000	£900	-
P6 2000 SC Series 2	1980/4	1970-73	£2,000	£900	-
P6 2000 SC Auto Series 2	1980/4	1970-73	£1,500	£800	-
P6 2000 TC Series 2	1980/4	1970-73	£2,000	£900	-
P6 3500 Series 1	3500/8	1968-70	£2,500	£1,400	-
P6 2200 SC	2200/4	1974-77	£1,750	£850	-
P6 2200 SC Auto	2200/4	1974-77	£2,500	£1,000	-
P6 2200 TC	2200/4	1974-77	£2,000	£1,000	-
P6 3500 Series 2	3500/8	1971-77	£3,000	£1,700	-
P6 3500 S Series 2	3500/8	1971-77	£2,000	£1,500	-

1971 Rover 2000 Saloon, 4 cylinders, 1978cc, very good condition.
Est. £1,400–1,600 *ADT*

1974 Rover 2200 SC Sports Saloon, 26,000 miles, original manufacturer's specification throughout.
£750–800 *S*

1976 Rover P6 Saloon, very good original condition overall.
£700–750 *HOLL*

1966 Rover P5 3 Litre Coupé Automatic, requires restoration and MOT, but in good running order.
£500–550 *Mot*

1972 Rover 3½ Litre P5B 5 Seater Coupé, automatic transmission, Sundym glazing, headrests, radio, tow ball, right hand drive but speedometer calibrated in kilometres, very good condition throughout.
£4,400–4,800 *S*

SCANIA

The Swedish firm of Scania, perhaps best known for commercial vehicles, can trace its origins back to the 1890s when the English bicycle manufacturer of Humber established a Swedish subsidiary in Malmo. In 1900 this firm was taken over and became known as Scania.

1973 Rover P6 3500 Coupé, original condition, a few blemishes to paintwork.
£2,800–3,000 *C*

SÉNÉCHAL

1926 Sénéchal 2 Seater Sports, offset seating, cable brakes to all 4 wire wheels, single aero fold-flat screen, leather strapped bonnet, finished in French blue livery with blue upholstery, paintwork requires attention, museum displayed for many years.
£5,000–5,400 *S*

c1902 Scania 8hp Single Cylinder, coachwork renewed, eligible for the Brighton Run.
£17,000–18,000 *C*

SIATA

Siata was founded in 1926 by enthusiastic amateur racing driver Georgio Ambrosini. Short for Societa Italiana Applicazione Transformazione Automobilistiche, Siata began by specialising in providing tuning equipment for various cars, mainly Fiats.

1953 Siata Tipo 201 Sport, 4 cylinders, 1400cc Fiat engine, Abarth exhaust system, twin downdraught Weber carburettors, top speed of over 90mph, large drum brakes, alloy rimmed Borrani wire wheels, good condition. **£24,000–26,000** *COYS*

1947 Singer 9 Roadster, 4 cylinders, 1074cc, single overhead camshaft engine, dry stored, 3 speed manual gearbox, good condition. Est. **£4,500–5,500** *ADT*

Singer Vogue

- The Singer Vogue was the de luxe version of the Singer Gazelle.
- Hillman Minx and the Super Minx were other badge engineered Singer models.
- Initially powered by a 1592cc engine, it was uprated to 1725cc in line with the other Chrysler Corporation models from Sunbeam and Hillman.

> *A rebuilt car is not necessarily more valuable than a car in good original condition, even if the restoration has been costly.*

SIMCA

1956 Simca Aronde De Luxe Saloon, left hand drive, original condition. Est. **£1,000–1,500** *S*

SINGER

1930 Singer Junior, complete body-off restoration, very good condition. **£5,250–5,750** *Mot*

1965 Singer Vogue 1725cc Estate, engine overhauled, gearbox reconditioned, stored for 8 years, requires cosmetic attention. **£150–200** *S*

SINGER Model	ENGINE cc/cyl	DATES	CONDITION		
			1	2	3
10	1097/4	1918-24	£5,000	£2,000	£1,000
15	1991/6	1922-25	£6,000	£3,000	£1,500
14/34	1776/6	1926-27	£7,000	£4,000	£2,000
Junior	848/4	1927-32	£6,000	£3,000	£1,500
Senior	1571/4	1928-29	£7,000	£4,000	£2,000
Super 6	1776/6	1928-31	£7,000	£4,000	£2,000
9 Le Mans	972/4	1932-37	£12,000	£8,000	£5,000
Twelve	1476/6	1932-34	£10,000	£7,000	£6,000
1.5 litre	1493/6	1934-36	£3,000	£2,000	£1,000
2 litre	1991/6	1934-37	£4,000	£2,750	£1,000
11	1459/4	1935-36	£3,000	£2,000	£1,000
12	1525/4	1937-39	£3,000	£2,000	£1,000

SIRRON

Captain H. G. Cresswell and H. G. Norris started dealing in motor cars in Piccadilly in February 1909. The name Sirron was derived from Norris's name reversed and these cars, offered at 200 guineas, were powered by a 1944cc, 4 cylinder, side valve engine, with cylinders cast in pairs, a 3 speed gate change gearbox and a three seater body.

1909 Sirron 10/14hp 2 Seater with Dickey, P & M lighting, oil side and tail lamps, acetylene headlamps, folding brass framed windscreen, hand-operated wiper, excellent condition.
£9,250–9,500 *S*

1933 SS I 2.5 Litre Four Seater Tourer, bodywork sound, requires repainting.
£19,500–20,000 *BKS*

Did you know?
MILLER'S Collectors Cars Price Guide *builds up year-by-year to form the most comprehensive photo-reference library system available.*

STANDARD

1913 Standard Rhyl 1.1 Litre 9.5hp Special All Weather Tourer, well maintained, good usable condition.
Est. £12,000–16,000 *BKS*

SQUIRE

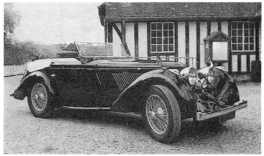

1937 Squire 1½ Litre Drophead Coupé, coachwork by Corsica, supercharged Anzani 4 cylinder, twin overhead camshaft, 1496cc engine, 100bhp at 3000rpm, 4 speed manual gearbox, drum brakes, semi-elliptical front and rear suspension with Houdaille shock absorbers, right hand drive, fair overall cosmetic condition, older restoration, requires some attention.
Est. £47,000–60,000 *CNY*

SS

The origins of SS lie in the manufacture of motorcycle sidecars and Swallow Sidecars gave rise to the famous SS title when the first cars were produced in 1931. Swallow previously built extremely attractive coachwork on Austin, Swift, Wolseley and Fiat cars.

1933 SS I 3.4 Litre Four Light Saloon, XK150 engine, paintwork crazed, re-trimmed in red vinyl, ideal restoration project.
£9,250–9,500 *BKS*

1934 SS I Four Seater Tourer, engine and gearbox overhauled, rewired, good condition throughout.
£21,000–22,000 *S*

1930 Standard 9 Four Seater Tourer,
well restored, good weather equipment,
original in all major respects, requires
re-commissioning.
£6,250–6,500 *S*

1937 Standard Flying 12, 4 cylinders,
1608cc, stored for some time, requires
re-commissioning.
Est. £6,000–8,000 *ADT*

*Priced at £249 for the standard 4 door saloon,
the engine was described as providing
'buoyant power', housing a 3 bearing
crankshaft, aluminium pistons, down-
draught carburettor and coil ignition.*

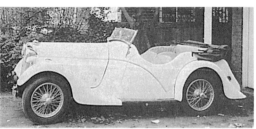

**1934 Standard Avon 10hp Sports
2 Seater,** recently restored, very good
condition throughout.
£6,000–6,500 *S*

*By 1928 the 9hp model had become very
successful, and William Lyons marketed
a series of special bodies on this Standard
9 chassis. In 1929 the first of the Avon
Standard Specials was produced, a low
built 2 seater styled by the Jensen brothers
and the Avon was to continue on many
Standard chassis from the 9hp to the 20hp
up to 1938.*

**1946 Standard Flying 8 Four Seater
Drophead Coupé,** 54,000 miles, engine
rebuilt, excellent condition.
£5,200–5,600 *S*

1947 Standard 8 Two Door Saloon,
original upholstery, good condition.
£2,200–2,400 *S*

1957 Standard Eight 4 Door Saloon,
completely restored, museum exhibited.
£1,200–1,400 *S*

STANDARD Model	ENGINE cc/cyl	DATES	CONDITION 1	2	3
SLS	1328/4	1919-20	£5,000	£4,000	£1,000
VI	1307/4	1922	£5,000	£4,000	£1,000
SLO/V4	1944/4	1922-28	£5,000	£4,000	£1,000
6V	2230/6	1928	£10,000	£8,000	£5,000
V3	1307/4	1923-26	£4,000	£3,000	£1,000
Little 9	1006/4	1932-33	£4,000	£2,000	£1,000
9	1155/4	1928-29	£4,000	£3,000	£1,000
Big 9	1287/4	1932-33	£4,500	£3,250	£2,000
15	1930/6	1929-30	£6,000	£4,000	£2,000
12	1337/6	1933-34	£4,000	£3,000	£1,500
10hp	1343/4	1933-37	£4,000	£2,500	£1,000
9	1052/4	1934-36	£4,000	£2,500	£1,000
Flying 9	1131/4	1937-39	£3,000	£1,800	£750
Flying 10	1267/4	1937-39	£3,250	£2,000	£750
Flying 14	1176/4	1937-48	£4,000	£2,000	£1,000
Flying 8	1021/4	1939-48	£3,000	£1,800	£750

1955 Standard 8 Saloon, original specification, good condition. **Est. £600–800** *S*

At £339, plus £142 purchase tax, the Standard 8 compared favourably with its direct competitors, the Austin A30 and Morris Minor.

Miller's is a price GUIDE not a price LIST

STANDARD Model	ENGINE cc/cyl	DATES	CONDITION 1	2	3
12	1609/4	1945-48	£2,000	£950	£250
12 DHC	1509/4	1945-48	£3,200	£2,000	£500
14	1776/4	1945-48	£3,000	£950	£250
Vanguard I/II	2088/4	1948-55	£1,800	£750	£150
Vanguard III	2088/4	1955-61	£1,500	£750	£150
Vanguard III Est	2088/4	1955-61	£2,000	£800	£150
Vanguard III Sportsman	2088/4	1955-58	£2,000	£800	£200
Vanguard Six	1998/6	1961-63	£1,500	£700	-
Eight	803/4	1952-59	£1,250	£500	-
Ten	948/4	1955-59	£1,400	£800	-
Ensign I/II	1670/4	1957-63	£1,000	£800	-
Ensign I/II Est	1670/4	1962-63	£1,000	£850	-
Pennant Companion	948/4	1955-61	£1,800	£850	£300
Pennant	948/4	1955-59	£1,650	£825	£250

STAR

Commencing in business in 1898, the Star Motor Company quickly established a good reputation. Their works were in Frederick Street, Wolverhampton, and the company continued in business until 1932.

1920 Star 15.9hp 5 Seater Open Tourer, engine and back axle rebuilt, very good mechanical condition. **£12,000–13,000** *S*

STIRLING

In 1899 Adolphe Clément acquired from Panhard et Levassor the licence to build a light voiturette adopting a rear mounted, single cylinder engine which was to be known as the Clément Panhard. It was marketed in the UK by Stirlings of Edinburgh, variously known as the Stirling-Panhard, the Clément-Stirling, or simply the Stirling.

1901 Stirling 5hp Light Dogcart, excellent original condition. **£13,500–14,000** *S*

STONELEIGH

1924 Stoneleigh Chummy 4 Seater Tourer, very good restored condition. **£7,800–8,200** *Bro*

During the 1920s, Armstrong-Siddeley produced a light car, the Stoneleigh. It was powered by a 90° V-twin, air-cooled overhead valve engine of 998cc. This is a very rare surviving motor car.

STUTZ

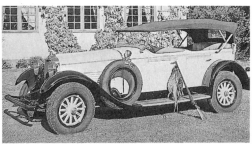

1928 Stutz Model BB Tourer, original specification in all major respects, dashboard instrumentation incomplete, requires re-commissioning after museum display.
£19,000–21,000 *S*

1933 Stutz DV 32 Sedan, straight 8 cylinder, double overhead camshaft, 322cu in engine, 156bhp at 3900rpm, 3 speed gearbox, 4 wheel hydraulic brakes, semi-elliptical leaf spring suspension front and rear, left hand drive, older restoration, good overall condition.
£9,000–11,000 *CNY*

SUNBEAM

1934 Sunbeam 20hp Saloon, major refurbishment and chassis-up restoration, excellent condition.
£18,000–19,000 *COYS*

Powered by a 2194cc, overhead valve 6 cylinder engine, rated at 18.2hp, it featured a 4 speed gearbox with synchromesh on 3rd and 4th, a new cross-braced chassis, featuring all-round semi-elliptic springs and hydraulic brakes.

1959 Sunbeam Alpine Sports, chassis-up restoration, engine fully rebuilt, left hand drive.
£4,600–4,800 *H&H*

1961 Sunbeam Alpine 1600cc Series I 2+2 Seater Sports, engine rebuilt, good condition throughout.
£4,800–5,200 *S*

1954 Sunbeam 90 MkIII Saloon, 4 cylinders, 2267cc, 4 speed gearbox with overdrive, good usable condition.
Est. £3,500–4,500 *ADT*

1957 Sunbeam MkIII Supreme Saloon, 3 year restoration, bodywork re-sprayed, engine rebuilt, good coniditon throughout.
£9,500–10,000 *S*

1966 Sunbeam Rapier Series V, requires cosmetic attention.
£750–850 *LF*

1962 Sunbeam Harrington Le Mans,
4 cylinders, 1592cc, excellent general condition.
£6,400–6,800 *ADT*

The Le Mans cars were converted by Thomas Harrington Ltd., and featured a special fibreglass fastback upper half as well as improved interior appointments, and a Hartwell tuned engine.

1961 Sunbeam Alpine Sports, works hard top, stainless steel exhaust, alloy wheels, overdrive, original right hand drive, very good condition.
£2,200–2,400 *H&H*

1964 Sunbeam Alpine 2 Seater Sports Coupé, good condition throughout.
Est. £4,000–5,000 *S*

This example has a 4 speed manual gearbox, although a 3 speed Borg-Warner option was offered.

1966 Sunbeam Tiger V8 5 Litre Sports 2 Seater, rebuilt to an excellent standard throughout.
£10,500–11,000 *S*

c1968 Sunbeam Tiger 2 Seater Sports, fully restored, good all-round condition.
£9,500–10,000 *S*

The Sunbeam Tiger was built for Rootes in the Jensen works at West Bromwich, and was inspired by the success of the AC Cobra, in which a large American built V8 engine was fitted into a traditional British sports car.

SUNBEAM Model	ENGINE cc/cyl	DATES	CONDITION		
			1	2	3
12/16	2412/4	1909-11	£20,000	£14,000	£10,000
16/20	4070/4	1912-15	£32,000	£22,000	£15,000
24	4524/6	1919-22	£28,000	£18,000	£10,000
3 litre	2916/6	1925-30	£48,000	£30,000	£20,000
16	2040/6	1927-30	£16,000	£12,500	£10,000
20	2916/6	1927-30	£22,000	£15,000	£10,500
Speed 20	2916/6	1932-35	£15,000	£10,000	£8,000
Dawn	1627/4	1934-35	£8,000	£5,000	£3,500
25	3317/6	1934	£10,000	£8,000	£4,000
Prices can vary depending on replica bodies, provenance, coachbuilder, drophead, etc.					

SUNBEAM-TALBOT

The two famous British car manufacturers, Sunbeam and Talbot, first had links in 1920 when they became embroiled in the STD group. The two names were combined on a car in 1938 under the aegis of the Rootes brothers, and the partnership continued until 1954.

1940 Sunbeam-Talbot 10 Supreme, 1184cc, side valve engine, minor cosmetic restoration required.
£3,500–4,000 *STAR*

SUNBEAM-TALBOT/ SUNBEAM Model	ENGINE cc/cyl	DATES	CONDITION		
			1	2	3
Talbot 80	1185/4	1948-50	£4,000	£2,250	£1,000
Talbot 80 DHC	1185/4	1948-50	£6,000	£4,500	£2,000
Talbot 90 Mk I	1944/4	1949-50	£4,000	£2,100	£750
Talbot 90 Mk I DHC	1944/4	1949-50	£7,000	£4,750	£2,000
Talbot 90 II/IIa/III	2267/4	1950-56	£5,000	£3,000	£1,500
Talbot 90 II/IIa/III DHC	2267/4	1950-56	£6,000	£4,500	£2,250
Talbot Alpine I/III	2267/4	1953-55	£9,000	£7,500	£3,750
Talbot Ten	1197/4	1946-48	£3,500	£2,000	£750
Talbot Ten Tourer	1197/4	1946-48	£7,000	£4,000	£2,000
Talbot Ten DHC	1197/4	1946-48	£6,500	£4,000	£2,000
Talbot 2 litre	1997/4	1946-48	£4,000	£2,500	£1,000
Talbot 2 litre Tourer	1997/4	1946-48	£7,500	£4,000	£2,250
Rapier I	1392/4	1955-57	£1,200	£700	£300
Rapier II	1494/4	1957-59	£1,800	£900	£300
Rapier II Conv	1494/4	1957-59	£3,000	£1,500	£450
Rapier III	1494/4	1959-61	£2,000	£1,200	£400
Rapier III Conv	1494/4	1959-61	£3,500	£1,600	£600
Rapier IIIA	1592/4	1961-63	£2,000	£1,200	£400
Rapier IIIA Conv	1592/4	1961-63	£3,600	£1,700	£650
Rapier IV/V	1592/ 1725/4	1963-67	£2,000	£700	£250
Alpine I-II	1494/4	1959-62	£6,000	£3,500	£1,800
Alpine III	1592/4	1963	£6,500	£4,000	£1,250
Alpine IV	1592/4	1964	£6,500	£4,000	£1,250
Alpine V	1725/4	1965-68	£7,000	£4,000	£1,250
Harrington Alpine	1592/4	1961	£8,000	£4,750	£1,250
Harrington Le Mans	1592/4	1962-63	£10,000	£6,500	£3,000
Tiger Mk 1	4261/8	1964-67	£12,000	£9,000	£5,000
Tiger Mk 2	4700/8	1967	£9,000	£7,500	£5,000
Rapier Fastback	1725/4	1967-76	£1,100	£700	£250
Rapier H120	1725/4	1968-76	£1,500	£800	£300

1952 Sunbeam-Talbot MkII Saloon, body repainted, engine in running condition, some cosmetic attention required.
£900–1,000 *C*

1957 Sunbeam-Talbot MkIII Saloon, restored to concours winning standard.
£4,100–4,300 *S*

TALBOT

1915 Talbot Model 15/20 Roadster, 4 cylinder single side valve, 2 litre engine, 4 speed right hand change gearbox, channel section chassis with beam axles carried on semi-elliptic springs front and rear, drum type brakes on rear wheels, centre lock wire type wheels with 5.00 x 24 tyres, almost complete, not in running condition.
£11,000–13,000 *C(A)*

The relatively high survival rate of Edwardian Talbots is proof of their popularity and sound engineering.

TALBOT Model	ENGINE cc/cyl	DATES	CONDITION		
			1	2	3
25hp and 25/50	4155/4	1907-16	£35,000	£25,000	£15,000
12hp	2409/4	1909-15	£22,000	£15,000	£9,000
8/18	960/4	1922-25	£8,000	£5,000	£2,000
14/45	1666/6	1926-35	£16,000	£10,000	£5,000
75	2276/6	1930-37	£22,000	£12,000	£7,000
105	2969/6	1935-37	£28,000	£20,000	£15,000

Higher value for tourers and coachbuilt cars.

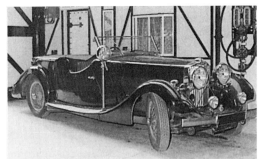

1934 Talbot 110 Type BA Tourer,
fold-flat windscreen, adjustable ride
suspension, pre-seletor gearbox, Jaeger
instruments, Lucas bull's-eye headlights,
Stephen Grebel pillar spotlight, requires
re-commissioning.
£16,000–16,500 *S*

1954 Talbot-Lago Type 26 Grand Sport,
6 cylinders, 4482cc, very good condition.
Est. £24,000–30,000 *COYS*

*This is believed to be the only such example
currently in Britain.*

TAMPLIN

**1921 Tamplin 8.9hp Tandem 2 Seater
Cyclecar,** good overall condition.
£6,800–7,200 *S*

*Designed by Captain Carden, who had also
been responsible for the Carden cyclecar and
the AV Monocar, the Tamplin was powered
by a 986cc JAP engine transmitting drive by
chain to a Sturmey-Archer gearbox,
incorporating a clutch and internal kick start.*

TRIKING

**1982 Triking 944cc 3 Wheeler 2 Seater
Sports,** totally re-built to as-new condition.
Est. £9,000–10,000 *S*

TALBOT-LAGO

Following the merger of the Sunbeam-Talbot
Darracq empire into the Rootes Group in
1935, Major Tony Lago took control of the
Talbot factory at Suresnes. His new 4 litre,
6 cylinder cars, with their triple carburettors,
developed 165bhp at 4200rpm, and with this
engine Talbot-Lago achieved victory in the
1937 Tourist Trophy and the French Grand
Prix in that year.

1948 Talbot-Lago Type 26 Record,
very original, right hand drive, requires
re-commissioning.
£18,000–20,000 *Bro*

TATRA

c1928 Tatra Type 12 Torpedo Tourer,
museum stored, mostly original specification,
good original condition.
£4,800–5,200 *S*

TRABANT

1966 Trabant 601 Saloon, good
general condition.
£350–375 *H&H*

*The Trabant 601 Saloon was a neat compact
design with front wheel drive and air-cooled
2 cylinder, 2 stroke engine which developed
26bhp and a top speed of 62mph.*

TRIUMPH

The Triumph TRs were the first successful sports cars produced by the Standard Triumph Company. They were designed to compete with the Austin Healey and MG range, which was a market almost solely for the sports enthusiast who perhaps could not afford the more expensive British products, such as Jaguar XK140.

There was no TR1 as such, only the prototype, and the TR2, launched at the 1952 Motor Show, was the cheapest 100mph car on the market at £555. Over 80,000 'sidescreen' TRs (TR2, TR3 and TR3A) were built. The TR4 was introduced in 1961. It is a relatively easy conversion from left to right hand drive. However, anything up to 15–20% should be added to the value of an original British right hand drive model over the more numerous export models.

1949 Triumph 2000 Roadster, full chassis-up rebuild to original specification.
£10,250–10,750 *LF*

1949 Triumph Roadster, good unrestored condition.
£6,000–6,300 *GES*

1957 Triumph TR3, converted from left hand drive, incorrect front bumper, good condition.
£6,500–6,750 *NTC*

TR2/3

- **The early TR2s and TR3s were the best selling sports cars of their time.**
- **Over 58,000 TR3As were built, but only about 2,000 stayed in the UK.**
- **A very strong 4 cylinder, 2 litre engine led to many rally victories, notably a famous 1st and 2nd in the RAC Rally of 1954.**

1959 Triumph TR3A Sports Convertible, left hand drive, original specification very good condition.
£7,000–8,000 *S*

1965 Triumph TR4A, totally restored throughout, very good condition.
£10,000–10,250 *BLE*

1965 Triumph TR4A, 4 cylinders, 2138cc, excellent condition.
£6,500–7,000 *ADT*

TRIUMPH	ENGINE	DATES	CONDITION		
Model	cc/cyl		1	2	3
TLC	1393/4	1923-25	£6,000	£4,000	£1,500
TPC	2169/4	1926-30	£6,000	£4,000	£2,000
K	832/4	1928-34	£4,000	£2,000	£1,000
S	1203/6	1931-33	£5,000	£3,000	£1,500
G12 Gloria	1232/4	1935-37	£6,000	£4,000	£2,000
G16 Gloria 6	1991/6	1935-39	£7,000	£4,500	£2,000
Vitesse/Dolomite	1767/4	1937-39	£14,000	£10,000	£6,000
Dolomite	1496/4	1938-39	£7,000	£4,000	£2,000

1964 Triumph TR4, original UK car, with Surrey top, wire wheels, good condition.
£8,000–8,250 *NTC*

1966 Triumph TR4A, 4 cylinders, 2138cc, left hand drive, very good overall condition.
£5,400–5,800 *ADT*

1967 Triumph TR4A, 4 cylinders, 2138cc, body original but re-painted, new chrome wire wheels, good condition throughout.
Est. £7,000–9,000 *ADT*

1967 Triumph TR4A IRS 2 Seater Sports, engine in excellent condition, original upholstery, very good condition throughout.
£11,500–11,750 *S*

1968 Triumph TR5, 6 cylinders, 2498cc, very good condition.
Est. £12,000–13,000 *ADT*

Although the bodyshell for the TR5 remained the same as the TR4, the use of a 6 cylinder engine for the first time in a TR heralded a new era for Triumph. In the short 15 month production period just 2,950 TR5s were built, 1,200 of which were UK cars.

1967 Triumph 2000 MkI, automatic transmission, very good condition.
£1,500–2,000 *OMH*

1972 Triumph 2000 Automatic Estate, unused recently, good general condition.
£625–675 *S*

Triumph 2000

- **The long low look coachwork was interpreted by Michelotti, and featured twin headlights.**
- **The 1998cc engine developed 90bhp, with a top speed of about 100mph.**
- **The car was generously equipped with well-upholstered reclining front seats, vanity mirrors, cigar lighter, and wooden door cappings.**

1970 Triumph 1300 Saloon, 31,000 miles recorded, manual gearbox, very good condition throughout.
£900–950 *LF*

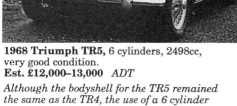

1972 Triumph 2000 MkII, one owner,
45,000 miles, rust-proofed from new.
£3,750–4,250 *Bro*

1973 Triumph Dolomite, 4 cylinders,
1854cc, fair to good condition throughout.
Est. £1,300–1,700 *ADT*

1976 Triumph Dolomite Sprint,
4 cylinders, 1998cc, good original condition.
Est. £1,500–1,800 *ADT*

**1976 Triumph 2500 S Automatic 4 Door
Saloon,** average mechanical condition,
paintwork, upholstery and interior trim good,
requires cosmetic restoration.
£775–825 *S*

*Based on the 2 litre, 2000 model introduced in
1964, the 2.5 litre version arrived with a
petrol injection de-tuned TR6 engine in 1969.
Production continued until 1977, latterly with
twin carburettors, the same year as the V8
Stag was discontinued.*

1980 Triumph Dolomite Sprint,
4 cylinders, 1998cc, good overall condition.
£1,000–1,100 *ADT*

Triumph GT6

- **Produced between 1966 and 1973,
  the GT6 evolved through 3 differing
  stages of tune, although all relied on
  the 6 cylinder, 1998cc Triumph engine.**
- **The MkI was capable of more than
  100mph although the handling was
  criticised for having understeer.**
- **The MkII model had a revised lower
  wishbone set-up as well as an uprated
  specification engine.**
- **The MkIII was the best of the range
  with 104bhp and the basic price in
  1970 was £970, which by 1973 had
  risen to £1,285.**

1969 Tiumph Herald 13/60 Convertible,
very good overall condition.
£1,400–1,600 *LF*

*This model evolved over the years, culminating
in the 13/60, which denotes the capacity of
1296cc and 60bhp, and is distinguishable from
the earlier models by the Vitesse style grille.*

1973 Triumph GT6, 6 cylinders, 1998cc,
excellent condition throughout.
Est. £6,500–8,500 *ADT*

1959 Triumph Italia 2000, 4 cylinders, 1991cc, 2 door coupé, manual transmission, left hand drive, excellent restored condition. **£9,000–9,500** *ADT*

The styling consultant, Michelotti, combined his talent with that of Vignale to produce the Triumph Italia. The car was mechanically identical to the TR3A but retailed in Italy.

1972 Triumph TR6, 6 cylinders, 2498cc, manual 4 speed gearbox with overdrive on 2nd, 3rd and 4th, engine recondiitioned, excellent restored condition. **Est. £9,000–12,000** *ADT*

1978 Triumph TR8 Fixed Head Coupé, 3528cc engine, converted to right hand drive, very good condition throughout. **£5,000–5,500** *HOLL*

1973 Triumph Stag, some mechanical components require attention but complete and basically sound. **£2,300–2,500** *ADT*

1970 Triumph TR6, 6 cylinders, 2498cc, very good condition throughout. **£8,000–8,500** *ADT*

1972 Triumph TR6, 6 cylinder, 2498cc engine, left hand drive, very good panelwork and mechanics, no overdrive. **£3,600–3,800** *ADT*

1980 Triumph TR7 2 Seater Sports Convertible, excellent condition throughout. **£3,800–4,200** *S*

Introduced in 1975 as a replacement for the TR6, Triumph's TR7 used the 2 litre Dolomite Sprint engine in a unitary hull with all coil springing, rack-and-pinion steering, and initially with power disc/drum brakes. The original 4 speed gearbox was replaced in 1977 with a Rover 5 speed unit.

1975 Triumph Stag, 8 cylinders, 2997cc, automatic gearbox, rear axle and suspension in good condition, interior sound, very good condition throughout. **£3,200–3,500** *ADT*

1976 Triumph Stag, automatic gearbox, very good overall condition.
£5,500–6,000 *ADT*

1977 Triumph Stag Sports Convertible new automatic gearbox, with hard top, good condition.
Est. £4,750–5,750 *S*

Introduced in 1970, the Triumph Stag was designed by Michelotti. With hard and soft tops, 4 seats and a 3 litre, V8 engine, it was capable of 117mph.

TRIUMPH Model	ENGINE cc/cyl	DATES	CONDITION 1	2	3
1800/2000 Roadster	1776/ 2088/4	1946-49	£10,000	£7,500	£2,500
1800	1776/4	1946-49	£4,200	£2,000	£950
2000 Renown	2088/4	1949-54	£4,200	£2,000	£950
Mayflower	1247/4	1949-53	£1,700	£750	£350
TR2 long door	1247/4	1953	£10,000	£8,000	£5,000
TR2	1247/4	1953-55	£9,000	£6,000	£5,000
TR3	1991/4	1955-57	£9,000	£8,500	£3,500
TR3A	1991/4	1958-62	£9,500	£8,500	£3,500
TR4	2138/4	1961-65	£9,000	£6,000	£3,000
TR4A	2138/4	1965-67	£9,000	£6,500	£3,000
TR5	2498/6	1967-68	£10,000	£8,500	£4,000
TR6 (PI)	2498/6	1969-74	£9,000	£7,500	£3,500
Herald	948/4	1959-61	£800	£400	£150
Herald FHC	948/4	1959-61	£1,200	£550	£300
Herald DHC	948/4	1960-61	£2,000	£800	£350
Herald 'S'	948/4	1961-64	£800	£400	£150
Herald 1200	1147/4	1961-70	£1,100	£500	£200
Herald 1200 FHC	1147/4	1961-64	£1,400	£800	£300
Herald 1200 DHC	1147/4	1961-67	£2,000	£900	£350
Herald 1200 Est	1147/4	1961-67	£1,300	£700	£300
Herald 12/50	1147/4	1963-67	£1,200	£600	£250
Herald 13/60	1296/4	1967-71	£1,300	£600	£200
Herald 13/60 DHC	1296/4	1967-71	£2,000	£1,200	£400
Herald 13/60 Est	1296/4	1967-71	£1,500	£650	£300
Vitesse 1600	1596/6	1962-66	£2,000	£1,250	£550
Vitesse 1600 Conv	1596/6	1962-66	£2,800	£1,350	£600
Vitesse 2 litre Mk I	1998/6	1966-68	£1,800	£800	£300
Vitesse 2 litre Mk I Conv	1998/6	1966-68	£3,000	£1,500	£650
Vitesse 2 litre Mk II	1998/6	1968-71	£2,000	£1,500	£300
Vitesse 2 litre Mk II Conv	1998/6	1968-71	£4,000	£1,750	£650
Spitfire Mk I	1147/4	1962-64	£2,000	£1,750	£300
Spitfire Mk II	1147/4	1965-67	£2,500	£2,000	£350
Spitfire Mk III	1296/4	1967-70	£3,500	£2,500	£450
Spitfire Mk IV	1296/4	1970-74	£2,500	£2,000	£350
Spitfire 1500	1493/4	1975-78	£3,500	£2,500	£750
Spitfire 1500	1493/4	1979-81	£4,500	£3,000	£1,200
GT6 Mk I	1998/6	1966-68	£5,000	£4,000	£1,200
GT6 Mk II	1998/6	1968-70	£6,000	£4,500	£1,400
GT6 Mk III	1998/6	1970-73	£7,000	£5,000	£1,500
2000 Mk I	1998/6	1963-69	£2,000	£1,200	£400
2000 Mk III	1998/6	1969-77	£2,000	£1,200	£500
2.5 PI	2498/6	1968-75	£2,000	£1,500	£900
2500 TC/S	2498/6	1974-77	£1,750	£700	£150
2500S	2498/6	1975-77	£2,500	£1,000	£150
1300 (FWD)	1296/4	1965-70	£800	£400	£150
1300TC (FWD)	1296/4	1967-70	£900	£450	£150
1500 (FWD)	1493/4	1970-73	£700	£450	£125
1500TC (RWD)	1296/4	1973-76	£850	£500	£100
Toledo	1296/4	1970-76	£850	£450	£100
Dolomite 1500	1493/4	1976-80	£1,350	£750	£125
Dolomite 1850	1854/4	1972-80	£1,450	£850	£150
Dolomite Sprint	1998/4	1976-81	£6,000	£4,500	£1,000
Stag	2997/8	1970-77	£9,000	£4,250	£2,000
TR7	1998/4	1975-82	£4,000	£1,200	£500
TR7 DHC	1998/4	1980-82	£5,000	£3,500	£1,500

TVR

1972 TVR 1600M, one owner, only 42,000 miles recorded, excellent condition.
£4,250–4,500 *CCTC*

This is a very rare car.

1984 TVR 350i Convertible, V8 engine, manual gearbox, alloy wheels, only 28,000 miles recorded, excellent condition.
£8,000–10,000 *VIC*

TVR Model	ENGINE cc/cyl	DATES	CONDITION 1	2	3
Grantura I	1172/4	1957-62	£4,000	£3,000	£2,000
Grantura II	1558/4	1957-62	£4,300	£3,000	£2,000
Grantura III/1800S	1798/4	1963-67	£5,000	£3,000	£2,200
Tuscan V8	4727/8	1967 70	£12,000	£7,000	£6,000
Vixen S2/3	1599/4	1968-72	£5,000	£3,000	£1,500
3000M	2994/6	1972-79	£8,000	£4,000	£3,000
Taimar	2994/6	1977-79	£7,500	£5,000	£3,500

UNIC

In 1905 Georges Richard left the firm he founded and started building Unic cars at Puteaux, the name of the car relating to the new company's intended policy of offering but a single model. Although the policy was abandoned within 2 years, the name remained, and 4 cylinder models were introduced in 1906.

c1920 Unic Type J3 7/10 CV Rolling Chassis, complete rolling chassis, including radiator and bulkhead, mounted on wooden artillery wheels, all major chassis components present.
Est. £1,600–2,000 *S*

c1914 Unic Type M1 Coupé Chauffeur, coachwork by Vicard et Fils, roadworthy following museum storage, requires re-commissioning.
£15,000–16,000 *S*

> **Cross Reference**
> Restoration Projects

VANDEN PLAS

1978 Vanden Plas 1500, 67,000 miles, excellent original condition.
£1,400–1,600 *Mot*

VANDEN PLAS Model	ENGINE cc/cyl	DATES	CONDITION 1	2	3
3 litre I/II	2912/6	1959-64	£4,000	£2,000	£700
4 litre R	3909/6	1964-67	£4,300	£2,500	£700
1100 Princess	1098/4	1964-67	£2,000	£1,000	£250
1300 Princess	1275/4	1967-74	£2,200	£1,500	£500

VAUXHALL

1923 Vauxhall 23/60 OD Kingston Tourer, engine recently rebuilt, excellent condition throughout.
Est. £32,000–37,000 *S*

The Kingston Tourer was a handsome car with a rather barrel-sided body accommodating 5 people in comfort. The radiator and bonnet have the traditional Vauxhall flutes which date back to 1903.

1924 Vauxhall 30/98 Velox Tourer, original specification, a dream 'barn discovery', straightforward restoration project.
£72,000–74,000 *S*

1923 Vauxhall 30/98 OE Sports Tourer, suitable for restoration.
£37,000–38,000 *S*

> **Cross Reference**
> Restoration Projects

1935 Vauxhall 14/6 Cabriolet, good, sound, reliable car.
Est. £4,000–6,000 *ALC*

A rare 4 seater tourer, being one of the relatively small number fitted with Cabriolet convertible bodywork by Wingham to the 6 cylinder chassis.

VAUXHALL Model	ENGINE cc/cyl	DATES	CONDITION 1	2	3
D/OD	3969/4	1914-26	£32,000	£24,000	£18,000
E/OE	4224/4	1919-28	£80,000	£40,000	£25,000
Eighty	3317/6	1931-33	£10,000	£8,000	£5,000
Cadet	2048/6	1931-33	£7,000	£5,000	£3,000
Lt Six	1531/6	1934-38	£5,000	£4,000	£1,500
14	1781/6	1934-39	£4,000	£3,000	£1,500
25	3215/6	1937-39	£5,000	£4,000	£1,500
10	1203/4	1938-39	£4,000	£3,000	£1,500
Wyvern LIX	1500/4	1948-51	£3,000	£1,000	£500
Velox LIP	2200/6	1948-51	£3,000	£1,000	£500
Wyvern EIX	1500/4	1951-57	£3,000	£1,320	£400
Velox EIPV	2200/6	1951-57	£3,000	£1,650	£400
Cresta EIPC	2200/6	1954-57	£3,000	£1,650	£400
Velox/Cresta PAS/PAD	2262/6	1957-59	£2,850	£1,300	£300
Velox/Cresta PASY/PADY	2262/6	1959-60	£2,700	£1,500	£300
Velox/Cresta PASX/PADX	2651/6	1960-62	£2,700	£1,300	£300
Velox/Cresta PASX/PADX Est	2651/6	1960-62	£2,700	£1,300	£300
Velox/Cresta PB	2651/6	1962-65	£1,600	£800	£100
Velox/Cresta PB Est	2651/6	1962-65	£1,600	£800	£100
Cresta/Deluxe PC	3294/6	1964-72	£1,500	£800	£100
Cresta PC Est	3294/6	1964-72	£1,500	£800	£100
Viscount	3294/6	1964-72	£1,700	£900	£100
Victor I/II	1507/4	1957-61	£2,000	£1,000	£250
Victor I/II Est	1507/4	1957-61	£2,100	£1,100	£300
Victor FB	1507/4	1961-64	£1,500	£900	£200
Victor FB Est	1507/4	1961-64	£1,600	£1,000	£300
VX4/90	1507/4	1961-64	£2,000	£900	£150
Victor FC101	1594/4	1964-67	£1,600	£900	£150
Victor FC101 Est	1594/4	1964-67	£1,800	£1,000	£200
101 VX4/90	1594/4	1964-67	£2,000	£1,500	£250
VX4/90	1975/4	1969-71	£700	£600	£100
Ventora I/II	3294/6	1968-71	£500	£375	£100
Viva HA	1057/4	1963-66	£500	£350	£100
Viva SL90	1159/4	1966-70	£500	£350	£100
Viva Brabham	1159/4	1967-70	£1,200	£500	£100
Viva	1600/4	1968-70	£500	£350	£100
Viva Est	1159/4	1967-70	£500	£400	£100

1960 Vauxhall Victor SL, 4 cylinder, 1507cc engine, good original condition.
£1,800–2,000 *ADT*

1937 Vauxhall 14/6 Saloon, good condition throughout.
£4,750–5,250 *OMH*

1966 Vauxhall Victor 101 De Luxe 4 Door Saloon Special, very good condition.
Est. £2,000–3,000 *S*

Outwardly there is little to distinguish the car from the standard Vauxhall Victor 101 de Luxe model. The front end incorporates a space frame specially built to accommodate a Rover V8 engine and 3 speed transmission. It is also fitted with alloy wheels.

1963 Vauxhall VX 4/90 Saloon, re-sprayed, excellent condition throughout.
£2,200–2,400 *LF*

The FB Victor was introduced in 1961 and with it came the sporting twin carb VX 4/90. Easily distinguishable from the contemporary Victor by the grille and the side flashes, the car has a floor change with 4 speeds and developed some 71bhp.

1975 Vauxhall FE VX 490, 4 cylinders, good overall appearance, brakes require attention.
£500–600 *ADT*

VOLKSWAGEN

Developed between 1934 and 1939 with help from Ferdinand Porsche, only prototype Volkswagens were available prior to WWII and these had 984cc air-cooled engines. After the war the Volkswagen factory came under British control and a number of cars were assembled from parts. In 1945 a total of 1,785 cars were produced, the number being increased to 10,000 in 1946. In 1954 the engine was developed to 1192cc, with an output of 30bhp, with a further increase in engine output in 1960. Production of the ubiquitous 'Beetle' has continued somewhere in the world ever since.

1955 Volkswagen Saloon, 4 cylinders, 1192cc, original engine in good working condition, small oval rear window, spats and other early features.
Est. £5,000–6,000 *ADT*

1960 Volkswagen Beetle, 4 cylinders, 1192cc, comprehensively rebuilt, excellent condition.
Est. £4,000–5,000 *ADT*

VOLKSWAGEN Model	ENGINE cc/cyl	DATES	CONDITION 1	2	3
Beetle (split rear screen)	1131/4	1945-53	£5,000	£3,500	£2,000
Beetle (oval rear screen)	1192/4	1953-57	£4,000	£2,000	£1,000
Beetle (slope headlamps)	1192/4	1957-68	£2,500	£1,000	£600
Beetle DHC	1192/4	1954-60	£6,000	£4,500	£2,000
Beetle 1500	1493/4	1966-70	£3,000	£2,000	£1,000
Beetle 1302 LS	1600/4	1970-72	£2,500	£1,850	£850
Beetle 1303 S	1600/4	1972-79	£3,000	£2,000	£1,500
1500 Variant/1600	1493/ 1584/4	1961-73	£2,000	£1,500	£650
1500/1600	1493/ 1584/4	1961-73	£3,000	£2,000	£800
Karmann Ghia/I	1192/4	1955-59	£5,000	£3,000	£1,000
Karmann Ghia/I DHC	1192/4	1957-59	£8,000	£5,000	£2,500
Karmann Ghia/I	1192/4	1960-74	£5,500	£3,000	£1,800
Karmann Ghia/I DHC	1192/4	1960-74	£7,000	£4,500	£2,000
Karmann Ghia/3	1493/4	1962-69	£4,000	£2,500	£1,250

1970 Volkswagen Beetle, 4 cylinders, 1300cc, left hand drive, requires attention. **£240–280** *ADT*

1971 Volkswagen 1032S Beetle, 4 cylinders, 1584cc, good mechanics, fair general condition. **£700–800** *ADT*

1973 Volkswagen 1300S, fair to good overall condition. **Est. £1,300–1,500** *ADT*

1974 Volkswagen Beetle, fully reconditioned 1600cc engine, good condition throughout. **£600–700** *ADT*

1971 Volkswagen Karmann Ghia 2+2 Coupé, nearside trim missing, bumpers require re-chroming, very good condition. **Est. £2,200–2,800** *S*

1974 Volkswagen Trekker Type 181, good condition throughout. **£1,600–1,800** *S*

VOLVO

1966 Volvo 121 Amazon 4 Door Sports
Saloon, extensively restored, excellent high
specification car.
Est. £3,800–4,500 *S*

1971 Volvo P1800E 2 Door Sports Coupé,
excellent restored condition.
Est. £3,000–4,000 *S*

VOLVO Model	ENGINE cc/cyl	DATES	CONDITION 1	2	3
PV444	1800/4	1958-67	£4,000	£1,750	£800
PV544	1800/4	1962-64	£4,000	£1,750	£800
120 (B16)	1583/4	1956-59	£3,000	£1,000	£300
121	1708/4	1960-67	£3,500	£1,500	£350
122S	1780/4	1960-67	£4,500	£1,500	£250
131	1780/4	1962-69	£4,000	£1,500	£350
221/222	1780/4	1962-69	£2,500	£1,500	£300
123Gt	1986/4	1967-69	£3,000	£2,500	£750
P1800	1986/4	1960-70	£3,500	£2,000	£1,000
P1800E	1986/4	1970-71	£4,000	£2,500	£1,000
P1800ES	1986/4	1971-73	£5,000	£3,000	£1,000

1972 Volvo 1800E Sports, automatic
gearbox, maintained regardless of cost.
£4,000–4,400 *H&H*

1972 Volvo 1800ES, requires some attention.
£2,400–2,800 *ADT*

1972 Volvo 1800ES, 4 speed gearbox with
overdrive, very good condition throughout.
Est. £2,500–3,500 *ADT*

1972 Volvo 1800ES, excellent original
condition throughout.
£2,750–3,000 *ADT*

WILLYS KNIGHT

Don't Forget!
*If in doubt please refer
to the 'How to Use'
section at the beginning
of this book.*

1928 Willys Knight 6 Light Limousine,
3 owners from new, very original example.
£6,000–8,000 *Bro*

WOLSELEY

The first Wolseley appeared in 1895, designed by Herbert Austin. Initially a 3 wheeler similar to a French Léon Bollée, it was 4 years before the first 4 wheeled Wolseley appeared. The marque had Royal patronage from an early stage as H. M. Queen Alexandra owned a landaulette.

With the outbreak of WWI, the company built the SE5 aero engine, designed by Hispano-Suiza. Aero engine production inspired the manufacturer in its designs for post-war car production.

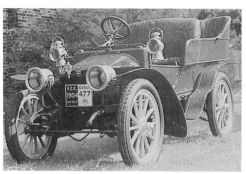

1904 Wolseley 8hp Rear Entrance Tonneau, excellent condition throughout. **£42,000–44,000** *BKS*

1923 Wolseley A9 15.6hp Open Drive Landaulette, recently restored, good overall condition. **Est. £15,000–17,000** *S*

1926 Wolseley 11/22hp Type E4 4 Seater Tourer, original rexine upholstery, mostly original condition, requires careful re-commissioning. **£5,600–5,800** *S*

1935 Wolseley Hornet Special, complete and to original specification, straightforward restoration project. **£6,400–6,800** *S*

The engine was essentially a 6 cylinder version of the overhead camshaft engine used in the Morris Minor and MG Midget. The early Hornet Specials had 1271cc capacity with twin SU carburettors, raised compression, domed pistons and double valve springs.

WOLSELEY (Veteran & Vintage) Model	ENGINE cc/cyl	DATES	CONDITION		
			1	2	3
10	987/2	1909-16	£16,000	£12,500	£9,000
CZ (30hp)	2887/4	1909	£18,000	£13,000	£9,000
15hp and A9	2614/4	1920-27	£12,000	£10,000	£8,000
20 and C8	3921/ 3862/6	1920-27	£11,000	£8,000	£6,000
E4 (10.5hp)	1267/ 1542/4	1925-30	£6,000	£4,000	£3,000
E6 and Viper and 16hp	2025/6	1927-34	£15,000	£12,000	£8,000
E8M	2700/8	1928-31	£18,000	£15,000	£12,000
Hornet	1271/4	1931-35	£10,000	£8,000	£4,500
Hornet Special	1271/ 1604/6	1933-36	£12,000	£8,000	£5,000
Wasp	1069/4	1936	£7,000	£5,000	£3,500
Hornet	1378/6	1936	£8,000	£6,000	£4,000
21/60 and 21hp	2677/ 2916/6	1932-39	£11,000	£6,000	£4,000
25	3485/6	1936-39	£11,000	£6,500	£4,000
12/48	1547/4	1937-39	£5,000	£3,000	£1,750
18/80	2322/6	1938-39	£11,000	£6,750	£4,000

Early Wolseley cars are well made and very British and those with coachbuilt bodies command a premium of at least +25%.

WOLSELEY Model	ENGINE cc/cyl	DATES	CONDITION 1	2	3
8	918/4	1939-48	£1,800	£1,000	£500
10	1140/4	1939-48	£2,500	£1,000	£500
12/48	1548/4	1939-48	£2,500	£1,000	£500
14/60	1818/6	1946-48	£2,500	£1,200	£500
18/85	2321/6	1946-48	£3,000	£1,200	£500
25	3485/6	1946-48	£2,500	£1,000	£500
4/50	1476/4	1948-53	£1,900	£600	£300
6/80	2215/6	1948-54	£2,000	£1,000	£400
4/44	1250/4	1952-56	£2,000	£850	£500
15/50	1489/4	1956-58	£1,850	£850	£350
1500	1489/4	1958-65	£2,500	£1,000	£500
15/60	1489/4	1958-61	£2,000	£700	£300
16/60	1622/4	1961-71	£1,800	£800	£300
6/90	2639/6	1954-57	£2,000	£1,000	£500
6/99	2912/6	1959-61	£2,000	£1,000	£500
6/110 MK I/II	2912/6	1961-68	£1,500	£800	£400
Hornet (Mini)	848/4	1961-70	£1,500	£450	£250
1300	1275/4	1967-74	£1,250	£750	£200
18/85	1798/4	1967-72	£950	£400	£150

COMMERCIAL VEHICLES

1932 Wolseley 9, 4 cylinders, 1018cc, good condition throughout.
£5,000–5,500 *ADT*

1926 Austin 7hp Light Van, comprehensive restoration, excellent condition throughout.
£4,200–4,400 *S*

1932 Austin 7hp Milk Delivery Car, good running order.
Est. £6,500–8,000 *S*

1951 Austin K8 Breakdown/Recovery Van, original condition throughout.
Est. £1,800–2,200 *S*

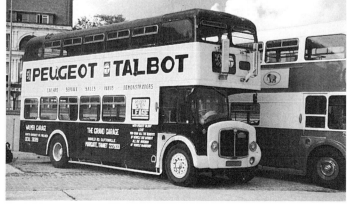

1964 AEC Regent V/Park Royal Double Decker Bus, body and mechanics in good condition.
Est. £1,500–1,800 *LF*

1951 Austin A40 Devon Van, well restored to original specification throughout.
£3,600–3,800 *S*

1955 Austin Loadstar 3 Ton Horse Box/Livestock Lorry, original Tiverton body, excellent condition.
£6,250–6,750 *Bro*

1970 Austin Morris Minor Van, bodywork and mechanics in good condition.
£600–700 *S*

1971 Austin Morris Pick-Up, good condition.
£2,400–2,500 *HOLL*

1969 Bedford Type CA Van, 4 cylinders, 1595cc, stored, requires attention.
£70–80 *ADT*

1929 Dennis Type ES 32 Seater Single Decker Bus, excellent condition throughout.
Est. £18,000–25,000 *S*

The Type ES of 1929 was powered by a 4 cylinder, 5700cc, side valve petrol engine.

1914 Ford Model T 2 Seater Pick-Up Truck, paintwork and mechanics in good condition, roadworthy but no MOT.
Est. £10,000–12,000 *S*

Cross Reference
Ford

1926 Ford Model TT One Ton Van, engine rebuilt, completely restored.
£7,500–8,000 *S*

1926 Ford Model T Van, complete with
14 beer barrels and working beer pumps,
sliding driver and passenger doors, full
engine, gearbox and chassis rebuilt in 1988,
excellent condition.
£11,500–12,000 *Bro*

1960 Ford Thames 300E Van, very good
original condition.
Est. £800–1,200 *LF*

*This is the larger, 7cwt van version of the
renowned 100E Ford. The Commercials were
known as the 300Es and were powered by the
same 1172cc engine through a 3 speed gearbox.*

1960 Ford Thames 7cwt Van, 4 cylinders,
1172cc, good overall condition.
Est. £1,800–2,200 *ADT*

1936 Lanchester 8 Seater Minibus,
only 2 owners, chassis, engine and gearbox
overhauled, re-sprayed and re-trimmed,
good condition.
£6,000–6,250 *Bro*

This is probably the only bus with wire wheels.

**1929 Morris Commercial Series R 25cwt
Breakdown Truck,** new van body, 30cwt
Harvey Frost crane, original cab interior,
unused for 20 years.
£3,800–4,000 *S*

1966 Morris Minor Pick-Up Special,
automatic gearbox, MG Midget differential,
front disc brakes, chassis-up rebuild.
Est. £1,500–2,000 *LF*

*This pick-up was originally fitted with a
Morris Minor 1000 engine, but now has a
Ford 1600cc engine with automatic gearbox.*

1946 Morris Series Y 10cwt GPO Van,
extensively restored to almost original
specification, good condition throughout.
£3,000–3,300 *S*

*Morris Z and Y Series vans were widely used
by the General Post Office.*

1972 Morris 6 cwt Van, original condition,
requires light restoration.
£500–800 *OMH*

FIRE APPLIANCES

1929 Dennis 45hp Turbine Fire Engine with Extension Ladder, excellent restored condition.
Est. £11,500–12,500 *S*

This vehicle is equipped with 4 lengths of new 5in suction hose, the extension ladder and pump giving 4 x 500/600 gallons of water per minute, and has regularly passed the fire service pumping tests.

Dennis Bros Ltd., produced their first commercial vehicle in 1904 having previously founded the company as a cycle manufacturer and subsequently quadricycles. The first Dennis fire engine incorporated an overdrive gearbox as early as 1908, as well as a Gwynne pump which could pump 400 gallons a minute.

1975 Land Rover Fire Tender, 4 cylinders, 2600cc, twin front foam taps mounted on a large girder style bumper, fully pressurised water pumps, twin flashing beacons, horns and water cannon, stored for last 5 years, very good original condition.
£3,000–4,000 *ADT*

1952 Dennis F7 Series 4¼ Litre Fire Engine, 'The Queen Mary', dry stored for many years, Ajax ladder, over-slung bell, twin hose reels, some uniforms, good overall condition.
£2,500–3,000 *BKS*

1958 Bedford S Type Turntable Ladder, crew cab body by Wilsdon, 100ft turntable ladder by Magirus, record book of all journeys undertaken whilst on active service.
£2,000–2,200 *LF*

> **Cross Reference**
> Land Rover

MILITARY VEHICLES

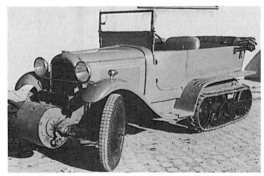

1934 Citroën Kegresse Type P17 D Half Track Vehicle, a remarkable and rare survivor.
£5,600–5,800 *S*

Citroën produced a half-track vehicle in pre-war years primarily for military service as an artillery carrier, but also for use by the engineers for more remote and inaccessible tasks.

1952 Austin Champ, 4 cylinders, 2828cc, restored over 5 years, mostly original, new lights and indicators.
£2,200–2,400 *ADT*

Although some 13,000 Champs were built by 1955, they were extremely expensive and highly sophisticated, so the Armed Forces looked to the Land Rover as soon as they could. This is chassis number 001, and military records confirm that it was first commissioned in May 1952.

c1963 Daimler MkIII Ferret Scout Car, little used although regularly serviced, good general condition.
Est. £3,000–4,000 *ADT*

Equipped with a Rolls-Royce B60 6 cylinder water-cooled engine of 4.26 litres, it was able to develop 129bhp. Weighing approximately 5 tons, the vehicle was able to achieve 45mph through its 5 speed, pre-selector gearbox. Other features of the machine include a 21 gallon fuel tank, 900 x 16 tyres, 2 speed 225 amp generator and 12 volt electricity.

1954 Volvo Military 4x4 Command/Radio Car, good overall condition.
Est. £3,500–4,500 *S*

Only 720 models of the 915 'Radiopersonterrang' were constructed between 1953 and 1956. They utilised a light truck chassis with a 6 cylinder side valve petrol engine.

1947 Willys Jeep Type CJ2 4x4, engine overhauled, wiring renewed, bodywork restored.
£3,200–3,500 *S*

RACING CARS

The Ex-Antony Powys-Lybbe Alvis 12/60 Racing Special, not raced for some years, substantially dismantled in a well-advanced state of restoration.
£18,500–20,000 *S*

This car is perhaps one of the most famous of Alvis's 12/50 and 12/60 cars, having a distinguished pre-WWII history in the hands of Antony Powys-Lybbe.

1961 Cannon Trials Car, same condition as when last raced.
£1,800–2,000 *S*

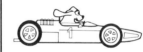

1960 Bandini Formula Junior,
excellent condition.
£25,000+ *Car*

This was to be the Italian's answer to the Lotus 18, however, only one was built!

1957 Cooper T43 Climax Formula Two,
chassis number FII-26-57, owned by Tommy Atkins, driven by Sir Jack Brabham and Roy Salvadori, very original condition.
£55,000+ *Car*

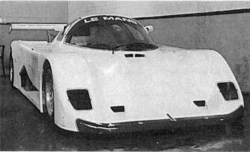

1984 Harrier LR4, 8 cylinders, 5700cc,
5.7 GM Dallas Motorsport engine capable of 560bhp, set up for endurance spec. racing, unused for 3 years, requires full re-commissioning.
£10,000–10,500 *ADT*

1929 Cagle-Ford Dirt Track/Sprint Single Seater, very good condition.
Est. £5,800–7,500 *S*

This special single seater was built in the USA in 1929 by J. C. Cagle of Illinois, using Ford Model A parts for dirt track use.

1969–72 Crossle-Chevrolet 5 Litre Mk15F Historic Formula 5000 Racing Single Seater, FIA and HSCC Historic Car papers, excellent usable condition.
£16,500–17,000 *BKS*

1975 Fiat 124 Coupé Racing Saloon,
4 cylinders, 1600cc, dry stored for 4 years, fibreglass boot lid, deep front air dam, engine modified from original 1800cc to race prepared 1600cc unit.
£2,400–2,800 *ADT*

1979 March BMW M1, 6 cylinders, 3453cc,
prepared to original specification, restored to original profile.
Est. £50,000–60,000 *COYS*

In 1973, March Engineering was granted exclusive use of the 2 litre BMW engine in Formula Two and sports car racing.

1955 HWM–Jaguar Open Sports-Racing, 6 cylinders, 3781cc, restored, excellent overall condition.
Est. £70,000–85,000 *COYS*

HWM was a partnership between John Heath and George Abecassis.

1967 MGB Roadster, Historic Race/Rally prepared, all safety equipment, roll bar, fire extinguisher, 72 spoke wire wheels, left hand drive, USA imported.
£8,500–9,000 *HRR*

1988 Van Diemen Formula First.
£2,000–2,250 *Car*

> **Cross Reference**
> MG

1971 Merlyn Mk20 Historic Formula Ford, restored.
£15,000–15,500 *Car*

1967 TVR 1800s Mk4, MGB 1800 engine, overdrive and wire wheels, restored 5 years ago, FIA registered, race eligible, very rare right hand drive, very good condition.
£6,500–7,000 *HRR*

REPLICA VEHICLES

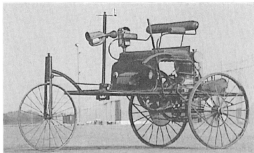

c1980 Benz Tricycle Replica, 1 cylinder, 350cc Briggs and Stratton vertically mounted engine, belt and chain final drive.
£2,000–2,200 *ADT*

This Tricycle has a passing resemblance, albeit half size, to that manufactured by Karl Benz in 1886.

1991 Replica Ferrari 250 GTO, 6 cylinders, 2600cc, totally reconditioned, triple 40DCOE Weber carburettors, reconditioned 5 speed Nissan gearbox.
Est. £7,000–8,000 *ADT*

This car was built around a Datsun 260Z, from a kit supplied by Classic Cars Limited, and powered by a Datsun 2.6 litre reconditioned engine.

1988 Daytona Spyder 2 Seater Sports Roadster, Jaguar V12, 5348cc fuel injected engine, Jaguar suspension, Getrag 4 speed gearbox, excellent bodywork, nearly new transmission and gearbox, good general condition.
Est. £14,000–18,000 *S*

1977 Kennedy Squire, rare, hand built, good condition.
£8,500–10,000 *OMH*

1978/88 RS Daytona Spyder, 5343cc, Jaguar V12 fuel injected engine, Rolls-Royce automatic 3 speed transmission.
£10,000–12,000 *ADT*

The donor car for this replica was a 1978 Jaguar XJ12L.

1977 Bugatti Type 35 Two Seater Replica Sports Racer, Triumph Vitesse 1.6 litre overhead valve engine, twin carburettors, 4 speed manual gearbox, chrome wire wheels, good condtion throughout.
£6,200–6,800 *S*

1960 Jaguar XK150S based SS100 Special Replica, fitted with Jaguar 4.2 litre engine, fabricated aluminium coachwork.
£18,000–18,500 *S*

c1986 Wingfield Jaguar D-Type, 6 cylinders, 3781cc, 3.8 litre XK engine, 3 double-barrelled Webers, based on a 1962 E-Type, featuring a monocoque construction very similar to the original, excellent condition.
Est. £45,000–60,000 *COYS*

RESTORATION PROJECTS

1968 Alfa Romeo Tipo 33/2 2.5 Litre,
8 cylinder, 2500cc engine.
£110,000–115,000 *COYS*

*This car is still in the same condition as when it
was discovered in Angola, virtually untouched
since the day it last raced. It is possibly the most
exciting discovery of recent years.*

1962 Aston Martin DB4 Vantage, in the
process of being restored.
£25,000–30,000 *DJR*

1928 Austin 12hp 4 Door Fabric Saloon,
interior reflects careful use throughout its
life, starts and runs well.
£7,400–7,800 *S*

1969 Aston Martin DB6 Convertible,
complete with engine and automatic
transmission, right hand drive.
Est. £18,000–20,000 *ADT*

**c1958 Ex-War Department Austin
Champ Military Type Jeep,** no canvas
hood, rear seats missing, brakes seized on,
right hand drive.
£400–500 *S*

*Introduced in 1952 by the Austin Motor
Company as a military replacement for the
Jeep, the Champ remained in army service
until 1966. It featured all independent
suspension, a 5 speed gearbox, and was
powered by a 4 cylinder inlet over exhaust
Rolls-Royce engine of 2.8 litres.*

1955 Austin Healey 100 BN2, big block
Chevrolet engine, automatic gearbox,
bodywork in good condition.
£2,600–2,800 *CCTC*

c1932/34 Hispano-Suiza T60 Rolling Chassis, body removed, P100 headlights, some restoration already carried out.
£3,800–4,000 *S*

1966 Morgan 4/4, Ford 1500 engine, left hand drive Californian car, complete for easy restoration.
£5,250–5,500 *CCTC*

Morgan restoration projects are very popular, and always sought after.

1960 Porsche 356B Cabriolet, imported from California, left hand drive, complete, engine runs, floor very rusty.
£8,750–9,000 *CCTC*

1975 Triumph TR6, running order, rust free body and chassis, USA import, left hand drive.
£3,000–3,250 *CCTC*

1961 Lotus Elite Factory Built Special Equipment Model, Coventry Climax FWE 1216cc engine, approx. 85bhp at 6100rpm, 4 speed ZF close ratio manual gearbox, disc brakes all-round, inboard at rear, independent front suspension by wishbone, combined coil spring, shock absorber, anti-roll bar, rear Chapman strut coil spring shock absorber, trailing arm, right hand drive.
£10,000–10,500 *C*

A classic 'barn find' of a classic English sports racing car.

1936 Riley 15/6 Kestrel 4 Door Saloon, complete, interior original and restorable, right hand drive.
£3,000–3,300 *C*

1929 Rolls-Royce 20/25 Tourer, restoration well advanced.
Est. £10,000–12,000 *S*

1961 TVR Grantura MkII, MGA 1600 engine, wire wheels, unused for many years, rare and interesting.
£1,400–1,500 *CCTC*

MICROCARS (BUBBLE CARS)

Bubble cars, as they were known, came in a variety of shapes and sizes, and were produced by a number of makers. Today, these cars are more often known as Microcars, with several clubs worldwide catering for the various types.

It was at the time of the Suez crisis, and the subsequent petrol rationing, that demand increased for this type of small runabout. With low annual road tax and running costs, the bubble car was a natural development from two-wheeled transport, offering full protection from the elements and the ability to carry a small amount of luggage or shopping. They were convenient for the heavy traffic of big towns, with many of the features of larger cars, and also reliable for long distance travel.

Better known makes included the Isetta, Messerschmitt, Heinkel/Trojan, Bond and Reliant, but there were also numerous other unusual marques like the Scootacar, Frisky, Nobel, Lloyd, Peel, Berkeley, Vespa, Allard, Zundapp, Gordon, and Coronet. Increasing affluence and competitive prices saw the decline of the bubble car in the mid-1960s and the introduction of small four-wheeled cars like the Austin 7 Mini.

1959 BMW Isetta Superplus, 1 cylinder, 298cc, good sound example.
£1,100–1,300 *ADT*

1960 BMW Isetta 300cc Bubble Car, totally rebuilt, excellent original specification throughout.
£5,200–5,400 *S*

BMW built under licence Renzo Rivolta's mini car, the Isetta, which was launched in 1953, and by 1955 the BMW version had been launched. Initially with a 250cc twin cylinder 2 stroke engine, BMW now fitted their 250cc single cylinder, 12bhp, 4 stroke unit, later to be uprated to 300cc. The cars were to be introduced into the UK and produced under licence at Brighton in 1957.

1960 BMW Isetta 300, excellent restored condition.
£3,250–3,750 *ScR*

1964 Trojan 200 Bubble Car, 198cc, re-painted, good overall condition.
Est. £3,000–3,500 *S*

The Trojan 200 was a licence-built Heinkel 3 wheel tricycle or Bubble Car produced by Trojan of Croydon. Ernst Heinkel's cabin cruiser was originally manufactured in Stuttgart-Zuffenhausen with 175cc engines, but these were later enlarged to 198cc.

1958 Bond MkE, Villiers 197cc 2 stroke engine.
£1,100–1,300 *ScR*

1960 Nobel, Sachs 200L, 191cc, single
cylinder 2 stroke engine, fibreglass body,
plywood floor, steel chassis.
£450–550 *ScR*

*Approximately 1,000 cars were produced
between 1958 and 1962, and only about
50 are currently known to survive.*

1963 Scootacar MkII, modified by the
designer to include a flat roof.
£1,400–1,600 *ScR*

1960 Messerschmitt KR200,
completely rebuilt.
£5,250–5,750 *Mot*

**1955 Messerschmitt KR200 Cabin
Scooter,** Sachs 1 cylinder, 191cc engine,
10.2bhp at 5250rpm, 4 speed gearbox, re-
painted, original interior, chrome pitted,
speedometer and pieces of trim missing.
£5,500–6,000 *CNY*

1960 Messerschmitt, restored.
£2,850–3,250 *ScR*

c1980 Vespacar P601V, 200cc,
completely restored.
£1,500–2,000 *ScR*

l. **1961 Lambretta FLI 175 3 Wheeler Fire
Engine,** 173cc, restored.
£4,250–4,500
c. **1984 Lambretta Innocenti Lambro 175
Works Pick-Up Truck,** 200cc, restored.
£2,250–2,500
r. **1958 Lambretta FDC Rickshaw
3 Wheeler,** specially designed for Innocenti
by Ghia, 148cc, wicker seats, hand lever
start, restored.
£4,750–5,000 *EP*

1988 Cursor 2 Seater Prototype.
£2,000–2,500 *ScR*

*Approximately 50 of these cars were built,
powered by Honda Vision engines. Most had
a single seat, but this was probably the last
car manufactured and was a prototype with
2 seats and conventional doors.*

A French ebonite gear knob, with
silver and enamel Saint Christopher
design, 1930s.
£200–250 *BCA*

An English silver and enamel Saint
Christopher plaque, for attaching
to a dashboard, 1930s.
£200–300 *BCA*

A silk pennant,
awarded for 2nd place
in Brooklands 500 Mile
Race 1935, 26in (66cm)
high, framed.
£440–480 *BKS*

A signpost arm, with road number added in the early
1920s during the road numbering campaign.
£45–55 *MSMP*

An Art Deco teapot, by Sadler & Co.,
marked 'OK-T-4-2', 1930s.
£180–220 *SIG*

A Continental silver card/cigarette
case, decorated with enamelled road
signs, 1930s.
£220–290 *BCA*

An illuminated sign,
late 1930s, 28in
(71cm) high.
£150–200 *PMB*

The steering wheel from the
Mercedes-Benz W25 Grand
Prix car when tested by
Richard Seaman in 1937,
engraved by Alfred Neubauer.
Est. £4,000–5,000 *BKS*

A French Automobile pocket
watch, c1900.
£300–350 *BCA*

A silver plated trophy,
'Coupe des Glaciers',
engraved, 1932, 10½in
(26.5cm) high.
£1,600–1,800 *CNY*

A Bristol 100 D2 engine, 6 cylinders,
1971cc, suitable for an AC Ace or
Aceca, re-built.
£6,400–6,600 *COYS*

A Panhard et Levassor
radiator and grille, 1920s.
£250–300 *C(A)*

An MG desk companion, with octagonal desk
calendar, inkwell, pen rest, and pen, ex-MG
Abingdon factory, 1950s.
£400–500 *MCh*

An American racing
helmet and visor, by
Hurst, with silk and
leather lining, c1952.
£425–450 *BKS*

A Watford mechanical car
clock, from a Rolls-Royce
Silver Ghost, 1920s.
£250–350 *MCh*

Two rosebud vases, for attaching to
dashboards of light cars, 1920s.
£80–120 *MCh*

A pair of Foden lapel
badges, 1900s.
£80–90 each *MSMP*

A pennant flag from a WWII German Officer's
Mercedes-Benz staff car.
£100–150 *MCh*

An Edwardian Dunlop
brass stirrup pump.
£100–140 *MCh*

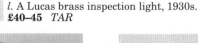

l. A Lucas brass inspection light, 1930s.
£40–45 *TAR*

A Wedgwood Rolls-Royce Spirit of Ecstasy
ashtray, 1930s, 4½in (11.5cm) diam.
£25–30 *TAR*

A French veteran motor car hot water
bottle/foot warmer, 1902–04.
£120–140 *MCh*

A Royal Automobile Club
of Egypt badge, c1940.
£160–180 *MSMP*

An AA badge, numbered and
marked 'Stenson Cooke', 1909–10.
£200–250 *MCh*

An AA solid nickel badge, 1918–20.
£100–140 *MCh*

A New Zealand AA
badge, post-war.
£20–30 *MSMP*

A Variety Club of Guernsey
chrome plated and enamelled
car badge, 1950–60.
£50–60 *MCh*

A Burma Star badge,
by J. R. Gaunt Ltd.,
London, 1950s.
£80–100 *MCh*

l. An Edwardian RAC Associate's
badge, nickel and coloured
enamel, boxed, unused.
£200–250 *MCh*

A Stafford District Car Club full member's, chrome
plated and enamelled car badge, c1950.
£80–120 *MCh*

A Sunbac full member's chrome plated and
enamelled car badge, 1930s.
£70–80 *MCh*

An Order of the Road
aluminium and enamelled
car badge, 1930s.
£50–60 *MCh*

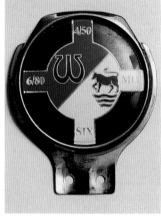

A Wolseley/Morris Car Club full
member's badge, 1950s.
£50–70 *MCh*

A Bristol Owners Club chrome
plated and enamelled full
member's car badge, 1960–70.
£50–60 *MCh*

A British Automobile Racing
Club chrome plated and
enamelled car badge, 1950s.
£70–80 *MCh*

A Brooklands Junior Car
Club racing badge, 1930s.
£120–130 *MCh*

A Motor Car Club full
member's car grille
badge, 1930s.
£40–50 *MCh*

A Three Services Golfing Society
chrome plated and enamelled
car badge, 1950s.
£50–70 *MCh*

A Crusader Car Club full member's
car badge, 1950s.
£40–50 *MCh*

A Silverstone Racing Club
chrome plated and
enamelled car badge, with
laurel leaf decoration, 1950s.
£60–80 *MCh*

A collection of 12 Road Fund Licence discs, 1953–79.
£25–30 *MCh*

A Morris Trucks double-sided enamel sign, c1928, 20 by 12in (50.5 by 30.5cm).
£700–800 *PMB*

An Apollo Electric Motor Horn board sign, c1915.
£70–75 *PMB*

A Wills's Star Cigarettes plastic coated tin sign, c1938, 20 by 15in (50.5 by 38cm).
£600–700 *PMB*

A collection of driver's licences, 1930s.
£50–60 *MCh*

Two greetings postcards from Tadcaster and Sheringham, 1920s.
£5–10 each *PMB*

The Book of the Austin 7, by Gordon Goodwin, c1936.
£10–12 *PMB*

A Chrysler 8 page broadsheet, 1951, 12 by 10in (30.5 by 25cm).
£10–12 *PMB*

The Motor, dated 3rd April, 1934.
£10–12 *PMB*

The Vauxhall Motorist, house magazine for Vauxhall Motors Limited, c1934.
£8–10 *PMB*

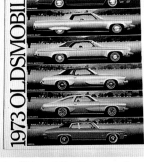

An Oldsmobile 48 page sales brochure, 1973, 10 by 8in (25 by 20cm).
£7–8 *PMB*

A *Metropolitan 1500* 4 page colour folder, 1958, 11 by 8in (28 by 20cm).
£8–10 *PMB*

A Vesta Rearlite Cycle Lamp, boxed,
unused, 1950s.
£35–45 *MCh*

A Miller's battery-powered
bicycle headlamp, 1940s.
£30–40 *MCh*

A Lucas oil rear lamp,
from a Rolls-Royce Silver
Ghost, 1908–10.
£250–350 *MCh*

A pair of BRC electric
headlamps, c1930.
£250–350 *MCh*

A pair of Edwardian Lucas King
of the Road oil rear lamps.
£650–850 *MCh*

A 2 person picnic basket,
from an Austin 7, 1930s.
£150–200 *MCh*

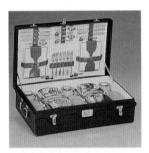

A Coracle 6 person picnic
set, with black Rexine
covered case, 1920s,
26in (66cm) wide.
£2,000–2,300 *S*

A 4 person wicker picnic basket, with
wood lined base, red Rexine lined lid,
25in (63.5cm) wide.
£2,250–2,500 *S*

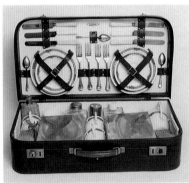

A 6 person picnic case, by Bandalasta
of London, 1930–35.
£400–600 *MCh*

A Brexton 4 person picnic set,
unused, 1950s.
£120–150 *MCh*

A 2 person picnic basket, 1930s.
£150–250 *MCh*

A Desmo horse and jockey mascot, 1930s, 6in (15cm) high.
£200–250 *TAR*

A Lalique falcon mascot, with moulded markings, on an illuminated base, 1930s, 9¾in (24.5cm) high.
£2,000–3,000 *SIG*

A mascot depicting a German Shepherd dog, on a radiator cap, 1920s, 4in (10cm) high.
£110–130 *MSMP*

A Desmo chrome mascot of the Duke of Windsor playing golf, c1935, 6½in (16.5cm). **£500–600** *SIG*

l. A Latil mascot, by F. Bazin, signed, c1925, 6½in (16.5cm) wide, on a wooden base.
£1,800–2,000 *S*

A chrome plated mascot of a fireman, pre-WWII, 6in (15cm) high.
£220–240 *MSMP*

A Lalique Epsom mascot, embossed 'R. Lalique, France', c1930, 7½in (19cm) wide, mounted on a radiator cap.
£4,800–5,200 *S*

A Lalique Epsom amethyst mascot, on a black base with a plated screw stand, some damage to fitting, moulded mark, 5in (13cm) high.
£2,500–2,750 *Bea*

A mascot of a leaping salmon, 1930s, 5in (12.5cm) high.
£100–135 *TAR*

A Harrods of London Royal Warrant mascot, on a later radiator cap, c1910, 7in (17.5cm) high.
£180–240 *SIG*

A Hispano-Suiza stork mascot, used on H6B and V12 models, signed 'F. Bazin', numbered beneath, c1920–30, 6½in (16.5cm).
£1,000–1,500 *SIG*

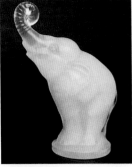

A Sabino mascot, 1950s,
4½in (11.5cm) high.
£250–350 *SIG*

A Red Ashay glass mascot, with
propeller driven coloured filters,
moulding mark on shoulder, with
illuminated base and radiator cap on
wooden base, 1930s, 5½in (14cm).
£2,000–2,800 *S*

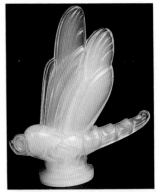

A Sabino dragonfly mascot,
moulded and etched markings,
1930s, 6in (15cm) high.
£275–325 *SIG*

'The Beck' mascot, 'Vertige
de la Vitesse', by Finnigans
of London, signed 'G. Poitvin',
numbered and inscribed,
c1920, 9in (22.5cm) high.
£850–1,250 *SIG*

An 'Old Bill' mascot, by
Bruce Bairnsfather,
c1914–18, 4½in (11.5cm).
£200–300 *SIG*

A Lalique mascot of a cockerel,
post-WWII, 8in (20cm) high.
£300–500 *SIG*

An aluminium reproduction of
Whisper, in the style of Charles
Sykes, c1960, 8in (20cm) high.
£100–150 *SIG*

A mascot of an Italian lady,
1930s, 5½in (14cm) high.
£165–180 *TAR*

A Mack truck gold plated
mascot, designed by Masury,
1932, 6in (15cm) wide.
£200–250 *TAR*

A mascot of a pug dog, by A. G.
Ward, 1930s, 2½in (6.5cm) high.
£120–140 *TAR*

A mascot of a terrier, 1930s,
2½in (6.5cm) high.
£65–80 *TAR*

A poster on linen, after Karl Bickel, IVme Course Internationale du Klausen, 1925, published by Wolfsberg, Zurich, 50½ by 35½in (128 by 91cm).
Est. £6,000–8,000 *ONS*

A 'Stop' Lamp cardboard sign, 1920s, 14 by 10in (36 by 25.5cm), framed and glazed.
£50–60 *PMB*

A Rudge-Whitworth enamel sign, c1900, 36 by 24in (92 by 61cm), framed and glazed.
£1,000–1,200 *PMB*

l. An original poster for the Lottery Grand Prix, by Martinati, Tripoli 1936, 60 by 48in (154 by 120cm). **£1,500–1,600** *BKS*

A poster by Geo. Ham, 1935 Monaco Grand Prix, 56 by 40in (142 by 101.5cm).
£1,100–1,200 *COYS*

A poster by Geo. Ham, 1933 Monaco Grand Prix,
£1,200–1,400 *COYS*

A poster by Codognato, XIII Gran Premio d'Italia, 55½ by 40in (140 by 101.5cm).
Est. £7,000–10,000 *CNY*

A poster of the Automobile Club Brescia XIX Mille Miglia, 1952, 39 by 27½in (99 by 70cm).
£2,200–2,400 *CNY*

An original lithographed race poster by Falcucci, 2me Grand Prix Automobile Monaco, 6 Avril 1930, autographed by René Dreyfus, winner of the race, 46½ by 31in (118 by 79cm).
Est. £3,500–5,500 *CNY*

A Renault advertising poster on linen, after De Bas, published by Minot, Paris, 38½ by 45½in (98 by 116cm).
£850–900 *ONS*

A BOAC International 500 poster, programme and scorecard, 13th April, 1969, signed by about 60 competitors, 30 by 21in (76 by 53cm).
£700–750 *CSK*

An original poster, after Michael Turner, Goodwood, 26th RAC Tourist Trophy Race, 1961, framed, 30 by 20in (76 by 51cm).
£240–260 *BKS*

An original lithographed poster, The Dunlop Trophy Race, Brooklands 1938, 30 by 20in (76 by 51cm).
£300–330 *BKS*

An original lithographed poster, Monaco Semaine Automobile, 20–25 Mars 1922, designed by Antony Noghès, 46½ by 31in (118 by 79cm).
Est. £5,400–6,600 *CNY*

Antony Noghès conceived the Monaco Grand Prix in 1928.

An original poster, The 8th International British Empire Trophy Race, Donington, c1938, 30 by 20in (76 by 51cm).
£300–330 *BKS*

An original poster, after Roy Nockolds, Goodwood, Whit Monday, showing Maserati 250F, c1954, 30 by 20in (76 by 51cm).
£200–230 *BKS*

An original linen backed poster, by R. T. Garcia, Spanish Grand Prix 1954, Penya Rhin, showing the 4½ litre Ferrari, minor tears, 22 by 26in (56 by 66cm).
£600–650 *BKS*

A BP Super globe, 1950s.
£280–320 MSMP

Originals are usually marked 'Hallware' and 'Property of Shell-Mex & BP Ltd.'

A Bowser alloy oil pump, with brass plate for Regent Oil Co., restored glass globe, post WWII.
£400–500 MSMP

A Raleigh Bicycle hanging glass sign, 1930s, 18 by 23in (46 by 56cm).
£180–200 PMB

A Mobil petrol globe in rare rectangular style, with flying horse logo, 1962.
£220–240 MSMP

A Patchquick counter top/window display unit, with 4 drawer storage section, includes mint condition tins sealed in display area, pre-WWI.
£550–650 MSMP

A Curfew petrol globe, post-WWII.
£180–200 MSMP

Right: Two petrol pumps:
l. An Epex twin bowl, c1925.
£650–750
r. A Plume 6 gallon, c1930.
£600–700 C(A)

A Champion promotional model sparking plug, c1974, 18in (46cm).
£15–20 WP

A Trident petrol globe, post-WWII.
£160–170 MSMP

A Dunlop Tyres promotional enamel clock, French, 1930s, 33in (84cm) diam.
£550–600 PMB

A Michelin man air compressor, by Luchard of Paris, with cabling No. B4 2661.
£1,000–1,500 C(A)

A Gargoyle Mobiloils enamel sign,
1920s, 18 by 24in (46 by 61cm).
£60–70 *PMB*

A Price's Motor Oils enamel sign,
1920s, 18 by 24in (46 by 61cm).
£80–100 *PMB*

A Duckham's
Oils enamel
thermometer,
1930s, 46 by 11in
(116.5 by 28cm).
£120–140 *PMB*

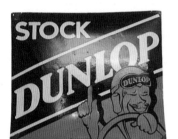

A Dunlop enamel sign,
German, 1920s, 18 by 24in
(46 by 61cm).
£225–250 *PMB*

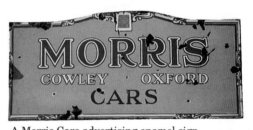

A Morris Cars advertising enamel sign,
fair condition, late 1920s.
£180–190 *MSMP*

A Blackstone Oil Engines enamel sign, 1920s,
18 by 30in (46 by 76cm).
£400–450 *PMB*

A Castrol 'R' advertising double-sided enamel
sign, 1930s, 16 by 20in (41 by 51cm).
£240–260 *MSMP*

A BP enamel sign, c1924, 40 by
30in (101.5 by 76cm).
£1,750–2,000 *PMB*

An AA Caution school sign,
poor condition, early 1900s.
£100–120 *MSMP*

A BP advertising double-
sided enamel sign, c1930.
£170–190 *MSMP*

A Shellmex petrol pump globe, post-war.
£90–150 *ALC*

A Duckham's Q5500 Super Lubricant 5 gallon can, 1930s.
£25–30 *MSMP*

A Champion sparking plug enamel sign, 1930s, 27 by 19in (69 by 48cm).
£220–240 *PMB*

An AA enamel garage sign, c1930.
£180–200 *PMB*

A First Oil enamel advertising sign, French, pre-war.
£40–60 *ALC*

An Empire Lamp Oil enamel sign, 1930s, 15 by 24in (38 by 61cm).
£280–300 *PMB*

A Cleveland Discol enamel sign, 1930s.
£160–180 *PMB*

A Telamite Service tin sign, 1950s.
£70–75 *MSMP*

A Michelin tyre compressor, with original pressure gauge and carrying handle, pre-war.
£320–340 *ALC*

A Lodge cardboard display sign and plug, mid-1920s.
£50–70 *MCh*

A Prices' Motor Oils enamel sign, with a ship emblem, pre-war.
£50–100 *ALC*

l. A Wakefield Castrol 2 gallon oil can,
pre-WWII. **£90–110**
r. A Castrol Motor Oil 2 gallon oil can,
post-WWII. **£55–65** *MSMP*

A collection of 12 oil and acetylene
reservoir tins of burning oil and
acetylene, 1900–20.
£150–180 *MCh*

A collection of 5 Dunlop tube and tyre repair sets,
1930–40s.
£70–80 *MCh*

A toffee tin, depicting a motoring
scene, 1920s.
£50–70 *MCh*

Two Victorian tins of Neatsfoot
Oil, for maintaining harness
and carriage leather.
£70–100 *MCh*

Three oil containers, with bulkhead clips, c1930s.
£60–70 each *MCh*

A tydol motor spirit
4 gallon drum and pourer.
£60–80 *C(A)*

Three anti-freeze tins:
l. Smith's Bluecol, 1930s. **£30–40**
c. Zero Radiator Glycerine, with contents, 1900s. **£90–110**
r. Chemico 'Stop-It' Freezing, 40fl.oz., with directions in English and
German, 1920s. **£40–50** *MSMP*

S. C. H. Davis, Le Mans 1927, White House Crash, oil on canvas, signed, mounted in gold leaf frame, together with a signed letter describing the event, 21 by 24in (53 by 61cm).
£1,400–1,500 *BKS*

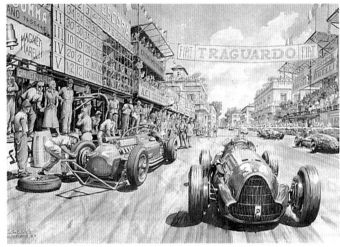

Michael Wright, Pescara Grand Prix 1950, watercolour and gouache, depicting Fangio in the 158 Alfa Romeo, signed, captioned to reverse, mounted, framed and glazed, 30 by 40in (76 by 101.5cm).
£1,700–1,800 *BKS*

Roy Nockolds, Bugatti T51 driven by Achille Varzi, oil on board, framed and glazed, 1950s, 24 by 34in (61 by 86cm).
£680–700 *BKS*

Nick Watts, the winning Bentley at Le Mans 1928, acrylic and gouache on canvas, framed, 28 by 42in (71 by 106.5cm).
£1,500–1,600 *BKS*

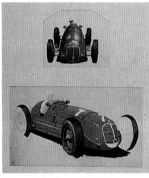

Two original pre-WWII watercolour and gouache studies of the Maserati 8CTF, one unfinished, framed, 21 by 17in (53 by 43cm).
£240–260 *BKS*

Roy Nockolds, Brooklands, the 1½ litre Delage, watercolour and gouache, signed and framed, 1930s, with a BRDC member's cloth overall badge and description of the race.
£650–680 *BKS*

Graham Turner, Jim Clark and the Aston-Martin DBR1, TT Race, Goodwood, watercolour and gouache, signed, framed, c1986.
£925–975 *BKS*

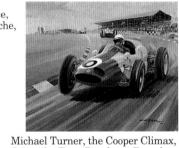

Michael Turner, the Cooper Climax, driven by Tony Brooks at Brands Hatch, oil on canvas, signed and dated '1960', framed, 24 by 29in (61 by 74cm). **£900–950** *BKS*

The Ferrari P3/4, Targa Florio 1967, a signed Dexter Brown colour print on 50% cotton Fabriano stock, 1985, 24 by 30in (61 by 76cm).
£240–250 *JAR*

Roy Nockolds, pencil, charcoal and wash drawing, framed and glazed, c1930.
Est. £300–400 *BKS*

A photograph of Ayrton Senna, in a McLaren Ford, at the 1993 Monaco Grand Prix, by Nigel Snowdon, 12 by 9in (30.5 by 22.5cm). **£55–65** *JAR*

A photograph of Gilles Villeneuve, in a Ferrari, at the Brazilian Grand Prix, 1981, by Nigel Snowdon, 9 by 12in (22.5 by 30.5cm). **£55–65** *JAR*

A photograph of Marie Térèse de Filippis' Maserati, at the Italian Grand Prix, 1958, signed, 12 by 9in (30.5 by 22.5cm). **£70–75** *JAR*

A photograph of Mike Hawthorn in a Ferrari, at the Dutch Grand Prix at Zandvoort, 1958, by Edward Eves, 9 by 12in (22.5 by 30.5cm). **£55–65** *JAR*

Jan Manuel Fangio in a BRM, at Silverstone, 1953, by T. C. March, 9 by 12in (22.5 by 30.5cm). **£50–55** *JAR*

A photograph of Maseratis, at Silverstone, 1950, by Tom March, 9 by 12in (22.5 by 30.5cm). **£55–65** *JAR*

A photograph of the Targa Florio, 1958, by Edward Eves, 12 by 9in (30.5 by 22.5cm). **£60–65** *JAR*

A photograph of Graham Hill in a BRM, at the British Grand Prix at Silverstone, 1965, by Colin Waldeck, 9 by 12in (22.5 by 30.5cm). **£55–65** *JAR*

A signed photograph of Stirling Moss in a Vanwall, at the Monaco Grand Prix, 1958, by Edward Eves, 9 by 12in (22.5 by 30.5cm). **£80–90** *JAR*

A photograph of Michael Schumacher in a Benetton Ford, winning the Monaco Grand Prix, 1994, 9 by 12in (22.5 by 30.5cm). **£55–65** *JAR*

AUTOMOBILE ART

Le Mans 1929, oil on canvas, framed, 29½ by 39½in (75 by 100cm).
£780–800 *S*

Gamy (Marguerite Montaut), La Voiture Th.Schneider 1912 Gagne a Dieppe Dinant et a la Sarthe, original lithograph in colours, Mabileau & Co., Paris, copyright 1912, unframed, 18 by 35½in (46 by 90cm).
£680–740 *CSK*

After Geo Ham, Rudolf Caracciola, his original Christmas card for 1938, designed by the artist, and a signed photograph of the subject, together in common mount, framed and glazed, 15 by 18in (38 by 46cm).
£150–175 *BKS*

Frederick Gordon Crosby, 1914 Isle of Man Tourist Trophy, Kenelm Lee Guiness on route to victory in the Sunbeam, watercolour, pencil heightened with white, signed and dated '1920', unframed, 18 by 16in (46 by 41cm).
£6,400–6,800 *CSK*

Excelsior Gummiwerke A. G., motoring through the tunnel, original lithograph in colours, printed by Hollerbaum & Schmidt, Berlin, late 1920s, 27½ by 37½in (70 by 95cm).
£500–540 *CSK*

Geo Ham (Georges Hamel 1900–72), Racing Peugeot, c1914, watercolour and gouache on paper, signed, 18 by 13in (46 by 33cm), mounted, framed and glazed.
£800–850 *S*

After Frederick Gordon Crosby, 1932 Targa Florio, 25½ by 30in (65 by 76cm).
£800–850 *CSK*

L'Automobilisme Militaire, original oil design for a magazine cover by Carey, unsigned, c1920, framed, 15½ by 10½in (40 by 27cm).
£180–200 *ONS*

Seven views of Rolls-Royce, Lanchester, Crossley and Vickers-Guy WWI and WWII armoured cars, together with 6 views of British MK IV Churchill, 7 of Crusader MK VI and 5 others, by Terence Halder and others, for Profile and similar publications.
Est. £150–200 *CSK*

Terence Cuneo, Bentleys at Le Mans 1929, artist's preliminary pencil drawing, with handwritten notes and amendments, signed, 10 by 12in (25 by 30.5cm), mounted, framed and glazed.
£2,700–3,200 *S*

Geo Ham, 1950s Endurance Race poster design, watercolour and gouache on paper, creased, signed, 19½ by 15½in (49.5 by 39.5cm), mounted, framed and glazed.
£900–950 *S*

George Lane, A Streamlined Car, watercolour and pastel heightened with white, late 1930s, c1920, 11¼ by 15in (29 by 38cm).
Est. £250–350 *CSK*

Phil May, 1921 Rolls-Royce Silver Ghost, Gordon Bennett Barker Torpedo tourer, pastel, signed, c1982, 8¼ by 10¾in (21 by 27cm).
£160–180 *HOLL*

Jameson, Brakes!, pencil drawing depicting an accident about to happen, signed and dated '36', torn, creased and stained, 12⅝ by 19¼in (32 by 49cm), mounted on card, framed and glazed.
£375–400 *S*

George Lane, 1948 Grosser Preis von Europa, Felice Trossi about to pass Guiseppe Farina, pencil, black ink, crayon heightened with white, late 1940s, 8 by 8¼in (20 by 21cm).
Est. £200–300 *CSK*

Lawler, 1988 Monaco Grand Prix, Prost leading Berger through Casino Square, oil on canvas, signed and dated '93', unframed, 30in (76cm) square.
Est. £300–500 *CSK*

Attributed to Geo Ham, 1950s Endurance Race poster design, watercolour and gouache on paper, 18 by 13in (46 by 33cm), mounted, framed and glazed.
£620–660 *S*

N.M., After the Drive, watercolour, initialled, mounted, framed and glazed, c1910, 9 by 6in, (23 by 15cm).
£390–420 *S*

Trevor Holder, 1912 Rolls-Royce Silver Ghost, chassis number 1921, watercolour, signed and dated '74', 21 by 31in (53 by 79cm), framed and glazed.
£370–400 *S*

Ernest Montaut, Coupés des Voiturettes 1907, Sizaire et Naudin, original lithograph in colours, 20 by 36½in (51 by 93cm).
£400–440 *CSK*

Blitzen Benz at Brooklands, oil on canvas, pre-WWI, 29½ by 39½in (75 by 100cm), framed.
£250–280 *S*

Trevor Holder, 1914 Rolls-Royce Silver Ghost, chassis number 30ED, watercolour, signed and dated '75', 21 by 31in (53 by 79cm), framed and glazed.
£270–290 *S*

Ernest Montaut, Le Virage, an early racing car taking a corner at speed, pencil and watercolour, 15 by 33½in (38 by 85cm).
£1,500–2,000 *CNY*

A very rare example of original art by this famous automotive artist. Montaut was one of the first artists in the history of motoring to capture the speed and excitement of the early road races.

Dion Pears, The White House Crash, Le Mans 1927, acrylic on canvas, signed, unframed, 28½ by 36in (72 by 92cm).
£340–380 *S*

Bob Murray, 1934 French Grand Prix at Montlhéry, watercolour and gouache on watercolour board, depicting Chiron in the wide bodied Tipo B leading Caracciola in the Mercedes-Benz W25 at the start of the race, signed, 21½ by 28in (54.5 by 71cm), mounted, framed and glazed.
Est. £500–600 *S*

Fritz Peters, Mediterranean Grand Prix local favourite, oil on canvas, signed, 1930s, 19 by 23in (48 by 58.5cm), framed.
Est. £300–400 *S*

Dion Pears, Fangio, Maserati 250F, oil on canvas, signed, 1950s, 24 by 36in (61 by 92cm), framed.
£400–440 *S*

George Lane, Off the start line at Prescott, black crayon and wash heightened with white, late 1940s, 7¼ by 12¾in (18 by 33cm).
Est. £180–200 *CSK*

Michael Turner, 1958 Monaco Grand Prix, Trintignant leads Musso and Hawthorn out of the tunnel, watercolour on paper, signed, dated '59', 16 by 22in (41 by 56cm), mounted, framed and glazed.
Est. £700–900 *S*

Barry Rowe, Lautenschlager, Mercedes, 1914 French Grand Prix, acrylic on canvas board, signed, 15½ by 19½in (39.5 by 50cm), framed.
£480–520 *S*

Barry Rowe, Duncan Hamilton, C-Type Jaguar, Le Mans 1953 24 Hour Race, acrylic on canvas board, signed, 19½ by 23½in (50 by 60cm), framed.
Est. £400–600 *S*

l. Barry Rowe, Tony Brooks Vanwall 1958 Italian Grand Prix Monza, acrylic on canvas board, signed, 19½ by 23½in (50 by 60cm), framed.
£320–360 *S*

Barry Rowe, Bugatti T35, Targa Florio 1926, acrylic on canvas board, signed, 15½ by 19½in (40 by 50cm), framed.
£550–600 *S*

Barry Rowe, Stirling Moss, Monaco 1955, acrylic on canvas board, signed, 9½ by 13½in (24 by 34cm), framed.
£250–280 *S*

Barry Rowe, Mille Miglia 1955, acrylic on canvas board, signed, 19¾ by 23½in (50 by 60cm), framed.
Est. £300–400 *S*

Barry Rowe, Graham Hill, BRM, acrylic on canvas board, signed, 1960s, 8½ by 11¼in (21 by 29cm), framed.
£330–350 *S*

Barry Rowe was the winner of the Transport Trust Award 1994.

Barry Rowe, Mike Hawthorn Dino 246 Ferrari, Monza 1958, acrylic on canvas board, signed, 15½ by 19½in (40 by 50cm), framed.
Est. £450–550 *S*

l. N. A. Watts, Le Mans 1955, watercolour, mounted on board, signed and dated '79', 11½ by 15in (29 by 38cm).
Est. £1,100–1,300 *S*

N. A. Watts, Fangio and Brooks, Monaco Grand Prix 1957, watercolour and gouache, depicting Fangio's Maserati cornering at Gasworks bend, in front of the Vanwall of Brooks, signed, 27½ by 41in (70 by 104cm), framed and glazed.
£1,500–1,700 *S*

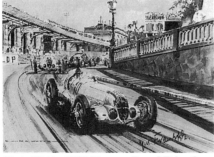

N. A. Watts, 1937 Monaco Grand Prix, the Mercedes W125 of Manfred von Brauchitsch, leading Rudolf Caracciola's Mercedes out of the Station Hairpin, watercolour and gouache, signed by the artist and Manfred von Brauchitsch, 14 by 20in (36 by 51cm), mounted, framed and glazed.
£1,000–1,400 *S*

r. Michael Wright, Alpine Retrospective, watercolour and gouache depicting Alan Clark's Rolls-Royce Silver Ghost, signed, 19¾ by 25½in (50 by 65cm), mounted, framed and glazed.
Est. £1,300–1,500 *S*

AUTOMOBILIA

A Ford V8 engine and gearbox, 21 stud, complete but in need of restoration.
£50–100 *C(A)*

A Sheffield Simplex Motor Works Ltd. presentation tray, by Walker and Hall, engraved with presentation details to Bernard Incledon Day, 1913, 25½in (65cm) wide.
£840–880 *S*

A Fodens Ltd. brass 'By Appointment' plate, c1914, 6in (15cm) high.
£140–160 *MSMP*

A BARC Brooklands 120mph badge, presented to E. A. Eldridge, engraved, enamelled in eight colours, 1930s, 4in (9.5cm) high, on a wooden base, and a pair of Eldridge's custom-made driving goggles, by E. B. Mayrowitz, Paris, with blacked-out right eyepiece, in original leather case.
£1,700–1,900 *S*

1924 was a successful year for Eldridge. On 12th July he drove 'Mephistopheles' to a World Land Speed Record of 146.01mph along the Arpajon Road in France.

Four patented designs for exhaust ends in the form of a leopard's head, a bird's head and two hound's heads.
£275–300 *CSK*

A silver toast rack in the form of a veteran motor car, hallmarked Sheffield 1905, 8½in (21.5cm) wide.
£630–650 *CSK*

A BARC Brooklands attendance counter, early 1930s.
£180–200 *MCh*

A four note exhaust whistle, from a Ford Model T Roadster, c1912.
£140–185 *MCh*

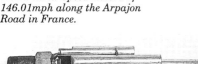

A Brooklands BARC clubhouse bar EPNS wall plate, c1930.
£120–140 *MCh*

A Rolls-Royce factory EPNS cocktail shaker flask, 1930s.
£350–375 *MCh*

A Rolls-Royce chauffeur's school cap badge, No. 359, solid silver with red enamel lettering, 1930s, ¾in (2cm) high.
£330–360 *S*

These badges were awarded upon successful completion of the driving course, and if lost were only replaced by Rolls-Royce with un-numbered black enamelled versions.

A Rolls-Royce radiator assembly, with a red enamel badge and mascot-type radiator cap, registered design dated '1913'.
£1,600–1,700 *S*

A chassis plate, bulkhead plate, red enamelled radiator badge, starting handle cover, and solid nickel mascot from a Rolls-Royce, c1920.
£350–450 *MCh*

A brass interior light from a vintage limousine, in wooden mount.
£100–150 *MCh*

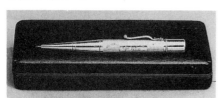

A personalised Barker's 'Major' pointer silver propelling pencil, with inscription from Donald Campbell to Peter Reynolds, hallmarked Birmingham, 1962.
£520–550 *S*

Donald Campbell was a great friend of Peter Reynolds for many years, and was to have acted as Best Man at his wedding but had to change his plans and return to the lakes for an attempt on the World Water Speed record.

An Aston Martin Lagonda Limited stainless steel chassis plate, 1980 onwards.
£80–140 *MCh*

A Rolls-Royce stainless steel radiator surround, with fixed vertical shutters and kneeling Spirit of Ecstasy mascot, post-WWII.
£250–275 *S*

A Shell Motor Spirit garage 'wash and brush-up' wall panel, 1920s.
£140–180 *MCh*

A Michelin Bibendum tyre compressor unit, incomplete.
£220–240 *CSK*

A Burglow cable-operated mechanical hand signal, with operating mechanism, 1930s.
£200–300 *MCh*

An unused bottle of motor car varnish, in original box, c1902.
£40–70 *MCh*

A copper hot water foot warmer, for an Edwardian limousine.
£60–85 *MCh*

Advertising & Promotional Items

A Castrol Lubrequipment oil cabinet, painted green and black with sliding front door, post-WWII, 61in (155cm) high.
£385–400 *S*

An Edwardian brass Austin Motor Company claret corkscrew.
£150–200 *MCh*

Three 1930s Morris dealership double-sided enamel signs, comprising circular Sales and Service, 28½in (72.5cm) diam., Cowley Oxford Cars with radiator decoration, 36in (91.5cm) wide, and Morris Cars, 37in (94cm) wide.
£520–550 *S*

A bronze wall plate, by J. R. Pearson of Birmingham, makers and suppliers of lifts at the Austin Motor Co. factory, 1920s.
£180–260 *MCh*

An AA badge from a service garage wall, enamelled in AA yellow colour, 1920s, 14in (35.5cm) high.
£150–180 *MCh*

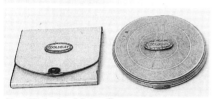

Two Wolseley Motor Company promotional lady's powder compacts, c1930–40s.
£60–120 each *MCh*

Two MG factory promotional items, 1950s.
£140–200 *MCh*

Cross Reference
Smoking

A Minerva Automobiles embossed tin advertising sign, maroon and cream, 1930s, 24in (61cm) diam., mounted on a framed display board.
£1,100–1,200 *S*

A printed Rolls-Royce Ltd. advertising glass panel, printed in black and white, originally a decorative mirror now mounted on red card, 1960s, 18 by 24in (46 by 61cm), framed.
£375–400 *S*

> **Cross Reference**
> Signs

After Leslie Ellis, Gaymer's Cyder 'Safe for Motorists' laminated showcard, 1930s, 9 by 6in (23 by 15cm).
£70–80 *ONS*

A Bentley illuminated showroom hanging sign, with plastic box surround, post-WWII, 39½in (100cm) wide.
£400–440 *S*

Four Jaguar presentation items, comprising: a jotter with calendar, lighter, ashtray, and drinks tray.
£660–680 *S*

A Bentley Icarus showroom display mascot, from Bentley Motors, Cricklewood, 1927.
£1,500–2,000 *MCh*

> **Cross Reference**
> Mascots

An AA double-sided cut-out garage hanging enamel sign, yellow and black, 1950s, some overpainting, 25in (63.5cm) high.
£330–360 *S*

> **Cross Reference**
> Petrol Pumps

A Hispano-Suiza lady's powder compact, c1926.
£180–250 *MCh*

Badges

An RAC badge, unused condition, c1970.
£40–50 *MCh*

A Royal Automobile Club Associate Member's brass car badge, c1912.
£140–185 *MCh*

A Premier Motor Racing Club enamel badge and rule book, chrome plated badge painted with five colours, late 1950s, 4½in (11cm) high.
£110–130 *S*

An RAC Associate Member's polished brass badge, with Liverpool Automobile Club enamel centre, c1910, 4½in (11cm) high.
£270–290 *S*

An Edwardian RAC Full Member's car badge, 1920s.
£180–240 *MCh*

An RAC nickel plated brass badge, with enamelled centre disc, bulkhead fitting, 1920s.
£140–160 *MCh*

Top. An RAC Associate Member's badge, c1930.
£60–80
Bottom. An RAC Full Member's badge, c1950.
£40–60 *MCh*

A National Motorist's Association car badge, with logo 'Omnium Saluti', late 1930s.
£250–350 *MCh*

An RAC Associate Member's car badge, late 1920s.
£80–100 *MCh*

An AA Committee Member's nickel plated brass car badge, c1910.
£350–450 *MCh*

Three AA Full Member's car badges:
l. base fitted, c1940. **£50–60**
c. side fitted, c1950. **£20–25**
r. for a small car or motorcycle, c1950.
£20–30 *MCh*

Two AA industrial vehicle badges.
l. c1920–30. **£80–100**
r. c1950. **£40–60** *MCh*

An Aston Martin Owners' Club Full Member's car badge, mounted to wooden wall display board, post-WWII.
£80–100 *MCh*

A Brookland's Junior Car Club Full Member's car badge, chrome plated and enamelled, 1930s.
£220–270 *MCh*

An Order of the Road enamelled and chrome plated brass badge, 1930s.
£140–160 *MCh*

A Boyce Motometer, with wings on hinged integral cap, from a Hudson Straight 8 Tourer, late 1920s.
£200–250 *MCh*

A Birmingham Motoring Club Full Member's car badge, plated and enamelled in blue, red and orange, 1930s.
£200–250 *MCh*

Cross Reference
Clocks & Instruments

A British Racing Drivers Club Full Member's car badge, by Collins of London, in chrome plated and multi-coloured enamels, c1930.
£250–350 *MCh*

A BARC Full Member's car badge, chrome plated and enamelled, post-WWII.
£80–100 *MCh*

Three BARC Brooklands badges: a Racing Club, Junior Car Club and Brooklands Aero Club, 1930s, all in mint condition.
£2,000–2,500 *MCh*

A Bentley Owners' Club Full Member's car badge, enamelled and chrome plated finish, 1929–38.
£180–250 *MCh*

A Midland Automobile Club Full Member's car badge, enamelled and chrome plated, 1930s.
£100–150 *MCh*

A Disabled Driver's Motor Club radiator cap mounted mascot badge, late 1920s.
£100–140 *MCh*

A BARC Full Member's Racing Club badge, enamelled and chrome plated, 1930s.
£400–500 *MCh*

Radiator Badges

An MG TF sports car radiator badge, c1954.
£60–75 *MCh*

A Rover 90 grille badge, 1950s–60s.
£20–30 *MCh*

Two Rolls-Royce radiator
badges, pre-war and post-war.
£200–250 MCh

An Essex Motors radiator
badge, American, c1928.
£80–100 MCh

An Aston Martin Vantage
radiator badge, 1985.
£60–80 MCh

Miscellaneous Badges

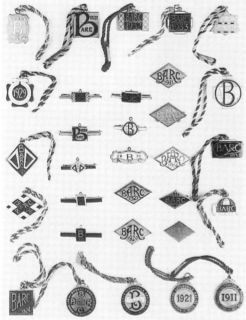

r. An AA metal
GB plate, 1930s.
£45–65 MCh

r. An RAC metal
enamelled GB
plate, 1950s.
£60–70 MCh

r. An Automobile Club of
Great Britain and Ireland,
Gordon Bennett Race
Steward's enamel badge,
1903, 2in (5cm) high,
complete with cord, in
original box.
£700–730 S

A collection of Brooklands Automobile Racing Club
enamelled lapel badges, 1911–1939.
£1,350–1,450 CSK

Clocks & Instrument Clocks

An eight-day car clock, in an
angled brass case, chipped lens,
Swiss made, c1910, bezel 2½in
(6cm) diam.
£140–160 S

r. A motoring aneroid
barometer by W. Batty
& Sons Ltd., outer
marking ring stuck,
1930s, bezel 2½in
(6cm) diam.
£300–330 S

An MG octagonal factory
mantlepiece clock, handmade
for Abingdon MG, 1930s.
£300–400 MCh

A Short & Mason motoring
aneroid barometer, with
adjustable ring for ascent
or descent, 1920s, bezel 2in
(5cm) diam.
£350–370 S

A calorimeter from a Morris
car, 1930s.
£60–80 MCh

A Jaeger-Paris eight-day
dashboard clock, for Delage,
Swiss made, 1920s, bezel 3in
(8cm) diam.
£150–170 *S*

A Smiths type 'Time of Trip'
motoring chronometer, 1920s,
second hand loose, bezel 3in
(7.5cm) diam.
£320–340 *S*

A Smiths silver faced
mechanical car clock, 1920s.
£50–75 *MCh*

An Octo eight-day car clock, in
an angled brass case, Swiss
made, 1910–20, bezel 2⅜in
(6cm) diam.
£320–340 *S*

An MG factory desk clock,
Abingdon, 1930s–50s.
£200–300 *MCh*

A Jaeger-Paris eight-day car
clock, with side winder,
Swiss made, 1920s, bezel
3in (7.5cm) diam.
£170–190 *S*

An American brass car clock,
c1906–08.
£200–250 *MCh*

A Rolls-Royce radiator clock,
post- WWII.
£360–380 *S*

r. An S. Smith & Son
Ltd., car clock, in an
angled brass case,
chipped lens, Swiss
made, c1910, bezel
3in (7.5cm) diam.
£360–380 *S*

A Jaeger-Paris eight-day
mechanical time clock, for
a 1927 Hispano-Suiza H6B.
£300–400 *MCh*

l. An auto altimeter motoring
aneroid barometer, 1930s,
bezel 2in (5cm) diam.
£365–385 *S*

A calorimeter by Boyce
Motometer Company, 1920s.
£90–120 *MCh*

The tachometer from Malcolm
Campbell's Bluebird, by
Smith & Sons Ltd., 1933, in
octagonal mahogany surround,
applied with silvered engraved
plaque, the dial with mounting
ring engraved with speeds '256,
264, 270, 280, 290, 299, 309'.
£5,000–5,500 *S*

*At Daytona, on 22nd February
1933, Sir Malcolm Campbell
drove the V12, 36.5 litre 2,300bhp
Bluebird with a Rolls-Royce 'R'
engine, to a new World Land
Speed Record. He beat his own
record of 253.97mph, set only
363 days earlier, with a final
speed set at 272.463mph.*

Clothing

A pair of fur and leather motoring gloves, 1908.
£80–100 *MCh*

Andrea de Cesaris' Bell Helmet, (McLaren) used during the 1981 season.
Est. £800–1,000 *S*

Two 1950s racing drivers' silk scarves:
l. A British scarf depicting Donington, Silverstone, Douglas and Brooklands tracks, 33½in (85cm) square. **£250–300**
r. A 1957 Mille Miglia scarf depicting the route in a brightly patterned border, 34in (86cm) square.
£425–450 *S*

A pair of Alan Jones' Linea Sport Racing overalls, post-1975.
Est. £1,000–1,500 *S*

A Stand 21 racing suit, worn by Damon Hill during the 1993 Formula One season.
Est. £1,500–1,800 *S*

A Bell racing helmet, signed by Formula One drivers and personalities, 1979.
Est. £2,500–3,000 *S*

Desk Accessories

A Rolls-Royce showroom clock and barometer desk piece, 1920s.
£380–450 *MCh*

A Rolls-Royce desk blotter, 1920s.
£280–350 *MCh*

A Bakelite and enamelled desk set, 1930s.
£60–70 *MCh*

A Rolls-Royce factory presentation paperknife, 1960s.
£100–150 *MCh*

A brass desk calendar and notepad, presented to A. D. Tarrant of Hampshire and Dorset Tyres Ltd. on his retirement, Christmas 1929.
£100–120 *MCh*

A Rolls-Royce presentation table lamp, with revolving perpetual calendar, 1950s.
£200–240 *MCh*

A BARC and Brooklands Aero Club Bakelite desk blotter, 1930s.
£200–250 *MCh*

A Frazer-Nash factory desk calendar, 1930s.
£120–160 *MCh*

A Lagonda gold plated and enamelled showroom revolving perpetual calendar, 1960s.
£160–200 *MCh*

A desk calendar from Bentley Motors Cricklewood factory, late 1920s.
£300–400 *MCh*

A showroom advertising pen holder set, 1960s.
£60–80 *MCh*

An advertising desk inkwell, for Morrisol Oils, c1929.
£80–100 *MCh*

A Vauxhall Motors desk top ink blotter, unused, in box, 1950s.
£70–80 *MCh*

An MG showroom promotional perpetual desk calendar, 1950s.
£80–140 *MCh*

Ephemera

l. A collection of seven manufacturers' sales and other booklets and pamphlets, relating to steam wagons and carts, c1901.
£180–200 *CSK*

r. A set of 50 John Player & Sons cigarette cards, 'Motor Cars', c1936.
£60–120 *ACC*

A Morgan psychodelic design, c1973, and another, First of the Real Sports Cars.
£12–15 *ONS*

A Bleriot Limited sales catalogue, English text, 54 pages, 1912.
£375–395 *S*

A set of 50 W. D. & H. O. Wills cigarette cards, 'Safety First', c1934.
£40–80 *ACC*

An autographed table reservations card, signed on the reverse by Richard Seaman, M. V. Brauchitsch, John Cobb, Rudolf Caracciola, Neubauer, and Bernd Rosemeyer, slight creasing, late 1930s, 5½ by 3in (14 by 7.5cm).
£500–550 *S*

A Rolls-Royce illuminated Long Service certificate, presented to Bertram Coles for 25 years service, dated '1948', 16½ by 11in (42 by 28cm), mounted, framed and glazed.
£160–180 *S*

Twenty printed tin badges of famous marques, contained in *The Magnet* Car Badge Album, 19th January, 1929, on original card.
£90–100 *ONS*

A Bleriot Lamps sales catalogue, English text, card covers, cord bound, 32 pages, one detached, 1907.
£250–270 *S*

A Mercedes 6 cylinder Supercharger Models sales catalogue, card covers, 1925–26, together with thirteen inserts, road tests and other sales sheets.
Est. £400–500 *S*

Horns

A foot-operated, floor-mounted horn, by Birdie Horns Ltd., London, early 1920s.
£100–150 *MCh*

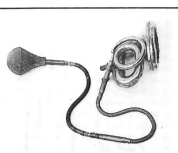

A rubber and brass bulb horn, c1908–11.
£180–240 *MCh*

r. A Howes & Burley ('H & B') brass coiled bulb horn, 1908–12.
£180–200 *MCh*

A Bosch 12 volt electric car horn, from a Lagonda Tourer, chrome finish, c1930.
£200–300 *MCh*

A pair of 12 volt electric chrome plated long trumpet horns, each with mounting bracket and red painted fly mesh, 1930s, 12in (30.5cm).
£170–190 *S*

A brass electric klaxon horn, from a Rolls-Royce Silver Ghost, 1914–25.
£375–450 *MCh*

A boa constrictor nickel plated
serpent's head bulb horn, with
tapered tube, c1910, 72in
(182.5cm) long.
£800–1,100 *MCh*

r. A Joseph Lucas brass
bulb horn, suitable for
early 1920s medium
sized vehicles.
£140–160 *MCh*

A Joseph Lucas brass
bulb horn, c1920.
£100–150 *MCh*

*This type of bulb horn fitted
through the bulkhead by
the windscreen.*

A cyclist's horn and silver
banded warning trumpet, c1870.
£200–300 *MCh*

Two cyclists' trumpets, c1880,
and a cyclist's whistle, c1890.
£300–400 *MCh*

Lamps

A pair of Stephen Grebel brass
headlamps, with original
lenses, early 20thC, lenses
9in (23cm) diam.
£440–480 *CSK*

A pair of Lucas King of the Road
self-generating acetylene
headlamps, c1907, with 5½in
(13.5cm) diam. convex lenses.
£700–750 *S*

A pair of Lucas brass oil rear
lamps, c1904–12.
£650–850 *MCh*

A Lucas brass oil side
lamp, c1904–12.
£140–160 *MCh*

A pair of Edwardian brass
Joseph Lucas veteran 700
series oil sidelamps.
£500–600 *MCh*

A pair of bell-shaped electric
headlamps, by C.A. Vandervell &
Co., patented 1911, with bevelled
glass lenses, 10in (25cm) diam.
£600–640 *S*

A pair of Marchal pillar-mounted
bull's-eye type 43 headlamps,
with Marchal Sunburst trade
shield, mounted on a three bulb
bar, restored, c1930, 1½in (4cm)
diam. bull's-eye, behind 9in
(23cm) diam. lenses.
£1,500–1,550 *S*

A pair of Model G bell-shaped
electric headlamps, by C.A.
Vandervell & Co., registered
design 1909, with polished
reflectors and bevelled glass
lenses, 10in (25cm) diam.
£600–625 *S*

A pair of Bleriot black enamelled and nickelled brass oil side lamps, c1908–10.
£1,250–1,600 MCh

A pair of Rotax self-generating acetylene road lights, c1906, 5½in (13.5cm) diam.
£500–540 S

A pair of Powell & Hanmer combination front/rear lamps, with side fitting, oil powered, for the Eldorado Ice Cream Company, pre-WWI.
£100–140 MCh

A pair of Edwardian nickelled brass S.E.M. opera side lamps, oil and electric powered, French.
£450–550 MCh

An acetylene self-generating brass headlamp, from a 1903 Lagonda.
£200–240 MCh

A pair of Victorian carriage lamps, from a Panhard Pioneer motor carriage, German, c1890.
£300–400 MCh

A French oil rear lamp, unused, 1902–06.
£200–250 MCh

An Edwardian nickel plated brass electric motor rear lamp, by Salsbury of London.
£140–160 MCh

A pair of Victorian coach lamps, converted to electricity, c1900.
£100–150 MCh

A pair of Victorian candle carriage lamps, c1890.
£200–300 MCh

An oil rear lamp, by Wyncott & Co., Birmingham, c1903–06.
£250–350 MCh

A pair of C. A. Vandervell bell-shaped nickelled brass electric headlamps, each with correct fork brackets.
£500–700 MCh

A pair of Shand Mason & Co., oil illuminated fire engine lanterns, converted to electricity, each with copper body, brass fittings and makers plaque, c1900, main lenses 5½in (14cm) diam.
£540–580 *S*

A Lucas King's Own No. F141 brass oil side lamp, c1900–20.
£180–250 *MCh*

A pair of Powell & Hammer of Birmingham oil rear lamps, c1900.
£300–400 *MCh*

A pair of Carl Zeiss Jena electric headlamps, from a 1930s Mercedes-Benz Cabriolet.
£2,500–3,500 *MCh*

A 1920s Lucas black enamelled oil bicycle tail lamp, with box, unused.
£100–120 *MCh*

A pair of Victorian candle coachlamps, for Benz or Panhard, c1900.
£300–400 *MCh*

A pair of brass oil side lamps, by Howes & Burley Ltd., c1905.
£380–470 *MCh*

A Lucas King of the Road brass acetylene lamp generator, with twin acetylene outlets, c1908.
£300–400 *MCh*

A pair of candle coach lamps, with mounting brackets, c1890.
£200–300 *MCh*

A Motex black enamelled motorcycle acetylene lamp generator, boxed, c1920.
£100–120 *MCh*

A Lucas acetylene lamp, with spare burners, tools and instructions, unused, c1909–12.
£300–400 *MCh*

A pair of Edwardian nickel plated brass oil side lamps, by Powell & Hanmer.
£280–380 *MCh*

A Lucas GPO acetylene front lamp, c1910, with case, unused.
£55–60 *HOLL*

An Edwardian running board mounted acetylene generator, by H & B Ltd.
£250–320 *MCh*

A Lucas Calcia Major nickel plated acetylene lamp, c1925.
£80–120 *MCh*

Luggage & Picnic Sets

A Coracle six person picnic basket, with copper kettle, burner, ceramic cups and saucers, wicker covered bottles and glasses, food boxes, condiments and butter jars, 1920s, 28½in (72.5cm) wide, with original canvas and leather cover.
£2,700–2,800 *S*

A set of three Lucas oil lamps, comprising a pair of sidelamps and a rearlamp, spade fitted, with loop handles, c1900.
£500–700 *MCh*

A four person 'en route' tea basket, by Drew & Sons, the wicker basket with lid and fitted interior containing kettle, burner, saucepan, warming plate, five metal boxes, knives and forks, ceramic saucers and three plates, 1912, 18½in (47cm) wide.
£330–360 *S*

An overnight vanity case, by Elkington & Co. Ltd., with foul weather cover, silk lined fitted interior, four silver topped bottles hallmarked London 1911, four silver backed brushes hallmarked London 1910, silver buttonhook, shoehorn and glove stretcher hallmarked Birmingham 1911, and other accessories.
£350–375 *S*

A lady's motoring vanity case, c1910.
£400–600 *MCh*

A four person picnic case, from a Bentley, in excellent condition, c1928.
£480–650 *MCh*

A Brexton vintage car picnic case for four persons, 1920s.
£220–280 *MCh*

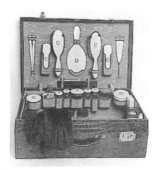

A Coracle four person wicker picnic basket, the fitted interior with kettle and burner, ceramic cups, saucers, plates and preserve jars, two wicker covered bottles and food boxes and cutlery, some pieces restored or replaced, c1920s, 25½in (65cm) wide.
£1,000–1,100 *S*

A crocodile skin travelling vanity case, with gold, silver and ivory capped and cased fittings, from a Rolls-Royce, 1928.
£3,000–4,000 *MCh*

A gentleman's crocodile skin travelling vanity case, with silver accessories, by Harrods, 1928.
£480–650 *MCh*

A four person 'en route' picnic set, by A. Drew & Sons, with green leather cloth case, kettle and burner, cups and saucers, enamel plates, cutlery, wicker covered bottles, glasses, food boxes, vesta case, condiment jars, and other accessories, c1920s, 31in (78.5cm) wide.
£5,000–5,500 *S*

A lady's travelling vanity case, with gold and enamelled finished fittings, c1908.
£750–1,150 *MCh*

A motorist's travelling vanity case, by Asprey & Co, 1920s.
£400–600 *MCh*

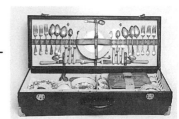

A six person picnic case, from a Rolls-Royce Phantom I, c1926–28.
£800–1,200 *MCh*

Mascots

Glass

A Lalique Grande Libelule glass mascot, repaired, 1930s.
£500–700 *MCh*

A Sabino glass mocking bird mascot, on illuminating mount, c1930.
£700–800 *MCh*

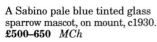

A Sabino pale blue tinted glass sparrow mascot, on mount, c1930.
£500–650 *MCh*

A Sabino glass cockerel mascot, on mount, 1920s.
£600–800 *MCh*

A glass angel fish mascot, mounted in a metal ring above a radiator cap, on wooden stand, probably French, 1920s, 5in (12.5cm) high.
£250–275 *S*

A Warren-Kessler glass salmon mascot, 1920s.
£400–600 *MCh*

A French clear glass sparrow mascot, on plated cap mount, late 1920s.
£400–500 *MCh*

A Lalique Tête d'Epervier, clear glass mascot, in a Brèves Galleries illuminated base with blue filter, embossed mark, large chip, 1920s–30s.
£675–700 *S*

A Lalique glass St. Christopher mascot, intaglio moulded with impressed mark, on a Brèves Galleries base, 1930s, 4½in (11cm) high.
£375–400 *S*

Metal

A Red Ashay Mephistopheles glass mascot, on metal mount, late 1920s, 5½in (14cm) high.
£1,250–1,350 *S*

A Red Ashay Charioteer glass mascot, on an illuminated base with wind powered rotating coloured filters, and wooden base, 1930s, 9½in (24cm) high.
£1,450–1,650 *S*

A baby's dummy or pacifier mascot, produced as an accessory for the Austin 7 car, 1920s.
£200–250 *MCh*

A skull and cross bones illuminating mascot, late 1920s.
£300–400 *MCh*

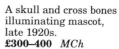

A Pyrene promotional fire extinguisher mascot on radiator cap, late 1920s.
£240–280 *MCh*

A Warwick vase mascot,
from a vintage charabanc that
transported staff to Warwick
Castle, 1920s.
£250–300 *MCh*

A skull and cross bones
mascot, 1930s.
£200–250 *MCh*

A Praga cars Laurels of Victory
mascot, patinated bronze, with
hole through back, mounted on
a marble base, Czechoslovakian,
1927, 6in (15cm) high.
£250–270 *S*

A Bridges Drills chrome plated
publicity mascot, post-WWII.
£150–180 *MCh*

A three bells mechanical mascot,
on cap, late 1920s.
£100–150 *MCh*

A flying bird mechanical mascot,
with flapping wings, by Flying
Mascots Ltd., early 1930s.
£200–300 *MCh*

The personal mascot of racing
driver Prince Bira, from his
Bentley 'The Bira Tiger',
with jewelled eyes, signed
'B. Bira', 1930s.
£650–850 *MCh*

A brass cat mascot, marked
'Sans Peur', French, early 1920s.
£250–320 *MCh*

A chrome plated brass
elephant mascot, probably
Indian, 1930s, 7½in (19cm)
high, on a wooden base.
£570–590 *S*

A plated bronze stork
mascot, c1925–28.
£180–220 *MCh*

A hornet mascot, with ruby
coloured inset eyes, stamped
'Asprey-London', 1920s,
wingspan 8in (20cm).
£900–950 *CSK*

A snowgoose solid nickel
mascot, on a cap, c1925.
£180–200 *MCh*

A French 'wise owl on the book of learning' mascot, early 1920s.
£300–360 *MCh*

A brass dog mascot on cap, for an Austin 7 Chummy, c1928.
£180–200 *MCh*

An enamelled brass mascot of a squirrel eating an acorn, c1914.
£180–240 *MCh*

A Molly the Dog cold enamel and bronze mascot, by A.E.L., 1930s.
£120–150 *MCh*

A chrome on brass greyhound mascot, early 1930s.
£100–120 *MCh*

A bronze teal mascot, by G. H. Laurent, signed and stamped, French, 1920s, 4in (10cm) high.
£430–460 *S*

A Desmo chrome plated brass Scottie dog mascot, 1950s.
£80–120 *MCh*

A nickel plated bronze bull mascot, on a metal base, 1920s, 3½in (9cm) high.
£250–275 *S*

A mascot from a Hispano-Suiza H6B town car, by F. Bazin, c1927.
£1,250–1,650 *MCh*

A saucy witch mascot, nickel plated and mounted on 'dog bone' radiator cap, c1922, 4½in (11cm) high.
£550–575 *S*

A chrome plated Fox's bear mascot, for Fox's Mints delivery lorry, dated '1932.'
£130–140 *MCh*

A chrome plated horse's head mascot, on cap, late 1920s.
£120–160 *MCh*

A nickel and brass mascot of
an otter with a salmon in his
mouth, 1932.
£180–240 *MCh*

A chromed brass aeroplane
mascot, on radiator cap,
early 1950s.
£150–200 *MCh*

A spelter hare mascot, after a
design by Bequerel, mounted
on a radiator cap, 1930s, 7½in
(19cm) high.
£120–130 *S*

A chrome plated WWII
Hurricane mascot.
£200–250 *MCh*

Cross Reference
Advertising & Promotional

A silver and enamelled British
Airways Concorde aircraft mascot,
from a limited edition, 1970.
£280–375 *MCh*

A silver plated brass Schneider
S6B seaplane mascot, late 1920s.
£250–375 *MCh*

A policeman mascot, with
movable porcelain head,
known as 'The Robert Mascot'
by J. Hassall, mid-1920s.
£280–370 *MCh*

A chrome plated aeroplane
mascot, with spinning
two-bladed propellers, on
radiator cap, c1950.
£140–180 *MCh*

A brass and nickel Hassall
aviator mascot, the aeroplane
with spinning propeller and
spring-loaded movable
aviator's head, c1914.
£500–600 *MCh*

A brass mascot of a golfer
on a golf ball, mid-1920s.
£180–220 *MCh*

A nickel plated brass Schneider
S6B seaplane mascot, by Rolls-
Royce Ltd., stamped on float,
early 1930s.
£500–750 *MCh*

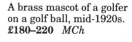

A bronze statuette mascot, mounted on a radiator cap, probably French, c1910, 9in (23cm) high.
£250–270 *S*

A silver plated brass cherub mascot, c1911.
£140–180 *MCh*

A silver plated brass Mr Punch mascot, from Stellite car, on correct cap, c1914.
£380–450 *MCh*

An Edwardian nickel plated brass head of the goddess Minerva mascot, signed 'P. de Soete'.
£350–450 *MCh*

A nickel plated brass griffin mascot, by AEL, c1930.
£240–280 *MCh*

A brass harp mascot, mounted on a radiator cap, 1920s.
£140–160 *MCh*

A nickel plated brass Speed God in the Wheel mascot, by Cottin, c1914.
£400–500 *MCh*

A Vulcan bronze lorry mascot, on radiator cap, 1920s.
£200–240 *MCh*

An English brass traffic policeman mascot, 1928.
£240–280 *MCh*

A Desmo chrome and brass downhill skier mascot, on radiator cap, 1930s.
£200–250 *MCh*

A chrome and brass smoking ballerina mascot, c1930.
£200–250 *MCh*

A chrome plated le hurler mascot, French, 1930s, 7½in (19cm) high.
£1,900–2,000 *S*

A nickel plated Mr Punch mascot, stamped 'Willoughby 57841-Finnigans London', 1930s, 6in (15cm) high.
£220–240 *CSK*

A brass mascot of William Shakespeare, c1910.
£200–250 *MCh*

These accessories were sold to motorists in Stratford-upon-Avon garages.

A nickel plated brass fantasy mascot of Mr Punch, Judy, the baby and Toby the dog, early 1920s.
£200–250 *MCh*

A bronze mascot, of a youth thumbing his nose, wearing oversize boots, mounted on a wooden base, pre-WWII, 6in (15cm) high.
£180–200 *CSK*

A chrome plated brass mascot of Sir Walter Raleigh, from a 1930s Raleigh light car.
£200–250 *MCh*

A plated bronze helmsman mascot, 1920s–30s.
£250–320 *MCh*

l. A nickel plated bronze mascot of a WWI fusilier, made in London.
£200–250 *MCh*

r. A chrome plated brass mascot, of a girl with a beach ball, numbered, 1930s.
£80–140 *MCh*

A nickel plated brass pixie mascot, for a vintage car, 1920s.
£160–200 *MCh*

A brass lifeboatman mascot,
early vintage, 1920s.
£120–160 *MCh*

A Finnegan's nickel Icarus
mascot, by Colin George, signed
and numbered, pre-1924.
£400–500 *MCh*

A chrome plated brass Lord
Nelson mascot, early 1920s.
£200–260 *MCh*

An Art Deco silver plated brass
mascot, by J'Aland, early 1930s.
£350–450 *MCh*

A brass mascot, The
Motorist, c1928.
£220–240 *MCh*

A chrome plated brass mascot,
The Skipper, signed in various
places, c1927.
£260–320 *MCh*

l. An Egyptian brass Pharoah
mascot, 1930s.
£240–300 *MCh*

A nickel wind-operated
mechanical Batgirl
mascot, 1920s.
£200–245 *MCh*

An Art Deco silver plated
brass golfer mascot, mounted
as a golfing award, 1928.
£375–400 *MCh*

A German silver on solid nickel
mascot, The Pathfinder, by
C. Poitvin, Finnigan's London,
retailed 1920s, London, Paris,
Rome and Madrid.
£450–500 *MCh*

A nickel plated brass mascot,
Cubitt's Cupid, from a 1920s
Cubitt light car.
£200–300 *MCh*

A brass mascot of a traffic policeman, mounted on a cap, c1920.
£200–225 *MCh*

A brass diving nymph mascot, on radiator cap, an accessory for light cars in 1920s.
£80–140 *MCh*

A Finnigan's nickel plated brass debutante mascot, mid-1920s.
£350–420 *MCh*

An American chrome plated spelter winged goddess mascot, c1928, with integral cap unit.
£240–290 *MCh*

Manufacturers' Mascots

A Rover chrome plated aluminium Viking's head mascot, 1930s.
£150–200 *MCh*

A Guy Motors Ltd., aluminium Indian head mascot, with 'Feathers in Our Cap' logo, 1930s.
£100–150 *MCh*

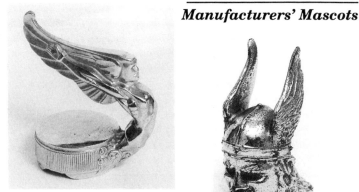

An American Chevrolet chrome plated mascot, designed by William Schnell, c1930.
£200–250 *MCh*

A Rover brass full-length Viking mascot, on radiator cap, c1920.
£250–320 *MCh*

An American Chrysler nickel plated brass winged helmet mascot, with integral cap, c1926.
£200–240 *MCh*

Two American Chevrolet car mascots, on radiator caps, late 1920s.
£180–240 each *MCh*

A nickel plated brass mascot, from the rare Crown Ensign car, c1920.
£300–400 *MCh*

An Edwardian brass windmill mascot, from an Old Mill light car, c1914.
£240–285 *MCh*

A chrome plated Lorraine Deitrich greyhound mascot, designed by Casimir Brau, French, 1931, 8in (20cm) long.
£430–460 *S*

An American Studebaker chrome plated and enamelled mascot, 1930s.
£200–220 *MCh*

An American Plymouth chrome plated mascot, by Jarvis & Company, designed by H. V. Henderson, c1931.
£180–220 *MCh*

A Buick nickel plated spelter mascot, known as 'Buick Goddess', by Ternstedt Manufacturing Company, USA, with integral radiator cap, c1928.
£240–270 *MCh*

An American General Motors Company truck mascot, pre-WWII.
£80–140 *MCh*

An Alvis nickel plated brass hare mascot, 1920s.
£250–270 *MCh*

A W. O. Bentley horizontal winged 'B' chrome plated brass mascot, by Joseph. Fray of Birmingham, for a Bentley 3 litre, 1923-26.
£350–450 *MCh*

A Straker-Squire nickel mascot, 1920s.
£400–600 *MCh*

A winged flying 'B' chrome plated brass mascot, on radiator cap, for 3½ and 4¼ litre Bentleys, 1930s.
£400–450 *MCh*

A nickel plated horizontal winged 'B' mascot, by Joseph Fray of Birmingham, for 4½ litre Bentley cars, 1928–31, wingspan 8in (20cm).
£500–600 *MCh*

An American Moon limousine nickel plated brass mascot, on radiator cap, c1924.
£240–280 *MCh*

A winged flying 'B' chrome plated
brass mascot, on radiator cap,
for Bentley Mk6 and R-Type,
mid-1950s.
£280–350 *MCh*

A Talbot chrome plated spelter
sail mascot, with integral
thermometer, 1930s.
£80–140 *MCh*

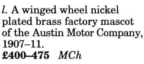

A Rolls-Royce stainless steel
Spirit of Ecstasy mascot, 1960s.
£200–250 *MCh*

A Rolls-Royce chrome on bronze
Spirit of Ecstasy mascot, on
radiator cap, for Rolls-Royce
20/25, 1930s.
£270–300 *MCh*

l. A winged wheel nickel
plated brass factory mascot
of the Austin Motor Company,
1907–11.
£400–475 *MCh*

A silver plated bronze
mascot, The Whisper,
by Charles Sykes, c1910.
£2,000–3,000 *MCh*
*This design was submitted
to Mr Royce of Rolls-Royce
Motors, but was rejected in
favour of the Spirit of Ecstasy.*

A Rolls-Royce solid silver Spirit
of Ecstasy mascot, signed
'Charles Sykes', for Rolls-Royce
Phantom II type, 1929, on a
display base, 5½in (14cm) high.
£1,000–1,100 *S*

A solid silver model of a Rolls-
Royce Silver Ghost, hallmarked
London 1976, on a wooden base,
9in (23cm) long.
£1,350–1,450 *S*

Models

A ¼ scale model Bugatti Type 35
Grand Prix, built by I.J.G. Carson,
with internal combustion engine
and aluminium body, 92in
(234cm) long.
£9,000–10,000 *CSK*

A diecast Ferrari 500 F2 Grand
Prix promotional model,
produced for the factory,
c1952, 16in (40cm) long.
£1,200–1,300 *BKS*

A steel, brass and aluminium ⅛th
scale model of a Bugatti Type 35
Grand Prix car by Art Collection
Auto, Vichy, 1975, with display
base, perspex cover and
literature, 22in (55.5cm) long.
£2,500–2,600 *CSK*

A model of the 1.5 litre BRM and driver Jackie Stewart winning the Monaco Grand Prix, on display base, 1960s.
£190–200 *BKS*

A Pocher ⅛th scale model of an Alfa Romeo, Type 8C 2300 Monza, c1931, built by R. A. Burgess, with display case, 27in (68.5cm) long.
£1,900–2,000 *CSK*

A model of the 1954 Maserati 250F, of Prince Birabongse Bhanubandh of Thailand, inscribed 'Conti M', 1954, 13½in (34cm) long.
£1,700–2,000 *CNY*

An Alfa Romeo P2 model, with fully working clockwork mechanism and steering front wheels, excellent condition, 20in (50.5cm) long.
£1,400–1,500 *COYS*

One of a limited edition released during 1930/31.

A collection of 50 1:43 scale models and toys, representing the winning cars from the inception of the Le Mans race to c1989.
£2,600–2,800 *BKS*

Pedal Cars

l. A pressed steel single seater racing pedal car, painted red, with solid rubber tyres, 47in (119cm) long.
£270–290 *S*

r. An enamelled metal pedal racing car, solid rubber tyres, electric horn and lights, by Giordiani, Bologna, 1950s, 52in (132cm) long.
£700–725 *AG*

A Mercedes-Benz Spider 500 pedal car, with plastic monocoque on a square section steel chassis frame, modern.
£85–95 *CARS*

l. A Tri-ang pedal car model of a De Dion car, with metalbody on a steel tubular frame, with solid rubber tyres.
£450–500 *CARS*

A Tri-ang Sharna Rolls-Royce Corniche, produced under licence, with moulded plastic body over steel box frame chassis. Electric powered. **£450–550** Pedal powered. **£200–300** *CARS*

These children's cars were produced in electric form from the early 1970s up to the early 1990s. The pedal powered series RRM 1–RRM 6 was discontinued in 1991.

Petrol Pumps

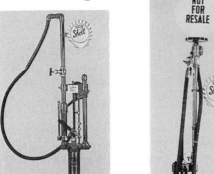

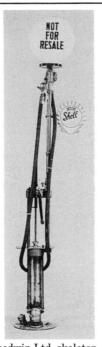

A Gilbert and Barker self measuring hand cranked petrol pump, with Super Shell plate, restored, 1920s, 84in (213cm) high.
£580–620 *S*

An H.J. Goodwin Ltd. skeleton hand petrol pump, painted red, restored, 85in (216cm) high.
£750–770 *S*

r. An H. J. Goodwin Ltd., hand cranked petrol pump, with Sealed Shell glass, painted red with polished brass, modern globe, restored, 1920s, 100in (254cm) high.
£200–225 *S*

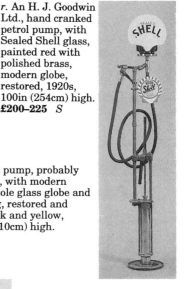

A hand petrol pump, probably Avery Hardoll, with modern National Benzole glass globe and guarantee flag, restored and repainted black and yellow, 1920s, 83in (210cm) high.
£500–550 *S*

A Gilbert and Barker hand operated petrol pump, repainted orange with black Pratts symbol painted on inside, white globe applied with black Pratts lettering, 1920s, 100in (254cm) high.
£1,500–1,600 *S*

An Avery Hardoll electric petrol pump, repainted yellow and black, with enamel National Benzole Mixture sign, glass petrol pump globe repaired, 1950s, 83in (210cm) high.
£400–440 *S*

A Bowser hand petrol pump, painted blue with BP stickers, restored, 1920s, 82in (208cm) high.
£1,100–1,200 *S*

A Beckmeter electric petrol pump, patented 1932-33, repainted red and black, modern glass globe, 80in (203cm) high.
£1,300–1,400 *S*

Globes

A BP glass petrol pump globe, lettered in yellow with black shading on green background, post-WWII, 16in (40.5cm) high.
£270–290 *S*

A BP Diesel glass petrol pump globe, lettered in yellow on green and black, 1950s, 18in (46cm) high.
£230–250 *S*

A BP Super glass petrol pump globe, green, yellow and black, registered design 1949, 18½in (47cm) high.
£230–250 *S*

A Regent Derv glass petrol pump globe, lettered in red and blue, slight crack to one side, late 1940s, 17in (43cm) high.
£100–110 *S*

An Esso Benzol Mixture glass petrol pump globe, base with rubber ring, some repainting, pre-WWII, 18½in (46.5cm) high.
£220–240 *S*

An Esso High Test glass petrol pump globe, with rubber ring, overpainted, slight chips to base, pre-WWII, 19in (48cm) high.
£160–180 *S*

A Mobil glass petrol pump globe, lettered in blue and red, dated '12.66', 12in (30.5cm) high.
£115–125 *S*

A National Benzole Mixture glass petrol pump globe, with green line around globe, 1930s, 19½in (49cm) high.
£175–185 *S*

A Munster and Simms glass petrol pump globe, in red and grey with yellow top and base, 1970, 14in (35.5cm) high.
£115–125 *S*

A Power glass petrol pump globe, with green lettering, black painted base and neck, 1950s, 19in (48cm) high.
£210–225 *S*

A Gulf glass petrol pump globe, in blue and orange, 1960s, 9in (48cm) high.
£240–260 *S*

A National Benzole Mixture three-sided glass petrol pump globe, decorated in yellow and black, pre-WWII, 16½in (42cm) high.
£260–280 *S*

A Power glass petrol pump globe, with green lettering, 1950s, 19in (48cm) high.
£180–200 *S*

A Sealed Shell 'fat' glass petrol pump globe, repainted, 1950s, 16½in (42cm) high.
£190–220 *S*

A Shell 'fat' glass petrol pump globe, overpainted in black, 1950s, 20½in (51.5cm) high.
£150–160 *S*

A Shell 'fat' glass petrol pump globe, lettered in red, with black base, dated '5.53', 19in (48cm) high.
£270–290 *S*

A Shell Mex Sealed glass petrol pump globe, overpainted in black, pre-WWII, 17in (43cm) high.
£210–230 *S*

A Shell glass petrol pump globe, lettered in red, dated 'L.9.49', 17in (43cm) high.
£110–120 *S*

A Shellmex 'fat' glass petrol pump globe, lettered in red with black base, slight damage, pre-WWII, 19½in (49cm) high.
£230–250 *S*

A Super Shell blue glass petrol pump globe, lettered in blue and red, c1940s, 17½in (44.5cm) high.
£290–320 *S*

Photographs

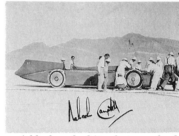

A black and white photograph of Blue Bird, autographed by Sir Malcolm Campbell, 5in (12.5cm) wide, together with a letter signed and dated '1936'.
£380–400 *CSK*

Two albums of photographs covering CanAm, American sports car races, NASCAR, Indianapolis, USAC and Trans-Am racing, mid–late 1960s.
£750–850 *CSK*

Two albums of photographs covering the Sports Car Championship, including Targa Florio, Nürburgring 1000kms, Le Mans and others, 1964–67.
£430–450 *CSK*

An album of 60 photographs, covering Formula One and Formula Two, with descriptions and publishers remarks on the reverse, 1966–67.
£280–300 *CSK*

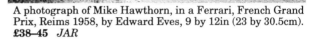

A photograph of Mike Hawthorn, in a Ferrari, French Grand Prix, Reims 1958, by Edward Eves, 9 by 12in (23 by 30.5cm).
£38–45 *JAR*

An album of 132 photographs of 'The Scottish Automobile Club Reliability Trials, 1909, on the Lanchester'.
£2,200–2,300 *CSK*

Two albums of photographs of rallying interest, mostly with descriptions on reverse, 1964–68.
£250–270 *CSK*

A photograph of Jean Popperato and Morris Rocco in the Sunbeam, Indianapolis 500, 1915, 9in by 10in (23 by 25cm).
£430–450 *CSK*

A collection of photographs mostly of Formula One drivers and team managers, including Rindt, Stewart, Ireland, Von Trips Ickx, Pedro Rodrigues and others, 1960s.
£320–340 *CSK*

r. A photograph of Jean Alesi, in the team Ferrari, Monaco Grand Prix 1994, by Nigel Snowdon, 9 by 12in (23 by 30.5cm).
£38–45 *JAR*

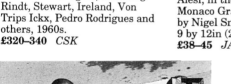

A photograph of Michael Schumacher, in the team Benetton Ford, Monaco Grand Prix 1994, by Nigel Snowdon. 9 by 12in (23 by 30.5cm).
£38–45 *JAR*

A photograph of Graham Hill, in a Jaguar, Crystal Palace 1963, by Colin Waldeck, 9 by 12in (23 by 30.5cm).
£38–45 *JAR*

A photograph of Peter Collins, in the team Ferrari, German Grand Prix, Nürburgring 1958, by Edward Eves, 9 by 12in (23 by 30.5cm).
£38–45 *JAR*

r. A photograph of Antonio Branca, in the team Maserati, Goodwood 1951, by Alan Smith, 9 by 12in (23 by 30.5cm).
£38–45 *JAR*

r. A photograph of
Juan-Manuel Fangio,
in a Maserati, Pescara
Grand Prix 1957, by
Edward Eves, 9 by 12in
(23 by 30.5cm).
£38–45 *JAR*

A photograph of Ayrton Senna,
in the team McLaren Honda,
Monaco Grand Prix 1992, by
Nigel Snowdon, 9 by 12in
(23 by 30.5cm).
£38–45 *JAR*

A linen backed lithograph in
colours, Standard Cars, 1933,
60½in (153.5cm) wide.
£300–330 *CSK*

Posters

After René Vincent, 'La Nouvelle
6 Cylindres Renault', a hand
coloured lithograph, signed,
published by Draeger, on linen,
c1910, 23in (58.5cm) wide.
£550–575 *ONS*

Cross Reference
Ephemera

A collection of thirty official
event posters covering,
1963–1993, 23½ by 16½in
(60 by 42cm).
£1,500–1,600 *CSK*

A lithograph in colours, 'Grand
Prix of Cuba 500km, Feb. 25 at
Havana', 1957, 28 by 19 in
(71 by 48cm) wide.
£260–280 *CSK*

A poster on linen, 'Grand Prix
Automobile Pau, 7 Avril 1947',
after Ch. V. Surreau, 47 by 30in
(119 by 77cm).
£550–575 *ONS*

A lithograph in colours, 'Premier
SZ1SZ Voiture Renault Sur
Pneus Michelin', by William
Cook, 1906, 18 by 26in
(45 by 66cm), framed.
£440–480 *ONS*

A linen poster, published by
Wall, Paris, 31½ by 23in
(80 by 59cm).
£140—160 *ONS*

Six Porsche achievements
posters, for World Sports Car
Championships, 1000kms
Osterreichring and de Spa 1971,
Interserie-Nürburgring, Imola
and Hockenheim 1972 and
Silverstone 1973.
£185–200 *CSK*

An autographed colour advertising poster, by Phil Hill, for the 1961 Le Mans 24 hour race, 22 by 15in (56 by 38cm).
£300–325 *CSK*

An original poster, by Hans Liska, of the 1937 Grossen Preis Von Monaco, Mercedes-Benz, dated '1937', 27½ by 16in (69.5 by 40cm), display mounted.
£440–480 *S*

A mounted poster, for 16 Internationales Adac Eifel Rennen Nürburgring, by Van Heusen, 34 by 24in (86 by 61cm).
£440–480 *S*

An original poster, Circuit International, by G. Gaudy, with J. E. Goosens lithographers stamp, dated '18 Juin 1906', 23 by 35in (59 by 89cm), framed and glazed.
£1,300–1,400 *S*

An original poster, Monza Lottery Grand Prix, colour lithograph depicting a Cooper racing car, mounted, framed and glazed, c1962, 16 by 12in (40.5 by 30.5cm).
£120–140 *BKS*

An original advertising poster, for the 51st Targa Florio, 1967, with artwork by Gordon Crosby, 39 by 27in (99 by 69cm).
£350–375 *CSK*

Signs

An advertising sign for Dodge Brothers, double-sided with flange mount, slight wear, pre-WWII, 21 by 32in (53 by 81cm).
£100–120 *S*

A double-sided enamel advertising sign, for Pratts Petrol & Oils, the Art Deco design in six colours, with tab mounting bracket, 1920s, 22in (56cm) wide.
£220–240 *S*

An enamel advertising sign for Sun Insurance, in four colours, some weathering, 1920s, 30 by 20in (76 by 51cm).
£475–500 *S*

A Willys-Overland Motor Cars double-sided enamel sign, in five colours, some wear, pre-WWII, 24in (61cm) wide.
£220–240 *S*

A double-sided National Benzole Mixture enamel sign, in black and orange on white, repaired, 1920s, 24in (61cm) diam.
£200–225 *S*

Cross Reference
Colour Review
Advertising &
Promotional

Smoking

A BARC Brooklands desk ashtray, by No Fume, Bakelite, with detachable chrome cap, 1930s.
£140–185 *MCh*

A Daimler Motor Company Royal family loyalty copper ashtray, 1911.
£60–90 *MCh*

A BARC Brooklands Bakelite and chrome plated clubhouse bar ashtray, 1930s.
£100–140 *MCh*

A Rolls-Royce showroom ashtray, 1933.
£200–300 *MCh*

A Rolls-Royce showroom ashtray, 1950s.
£180–250 *MCh*

An 18ct gold and enamel cigarette case, with a picture of a Ford Model T, engraved, London 1911, 4in (10cm) wide.
£1,200–1,300 *CSK*

A Lagonda Factory cigarette box, 1960s.
£140–170 *MCh*

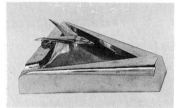

A Vauxhall showroom ashtray, c1930.
£200–240 *MCh*

A Bentley Motors promotional cigarette lighter, boxed, 1930s.
£100–140 *MCh*

An EPNS cigarette box, with a plaque of a Wolseley 30/40hp, 1920s, 6in (15cm) wide.
£420—450 *CSK*

This cigarette box was the property of the late William Deallow, financial director of Wolseley Motors from 1922-27.

A Rolls-Royce showroom ashtray, mounted with Spirit of Ecstacy mascot, 1960s.
£250–300 *MCh*

A Rolls-Royce Owners' Club desk ashtray, 1960-70.
£80–120 *MCh*

A brass ashtray, from AA approved South Ealing Garage, c1927.
£70–80 *MCh*

A tin of Bryant and May's motor matches, for illuminating oil lamps, c1904.
£80–100 *MCh*

A silver plated on brass ashtray, by Fakir Motors for Bentley, 1920s.
£100–140 *MCh*

A Rolls-Royce cigarette case, c1930.
£300–400 *MCh*

A Wolseley Motor Co. copper and silver showroom ashtray, 1913–19.
£100–125 *MCh*

An Elliott-Lucas showroom ashtray, c1930.
£60–85 *MCh*

A silver cigarette case, with enamel St. Christopher plaque to the front, the front folding down to form an ashtray, hallmarked Birmingham 1936, 3in (7.5cm) wide.
£160–180 *S*

A Rolls-Royce retailer's desk ashtray, mounted with Spirit of Ecstasy mascot, c1920.
£250–350 *MCh*

A 'Mr. Maymore' factory ashtray by May and Padmore, motoring and household match makers, c1920.
£300–350 *MCh*

A silver ashtray, from the Joseph Lucas, King Street, Birmingham factory, 1926.
£100–150 *MCh*

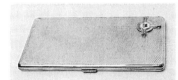

A Morris Motors of Cowley gentleman's cigarette case, c1950.
£50–75 *MCh*

A glass showroom ashtray for Solignum oils and greases, c1930.
£60–70 *MCh*

A Lesney desktop cigarette box, for W.O. Bentley, 1960s.
£40–60 *MCh*

A pair of EPNS cigarette cases, for BARC Brooklands, and Brooklands Aero Club, mid-1930s.
£250–350 *MCh*

r. An Austin Motor Co. gentleman's cigarette case, 1950s.
£50–60 *MCh*

Tools & Equipment

Two motor car fire extinguishers, c1920.
£50–75 each *MCh*

A Liquall brass two gallon can pouring spout, c1914–31.
£70–85 *MCh*

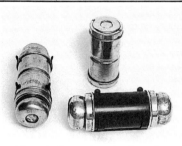

Three bulb carriers, by Joseph Lucas of Birmingham, c1914–31.
£70–80 each *MCh*

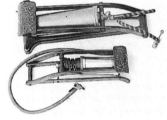

Two Dunlop brass and black enamelled footpumps, restored, 1920s–30s.
£70–80 each *MCh*

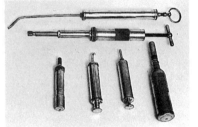

A collection of six brass grease guns and oil syringes, c1910–30.
£120–180 *MCh*

A brass electric inspection lamp, c1920s.
£80–140 *MCh*

A brass inspection lamp, by Joseph Lucas Ltd., Birmingham, with winding handle, pre-WWII.
£60–80 *MCh*

A Lucas King of the Road copper fuel tank filling funnel, c1910.
£80–90 *MCh*

Trophies & Medals

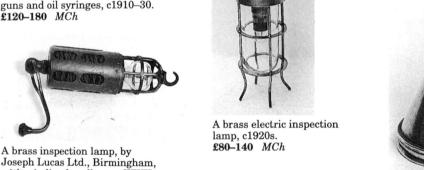

A Motor Union of Great Britain & Ireland winners silver medal, the obverse with design by H. von Herkanier, dated '1906', presented to Colonel F. W. Blood for the Cheshire Automobile Club Gymkhana, hallmarked Birmingham 1908, 3in (7cm) diam, with original case.
£220–250 *S*

A BARC Brooklands Trophy for the Easter Race, 1932.
£280–350 *MCh*

A BARC Brooklands silver cup, The Rupert Garside Challenge Cup, hallmarked 1936.
£250–350 *MCh*

GLOSSARY

We have attempted to define some of the terms that you will come across in this book. If there are any terms or technicalities you would like explained or you feel should be included in future please let us know.

All-weather - A term used to describe a vehicle with a more sophisticated folding hood than the normal Cape hood fitted to a touring vehicle. The sides were fitted with metal frames and transparent material, in some cases glass.

Berline - See Sedanca de Ville.

Boost - The amount of pressure applied by a supercharger or turbocharger.

Brake Horsepower - Bhp - This is the horse power of the combustion engine measured at the engine flywheel (See Horsepower).

Brake - A term dating from the days of horse drawn vehicles. Originally the seating was fore and aft, with the passengers facing inwards.

Cabriolet - The term Cabriolet applies to a vehicle with a hood which can be closed, folded half way, or folded right back. The Cabriolet can be distinguished from the Landaulette as the front of the hood reaches the top of the windscreen whereas the Landaulette only covers the rear quarter of the car.

Chain drive - A transmission system in which the wheels are attached to a sprocket, driven by a chain from an engine powered sprocket usually on the output side of a gearbox.

Chassis - A framework to which the car body, engine, gearbox, and axles are attached.

Chummy - An open top 2 door body style usually with a single door, 2 seats in the front and one at the rear.

Cloverleaf - A 3 seater open body style usually with a single door, 2 seats in the front and one at the rear.

Cone Clutch - One in which both driving and driven faces form a cone.

Convertible - A general term (post-war) for any car with a soft top.

Continental - This is a car specifically designed for high speed touring, usually on the Continent. Rolls-Royce and Bentley almost exclusively used this term during the 1930s and post-WWII.

Coupé - In the early Vintage and Edwardian period, it was only applied to what is now termed a Half Limousine or Doctor's Coupé which was a 2 door, 2-seater. The term is now usually prefixed by Drophead or Fixed Head.

Cubic Capacity - The volume of an engine obtained by multiplying the bore and the stroke.

De Ville - Almost all early coachwork had an exposed area for the driver to be in direct control of his horses, and so the motor car chauffeur was believed to be able to control the vehicle more easily if he was open to the elements. As the term only refers to part of the style of the car, i.e. the front, it is invariably used in connection with the words Coupé and Sedanca.

Dickey Seat - A passenger seat, usually for 2 people contained in the boot of the car without a folding hood (the boot lid forms the backrest). Known in America as a rumble seat.

Doctor's Coupé - A fixed or folding head coupé without a dickey seat and the passenger seat slightly staggered back from the driver's to accommodate the famous black bag.

Dog Cart - A horsedrawn dog cart was originally used to transport beaters and their dogs to a shoot (the dogs were contained in louvred boxes under the seats, the louvres were kept for decoration long after the dogs had gone).

Dos-à-dos - Literally back-to-back, i.e. the passenger seating arrangement.

Drophead Coupé - Originally a 2 door 2 seater with a folding roof, see Roadster.

Dry Sump - A method of lubricating engines, usually with 2 oil pumps, one of which removes oil from the sump to a reservoir away from the engine block.

Engine - Engine sizes are given in cubic centimetres (cc) in Europe and cubic inches (cu in) in the USA. 1 cubic inch equals 16.38cc (1 litre = 61.02cu in).

Estate Car - See Brake.

Fixed Head Coupé - FHC, a coupé with a solid fixed roof.

Golfer's Coupé - Usually an open 2 seater with a square-doored locker behind the driver's seat to accommodate golf clubs.

Hansom - As with the famous horse drawn cab, an enclosed 2 seater with the driver out in the elements either behind or in front.

Horsepower - The unit of measurement of engine power. One horsepower represents the energy expended in raising 33,000lb by one foot in 60 seconds.

Landau - An open carriage with a folding hood at each end which would meet in the middle when erected.

Laudaulette - Also Landaulet, a horsedrawn Landaulette carried 2 people and was built much like a coupé. A Landau was a town carriage for 4 people. The full Landau was rarely built on a motor car chassis because the front folding hood took up so much room between the driver's seat and the rear compartment. The roof line of a Landaulette has always been angular, in contrast to the Cabriolet and the folding hood, and very often made of patent leather. A true Landaulette only opens over the rear compartment and not over the front seat at all.

Limousine - French in origin, always used to describe a closed car equipped with occasional seats and always having a division between the rear and driver's compartments. Suffixes and prefixes are often inappropriately used with the term Limousine and should be avoided.

Monobloc engine - An engine with all cylinders cast in a single block.

Monocoque - A type of construction of car bodies without a chassis as such, the strength being in the stressed panels. Most modern mass produced cars are built this way.

OHC - Overhead camshaft, either single (SOHC) or double (DOHC).

OHV - Overhead valve engine.

Phæton - A term dating back to the the days of horsedrawn vehicles for an open body, sometimes with a Dickey or Rumble Seat for the groom at the rear. It was an owner/driver carriage and designed to be pulled by 4 horses. A term often misused during the Veteran period but remains in common use, particularly in the United States.

Post Vintage Thoroughbred (PVT) - A British term drawn up by the Vintage Sports Car Club (VSCC) for selected models made in the vintage tradition between 1931 and 1942.

Roadster - An American term for a 2 seater sports car. The hood should be able to be removed totally rather than folded down as a drophead coupé.

Roi des Belges - A luxurious open touring car with elaborately contoured seat backs, named after King Leopold II of Belgium. The term is sometimes wrongly used for general touring cars.

Rotary engine - An engine in which the cylinder banks revolve around the crank, for example the Wankel engine with its rotating piston.

Rpm - Engine revolutions per minute.

Rumble Seat - A folding seat for 2 passengers, used to increase the carrying capacity of a standard 2 passenger car.

Runabout - A low powered light open 2 seater from the 1900s.

Saloon - A 2 or 4 door car with 4 or more seats and a fixed roof.

Sedan - See Saloon.

Sedanca de Ville - A limousine body with the driving compartment covered with a folding or sliding roof section, known in America as a Town Car.

Sociable - A cycle car term meaning that the passenger and driver sat side-by-side.

Spider/Spyder - An open 2-seater sports car, sometimes a 2+2 (2 small seats behind the 2 front seats).

Station Wagon - See Brake.

Supercharger - A device for forcing fuel/air into the cylinder for extra power.

Surrey - An early 20thC open 4 seater with a fringed canopy. A term from the days of horse drawn vehicles.

Stanhope - A term from the days of horsedrawn vehicles for a single seat 2 wheel carriage with a hood. Later, a 4 wheeled 2 seater, sometimes with an underfloor engine.

Stroke - The distance a piston moves up-and-down within the cylinder. This distance is always measured in millimetres.

Tandem - A cycle car term, the passengers sat in tandem, with the driver at the front or at the rear.

Targa - A coupé with a removable centre roof section.

Tonneau - A rear entrance tonneau is a 4 seater with access through a centrally placed door at the rear. A detachable tonneau meant that the rear seats could be removed to make a 2 seater. Tonneau nowadays usually means a waterproof cover over an open car used when the roof is detached.

Torpedo - An open tourer with an unbroken line from the bonnet to the rear of the body.

Tourer - An open 4 or 5 seater with 3 or 4 doors, folding hood, with or without sidescreens, generally replaced the term torpedo, with seats flush with the body sides. This body design began in about 1910, but by 1920 the word tourer was used instead - except in France, where 'torpédo' continued until the 1930s.

Veteran - All vehicles manufactured before 31st December 1918, only cars built before 31st March 1904 are eligible for the London to Brighton Commemorative Run.

Victoria - Generally an American term for a 2 or 4 seater with a very large folding hood. If a 4 seater, the hood would only cover the rear seats.

Vintage - Any vehicles manufactured between the end of the veteran period and 31st December 1930. See Post Vintage Thoroughbred.

Vis-à-Vis - Face-to-face, an open car where one or 2 passengers sit opposite each other.

Voiturette - A French term meaning a very light car, originally used by Léon Bollée.

Wagonette - A large car for 6 or more passengers, in which the rear seats faced each other. Entrance was at the rear, and the vehicles were usually open.

Weyman - A system of construction employing Rexine fabric panels over a Kapok filling to prevent noise and provide insulation.

Wheelbase - The distance between the centres of the front and rear wheels.

MOTOR BOOKS

Leading specialists in automotive books for enthusiasts throughout the world.
Many thousands of general, technical, tuning and rating books in our catalogue for £1.00

MOTOR BOOKS, 33 St Martin's Court, St Martin's Lane, London WC2N 4AL	Tel: 0171-836 5376/6728/3800	Fax: 0171-497 2539
MOTOR BOOKS, 8 The Roundway, Headington, Oxford OX3 8DH	Tel: (01865) 66215	Fax: (01865) 63555
MOTOR BOOKS, 241 Holdenhurst Road, Bournemouth BH8 8DA	Tel: (01202) 396469	Fax: (01202) 391572
MOTOR BOOKS, 10 Theatre Square, Swindon SN1 1QN	Tel: (01793) 523170	Fax: (01793) 432070

MAIL ORDER: *Inland:* add 10% of order value, minimum £1.50, maximum £3.00. Orders over £50.00 post free.

Overseas: add 15% of order value on orders up to £150.00, minimum £5.00. Add 10% of order value

on orders over £150.00. For large orders we prefer insured parcel post (usually by air) which we will quote for.

CREDIT CARDS: Visa, Access, Mastercard, Eurocard, Diners Club, TSB, AMEX Please quote full card number and expiry date.

Official technical books. These are all originals or unedited re-issues of official factory publications, including workshop manuals and parts catalogues. Far more detailed than the condensed literature widely available, they are essential possessions for owners and restorers and are highly recommended.

Alfa Romeo '33' 1983–86 WSM £49.95

Alfa Romeo Montreal WSM £23.95

Alfa Romeo Montreal Parts £31.95

Alfa Romeo Spider May 1985 WSM £38.95

Alfa Romeo 105 Series Parts £26.95

Alfa Romeo 105 Series WSM £34.95

Alfa Romeo '75' Engine Manual.....................£49.00

Audi 80/Fox 1973–79 WSM £24.95
562 pages, 1020 ills/diagrams, 27 pages
wiring diagrams.

Audi 4000 Coupé (80) 1980–83 WSM £44.95
Petrol, diesel & turbo diesel, 880 pages,
1020 ills/diagrams, 27 pages
wiring diagrams.

Audi 4000S, CS & Coupé GT
1984–87 WSM £64.95
1600 pages, 2439 ills/diagrams,
327 pages electrical wiring.

Audi 5000 & S (100) 1977–83 WSM £44.95
Petrol & Turbo/Diesel & Turbo, 992
pages, 1856 ills/diagrams, 140 pages
wiring diagrams.

Audi 80, 90, Coupé Quattro 1988–91 WSM......£64.95
1222 pages, 3154 ills/diagrams,
no wiring.

Audi 80, 90 Coupé Quattro Electrical
Troubleshooting 1988–90 WSM £34.95

Audi 100, 200 1989–91 WSM.........................£110.00
3 vols, 1759 pages, thousands of
diagrams, 500 pages electrical & wiring.

Austin A40 Devon/Dorset WSM £17.95

Austin A40 Somerset WSM £23.95

Austin Healey 100 BN1 & BN2 WSM...........£19.95

Austin Healey 100/6 & 3000 WSM £19.95

Austin Healey Sprite Mk 1 'Frogeye' WSM ..£18.95
260 pages.

Austin Healey Sprite Mk 2, 3 & 4 and
Midget WSM £18.95

Austin Healey Sprite Mk 3 & 4 Parts £18.95

JAGUAR XJ6C SERIES 2
TWO DOOR

Operating, Maintenance and Service Handbook

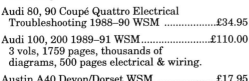

Bentley MkVI Parts £69.95

BMW 1502/2002 WSM £92.95

BMW 2500 3.3 Litre WSM £92.95

BMW 320/323i 6 cylinder (2 vols) WSM £83.95

BMW 520 6 cylinder WSM.............................£63.95

BMW 518-520 4 cylinder WSM £58.00

BMW 628/630/633Csi WSM...........................£92.95

BMW 720/730/730i (2 vols) WSM £104.95

Citroën 12 & 15 Factory Manual....................£19.95
256 pages, fully illustrated.

Daimler Dart Parts £18.95

Fiat X1/9 Technical Data WSM.....................£25.95

Ford Anglia 100E WSM £26.95

Ford Capri 1.3/1.6/2.0/2.3 & 3.0
from 1974 WSM, 600 pages.........................£29.95

Ford Capri 2.8i Supplement WSM £7.95

Jaguar XK 120/140/150 & Mk 7/8/9 WSM £46.95

Jaguar Mk 2/240/340 WSM £29.95

Jaguar Mk 10 & 420G WSM £27.95
Comprehensive information on maintenance
repair and servicing procedures, 364 pages,
fully illustrated.

Jaguar S-Type WSM £27.95

Jaguar E-Type 3.8/4.2 Series 1/2 WSM.........£35.95

Jaguar E-Type V12 Series 3 WSM £29.95

Jaguar 420 WSM £27.95

Jaguar XJ6 Series 1 WSM £29.95

Jaguar XJ6 Series 2 WSM £29.95

Jaguar XJ12 Series 2 WSM £29.95

Jaguar XJ6 & XJ12 Series 3 WSM £34.95

Jaguar XJS V12 (+ HE Supp) WSM £32.95
Comprehensive instructions covering all
components. Fully illustrated, 396 pages.

Jaguar Mk2 & 340 Parts £29.95

Jaguar E-Type Series 1 Parts £19.95

Jaguar E-Type 4.2 Series 1 Parts £19.95

Jaguar E-Type Series 2 GT Parts £24.95
With over 100 pages of illustrations.

Jaguar XJ6 Series 1 Parts £16.95

Jaguar XJ6 Series 2 Parts £29.95

Lamborghini Espada WSM £26.95

Lamborghini Diablo WSM £43.95

Lancia Fulvia, all models, WSM £52.80

Lancia Beta WSM...£31.95

Lancia Montecarlo WSM £35.95

Lancia Flaminia WSM £30.00

Lancia Flavia WSM £33.95

Lancia Stratos WSM £35.00

Lancia Thema WSM......................................£61.95

Lancia Dedra WSM £65.95

Lancia Prisma WSM £61.95

Land Rover Series 1 WSM £21.95

Land Rover Series 1 Parts 1948–53 ....£19.95
448 pages, includes Extra Equipment.

Land Rover Series 1 Parts 1954–58 ....£19.95

Land Rover Series 2 & 2A WSM £46.90

Land Rover Series 2 & 2A Parts £21.95

Land Rover Series 3 WSM £23.95

Land Rover Series 3 Parts £21.95

Land Rover 90/110/Defender to '93 WSM £39.95

Land Rover Military 101 F/C WSM................£27.95
  Official manual for the Military Land Rover
  enthusiast, 270 pages, fully illustrated.

Land Rover Military 101 F/C Parts................£24.95

Land Rover Military Series III (Lightweight)
  Factory Parts Catalogue, 200 pages. £19.95

Land Rover 90/110/Defender to 1993 WSM ..£39.95
  840 pages in 2 vols.

Lotus Cortina Mk2 WSM...............................£27.95
  A re-issue of the original factory manual,
  316 pages, fully illustrated.

Maserati Ghibli WSM £26.95

Maserati Bora WSM.......................................£26.95

Maserati 3500 GT WSM................................£21.95

Maserati 3500 GT Parts................................£26.95

Maserati Biturbo £72.95

Mercedes-Benz 170 (M136) 1950-53 WSM £63.00

Mercedes-Benz 190 1956-61 WSM £40.00

Mercedes-Benz 190SL Supplement WSM......£26.95

Mercedes-Benz 180/220/220S Supplement
  to 190 WSM £40.00

Mercedes-Benz 300SL WSM £63.00

Mercedes-Benz 190C – 300SEL from 1959....£40.00

Mercedes-Benz 108, 109, 111, 113 WSM £40.00

MG Midget TD & TF WSM £17.95

MG Midget Mk 1, 2 & 3 WSM £17.95

MG Midget 1500 WSM 260 pages £17.95

MGB WSM £21.95

MGB GT V8 Supplement WSM.....................£10.95

MG Midget Mk 2 & 3 Parts £17.95

MGB Tourer GT & V8 to Sept '76 Parts £19.95

MGC WSM £15.95

Mini 1959-76 WSM.......................................£19.95
  Covering the Saloon, Countryman,
  Traveller, Clubman, Estate, 1275GT, Van,
  Pick-up, Moke, Cooper and Cooper S.

Morris Oxford Series 'MO' WSM £23.95

Range Rover 1970-85 WSM £33.95

Range Rover 1986-93 WSM £49.95

Range Rover Parts Catalogue to October '85 ....£28.95
  410 pages, fully illustrated.

Reliant Scimitar GTE 3 Litre WSM £39.95

Reliant SST & SS1 WSM £31.95

Reliant SST & SS1 Parts £28.00

Riley 1½ – 2½ WSM £25.95

Riley 1½ – 2½ Parts £25.95

Rover P4 WSM £41.95

Sunbeam Alpine Series I to V WSM £31.95

Sunbeam Alpine Series I to V Parts £32.95

Triumph TR2 & 3 WSM £23.95

Triumph TR4 & TR4A WSM £23.95

Triumph TR6 WSM £24.95

Triumph Spitfire 1, 2, 3,
  Vitesse 6 & Herald WSM............................£20.95

Triumph Spitfire 4 WSM £17.95

Triumph Spitfire 1500 WSM £17.95

Triumph TR2 & 3 Parts £18.95

Triumph TR4 Parts £18.95

Triumph TR6 Parts to 1973..........................£18.95

Triumph TR6 Parts 1974-76 ....£18.95

Workshop Manual

Ninety
One Ten

Volume One

Including Workshop Manual
Supplements for Defender
Model up to 1993

REPAIR
OPERATION
MANUAL

TR6

Second
Edition

Incorporating IC and PI Models

Issued by
SERVICE DIVISION
TRIUMPH MOTORS BRITISH LEYLAND UK LIMITED
COVENTRY, ENGLAND

Triumph TR7 Parts 1975-78 ....£19.95

Triumph TR7 Parts 1979-On £19.95

Triumph Spitfire Mk3 Parts £15.95

Triumph Spitfire 1500 (75+) Parts £15.95

Triumph Stag WSM £24.95

Triumph Stag Parts £22.95

VW 1200 Beetle & 11.14 & 15
1961-65 WSM £64.95
1364 pages, 2622 ills/diagrams,
10 pages, wiring diagrams.

VW Beetle & Karmann Ghia
1966-69 WSM..£29.95
512 pages, 959 ills., 6 pages wiring diags.

VW Beetle & Karmann Ghia 1970-79 WSM ..£26.95
466 pages, 720 ills., 27 pages wiring diags.

VW Fastback/Squareback 1966-73 WSM £29.95
Type 3: 424 pages, 764 ills/diagrams,
9 pages wiring diagrams.

VW Dasher (Passat) 1974-81 incl. Diesel WSM £32.95
692 pages, 1125 ills/diagrams, 42 pages
wiring diagrams.

VW Passat 1990-92 incl. Wagon WSM £35.95
582 pages, 639 ills/diagrams, 247 pages
wiring diagrams.

VW Scirocco, Cabriolet 1985-93 WSM............£35.95
520 pages, 860 ills/diagrams.

VW Rabbit/Golf/Scirocco 1975-79 WSM £29.95
628 pages, 1000 ills/diagrams,
72 pages wiring diagrams.

Repair Operation Manual

Repair Operation Manual

VW Rabbit/Golf/Jetta Diesel 1977-84 WSM ..£29.95
624 pages, 973 ills/diagrams, 78 pages
wiring diagrams.

VW Rabbit/Golf/Scirocco/Jetta 1980-84 WSM ..£29.95
720 pages, 1151 ills/diagrams, 100 pages
wiring diagrams.

VW GTi/Golf/Jetta 1985-92 WSM £32.95
840 pages, 698 ills/diagrams, 299 pages
wiring diagrams.

VW Corrado 1990-94 WSM £79.95
1064 pages, 1235 ills/diagrams,
280 pages wiring diagrams.

VW Transporter 1963-67 WSM £64.95
All models incl. Kobi, Micro Bus, Micro
Bus de Luxe, Pick-up, Delivery Van and
Ambulance. 918 pages, 1450 ills/diagrams,
17 pages wiring diagrams.

VW Station Wagon/Bus 1968-79 WSM £26.95
464 pages, 753 ills/diagrams, 23 pages
wiring diagrams.

VW Vanagon 1980-91 WSM incl. Diesel,
Synchro and Camper £59.95
1388 pages, 2295 ills/diagrams,
247 pages wiring diagrams.

VW Quantum (Passat) 1982-86 WSM............£59.95

VW Fox (Jetta) 1987-89 WSM £19.95
440 pages, 570 ills/diagrams, 70 pages
wiring diagrams.

Volvo P1800 WSM £33.95

Volvo P1800ES WSM £37.95

Volvo Amazon 120 WSM £39.95

Volvo 121/122S WSM £27.95

Volvo PV544 (P210) WSM £38.95

We can also supply many handbook reprints for the above range of vehicles as well as
the original factory manuals for many other vehicles.

Prices Subject to Alteration

DIRECTORY OF CAR CLUBS

If you would like your Club to be included in next year's directory, or have a change of address or telephone number, please inform us by December 31st 1995. Entries will be repeated unless we are requested otherwise.

ABC Owners Club, D.S. Hales, Registrar, 20 Langbourne Way, Claygate, Esher, Surrey.
A.C. Owners Club, B.C. Clark, 60 Hillcrest Road, Camberley, Surrey GU15 1LG. Tel: 01276 676639
A.J.S. & Matchless Owners Club, 36 Childsbridge Lane, Kemsing, Sevenoaks, Kent.
Alexis Racing and Trials Car Register, Duncan Rabagliati, 4 Wool Road, Wimbledon, London SW20
Alfa Romeo Section (VSCC Ltd), Allan & Angela Cherrett, Old Forge, Quarr, Nr Gillingham, Dorset.
Alfa Romeo 1900 Register, Peter Marshall, Mariners, Courtlands Avenue, Esher, Surrey. Tel: 01223 894300
Alfa Romeo 2600/2000 Register, Roger Monk, Knighton, Church Close, West Runton, Cromer, Norfolk.
Alfa Romeo Owners Club, Michael Lindsay, 97 High Street, Linton, Cambs.
Allard Owners Club, Miss P. Hulse, 1 Dalmeny Avenue, Tufnell Park, London N7
Alvis 12/50 Register, Mr J. Willis, The Vinery, Wanborough Manor, Nr Guildford, Surrey GU3 2JR Tel: 01483 810308
Alvis Owners Club, 1 Forge Cottages, Bayham Road, Little Bayham, Nr Lamberhurst, Kent.
American Auto Club, G. Harris, PO Box 56, Redditch.
Pre-'50 American Auto Club, Alan Murphy, 41 Eastham Rake, Eastham, S. Wirral. Tel: 0151 327 1392
Amilcar Salmson Register, R.A.F. King, The Apple House, Wilmoor Lane, Sherfield on Lodden, Hants.
Armstrong Siddeley Owners Club Ltd, Peter Sheppard, 57 Berberry Close, Bourneville, Birmingham, B30 1TB.
Aston Martin Owners Club Ltd, Jim Whyman, AMOC Ltd, 1A High Street, Sutton, Nr Ely, Cambs. Tel: 01353 777353
Atlas Register, 38 Ridgeway, Southwell, Notts.
Austin J40 Car Club, B.G. Swann, 19 Lavender Avenue, Coudon, Coventry CV6 1DA.
Austin Atlantic Owners Club, 124 Holbrook Road, Stratford, London E15 3DZ. Tel: 0181 534 2682
A40 Farina Club, Membership Secretary, 113 Chastilian Road, Dartford, Kent.
1100 Club, Paul Vincent, 32 Medgbury Road, Swindon, Wilts.
Austin Cambridge/Westminster Car Club, Mr J. Curtis, 4 Russell Close, East Budleigh, Budleigh Salterton, Devon.
Austin Big 7 Register, R.E. Taylor, 101 Derby Road, Chellaston, Derby.
Austin Counties Car Club, David Stoves, 32 Vernolds Common, Craven Arms, Shropshire. Tel: 0158 477459
Austin Eight Register, 3 La Grange Martin, St Martin, Jersey, C.I.
Austin Gipsy Register 1958-1968, Mike Gilbert, 24 Green Close, Rixon, Sturminster Newton, Dorset.
Austin Healey Club, Colleen Holmes, Dept CC, 4 Saxby Street, Leicester LE2 OND.
Austin Healey Owners Club, c/o Mrs Carol Marks, 171 Coldharbour Road, Bristol BS6 7SX.
Austin Healey Club, Midland Centre, Mike Ward, 9 Stag Walk, Sutton Coldfield. Tel: 0121-382 3223
Association of Healey Owners, Don Griffiths, The White House, Hill Pound, Swan More, Hants. Tel: 01489 895813
750 Motor Club, 16 Woodstock Road, Witney, Oxon. Tel: 01993 702285
Austin Seven Mulliner Register, Mike Tebbett, Little Wyche, Walwyn Road, Upper Colwall, Nr Malvern, Worcs.
Austin Seven Owners Club (London), Mr and Mrs Simpkins, 5 Brook Cottages, Riding Lane, Hildenborough, Kent.
Austin Seven Sports Register, C.J. Taylor, 222 Prescot Road, Aughton, Ormskirk, Lancs.
Austin Seven Van Register, 1923-29, N.B. Baldry, 32 Wentborough Road, Maidenhead, Berks.
Austin Swallow Register, G.L. Walker, School House, Great Haseley, Oxford.
Austin A30-35 Owners Club, Andy Levis, 26 White Barn Lane, Dagenham, Essex. Tel: 0181 517 0198

Austin Maxi Club, Mr I. Botting, 144 Village Way, Beckenham, Kent.
Pre-War Austin Seven Club Ltd, Mr J. Tatum, 90 Dovedale Avenue, Long Eaton, Nottingham NG10 3HU. Tel: 0115 972 7626
The North East Club for Pre-War Austins, Tom Gatenby, 9 Townsend Crescent, Morpeth, Northumberland NE61 2XW.
Austin Ten Drivers Club Ltd, Mrs Patricia East, Brambledene, 53 Oxted Green, Milford, Godalming, Surrey.
Bristol Austin Seven Club Ltd, 1 Silsbury Cottages, West Kennett, Marlborough, Wilts.
Vintage Austin Register, Frank Smith, The Briars, Four Lane Ends, Oakerthorpe, Alfreton, Derbyshire DE5 7LN. Tel: 01773 831646
Scottish Austin Seven Club, 16 Victoria Gardens, Victoria Park, Kilmalcolm, Renfrew.
Solent Austin Seven Club Ltd, F. Claxton, 185 Warsash Road, Warsash, Hants.
South Wales Austin Seven Club, Mr and Mrs J. Neill, 302 Peniel Green Road, Llansamlet, Swansea.
Wanderers (Pre-War Austin Sevens), D. Tedham, Newhouse Farm, Baveney Wood, Cleobury, Mortimer, Kidderminster, Worcs.
Autovia Car Club, Alan Williams, Birchanger Hall, Birchanger, Nr Bishops Stortford, Herts.
Battery Vehicle Society, Keith Roberts, 29 Ambergate Drive, North Pentwyn, Cardiff.
Bean Car Club, G. Harris, Villa Rosa, Templewood Lane, Farnham Common, Bucks.
Old Bean Society, P.P. Cole, 165 Denbigh Drive, Hately Heath, West Bromwich, W. Midlands.
Bentley Drivers Club, 16 Chearsley Road, Long Crendon, Aylesbury, Bucks.
Berkeley Enthusiasts Club, Paul Fitness, 9 Hellards Road, Stevenage, Herts. Tel: 01438 724164
Biggin Hill Car Club, Peter Adams, Jasmine House, Jasmine Grove, Anerley, London SE20. Tel: 0181 778 3537
BMW Car Club, PO Box 328, Andover, Hants. Tel: 01264 337883
BMW Drivers Club, Sue Hicks, Bavaria House, PO Box 8, Dereham, Norfolk. Tel: 01362 694459
Bond Owners Club, Stan Cornock, 42 Beaufort Avenue, Hodge Hill, Birmingham.
Borgward Drivers Club, Ian Cave, Nateley House, Ridgway, Pyrford, Woking, Surrey. Tel: 01932 342341
Brabham Register, E.D. Walker, The Old Bull, 5 Woodmancote, Dursley, Glos. Tel: 01453 543243
Bristol Owners Club, John Emery, Uesutor, Marringden Road, Billingshurst, West Sussex.
British Ambulance Preservation Society, Roger Leonard, 21 Victoria Road, Horley, Surrey.
British Automobile Racing Club Ltd, Miss T. Milton, Thruxton Circuit, Andover, Hants.
British Racing and Sports Car Club Ltd, Brands Hatch, Fawkham, Dartford, Kent.
Brooklands Society Ltd, 38 Windmill Way, Reigate, Surrey.
Brough Superior Club, P. Staughton (Secretary), 4 Summerfields, Northampton.
BSA Front Wheel Drive Club, Godfrey Slatter, 14 Calstone, Calne, Wilts.
Bugatti Owners Club Ltd, Sue Ward, Prescott Hill, Gotherington, Cheltenham, Glos.
U.K. Buick Club, Alf Gascoine, 47 Higham Road, Woodford Green, Essex. Tel: 0181 505 7347
Buckler Car Register, Stan Hibberd, 52 Greenacres, Woolton Hill, Newbury, Berks. Tel: 01635 254162
Bullnose Morris Club, Richard Harris, PO Box 383, Hove, East Sussex, BN3 4FX.
C.A. Bedford Owners Club, G.W. Seller, 7 Grasmere Road, Benfleet, Essex.
Cambridge-Oxford Owners Club, COOC Membership, 6 Hurst Road, Slough.

Chester Vintage Enthusiasts Club,
Martin Hughes (Secretary), 33 Farndon Way, Oxton,
Birkenhead. Tel: 0151 653 9434
Chiltern Vehicle Preservation Group,
Chiltern House, Ashenden, Aylesbury, Bucks.
Tel: 01296 651283
Citroën Car Club. P.O. Box 348, Bromley,
Kent BR2 8QT
Traction Owners Club, Peter Riggs, 2 Appleby Gardens,
Dunstable, Beds.
Traction Enthusiasts Club, Preston House Studio,
Preston, Canterbury, Kent.
2CVGB Deux Chevaux Club of GB,
PO Box 602, Crick, Northampton.
(Citroën) The Traction Owners Club,
Steve Reed, 1 Terwick Cottage, Rogate,
Nr Petersfield, Hants.
Clan Owners Club, Chris Clay, 48 Valley Road,
Littleover, Derby. Tel: 01332 767410
Classic Corvette Club (UK), Ashley Pickering,
The Gables, Christchurch Road, Tring, Herts.
Classic Crossbred Club, 29 Parry Close,
Stanford Le Hope, Essex. Tel: 01375 671843
Classic and Historic Motor Club Ltd, Tricia Burridge,
The Smithy, High Street, Ston Easton, Bath.
Classic Saloon Car Club, 7 Dunstable Road, Caddington,
Luton. Tel: 01582 31642
Classic Z Register, Lynne Godber, Thistledown, Old
Stockbridge Road, Kentsboro, Wallop, Stockbridge, Hants.
Tel: 01264 781979
Clyno Register, J.J. Salt, New Farm, Startley,
Chippenham, Wilts. Tel: 01249 720271
Friends of The British Commercial Vehicle Museum,
c/o B.C.V.M., King Street, Leyland, Preston.
Commercial Vehicle and Road Transport Club,
Steven Wimbush, 8 Tachbrook Road, Uxbridge, Middx.
Connaught Register, Duncan Rabagliati,
4 Wool Road, Wimbledon, London SW20.
Crayford Convertible Car Club, Rory Cronin,
68 Manor Road, Worthing, West Sussex.
Tel: 01903 212828
Cougar Club of America, Barrie S. Dixon,
11 Dean Close, Partington, Manchester.
Crossley Climax Register, Mr G. Harvey,
7 Meadow Road, Basingstoke, Hants.
Crossley Register, Geoff Lee, 'Arlyn', Brickwall Lane,
Ruislip, Middx, and M. Jenner, 244 Odessa Road,
Forest Gate, London E7.
DAF Owners Club, S.K. Bidwell (Club Secretary),
56 Ridgedale Road, Bolsover, Chesterfield, Derbyshire.
Daimler and Lanchester Owners Club,
John Ridley, The Manor House, Trewyn, Abergavenny,
Gwent. Tel: 01873 890737
Datsun Z Club, Mark or Margaret Bukowska.
Tel: 0181 998 9616
Delage Section VSCC Ltd, Peter Jacobs,
17 The Scop, Almondsbury, Bristol BS12 4DU.
Delahaye Club GB, A.F. Harrison, 34 Marine Parade,
Hythe, Kent. Tel: 01303 261016
Dellow Register, Douglas Temple Design Group,
4 Roumella Lane, Bournemouth, Dorset.
Tel: 01202 304641
De Tomaso Drivers Club, Chris Statham, 2-4 Bank Road,
Bredbury, Stockport. Tel: 0161 430 5052
Diva Register, Steve Pethybridge, 8 Wait End Road,
Waterlooville, Hants. Tel: 01705 251485
DKW Owners Club, C.P. Nixon, Rose Cottage, Rodford,
Westerleigh, Bristol.
Droop Snoot Group, 41 Horsham Avenue,
Finchley, London N12. Tel: 0181 368 1884
Dunsfold Land Rover Trust, Dunsfold, Surrey.
Tel: 01483 200058
Dutton Owners Club, Rob Powell, 20 Burford Road,
Baswich, Stafford, Staffs.
Tel: 01785 56835
Elva Owners Club, R.A. Dunbar, Maple Tree Lodge,
The Hawthorns, Smock Alley, West Alley, West
Chiltington, West Sussex.
E.R.A. Club, Guy Spollon, Arden Grange, Tanworth-in-
Arden, Warwicks.
Facel Vega Owners Club, Roy Scandrett, Windrush,
16 Paddock Gardens, East Grinstead, Sussex.
Fairthorpe Sports Car Club, Tony Hill,
9 Lynhurst Crescent, Hillingdon, Middx.
Ferrari Club of GB, Betty Mathias, 7 Swan Close,
Blake Down, Worcs.
Tel: 01562 700009
Ferrari Owners Club, Peter Everingham.
Tel: 01485 544500

Fiat 130 Owners Club, Michael Reid, 28 Warwick
Mansions, Cromwell Crescent, London SW5.
Tel: 0171 373 9740
Fiat Dino Register, Mr Morris, 59 Sandown Park,
Tunbridge Wells, Kent.
Fiat Motor Club (GB), H.A. Collyer, Barnside, Chikwell
Street, Glastonbury, Somerset.
Tel: 01458 31443
Fiat Osca Register, Mr M. Elliott, 36 Maypole Drive,
Chigwell, Essex. Tel: 0181 500 7127
Fiat Twin–Cam Register, 3 Anderson Place, Bagshot,
Surrey GU19 5LX
X/19 Owners Club, Sally Shearman, 86 Mill Lane,
Dorridge, Solihull.
Fire Service Preservation Group, Andrew Scott,
50 Old Slade Lane, Iver, Bucks.
Pre–67 Ford Owners Club, Mrs A. Miller,
100 Main Street, Cairneyhill, Fife.
Five Hundred Owners Club Association,
David Docherty, Oakley, 68 Upton Park, Upton-by-
Chester, Chester, Cheshire. Tel: 01244 382789
Ford 105E Owners Club, Sally Harris, 30 Gower Road,
Sedgley, Dudley. Tel: 01902 671071
Ford Mk III Zephyr and Zodiac Owners Club,
John Wilding, 10 Waltondale, Woodside, Telford, Salop.
Tel: 01952 580746
Zephyr and Zodiac Mk IV Owners Club, Richard
Cordle, 29 Ruskin Drive, Worcester Park, Surrey.
Tel: 0181 330 2159
Model A Ford Club of Great Britain,
R. Phillippo, The Bakehouse, Church Street, Harston,
Cambs.
Ford Avo Owners Club, D. Hibbin, 53 Hallsfield Road,
Bridgewood, Chatham, Kent.
Ford Classic and Capri Owners Club,
Roy Lawrence, 15 Tom Davies House, Coronation Avenue,
Braintree, Essex. Tel: 01376 43934
Ford Corsair Owners Club, Mrs E. Checkley,
7 Barnfield, New Malden, Surrey.
Capri Club International, Field House, Redditch, Worcs.
Tel: 01527 502066
Ford Capri Enthusiasts Register, Liz Barnes,
46 Manningtree Road, South Ruislip, Middx.
Tel: 0181 842 0102
Capri Drivers Association, Mrs Moira Farrelly
(Secretary), 9 Lyndhurst Road, Coulsdon, Surrey.
Mk I Consul, Zephyr and Zodiac Club,
180 Gypsy Road, Welling, Kent.
Tel: 0181 301 3709
Mk II Consul, Zephyr, and Zodiac Club,
170 Conisborough Crescent, Catford.
Mk I Cortina Owners Club, R.J. Raisey,
51 Studley Rise, Trowbridge, Wilts.
Cortina Mk II Register, Mark Blows,
78 Church Avenue, Broomfield, Chelmsford, Essex.
Ford GT Owners, c/o Riverside School,
Ferry Road, Hullbridge, Hockley, Essex.
Ford Cortina 1600E Owners Club,
Dave Marson, 23 Cumberland Road, Bilston,
West Midlands. Tel: Bilston 405055
Ford Cortina 1600E Enthusiasts Club,
D. Wright, 32 St Leonard's Avenue, Hove, Sussex.
Savage Register, Trevor Smith, Hillcrest,
Top Road, Little Cawthorpe, Louth, Lincs.
Sporting Escort Owners Club, 26 Huntingdon Crescent,
off Madresfield Drive, Halesowen, West Midlands.
Ford Escort 1300E Owners Club, Robert Watt,
55 Lindley Road, Walton-on-Thames, Surrey.
Ford Executive Owners Register,
Jenny Whitehouse, 3 Shanklin Road, Stonehouse Estate,
Coventry.
Ford Granada Mk I Owners Club, Paul Bussey, Bay
Tree House, 15 Thornbera Road, Bishop's Stortford, Herts.
Granada Mk II & Mk III Enthusiasts' Club,
(incorporating Mk III Register), 515A Bristol Road,
Bournbrook, Birmingham B29 6AU.
Tel: 0121 426 2346
Pre 67 Ford Owners Club, Mrs A Miller,
100 Main Street, Cairneyhill, Fife.
Ford RS Owners Club, Ford RSOC, 18 Downsview
Road, Sevenoaks, Kent.
Tel: 01732 450539
Ford Sidevalve Owners Club, Membership Secretary,
30 Earls Close, Bishopstoke, Eastleigh, Hants.
Ford Model 'T' Ford Register of G.B,
Mrs Julia Armer, 3 Riverdale, Strong Close, Keighley,
W. Yorks. Tel: 01535 607978
Mk II Independent O/C, 173 Sparrow Farm Drive,
Feltham, Middx.

XR Owners Club, Paul Townend, 50 Wood Street, Castleford, W. Yorks.

Ford Y and C Model Register, Bob Wilkinson, Castle Farm, Main Street, Pollington, Nr Goole, Humberside DN14 0DJ. Tel: 01405 860836

Frazer-Nash Section of the VSCC, Mrs J. Blake, Daisy Head Farm, Caulcott, Oxford.

Friends of The British Commercial Vehicle, c/o BCVM, King Street, Leyland, Preston.

The Gentry Register, Frank Tuck, 1 Kinross Avenue, South Ascot, Berks. Tel: 01990 24637

Gilbern Owners Club, P.C. Fawkes, 24 Mayfield, Buckden, Huntingdon, Cambs. Tel: 01480 812066

Ginetta Owners Club, Dave Baker, 24 Wallace Mill Gardens, Mid Calder, West Lothian. Tel: 01506 8883129

Gordon Keeble Owners Club, Ann Knott, Westminster Road, Brackley, Northants. Tel: 01280 702311

Granada Enthusiasts Club, 515A Bristol Road, Bournbrook, Birmingham B29 6AU. Tel: 0121 426 2346

Gwynne Register, K. Good, 9 Lancaster Avenue, Hadley Wood, Barnet, Herts.

Heinkel Trojan Owners and Enthusiasts Club, Y. Luty, Carisbrooke, Wood End Lane, Fillongley, Coventry.

Hillman Commer Karrier Club, A. Freakes, 3 Kingfisher Court, East Molesey, Surrey. Tel: 0181 941 0604

Historic Commercial Vehicle Society, H.C.V.S, Iden Grange, Cranbrook Road, Staplehurst, Kent.

Historic Rally Car Register RAC, Martin Jubb, 38 Longfield Road, Bristol BS7 9AG.

Historic Sports Car Club, Cold Harbour, Kington Langley, Wilts.

HRG Association, I.J. Dussek, Little Allens, Allens Lane, Plaxtol, Sevenoaks, Kent.

Southern Counties Historic Vehicles Preservation Trust, Mrs. M. Leeves, 74 Welland Road, Tonbridge, Kent. Tel: 01732 366293

Holden U.K. Register, G.R.C. Hardy, Clun Felin, Woll's Castle, Haverfordwest, Pembrokeshire, Dyfed, Wales.

Honda S800 Sports Car Club, Chris Wallwork, 23a High Street, Steeton, W. Yorks. Tel: 01535 53845

Hotchkiss Association GB, Michael Edwards, Wootton Tops, Sandy Lane, Boars Hill, Oxford. Tel: 01865 735180

Humber Register, R.N. Arman, Northbrook Cottage, 175 York Road, Broadstone, Dorset BH18 8ES.

Post Vintage Humber Car Club, T. Bayliss, 30 Norbury Road, Fallings Park, Wolverhampton.

The Imp Club, Jackie Clark, Cossington Field Farm, Bell Lane, Boxley, Kent. Tel: 01634 201807

Isetta Owners Club, Brian Orriss, 30 Durham Road, Sidcup, Kent.

Jaguar Car Club, R. Pugh, 19 Eldorado Crescent, Cheltenham, Glos.

Jaguar/Daimler Owners Club, 130/132 Bordesley Green, Birmingham B9 4SU. Tel: 0121 426 2346

Jaguar Drivers Club, JDC Jaguar House, 18 Stuart Street, Luton, Beds. Tel: 01582 419332

Jaguar Enthusiasts Club, G.G. Searle, Sherborne, Mead Road, Stoke Gifford, Bristol. Tel: 0117 969 8186

Jensen Owners Club, Caroline Clarke, 45 Station Road, Stoke Mandeville, Bucks. Tel: 01296 614072

Jensen Owners Club, Brian Morrey, Selwood, Howley, Nr Chard, Somerset. Tel: 01460 64165

Jowett Car Club, Ian Priestley, (Membership Secretary), 626 Huddersfield Road, Wyke, Bradford, Yorks.

Junior Zagato Register, Kenfield Hall, Petham, Nr Canterbury, Kent. Tel: 01227 700555

Jupiter Owners Auto Club, Steve Keil, 16 Empress Avenue, Woodford Green, Essex. Tel: 0181 505 2215

Karmann Ghia Owners Club (GB), Eliza Conway, 269 Woodborough Road, Nottingham.

Kieft Racing and Sports Car Club, Duncan Rabagliati, 4 Wool Road, Wimbledon SW20.

Lagonda Club, Mrs Valerie May, 68 Saville Road, Lindfield, Haywards Heath, Sussex.

Lancia Motor Club, Dave Baker, (Membership Secretary), Mount Pleasant, Penrhos, Brymbo, Wrexham.

Landcrab Owners Club International, Bill Frazer, PO Box 218, Cardiff.

Land Rover Register (1947–1951), Membership Secretary, High House, Ladbrooke, Nr Leamington Spa.

Land Rover Series One Club, David Bowyer, East Foldhay, Zeal Monachorum, Crediton, Devon. Tel: 01363 82666

Land Rover Series Two Club, PO Box 1609, Yatton, Bristol.

Lea Francis Owners Club, R. Sawers, French's, Long Wittenham, Abingdon, Oxon.

Lincoln-Zephyr Owners Club, Colin Spong, 22 New North Road, Hainault, Ilford, Essex.

London Bus Preservation Trust, Cobham Bus Museum, Redhill Road, Cobham, Surrey.

London Vintage Taxi Association, Steve Dimmock, 51 Ferndale Crescent, Cowley, Uxbridge UB8 2AY.

Lotus Cortina Register, Fernleigh, Homash Lane, Shadoxhurst, Ashford, Kent.

Lotus Drivers Club, Lee Barton, 15 Pleasant Way, Leamington Spa. Tel: 01926 313514

Lotus Seven Owners Club, David Miryless, 18 St James, Beaminster, Dorset.

Club Lotus, PO Box 8, Dereham, Norfolk. Tel: 01362 694459

Historic Lotus Register, Mike Marsden, Orchard House, Wotton Road, Rangeworthy, Bristol.

Malaysia & Singapore Vintage Car Register, 2 Asimont Lane, Singapore 1130.

Manta A Series Register, Mark Kinnon, 87 Village Way, Beckenham, Kent.

Marcos Owners Club, 62 Culverley Road, Catford, London SE6. Tel: 0181 697 2988

Club Marcos International, Mrs I. Chivers, Membership Secretary, 8 Ludmead Road, Corsham, Wilts. Tel: 01249 713769

Marendaz Special Car Register, John Shaw, 107 Old Bath Road, Cheltenham. Tel: 01242 526310

The Marina/Ital Drivers Club, Mr J.G. Lawson, 12 Nithsdale Road, Liverpool.

Marlin Owners Club, Mrs J. Cordrey, 14 Farthings West, Capel St. Mary, Ipswich.

Maserati Club, Michael Miles, The Paddock, Old Salisbury Road, Abbotts Ann, Andover, Hants. Tel: 01264 710312

Masters Club, Barry Knight, 2 Ranmore Avenue, East Croydon.

Matra Enthusiasts Club, M.E.C, 19 Abbotsbury, Orton Goldhay, Peterborough, Cambs. Tel: 01733 234555

Mercedes-Benz Club Ltd, P. Bellamy, 75 Theydon Grove, Epping, Essex. Tel: Epping 73304

Messerschmitt Enthusiasts Club, Graham Taylor, 5 The Green, Highworth, Swindon, Wilts.

Messerschmitt Owners Club, Mrs Eileen Hallam, The Birches, Ashmores Lane, Rusper, West Sussex.

Metropolitan Owners Club, Mr N. Savage, Goat Cottage, Nutbourne Common, Pulborough, Sussex. Tel: 01798 13921

Register of Unusual Micro-Cars, Jean Hammond, School House Farm, Hawkenbury, Staplehurst, Kent.

The MG Car Club, PO Box 251 Abingdon, Oxon OX14 1FF. Tel: 01235 555552

MG Octagon Car Club, Harry Crutchley, 36 Queensville Avenue, Stafford. Tel: 01785 51014

MG Owners Club, R. S. Bentley, 2/4 Station Road, Swavesey, Cambs. Tel: 01954 231125

The MG Y Type Register, Mr J. G. Lawson, 12 Nithsdale Road, Liverpool.

Midget and Sprite Club, Nigel Williams, 15 Foxcote, Kingswood, Bristol. Tel: 0117 961 2759

Register of Unusual Micro-Cars, Jean Hammond, School House Farm, Hawkenbury, Staplehurst, Kent.

The Military Vehicle Trust, Nigel Godfrey, 8 Selborne Close, Blackwater, Camberley, Surrey.

Mini Cooper Club, Joyce Holman, 1 Weavers Cottages, Church Hill, West Hoathly, Sussex.

Mini Cooper Register, Mr R. Barfoot, Merlin, 28 London Road, Hitchin, Herts. Tel: 01462 453398

Mini Marcos Owners Club, Roger Garland, 28 Meadow Road, Claines, Worcester. Tel: 01905 58533

Mini Moke Club, Paul Beard, 13 Ashdene Close, Hartlebury, Worcs.

Mini Owners Club, 15 Birchwood Road, Lichfield, Staffs.

Morgan Sports Car Club, Mrs Christine Healey, 41 Cordwell Close, Castle Donington, Derby.

Morgan Three-Wheeler Club Ltd, K. Robinson, Correction Farm, Middlewood, Poynton, Cheshire.

Morris Cowley and Oxford Club,
Derek Andrews, 202 Chantry Gardens, Southwick,
Trowbridge, Wilts.
Morris 12 Club, D. Hedge, Crossways, Potton Road,
Hilton, Huntingdon.
Morris Marina Owners Club, Nigel Butler, Llys-Aled,
63 Junction Road, Stourbridge, West Midlands.
Morris Minor Owners Club, Jane White,
127-129 Green Lane, Derbyshire.
Morris Register, Arthur Peeling, 171 Levita House,
Chalton Street, London.
Moss Owners Club, David Pegler, Pinewood, Weston
Lane, Bath. Tel: 01225 331509
National Autocycle & Cyclemotor Club,
c/o R. Harknett, 1 Parkfields, Roydon, Harlow, Essex.
Norton Owners Club, Dave Fenner, Beeches, Durley
Brook Road, Durley, Southampton.
Nova Owners Club, Ray Nicholls, 19 Bute Avenue,
Hathershaw, Oldham, Lancs.
NSU Owners Club, Rosemarie Crowley,
58 Tadorne Road, Tadworth, Surrey.
Tel: 01737 812412
Octagon Car Club, 36 Queensville Avenue,
Stafford ST17 4LS. Tel: 01785 51014
The Ogle Register, Chris Gow, 108 Potters Lane,
Burgess Hill, Sussex. Tel: 01444 248439
Opel GT UK Owners Club, Martyn and Karen,
PO Box 171, Derby. Tel: 01773 45086
Opel Manta Owners Club, 14 Rockstowes Way,
Westbury-on-Trym, Bristol.
Opel Vauxhall Drivers Club, The Old Mill, Borrow Hall,
Dereham, Norfolk. Tel: 01362 694459
Manta A Series Register, Mark Kinnon,
87 Village Way, Beckenham, Kent.
Les Amis de Panhard et Levassor GB,
La Dyna, 11 Arterial Avenue, Rainham, Essex.
Panther Car Club Ltd, 35 York Road, Farnborough,
Hants. Tel: 01252 540217
Pedal Car Collectors Club, c/o A. P. Gayler,
4-4a Chapel Terrace Mews, Kemp Town, Brighton, Sussex.
Club Peugeot UK, Dick Kitchingman, Pelham, Chideock,
Bridport, Dorset.
Club Peugeot UK, Club Regs 504Cab/Coupé, Beacon
View, Forester Road, Soberton Heath, Southampton
SO32 3QG. Tel: 01329 833029
Piper (Sports and Racing Car) Club,
Clive Davies, Pipers Oak, Lopham Road,
East Harling, Norfolk.
Tel: 01953 717813
Porsche Club Great Britain, Ayton House,
West End, Northleach, Glos.
Tel: 01451 60792
Post Office Vehicle Club, 7 Bignal Rand Drive, Wells,
Somerset.
Post 45 Group, Mr R. Cox, 6 Nile Street, Norwich.
Post-War Thoroughbred Car Club,
87 London Street, Chertsey, Surrey
Potteries Vintage and Classic Car Club, B. Theobold,
78 Reeves Avenue, Cross Heath, Newcastle, Staffs.
The Radford Register, Chris Gow, 108 Potters Lane,
Burgess Hill, West Sussex.
Tel: 01444 248439
Railton Owners Club, Barrie McKenzie, Fairmiles,
Barnes Hall Road, Burncross, Sheffield.
Tel: 0114 246 8357
**Raleigh Safety Seven and Early Reliant Owners
Club,** Mike Sleap, 17 Courtland Avenue, London E4.
Range Rover Register, Chris Tomley, Cwm/Cochen,
Bettws, Newtown, Powys.
Rapier Register, D.C.H. Williams, Smithy, Tregynon,
Newton, Powys.
Tel: 01686 87396
Reliant Owners Club, Graham Close, 19 Smithey Close,
High Green, Sheffield.
Reliant Rebel Register, M. Bentley, 70 Woodhall Lane,
Calverley, Pudsey, West Yorks.
Tel: 01532 570512
Reliant Sabre and Scimitar Owners Club,
PO Box 67, Teddington, Middx.
Tel: 0181 977 6625
Rear Engine Renault Club, R. Woodall,
346 Crewe Road, Cresty, Crewe, Cheshire.
Renault Frères, J. G. Kemsley, Yew Tree House, Jubilee
Road, Chelsfield, Kent.
Renault Owners Club, C. Marsden, Chevin House,
Main Street, Burley-in-Wharfedale, Ilkley, West Yorks.
Tel: 01943 862700
Riley Motor Club Ltd, J. S. Hall, Treelands,
127 Penn Road, Wolverhampton.

Riley Register, J. A. Clarke, 56 Cheltenham Road,
Bishops Cleeve, Cheltenham, Glos GL52 4LY.
Riley R. M. Club, Mrs Jacque Manders, Y Fachell,
Ruthin Road, Gwernymynydd, Clwyd.
Ro80 Club GB, Simon Kremer, Mill Stone Cottage,
Woodside Road, Windsor Forest, Windsor, Berks.
Tel: 01344 890411
Rochdale Owners Club, Brian Tomlinson,
57 West Avenue, Birmingham.
Rolls-Royce Enthusiasts, Lt. Col. Eric Barrass,
The Hunt House, Paulersbury, Northants.
Rootes Easidrive Register, M. Molley,
35 Glenesk Road, London SE9.
Rover P4 Drivers Guild, Colin Blowers (PC),
32 Arundel Road, Luton, Beds.
Rover P5 Owners Club, G. Moorshead, 13 Glen Avenue,
Ashford, Middx. Tel: 01784 258166
Rover P6 Owners Club, PO Box 11, Heanor, Derbys.
Rover Sports Register, Cliff Evans, 8 Hilary Close,
Great Boughton, Chester.
British Saab Enthusiasts, Mr M. Hodges,
75 Upper Road, Parkstone, Poole, Dorset.
The Saab Owners Club of GB Ltd,
Mrs K. E. Piper, 16 Denewood Close, Watford, Herts.
Tel: 01923 229945
Salmons Tickford Enthusiasts Club, Keith Griggs,
40 Duffins Orchard, Ottershaw, Surrey.
British Salmson Owners Club, John Maddison,
86 Broadway North, Walsall, West Midlands.
Tel: 01922 29677
Savage Register, Trevor Smith, Hillcrest,
Top Road, Little Cawthorpe, Lough, Lincs.
Scimitar Drivers Club, c/o Mick Frost, Pegasus,
Main Road, Woodham Ferrers, Essex.
Tel: 01245 320734
Scootacar Register, Stephen Boyd, Pamanste,
18 Holman Close, Aylsham, Norwich,
Norfolk NR11 6DD. Tel: 01263 733861.
Simca Owners Register, David Chapman,
18 Cavendish Gardens, Redhill, Surrey.
Singer O.C., Martyn Wray, 11 Ermine Rise,
Great Casterton, Stamford, Lincs PE9 4AJ.
Tel: 01780 62740
Association of Singer Car Owners (A.S.C.O.),
Anne Page, 39 Oakfield, Rickmansworth, WO3 2LR.
Tel: 01923 778575
Skoda Owners Club of Great Britain,
Ray White, 78 Montague Road, Leytonstone, E11
South Devon Commercial Vehicle Club,
Bob Gale, Avonwick Station, Diptford, Totnes, Devon.
Tel: 01364 73100
South Hants Model Auto Club, C. Derbyshire,
21 Aintree Road, Calmore, Southampton, Hants.
Spartan Owners Club, Steve Andrews,
28 Ashford Drive, Ravenhead, Notts.
Tel: 01623 793742
Stag Owners Club, Mr H. Vesey, 53 Cyprus Road,
Faversham, Kent. Tel: 01795 534376
Standard Motor Club, Tony Pingriff, 57 Main Road,
Meriden, Coventry.
Tel: 01675 22181
Star, Starling, Stuart and Briton Register,
D. E. A. Evans, New Woodlodge, Hyperion Road, Stourton,
Stourbridge, Worcs.
Sunbeam Alpine Owners Club, Pauline Leese,
53 Wood Street, Mow Cop, Stoke-on-Trent.
Tel: 01782 519865
Sunbeam Rapier Owners Club, Peter Meech,
12 Greenacres, Downton, Salisbury, Wilts.
Tel: 01725 21140
Sunbeam Talbot Alpine Register, Derek Cook,
(Membership Secretary), 84 High Brooms Road, Tunbridge
Wells, Kent.
Sunbeam Talbot Darracq Register, R. Lawson,
West Emlett Cottage, Black Dog, Crediton, Devon.
Sunbeam Tiger Owners Club, Brian Postle, Beechwood,
8 Villa Real Estate, Consett, Co. Durham.
Tel: 01207 508296
The Swift Club and Swift Register, John Harrison, 70
Eastwick Drive, Great Bookham, Leatherhead, Surrey.
Tel: 01372 52120
Tame Valley Vintage and Classic Car Club,
Mrs. S. Ogden, 13 Valley New Road, Royton,
Oldham OL2 6BP.
Tornado Register, Dave Malins, 48 St Monica's Avenue,
Luton, Beds. Tel: 01582 37641
TR Drivers Club, Bryan Harber, 19 Irene Road,
Orpington, Kent.
Tel: 01689 73776

The TR Register, 1B Hawksworth, Southmead Industrial Park, Didcot, Oxon.
Tel: 01235 818866
Traction Enthusiasts Club, Preston House Studio, Preston, Canterbury, Kent.
Traction Owners Club, Peter Riggs, 2 Appleby Gardens, Dunstable Beds.
The 750 Motor Club Ltd., Courthouse, St. Winifred's Road, Biggin Hill, Kent.
Tel: 01959 575812
Trident Car Club, Ken Morgan, Rose Cottage, 45 Newtown Road, Verwood, Nr Wimborne, Dorset.
Tel: 01202 822697
The Triumph Dolomite Club, 39 Mill Lane, Arncott, Bicester, Oxon.
Tel: 01869 242847
Club Triumph Eastern, Mrs S. Hurrell, 7 Weavers Drive, Glemsford, Suffolk.
Tel: 01787 282176
Triumph Mayflower Club, T. Gordon, 12 Manor Close, Hoghton, Preston, Lancs.
Club Triumph North London, D. Pollock, 86 Waggon Road, Hadley Wood, Herts.
Pre–1940 Triumph Owners Club, Ian Harper, 155 Winkworth Road, Banstead, Surrey.
Triumph Razoredge Owners Club, Stewart Langton, 62 Seaward Avenue, Barton-on-Sea, Hants.
Tel: 01425 618074
The Triumph Roadster Club, Paul Hawkins, 186 Mawnay Road, Romford, Essex.
Tel: 01708 760745
Triumph Spitfire Club, Johan Hendricksen, Begijnenakker 49, 4241 CK Prinsenbeek, The Netherlands.
Triumph Sports Six Club Ltd, 121B St Mary's Road, Market Harborough, Leics.
Tel: 01858 34424
Triumph Sporting Owners Club, G. R. King, 16 Windsor Road, Hazel Grove, Stockport, Cheshire.
Triumph 2000/2500/2.5 Register, M. Aldous, 42 Hall Orchards, Middleton, King's Lynn, Norfolk.
Tel: 01553 841700
Turner Register, Dave Scott, 21 Ellsworth Road, High Wycombe, Bucks.
The Trojan Owners Club, D. Graham, 10 St Johns, Redhill, Surrey.
TVR Car Club, c/o David Gerald, TVR Sports Cars, The Green, Inkberrow, Worcs.
Tel: 01386 793239
United States Army Vehicle Club, Dave Boocock, 31 Valley View Close, Bogthorn, Oakworth Road, Keighley, Yorks.
Vanden Plas Owners Club, Nigel Stephens, The Briars, Lawson Leas, Barrowby, Grantham, Lincs.
Vanguard 1 & 2 Owners Club, R. Jones, The Villa, 11 The Down, Alviston, Avon.
Tel: 01454 419232
'F' and 'F.B.' Victor Owners Club, Wayne Parkhouse, 5 Farnell Road, Staines, Middx.
Victor 101 FC (1964-1967), 12 Cliff Crescent, Ellerdine, Telford, Shropshire.
The F-Victor Owners Club, Alan Victor Pope, 34 Hawkesbury Drive, Mill Lane, Calcot, Reading, Berks.
Tel: 01635 43532
Vauxhall Cavalier Convertible Club, Ron Goddard, 47 Brooklands Close, Luton, Beds.
Vauxhall Owners Club, Brian J. Mundell, 2 Flaxton Court, St Leonard's Road, Ayr, Scotland.
Vauxhall PA/PB/PC/E Owners Club, G. Lonsdale, 77 Pilling Lane, Preesall, Lancs.
Tel: 01253 810866
Vauxhall VX4/90 Drivers Club, c/o 43 Stroudwater Park, Weybridge, Surrey.
Vectis Historic Vehicle Club, 10 Paddock Drive, Bembridge, Isle of Wight.
The Viva Owners Club, Adrian Miller, The Thatches, Snetterton North End, Snetterton, Norwich.
Veteran Car Club of Great Britain, Jessamine Court, High Street, Ashwell, Herts.
Tel: 01462 742818
Vintage Sports Car Club Ltd, The Secretary, 121 Russell Road, Newbury, Berks.
Tel: 01635 44411
The Association of British Volkswagen Clubs, Dept PC, 66 Pinewood Green, Iver Heath, Bucks.
Volkswagen Cabriolet Owners Club (GB), Emma Palfreyman (Secretary), Dishley Mill, Derby Road, Loughborough, Leics.

Historic Volkswagen Clubs, 11a Thornbury Lane, Church Hill, Redditch, Worcs.
Tel: 01527 591883
Volkswagen Owners Club GB, R. Houghton, 49 Addington Road, Irthlingborough, Northants.
Volkswagen Owners Caravan Club (GB), Mrs Shirley Oxley, 18 Willow Walk, Hockley, Essex.
Volkswagen Split Screen Van Club, Brian Hobson, 12 Kirkfield Crescent, Thorner, Leeds.
Volkswagen '50–67' Transporter Club, Peter Nicholson, 11 Lowton Road, Lytham St Annes, Lancs. Tel: 01253 720023
VW Type 3 and 4 Club, Jane Terry, Pear Tree Bungalow, Exted, Elham, Canterbury, Kent.
Volvo Enthusiasts Club, Kevin Price, 4 Goonbell, St Agnes, Cornwall.
Volvo Owners Club, Mrs Suzanne Groves, 90 Down Road, Merrow, Guildford, Surrey.
Tel: 01483 37624
Vulcan Register, D. Hales, 20 Langbourne Way, Claygate, Esher, Surrey.
The Wartburg Owners Club, Bernard Trevena, 56 Spiceall Estate, Compton, Guildford, Surrey.
Tel: 01483 810493
Wolseley 6/80 and Morris Oxford Club, John Billinger, 67 Fleetgate, Barton-on-Humber, North Lincs.
Tel: 01652 635138
The Wolseley Hornet-Special Club, S. Ellin, The Poppies, 9 Cole Mead, Bruton, Somerset.
Wolseley Register, B. Eley, 60 Garfield Avenue, Dorchester, Dorset.
X/19 Owners Club, Sally Shearman, 86 Mill Lane, Dorridge, Solihull.
XR Owners Club, 20a Swithland Lane, Rothley, Leics.
The Yorkshire Thoroughbred Car Club, Bob Whalley, 31 Greenside, Walton, Wakefield WF2 6NN.

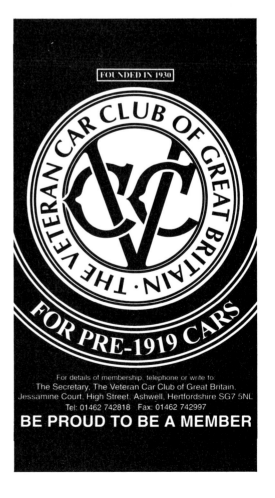

DIRECTORY OF AUCTIONEERS

United Kingdom

ADT Auctions Ltd., Blackbushe Airport, Blackwater, Camberley, Surrey, GU17 9LG. Tel: 01252 878555

Alcocks, Wyeval House, 42 Bridge Street, Hereford, HR4 9DG. Tel: 01432 344322

Bonhams, 65-69 Lots Road, London SW10 0RN. Tel: 0171-351 7111

Brooks, 81 Westside, London SW4 9AY. Tel: 0171-228 8000

Central Motor Auctions PLC, Central House, Pontefract Road, Rothwell, Leeds LS26 0JE. Tel: 0113 282 0707

Christie's, 8 King Street, St James's, London SW1Y 6QT. Tel: 0171-839 9060

Classic Motor Auctions, PO Box 20, Fishponds, Bristol BS16 5QU. Tel: 0117 970 1370

Coys of Kensington, 2-4 Queens Gate Mews, London SW7 5QJ. Tel: 0171-584 7444

Eccles Auctions, Unit 4, Gwydir St, Cambridge, CB1 2LG. Tel: Cambridge 01223 561518.

Evans & Partridge, Agriculture House, High Street, Stockbridge, Hants, SO20 6HF. Tel: 01264 810702

Greens Vintage and Classic Auction Sales, PO Box 25, Malvern, Worcs, WR14 2NY. Tel: 01684 575902

Hampson Ltd., Road 4, Winsford Industrial Estate, Winsford, Cheshire, CW7 3QN. Tel: 01606 559054

H & H Auctions, 385 London Road, Appleton, Nr. Warrington, WA4 5DN. Tel: 0161 747 0561 & 01925 860471

Holloways, 49 Parsons Street, Banbury, Oxon, OX16 8PF. Tel: 01295 253197

Husseys, Matford Park Road, Marsh Barton, Exeter, EX2 8FD. Tel: 01392 425481

Lambert & Foster, 97 Commercial Road, Paddock Wood, Tonbridge, Kent, TN12 6DR. Tel: 01892 832325

Phillips, West Two, 10 Salem Road, London W2 4DL. Tel: 0171-229 9090

RTS Auctions Ltd., 35 Primula Drive, Eaton, Norwich, NR4 7LZ. Tel: 01603 505718

Shoreham Car Auctions, 5-6 Brighton Road, Kingston Wharf, Shoreham-by-Sea, West Sussex. Tel: 01273 871871

Sotheby's, 34-35 New Bond Street, London W1A 2AA. Tel: 0171-493 8080

Sotheby's (Sussex), Summers Place, Billingshurst, West Sussex, RH14 9AD. Tel: 01403 783933

Thimbleby & Shorland, PO Box 175, 31 Great Knollys Street, Reading, Berks, RG1 7HU. Tel: 01734 508611

Truro Auction Centre, Calenick Street, Truro, Cornwall, TR1 2SG. Tel: 01872 260020

International

'The Auction', 3535 Las Vegas Boulevard, South Las Vegas, Nevada 89101, USA. Tel: 0101 702 794 3174

C. Boisgirard, 2 Rue de Provence, 75009 Paris, France. Tel: 010 33 147708136

Carlisle Productions, The Flea Marketeers, 1000 Bryn Mawr Road, Carlisle, PA 17013-1588, USA

Christie's Australia Pty Ltd., 1 Darling Street, South Yarra, Melbourne, Victoria 3141. Tel: 010 613 820 4311

Christie's (Monaco), S.A.M, Park Palace, 98000 Monte Carlo. Tel: 010 339 325 1933

Christie, Manson & Woods International Inc., 502 Park Avenue, New York, NY 10022. Tel: 0101 212 546 1000

Classic Automobile Auctions B.V., Goethestrasse 10, 6000 Frankfurt 1. Tel: 010 49 69 28666/8

Kruse International Inc., PO Box 190-Co. Rd. 11-A, Auburn, Indiana, USA 46706. Tel: 0101 219 925 5600

Paul McInnis Inc., Auction Gallery, Route 88, 356 Exeter Road, Hampton Falls, New Hampshire 03844, USA. Tel: 0101 603 778 8989

Orion Auction House, Victoria Bldg-13, Bd. Princess Charlotte, Monte Carlo, MC 98000 Monaco. Tel: 010 3393 301669

Silver Collector Car Auctions, E204, Spokane, Washington 99207, USA. Tel: 0101 509 326 4485

Sotheby's, 1334 York Avenue, New York, NY 10021. Tel: 0101 212 606 7000

Sotheby's, B.P. 45, Le Sporting d'Hiver, Place du Casino, MC 98001 Monaco/Cedex. Tel: 0101 3393 30 88 80

World Classic Auction & Exposition Co., 3600 Blackhawk Plaza Circle, Danville, California 94506, USA.

DIRECTORY OF MUSEUMS

Avon

Bristol Industrial Museum, Princes Wharf, City Docks, Bristol 1. Tel: 0117 925 1470

Bedfordshire

Shuttleworth Collection, Old Warden Aerodrome, Nr Biggleswade. Tel: 0196 727 288

Buckinghamshire

West Wycombe Motor Museum, Cockshoot Farm, Chorley Road, West Wycombe.

Cambridgeshire

Vintage M/C Museum, South Witham, Nr Peterborough.

Cheshire

Mouldsworth Motor Museum, Smithy Lane, Mouldsworth. Tel: 01928 31781

Cornwall

Automobilia Motor Museum, The Old Mill, St Stephen, St Austell.

Co. Durham

North of England Open Air Museum, Beamish.

Cumbria

Lakeland Motor Museum, Holker Hall, Cark-in-Cartmel, Nr Grange-over-Sands. Tel: 01448 53314

Cars of the Stars Motor Museum, Standish Street, Keswick. Tel: 017687 73757

Derbyshire

The Donington Collection, Donington Park, Castle Donington. Tel: 01332 810048

Devon

Totnes Motor Museum, Steamer Quay, Totnes. Tel: 01803 862777

Essex

Ford Historic Car Collection, Ford Motor Co, Eagle Way, Brentwood.

Gloucestershire

The Bugatti Trust, Prescott, Gotherington, Cheltenham. Tel: 01242 677201

Cotswold Motor Museum, Old Mill, Bourton-on-the-Water, Nr Cheltenham. Tel: 01451 821255

Hampshire

Gangbridge Collection, Gangbridge House, St Mary Bourne, Andover.

The National Motor Museum, Beaulieu. Tel: 01590 612345

Humberside

Peter Black Collection, Lawkholme Lane, Keighley.

Bradford Industrial Museum, Moorside Mills, Moorside Road, Bradford. Tel: 01274 631756

Hull Transport Museum, 36 High Street, Kingston-upon-Hull. Tel: 01482 22311

Museum of Army Transport, Flemingate, Beverley. Tel: 01482 860445

Sandtoft Transport Centre, Sandtoft, Nr Doncaster.

Kent

Historic Vehicles Collection of C. M. Booth, Falstaff Antiques, High Street, Rolvenden.

The Motor Museum, Dargate, Nr Faversham.

Ramsgate Motor Museum, West Cliff Hall, Ramsgate. Tel: 01843 581948

Lancashire

The British Commercial Vehicles Museum, King Street, Leyland, Preston. Tel: 01772 451011

Bury Transport Museum, Castlecroft Road, off Bolton Street, Bury.

Manchester Museum of Transport, Boyle Street, Manchester.

Tameside Transport Collection, Warlow Brook, Frietland, Greenfield, Oldham.

Leicestershire

Stanford Hall Motorcycle Museum, Stanford Hall, Lutterworth. Tel: 01788 860250

Lincolnshire

Geeson Brothers Motorcycle Museum and Workshop, South Witham, Grantham.

London

British Motor Industry, Heritage Trust, Syon Park, Brentford. Tel: 0181-560 1378

Science Museum, South Kensington, SW7. Tel: 0171-938 8000.

Norfolk

Caister Castle Car Collection, Caister-on-Sea, Nr Great Yarmouth. Tel: 01572 84251/84202.

Sandringham Museum, Sandringham. Tel: 01553 772675

Nottinghamshire

Nottingham Industrial Museum, Courtyard Buildings, Wallaton Park.

Shropshire

Midland Motor Museum, Stourbridge Road, Bridgnorth. Tel: 01746 761761

Somerset

Haynes Sparkford Motor Museum, Sparkford, Nr Yeovil. Tel: 01963 40804

Surrey

Brooklands Museum, Brooklands Road, Weybridge. Tel: 01932 859000

Dunsfold Land Rover Museum, Alfold Road, Dunsfold. Tel: 01483 200567

Sussex

Bentley Motor Museum, Bentley Wildfowl Trust, Halland. Tel: 0182 584711.

Effingham Motor Museum, Effingham Park, Copthorne.

Filching Manor Museum, Filching Manor, Jevington Road, Wannock, Polegate. Tel: 01323 487838/487933/487124

Tyne and Wear

Newburn Hall Motor Museum, 35 Townfield Garden, Newburn.

Warwickshire

Heritage Motor Centre, Banbury Road, Gaydon. Tel: 01926 641188

West Midlands

Birmingham Museum of Science and Industry, Newhall Street, Birmingham. Tel: 0121-235 1661

Black Country Museum, Tipton Road, Dudley.

Museum of British Road Transport, St Agnes Lane, Hales Street, Coventry. Tel: 01203 832425

West Yorkshire

Automobilia Transport Museum, Billy Lane, Old Town, Hebden Bridge. Tel: 01422 844775

Wiltshire

Science Museum, Red Barn Gate, Wroughton, Nr Swindon. Tel: 01793 814466

Eire

The National Museum of Irish Transport, Scotts Garden, Killarney, Co. Kerry.

Kilgarvan Motor Museum, Kilgarvan, Co Kerry. Tel: 010 353 64 85346

Isle of Man

Manx Motor Museum, Crosby. Tel: 01624 851236

Port Erin Motor Museum, High Street, Port Erin. Tel: 01624 832964

Jersey

Jersey Motor Museum, St Peter's Village.

Northern Ireland

Ulster Folk and Transport Museum, Cultra Manor, Holywood, Co Down. Tel: 01232 428428

Scotland

Doune Motor Museum, Carse of Cambus, Doune, Perthshire. Tel: 0178 684 203

Grampian Transport Museum, Alford, Aberdeenshire. Tel: 01336 2292

Highland Motor Heritage, Bankford, Perthshire.

Melrose Motor Museum, Annay Road, Melrose. Tel: 01896 822 2624

Moray Motor Museum, Bridge Street, Elgin. Tel: 01343 544933

Museum of Transport, Kelvin Hall, Bunhouse Road, Glasgow. Tel: 0141-357 3929

Myreton Motor Museum, Aberlady, East Lothian. Tel: 0187 57288

Royal Museum of Scotland, Chambers Street, Edinburgh. Tel: 0131-225 7534

Wales

Conwy Valley Railway Museum Ltd, The Old Goods Yard, Betws-y-Coed, Gwynedd. Tel: 01690 710568

INDEX TO ADVERTISERS

BIBLIOGRAPHY

Baldwin, Nick; Georgano, G.N.; Sedgwick, Michael; and Laban, Brian; The World Guide to Automobiles, Guild Publishing, London, 1987

Collins, Paul, and Stratton, Michael; British Car Factories from 1896, Veloce Publishing PLC., 1993.

Colin Chapman Lotus Engineering, Osprey, 1993.

Georgano, G.N.; ed: Encyclopedia of Sports Cars, Bison Books, 1985.

Georgano, Nick; Military Vehicles of World War II, Osprey 1994.

Golding, Rob; Mini 35 Years On, Osprey, 1994.

Harvey, Chris; Austin Sevens, Haynes, 1988.

Hay, Michael; Bentley Factory Cars, Osprey, 1993.

Hough, Richard; A History of the World's Sports Cars, Allen & Unwin, 1961.

Isaac, Rowan; Morgan, Osprey, 1994.

Key, Mike; Custom Beetle, Osprey, 1994.

McComb, F. Wilson; MG by McComb, Osprey, 1978.

Nye, Doug; Autocourse History of the Grand Prix Car 1966–1991, Hazleton Publishing, 1992.

Posthumus, Cyril, and Hodges, David; Classic Sportscars, Ivy Leaf, 1991.

Robson, Graham; Encyclopaedia of European Sports and GT Cars, Haynes, 1980.

Sieff, Theo; Mercedes Benz, Gallery Books, 1989.

Sparrow, David; Citroën DS, Osprey, 1994.

Sutton, Keith; Ayrton Senna: A Personal Tribute, Osprey, 1994.

Volkswagen Beetle Restoration, Osprey, 1994.

Walker, Mick; Moto Guzzi, Osprey, 1994.

Wherret, Duncan, and Innes, Trevor; Tractor Heritage, Osprey, 1994.

Wood, Jonathan; Wheels of Misfortune, Gidgwick and Jackson, 1988.

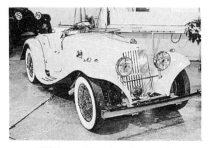

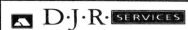

INDEX

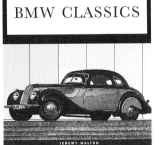
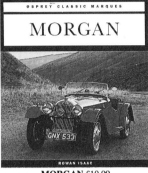
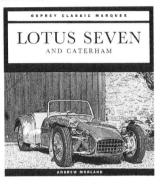